Uwe Sachse

Internationalisation and Mode Switching

GABLER RESEARCH

Uwe Sachse

Internationalisation and Mode Switching

Performance, Strategy
and Timing

With a foreword by Prof. Dr. Jan Freidank

GABLER

RESEARCH

Bibliographic information published by the Deutsche Nationalbibliothek
The Deutsche Nationalbibliothek lists this publication in the Deutsche Nationalbibliografie;
detailed bibliographic data are available in the Internet at http://dnb.d-nb.de.

Dissertation Edinburgh Napier University, 2011

1st Edition 2012

Cover design: KünkelLopka Medienentwicklung, Heidelberg
Printed on acid-free paper

ISBN 978-3-8349-3130-6

Foreword

Managing an international operation is seen by many as one of the most challenging activities in an enterprise. Generations of managers have therefore asked themselves similar questions such as: Firstly which foreign markets would be best to enter for my company, secondly, how can I best enter these markets, and thirdly what is the best development path for my enterprise once I have entered these markets? Even though these questions seem easy to answer reality shows that they are not. Looking only at numerous dimensions of market challenges it appears immediately that possible answers need to be supported by deep market insights and must acknowledge the complexity of the underlying questions.

Many highly reputable scholars as well as experienced practitioners have contributed valuable insights to these questions. However, looking at the high number of publications two trends can be seen: First of all, the great majority of research contributions try to answer the first two questions (1) foreign market selection and (2) market entry. Only a relatively small number of publications touch the third question of (3) market development after entry despite the fact that much of the long term success depends on the careful management and continuous development of foreign operation. Furthermore, due to the number of variables to be considered as well as their complex interactions many of the available studies include only a limited number of cases and markets. As a result they provide more qualitative than quantitative data.

In this research work Uwe Sachse is offering substantial answers to this third question of how companies behave after they have entered a particular foreign market. Starting with a comprehensive literature review reflecting current research progress in the field of internationalization process, managing foreign operations and switching foreign operation modes the author adds valuable knowledge to the field with an extensive empirical study. Despite the aforementioned difficulties of quantitative studies this empirical research is based on a combination of substantial qualitative and quantitative data to cover all relevant aspects of the study. 15 expert interviews of general managers in charge of the international operation of their company as well as an extensive survey of 192 small to medium German companies running an international operation provide a data base which so far has rarely be seen in this subject area. The use of this mixed method enables the author to support quantitative results with in depth qualitative data in order to deliver a rich and deep framework for successful foreign operation.

As with many studies attempting to give answers to complex questions there are no easy answers and all-embracing prescriptions. Nevertheless, several critical success factors and successful management behavior to optimize development paths of foreign operation are identified which clearly add to the existing body of knowledge. All results are carefully analyzed, interpreted and conclusively presented. Despite being written to satisfy highest academic and research standards this book offers a clear value to both scholars and practitioners.

Overall this work provides a substantial addition to the research field of foreign management operation.

Prof. Dr. Jan Freidank

Acknowledgements

This work was written during project breaks in my profession as a consultant and my time as a visiting lecturer at the THM Business School Giessen and substitute professor at the University of Technology, Business and Arts in Leipzig. It was submitted in August 2010 to the School of Management at Edinburgh Napier University.

The research project is part of a collaborative project between the universities in Edinburgh and Giessen and there are correspondingly many people to thank who have supported me in the past years as a guidance team and who have provided me with assistance both on the academic and personal level. Without the valuable suggestions, discussions and help of these kind people, this study would not have been possible.

First I would like to thank Prof. Dr. Marian Jones, Glasgow University, Centre for Internationalisation and Enterprise Research, and Prof. Dr. Thomas Peisl, University Munich as my external examiners. Many thanks also goes to Prof. Dr. John Adams, for his willingness to act as internal examiner in the oral defence ("viva ").

I would like to thank the director of studies Dr. Sajjad Haider. Dr. Haider awakened my interest in scientific-conceptual work and was always interested in critically and scientifically illuminating the work.

I would also very much like to thank Professor Dr. Robert Raeside for his guidance in Edinburgh. His assistance, particularly last year with the preparation and his critical evaluation of my work always led to the right questions and suggestions.

I would especially like to thank Professor Dr. Jan Freidank. He placed great faith in me and always gave advice and criticism where necessary and useful. He professionally guided me with high commitment throughout my scientific development through inspiring discussions regarding the "Global Model", regular meetings and the entire analysis. Furthermore, he granted me, as an external doctoral candidate, the required flexibility for the preparation of the dissertation, without which my work would have been considerably more difficult.

I was very glad to have the support of Prof. Dr. Martin Schmidt who, with his psychological skills and high interest in this work, coached me to a "victory" in the past few months.

Furthermore, I would like to thank Caroline Hayes and Ines von Weichs for their excellent support in the final phase of this work.

I would like to sincerely thank this team for the time taken for the study and the trust placed in me.

I would like to thank my dear parents, Pünktchen and Gerd Sachse, with my whole heart. This work is dedicated to you.

And, finally, I warmly thank my dear Tia for her understanding and moral support. It is thanks to her that a pleasant completion of this work was possible.

Dr. Uwe Sachse

Abstract

The subject of this thesis is the management of foreign operations and the switching of modes for international business. Contrary to research on the market entry, the focus here lies on the further development of the initially selected market entry strategy and the question of identifying the right timing and optimal approach for changing strategies (strategy change). Based on a comprehensive review of literature on internationalisation and mode switching, a theoretical concept for decision-making behaviour during a switch is formulated. The hypotheses derived from this are empirically assessed through interviews with top managers and a large-scale survey of 192 companies (51% switchers; 49% non-switchers). Here, the companies surveyed can be classified into five characteristic groups based on the preferred mode, corporate characteristics, timing of the mode decision and mode-switching probability. The results show that the mode switch is an important option for improving performance in foreign markets. Satisfaction with current performance of foreign operation is the main driver for or against the mode switch. When a firm makes the decision to switch modes, it is shown that, through the mode switch, success in the foreign market is significantly improved. Yet the switch is not in itself a prerequisite for success. The study shows that both switchers and non-switchers can be successful. The results also reinforce the assumed relationship between management style and the probability of a mode switch. Clear causal relationships are identified between systematic internationalisation planning and success. In addition, the dwelling time after market entry is shown to be critical; for example, it is established that the mode of "importers" is usually tied to a longer stay in a market than as with other mode strategies. This indicates a path-dependency with certain modes. This study shows that, over the duration of foreign business activity, companies pursue characteristic internationalisation pathways through their choice of mode. With regard to timing in the decision-making process, the conclusion is reached that there should be sufficient time and space for the development, negotiation and evaluation in the sense of using a co-evolutionary perspective. Timing is viewed as a result emerging from co-evolution of internationalisation activities, corporate characteristics, mode strategy, management style and industry influences. Areas for further research are identified and recommendations on how to improve decision making in the management of foreign operation are provided. The study concludes with an explanatory theory on mode switching, based on the theory of pathway dependency.

List of contents

List of tables

List of figures

XXII

„... but when I said that nothing had been done I erred in one important matter. We had definitely committed ourselves and were halfway out of our ruts. We had put down our passage money - booked a sailing to Bombay. This may sound too simple, but is great in consequence. Until one is committed, there is hesitancy, the chance to draw back, always ineffectiveness. Concerning all acts of initiative (and creation), there is one elementary truth the ignorance of which kills countless ideas and splendid plans: that the moment one definitely commits oneself, then providence moves too. A whole stream of events issues from the decision, raising in one's favour all manner of unforeseen incidents, meetings and material assistance, which no man could have dreamt would have come his way."

William Hutchison Murray (18 March 1913–19 March 1996)
was a Scottish Himalaya mountaineer

Chapter 1 Introduction

1.1 Internationalisation and mode switching

Alongside their domestic market, many companies are increasingly active in foreign markets and expand their business through internationalisation. The internationalisation of companies is a phenomenon which has long been empirically assessable and which has clear effects on the total performance of a company. The estimated share of export of the Gross Domestic Product (GDP), for 2007 (The World Bank 2010), was 12.1% in the U.S.; in Great Britain 26.4%; in France 26.5%; in China 39.7% and in Germany as much as 46.9%.[1] Companies in countries with developed export orientation often present export shares (percentage of foreign turnover against the total turnover) of over 50% and more. For example, the export share of the German engineering federation for 2009 was over 70%[2]. The type and manner of foreign operation has shown to be particularly critical to success in foreign business (Thiel 2007): in terms of the market operation, e.g. through partnerships with distributors, international license agreements, management contracts, local sales companies or subsidiaries in the foreign market.

---

[1] Exports of goods and services represent the value of all goods and other market services provided to the rest of the world. They include the value of merchandise, freight, insurance, transport, travel, royalties, license fees, and other services, such as communication, construction, financial, information, business, personal, and government services. They exclude compensation of employees and investment income (formerly called factor services) and transfer payments.

[2] VDMA: Verband Deutscher Maschinen- und Anlagenbau - German Engineering Federation

1

The reduction of trade restrictions and investment barriers, the strategic change from the isolation of single nation states to economic openness and cross-border mobility of material-, financial-, human- and know-how-related capital have been the main driving forces of globalisation (Lynch 2009). Demographic changes, the unbalanced distribution of raw materials, increasing budget deficits of some countries, rapid networking throughout the world, increasing penetration of poorer countries through the Internet, increasing significance of the middle class in Emerging Markets and various growth prognoses for the old markets in the U.S., Europe and Japan in comparison to China, India, Russia and Brazil – all are important influencing factors from today's perspective (Reinhart and Rogoff 2009; Roubini and Mihm 2010). It is no surprise that it can cause changes in demand volumes, the market entries of innovative providers, new customer requirements, new technologies and also changes in legal frame conditions. In summary, these changes can provoke a company to change its international strategies. The strategy change of foreign operation with focus on mode switch is the focus of this study.

The term "mode switching" refers to a change of previous mode of foreign management operation (Welch et al. 2007). An importer, for example, can be exchanged for a subsidiary; an agent is replaced by a new agent, and supplemented by yet another agent a few years later for stronger market penetration. Depending on the objective, firms have diverse options for structuring their foreign business. The foreign management operation can be extended, optimised, consolidated or reduced. In every case, however, barriers must be overcome for undertaking changes and successfully establishing a future internationalisation strategy. Decision makers are confronted with extensive connections, partnerships and networks with relationships and interests that should be considered for both minor and major changes (Zentes et al 2004; Kutschker and Schmid 2006).

1.2 Problem statement and research question

Internationalisation is not a "self-runner" but requires active management. The "how" of internationalisation is critical for success in international business. The selection of country, the market-entry strategy and the mode of market operation are important

2

decisions to be made. Depth of knowledge and experience in these areas is not evenly distributed in many organisations. But after market entry, feedback loops can improve the performance portfolio or optimise the relationship network. The question then arises as to how firms should ideally operate in foreign markets after market entry – a subject that is currently of high interest. In the current literature, far-reaching insights and recommendations for management regarding this subject and change-potential of foreign operations are lacking as suggested by Swoboda (2002), Welch et al. (2007) and Benito et al. (2009).

This leads to the key questions underlying the decision for this research field:
- Which factors influence the selected strategy after initial market entry has been made?
- Why do firms change or do not change their modes of foreign operation?
- How do firms decide to change the foreign operation mode?
- What role do timing-aspects play in the switch of foreign operation mode?
- How does the change of foreign operation mode influence the firm's success?
- Can success pattern of mode switching be identified?

The research questions are explained in more detail subsequent to the literature review in Chapter 3.

1.3 Main objectives

The research focus of this work is the analysis of foreign management operations with the aim of gaining better understanding of the switch of foreign operation mode. The analysis centres on company strategies after market entry and the further development of the operation mode. An attempt is made to explain decision making in the internationalisation process of firms and the management of foreign operations.

The focus of this study lies not on the contextual conditions in the foreign markets (although sector-influences and internal/external conditions in the environment will be analysed and considered), but on the underlying decision-making process and the strategic behaviour tied to a mode switch.

3

The practical relevance of the subject can be linked to two main aspects. Firstly, high importance is ascribed to the right mode of foreign operation for a company's success. For most firms, operations in foreign markets are already established and a part of the customary strategy programme. There is much knowledge and experience available regarding market entry. However, how firms should continue to operate after market entry in a foreign country and how they can improve their operation strategies is important for many firms and yet remains an open question. Secondly, from the practical perspective there is issue with the indicative factors for the benefits of a mode switch and the right timing. These culminate in a demand for practical statements regarding how internationalisation can best be-structured to allow for sustainable success as well as when a mode switch should be made.

A number of studies have dealt with the motives of internationalisation and key questions regarding country selection and, above all, market-entry strategies (see Chapter 2). Most of the studies, however, do not offer a holistic explanatory approach that extends beyond basic internationalisation decisions and goes beyond market entry mode or follows an empirically integrated approach.

As there are only very few empirical, large-scale studies on the management of foreign operations and no "mainstream" theoretical explanatory approach, it is the objective of this work to better understand fundamental determinants involved in mode switches (explored through the qualitative interviews with top managers) and to obtain indications of the significance of the mode switch and the determining factors through an extensive quantitative survey.

1.4 Theoretical approach

In research philosophy – what is given and actually existent should be the subject of research, so as to allow findings that can be empirically assessed. The objective here is therefore to critically discuss existing research literature on the subject of study and to observe foreign operations beyond market entry.

This work first pursues a more explorative, methodical approach with the general aim of better understanding, strategy and management after market entry and how practical use of these findings can be made. Based on a comprehensive review of research on the subject, qualitative interviews are then carried out. This structure-uncovering method is supplemented in the course of the work by a structure-validating method with a comprehensive survey of top managers. The combination of research methods allows a shift in perspective with the advantage that potential problem solutions can be holistically integrated in the company's reality.

In the first phase of the research process, the theoretical knowledge from the literature and existing and empirically verifiable determinants are identified and analysed. The aim here is to create a broad understanding of the internationalisation process of firms, the behaviour of decision makers with regard to a mode switch for foreign business and the identification of research gaps pertaining to the internationalisation process, decision-making behaviour and the mode switch. Propositions are deduced from the literature review.

The subsequent qualitative section observes past behaviour in the retrospective context and with the aid of exploratory interviews. It provides answers for "how" foreign operations should be managed; "which" structure, processes and strategies are affected; "what" should be changed or not changed and "why" switches are undertaken or not undertaken. In the large-scale survey and its quantitative parameters, the hypotheses will then be verified. Focus is placed on the analysis of the firm's behaviour with regard to "what exactly", "when", "how much" and "how often" in the context of the strategy after market entry. This provides the possibility to not only interpret the relations established but to also analyse their sensitivity and stability. In conclusion, the individual results are analysed and interpreted in context; an explanatory model is developed and recommendations derived.

1.5   Structure

This study is structured in nine chapters (see Figure 1.1), the content of which is presented in the following:

In the first chapter, the subject area is introduced. The background, the problem statement, the theoretical approach and the presentation of the work's structure provide orientation regarding the focus and the methodology.

The second chapter focuses on a detailed assessment of the current status of the subject. Based on a total of three theoretical levels – internationalisation research, research on switching and research on decision-making behaviour tied to mode switching – the theoretical foundation is developed. These partial theories are primarily presented and discussed based on what they can contribute to explaining strategy and management in the internationalisation process and behaviour after market entry. First, an overview of traditional and process-oriented internalisation theories will be provided along with the most important influencing factors, such as performance or timing, for the internationalisation process. This is followed by a comprehensive look at empirical- and more conceptual works on mode switching. Literature will be analysed in the context of the research question, the empirical basis and the core findings. This should allow the derivation of main research gaps. Based on the theoretical levels – decision-making behaviour before, during and after the switch of foreign operation mode is investigated as a first concept that has its basis in the previous and supplementing theory in the next section. The aim is to achieve a holistic perspective of the decision-making behaviour beginning with the start of internationalisation, market entry, and the preparation and implementation of the switch of foreign operation mode. In the third theoretical level, the previous individual findings will be set in descriptive form into the context of the decision-making process for mode switching.

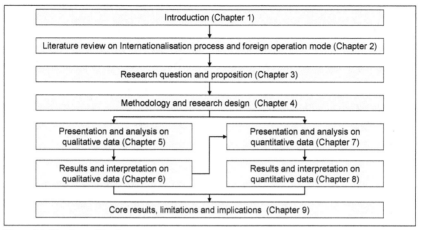

Figure 1.1: Structure of thesis

In the third chapter, the problem is defined more concretely with the aid of specific research questions and propositions. Based on the fundamental proposition that companies demonstrate certain behaviour after market entry, propositions are formulated regarding the mode switch, decision-making behaviour, the use of certain mode strategies, timing issues and the implications for performance. These serve as a conceptual frame of reference for the empirical section and present the subject of study.

In the fourth chapter, the selected research methodology is presented. The chapter begins with the philosophical foundation. Following this, the literature on mode switching will be analysed with regard to research methodology, sample characteristics and the emphasis on the research subject with the aim of identifying gaps and weaknesses. A description of the planning, implementation and evaluation of the exploratory interviews follows this. This section also comprises the interview guideline; the evaluation steps are explained. A further important section is the methodological presentation of the quantitative survey. Sample size, analysis approach and the employed methods of analysis are presented. The variables used and their coding as measurement criteria are also shown. A discussion regarding the quality criteria concludes this chapter.

Chapter 5 and 6 comprise the description, analysis and evaluation of the exploratory interviews. The sample group is characterised in detail and the results are presented from the fifteen exploratory interviews on strategy and management in the foreign markets most significant for the individual firms in Chapter 5. Interpretation of the results pertaining to the observed decision-making behaviour, mode-switching profiles, pathway patterns and mode-switching pathways forms the focus of the sixth chapter. This chapter closes with the further consideration of the propositions and the transfer into concrete and statistically assessable research hypotheses.

In the seventh and eighth chapter, selected hypotheses are analysed. First, the sample group of 192 firms is characterised in the seventh chapter with the aid of descriptive company indicators; sector and foreign market are shown; mode structures are analysed; the duration of the decision-making phase leading to the mode switch is presented along with the number of mode switches. Emphasis is placed on the characterisation of companies in the context of their foreign operation strategies. In the eighth chapter, the data is comprehensively and statistically evaluated with the use of distribution value-, mean value- and correlation analyses with emphasis on the individually most important foreign market. The measurement of dependencies between the influencing factors of managerial style, timing, mode strategy, mode switching and performance forms the analytical focus. Differences between non-switchers and switchers are shown; the question of how various behaviours in foreign operation management influence company success is answered. The analysis of the timing of mode switching supplies interesting findings with regard to when to switch modes depending on sector, country and mode strategy. The objective in this section is to uncover causal, systematic correlations in mode switching using comprehensive statistical methods in order to be able to formulate statements regarding the assumed hypotheses that are as deterministic as possible. The results of the validation of each hypothesis are addressed individually in each section of this chapter.

Following this in Chapter 9 the central theoretical and empirical results are summarised together with the derivation of the key conceptual and methodological implications for research. The main contribution in the context of existing literature is shown. Questions that still remain are discussed and future requirements for research indicated. Limitations arising from the holistic and empirical analysis are shown. Finally, recommendations are made for practitioners and the author gives his concluding observations regarding the management of foreign operations and mode switching. The explanatory theory on foreign operation and mode switching is derived based on the concept of path dependency. The aim is to create comprehensive understanding of the switch of a foreign mode between rigidity and impetus.

The objective of this chapter is to present the focus of the study, the challenges in the management of foreign operations and the aim of the study. Changing environmental conditions accelerate strategic and structural changes in companies and increase the importance of adjustment strategies. In the next chapter, the current status of the literature will be presented. This will show that there are firstly explanatory theories regarding the management of foreign operations and that there is also a great need for further research – in particular regarding influencing factors of the switch, successful mode strategies, and the timing of the switch and its effects on success.

Chapter 2 Theoretical framework of internationalisation process and switching foreign operation modes

2.1 Overview of key research approaches to internationalisation

The emphasis of this chapter is a comprehensive review of the literature at three theoretical levels: internationalisation research, research on mode switching and research on decision-making behaviour tied to mode switching. These partial theories are primarily presented and discussed in relation to their contribution to explaining strategy and management in the internationalisation process and the behaviour of firms following their international market entries.

Three perspectives to approach the concept of internationalisation and theory are presented in Figure 2.1.

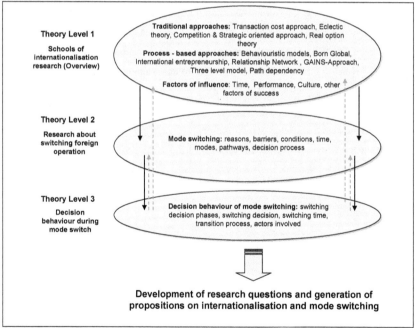

Figure 2.1: Theoretical framework of internationalisation process and mode switching

At the first theoretical level there will first be a general discussion of selected theories on internationalisation and developments based on research findings (Chapter 2.2). The more traditional perspective of internationalisation will then be extended to include theories on the process and behavioural perspectives of internationalisation with special consideration of mode switching and timing aspects (Chapter 2.3). Concluding this is a discussion of the influencing factors internationalisation carries with regard to firms (Chapter 2.4).

On the second theoretical level current research findings pertaining to mode switching will be presented and discussed, including the most important insights and research gaps. Insights gained from the discussion of internationalisation theories and findings of mode-switching research then form the basis for describing the decision-making behaviour tied to a mode switch (Chapter 2.5).

On the third theoretical level, and based on an assumed decision-making process, an in-depth analysis of the process of mode switching with regard to the three perspectives of "environment", "key actors" and "decision-making behaviour" is presented. Relevant theories on the actual research subject of the "mode switch" will be integrated and discussed (Chapter 2.7).

A total of five partial theoretical approaches form the basis of the literature review. The aim of the framework presented in Table 2.1 is a step-by-step, comprehensive understanding of the most important theories and their individual explanatory contributions, on the basis of which the research questions and propositions are derived (Chapter 3).

In light of the complexity of internationalisation and the firms behaviour after market entry, it should be noted that the explanatory theories are partial theories which contribute important findings but cannot claim comprehensive totality of theoretical approach. A comprehensive view is also not the intention. Rather, the aim is to develop a solid foundation for theoretical explanation of mode switching in the context of the internationalisation behaviour of a firm.

In view of the wide variety of theoretical models that have emerged in the last forty years on the subject of internationalisation of firms (Zentes et al. 2004; Macharzina and Wolf 2005, Becker 2005; Kutschker and Schmid 2006), a differentiation should be made here between the traditional perspective based on the economic stream of literature and the behavioural/process-related perspective of internationalisation which emphasises that internationalisation is an evolutionary, dynamic process (Benito and Welch 1994, Welch et al. 2007). A presentation of the most important influencing factors of internationalisation complements the two main explanatory approaches and completes the theoretical framework on level one.

Table 2.1: Theoretical framework and partial approaches to explaining behaviour during a switch of foreign operation mode.

Category	Theory level 1			Theory level 2	Theory level 3
Term of reference	Traditional approaches	Process-oriented approaches	Environmental factors in the internationalisation process	Research theories thus far on mode switching	Status of research on decision-making behaviour tied to mode switching
Conceptual aspects of emphasis	- Transaction cost approach - Eclectic theory - Competition & strategically oriented approach - Real option theory	- Behaviouristic models - Born Global - International entrepreneurship - Relationship Network - GAINS approach - Three-level model - Path dependency	- Internationalisation and time - Internationalisation and corporate culture - Success factors in internationalisation - Internationalisation and performance	- Reasons for - Barriers - Conditions - Main modes - Decision process - Path	- Optimal switch time - Switch decision - Transition process - Actors involved
Aim/ Objective	Overview and description of individual explanatory theories on internationalisation		Overview and presentation of selected theoretical aspects of internationalisation	Presentation of current research findings	Derivation of possible behavioural modes of actors in the decision process for a mode switch

2.2 The traditional (economic-based) approaches of internationalisation research

2.2.1 Transaction cost approach

The basic principles of the transaction cost approach were initiated by Coase (1937) and further developed by Williamson (1975, 1985). The central tenet of the transaction cost theory (Williamson 1975, 1985; Dunning 1981a, 1988; Buckley and Casson 1988; Rugman and Verbeke 2003) is that the decision between market and organisation will be made with consideration to the emerging cost. The amount of the costs determines which strategy is more cost-effective. If the costs of the market are lower, then the market solution is taken instead of the internalisation. As soon as the costs for the market have rise, a decision to internationalise is made. The discussion of the sum of costs of a market solution before and after a transaction supplies particularly important insights for mode-switch research (Buckley and Casson 1981; Williamson 1985). According to the transaction cost approach – the costs of the switch are higher, the greater the uncertainty, the more specific the transaction and the rarer the transaction is. Based on these considerations, Buckley and Casson (1981) developed a model for choosing between market (exporting), contracting (licensing) and performing an activity within the firm (hierarchy). On the basis of this model, Buckley and Casson (1981) examined the optimal timing for direct investments and the most favourable cost conditions and level of market presence when "switching" from licences to direct investments: "Foreign direct investment will occur when switching at time *t* from one mode to another mode generates lower recurrent variable costs and non-recoverable set-up costs." (Swoboda 2002; Welch et al. 2007). Firms therefore choose the organisational form and location with which overall transaction costs will be minimised. Transactions perceived to be high risk and requiring significant management time or other resource commitments are more likely to be internalised as part of a hierarchically structured organisation.

Furthermore, research that increases the focus on resource-based approaches in strategic management (Dhanaraj and Beamish 2003) reinforces the importance of internalising abilities and competencies in order to generate competitive advantages (Hymer 1976). In practice, businesses internalise materials and goods that represent their immaterial or intangible assets, namely international patents, licences and brand rights. The reason for this is obvious: the attainment of a sustained competitive advantage.

Despite a large number of publications produced by well-known researchers (Hennart 1982; Buckley and Casson 1991; Rugman 1997), the often-mentioned critical objections to this theoretical approach remain in internationalisation research. Coordination costs, for example, (costs of planning, organisation, management, communication) are only considered to a very limited degree in the comparison of costs of the organisation solution and company solution. Furthermore, transaction costs are extremely difficult to operationalise in international management. Finally, it is, of course, insufficient to observe the manifestations of changes with exclusion of the efficacy perspective (Kutschker and Schmid 2006). That is why, in the discussion of transaction costs, further considerations pertaining to risk, control and flexibility need to be investigated.

2.2.2 Agency theory

A further interesting theory for assessing the subject of research, one which is also a partial area of the new industrial economics, is Agency Theory. The basic problem between the principal (e.g. the owner of the company) and the agent (those acting on the principal's behalf, such as managers or employees; or external actors, such as intermediaries) is the existing asymmetry of information distribution and uncertainty regarding the behaviour of the individual partner (Welch et al. 2007; Petersen et al. 2000b). Often, the "agency problems" represent the basis for internationalising activities because possible transaction- and coordination costs are too high. Cooperation partners in the foreign market have a competitive edge due to their information advantages which they use to pursue their own objectives. With regard to behaviour of the transaction partner, Agency Theory assumes limited rationality and opportunism. Taking personal advantages, conniving or deceit, are assumed behaviours that cause transaction costs to rise (Kutscher and Schmid 2006). As the well-being of the principal is influenced by the actions taken by the agent, internationalising companies are placing increasing value on comprehensive controlling, the gradual development of knowledge and measures for promoting trust between the partners (Child et al. 2005; Welch et al. 2007).

2.2.3 Eclectic theory by Dunning

The eclectic paradigm developed by Dunning (1977, 1988b, 2000) is a multi-theoretical framework that attempts to integrate explanations of other theories and join them. Dunning argues that the success of firms' international business activities depends on three factors: ownership specific advantages (O), such as firm-specific assets; location-specific advantages (L) that describe the attractiveness of a foreign country; and internalisation advantages (I) which reflect a firm's ability to conduct a transaction efficiently within its hierarchical organisation. Dunning's eclectic paradigm, also referred to as the OLI framework, predicts that a firm will choose the internationalisation strategy most suited to the "advantages" it possesses. The core statement is that, for internationalisation, ownership advantages must be given. If, however, a firm exclusively has ownership advantages then, in its internationalisation, it will concentrate on contract-based transfer of resources (e.g. through licences). If there are internationalisation advantages in addition to this, then export is preferred. Finally, if there are also location advantages in the foreign country then direct foreign investments may be made (Kutschker 2006).

The main advantage of the eclectic paradigm in comparison with other theories is that it includes a large set of explanatory variables and, most importantly, it points out how different influencing factors interact. For example, a firm that generates an intangible asset by carrying out intense research and development (R&D) activities so that its product incorporates novel technology (the firm's ownership advantage) only chooses an integrated mode if it is also able to organise the distribution of its product abroad efficiently (the firm's internalisation advantage). However, the large set of explanatory variables is also the eclectic paradigm's greatest weakness. If all variables imaginable are included in a theory then it is difficult to derive testable hypotheses (Andersen 1997). According to Dunning (1993) the eclectic paradigm intends to explain "what is" rather than, in the normative sense, "what should be" a firm's type of internationalisation. Additionally, like most theories, it is a rather static theoretical approach (Swoboda 2002; Zentes et al. 2004; Kutschker and Schmid 2006).

2.2.4 Competition-oriented and strategic approach

Companies in a foreign market are initially at a disadvantage to the domestic competition. Knowledge and experience with customers, competition, product demand and partners etc. are usually missing (Hollensen 2007). This also applies to a mode switch. Only when the so-called "liability of foreignness" has been overcome and there is a competitive advantage can firms successfully internationalise. Behaviourism-based approaches do not consider competitive advantage but concentrate on the organisational learning process in internationalisation (Welch et al. 2007). For companies with monopolistic offers, these learning processes can be important. Therefore, if a company were to internationalise along these lines in a strictly incremental fashion then significant opportunity costs would arise (Becker 2005).

The researchers Prahalad and Doz (1987) viewed internationally active companies as finding themselves between the poles of necessary adaptation to local host-country conditions ("local responsiveness") and forces leading to a globally standardised approach ("global integration"). According to the authors, the management demands in an internationally active firm can be divided into three categories. Referred to by the authors as "building blocks", these are the "global integration of activities", the "global strategic coordination" and the "local responsiveness". In the sense of "building blocks", this creates a framework through which external environmental factors or sector-related forces exerting influence on the company may be observed. This perspective of the Integration-Responsiveness framework is consistent with the Structure-Conduct-Performance paradigm of industrial-organisation literature which purports that the sectoral structure, or the company's environment, co-determines the behaviour (conduct) of firms which in turn influences the company's success. Companies adjust their strategies in order to achieve a fit with the environment in which they are active. The role of the management lies in coordinating the company alignments. Companies which do not select the right/suitable strategy will not achieve the corresponding success necessary for surviving in this environment.

For Bartlett and Goshal (1989; 1990), firms have four options: internationalisation (international firms), localisation (multinational firms), globalisation (global firms) and combined localisation and globalisation (transnational firms). The strategic force decides which characteristics result in the organisation, management and coordination. To achieve competitive advantages, Bartlett et al. (2004) relied on economies of scale and economics of scope depending upon the strategic target.

According to Bartlett et al. (2004), the organisational structure crystallises in correspondence with the basic strategic orientation. For example, a globally-aligned company whose focus is placed on the achievement of advantages of scale forms a centrally-oriented organisational structure in order to achieve scale benefits from centrally planned value-creating activities. Bartlett and Goshal assume the existence of ideal-typical typologies of multinational firms (e.g. Stopford and Wells 1972). Such typologies are useful for reducing and better understanding the complexity of international organisations (Schwarz 2009). However, it remains open as to whether other forms can exist and what role the sector requirement has on the strategic alignment (Kutschker/Schmid 2006; Schwarz 2009).

According to these management concepts, the perception and interpretation of globalisation- and localisation necessities is decisive for success in the international competitive environment. In this, the individual mindset of the management and the company culture ("administrative heritage") play a vital role.

2.2.5 Real options theory

An interesting, economics-based approach for a further study of internationalisation is the real options theory (Amran and Kulatilaka 1999; Fisch 2004; Adner and Levinthal 2004; Copeland and Tufano 2004). The theory's basic premise is that, in the case of uncertainty, irreversible investments bear a risk of loss which can be reduced through a flexible timeframe. In essence, it is about the freedom to not have to decide right away but to be able to wait for more information. This freedom can be assigned value which grows in the face of increasing uncertainty. Basically, decision makers have the options to put off action (option to wait), discontinue action (option to withdraw), to expand (expansion option), or to use other resources than as originally planned (option to exchange). Real options may be successfully employed when future conditions can be predicted with high probability. Then suitable options can be planned for using this information/knowledge at an early stage as pointed out by Copeland and Tufano (2004).

In internationalisation, the real options theory becomes relevant in the case of decisions regarding international direct investment (Fisch 2004). For example, firms may refrain from making profitable investments when the loss of an option is involved and perhaps invest later when there are better conditions. On the flipside, firms will take an unprofitable foreign investment in their stride when it brings further options. The real options theory can also aid in defining stages of development in the internationalisation process. The phases of internationalisation can be understood as investments with varying optional character, which can help to explain leaps within the internationalisation process (Macharzina and Wolf 2005). For example, according to Macharzina and Wolf, "export strategy" can be interpreted as a "delayed investment", an international joint venture as a "real option" and a foreign sales subsidiary as an "immediate option" in the sense of the real option theory and thereby be better assessed with regard to the right timing of further internationalisation. In the theoretical discussion of dynamic internationalisation, the real options theory is often critically observed in comparison to simple finance options (Copeland and Tufano 2004). It is a young theory and there is little empirical data on the use of real options in internationalisation (Macharzina and Wolf 2005). "Nevertheless, not only the right decisions, but also the right timing makes for good management" (Copeland and Tufano p. 75, 2004). Hence, the real options theory seems to present an interesting perspective as supported by Fisch (2004).

2.3 The process-behavioural based approaches of internationalisation research

Supplementary to the traditional theoretical approaches based on the economic literature with a focus on rational decision-making processes, the behavioural/process-related perspective of internationalisation (which emphasises that internationalisation is an evolutionary, dynamic process) will now be discussed (see Table 2.1). The traditional theoretical approaches to internationalisation mainly focus on the question of "Why?" (causality of internationalisation) and "How?" (configuration of internationalisation). Dynamic internationalisation theories, however, ask not only "Why?" and "How?" but also place focus on "When?" (temporality/dynamics of internationalisation).

19

2.3.1 The process perspective

The process models assume a decision to initiate internationalisation that is largely conscious by nature and realised in a step-by-step approach along the "establishment chain". The first and most influential model was introduced by Johanson and Wiedersheim-Paul (1975) and then further developed by Johanson and Vahlne (1977, 1990). Often referred to as the Uppsala Model, it suggests that internationalisation activities occur incrementally and are influenced by increased market knowledge and commitment. While the model emphasises managerial learning, internationalisation is described in terms of market selection and the mechanisms used for market entry. For example, firms improve their foreign market knowledge through initial expansion using indirect exporting approaches to similar, "psychically close" markets. Over time, and through experience, firms increase their foreign market commitment, switching to direct export with independent distributors, to sales branches or sales subsidiaries, and then to foreign production. This, in turn, enhances market knowledge, leading to further commitment in more distant markets including equity investment in offshore manufacturing and sales operations. With regard to timing, it is perhaps the most important point of emphasis in this work that internationalisation commitment is a gradual process with incremental stages passed through over a relatively long period of time.

Market entry as the first step in the internationalisation process is observed particularly from the perspective of the right selection of market-entry strategy (Kutschker/Schmid 2006) and the overcoming of market-entry barriers (Brouthers 2002; Katsikea et al. 2003; Leonidou 2004; Brouthers and Hennart 2007). Firms can choose from a variety of strategic options (Brouthers/Brouthers 2003; Kutschker/Schmid 2006; Hollensen 2007). In a conclusion based on decades of research on market entry, Morschett et al. (2010) decided that market attractiveness, uncertainty in the host country, the legal environment of the host country and the culture of the home country have significant influence on entry-mode choice. For Leonidou et al. (2010), a stronger strategic orientation in the internationalisation process and the mode switch is necessary over time.

The internationalisation process models draws on organisational growth, behaviour and learning theory to capture internationalisation and are generally argued to be more dynamic than the Foreign Direct Investment theory (Johanson and Wiedersheim-Paul 1975; Welch and Luostarinen 1988; Johanson and Vahlne 1990; Melin 1992). Ongoing interaction between constants and variables leads the firm to develop incrementally and to increase internationality through learning processes. As such, the Uppsala model can be characterised as a combination of deliberate (or systematic) and emergent (or ad hoc) approaches (Yip et al. 2000). Although Johanson and Vahlne (1990) argue that the eclectic paradigm of foreign direct investment (FDI) and the Uppsala model are "inconsistent, as the basic assumptions are so different", the Uppsala model appears to reflect the essence of FDI and, in fact, complements Aharoni (1966) and builds on the theory of the growth of firms (Penrose 1959). The firm is ultimately expected to internalise its activities by moving over time from purely domestic operations to establishing foreign country production, based on a process of managerial learning.

It is assumed that, over the course of its lifecycle, a company passes through different stages of increased international activity and, depending on the stage, demonstrates typical behaviour (Cavusgil 1984; Zentes at al 2004). These models analyse export activity solely as a form of developing a market. Further steps of internationalisation, such as the establishment and management of foreign subsidiaries or production companies, are not taken into consideration. With regard to the factor of "time", the models give indirect indications of the sequence and duration of export stages. Specific definitions or descriptions are, however, not provided.

Other process-based models also argue that internationalisation is incremental, with various stages reflecting changes in the attitudinal and behavioural commitment of managers and the firm's resultant international orientation (Reid 1981; Czinkota 1982; Cavusgil 1984). These models argue that the perceptions and beliefs of managers bear influence and are shaped by incremental involvement in foreign markets. This involvement results in a pattern of evolution from managers having little or no interest in international markets, to evaluating psychically close markets and then carrying out trial initiatives. Managers then pursue active expansion into more challenging and unknown markets and become increasingly committed to international growth.

Furthermore, the process models of internationalisation underline the aspect that decision making in firms is predominantly influenced by a preference for familiar action patterns. New and less familiar alternatives are only accepted with a certain degree of scepticism or hesitation (Simon 2007). This so-called "lateral rigidity" has the effect that economic premises of the rational decision making are partially neglected (Luostarinen 1989; Simon 2007).

Despite the intuitive and commonsense appeal of the main ideas in the process perspective on company internationalisation, the empirical support for the theory is far from conclusive (Benito et al. 2005). The process models neglects both the potential leapfrogging of stages to accelerate internationalisation but also certain manifestations of internationalisation (e.g. joint ventures, web-based sales). Furthermore, its concept of internationalisation is future-oriented and focused on growth. The elements of the "stage-theory", for example, do not consider the relevant aspect of intentionally remaining within a stage as an indirect form of strategic sidestepping or withdrawal from a foreign market (Benito et al. 2005) at a certain point in time. Firms have seemed prone to leapfrog stages, entering distant markets in terms of psychic distance at an early stage, and the pace of the internationalisation process seems generally to have speeded up. The Internet has made it easier for a firm to become acquainted with foreign markets. Firms today also have quicker and easier access to knowledge about doing business abroad. In some cases, it is no longer necessary to build up in-house knowledge in a slow and gradual or trial-and-error process (Hollensen 2007). Some firms aim for international markets or even strive for global market presence right from founding on (Moen and Servais 2002; Gabrielsson et al. 2008).

2.3.2 Born-Global approach

Internationalisation research on born global companies focuses on how firms can internationalise and open up foreign markets immediately on their founding (Moen and Servais 2002; Gabrielsson and Kirpalani 2004; Gabrielsson et al. 2008). Gabrielsson and Kirpalani (2004) came to the conclusion that such companies can speed up their internationalisation through networking and by utilising the Internet. They do not necessarily have to take certain steps and gradually expand business from the domestic market to the selected foreign markets. They are immediately (on founding of the company and without a time gap) active in one or several foreign markets (Sharma and Blomstermo 2003). The internationalisation of "globals" is marked by knowledge gathered from available networks. The better the company's position in the network, the more likely it will be to gain the knowledge necessary to obtain a competitive edge (Sharma and Blomstermo 2003). Such companies are particularly creative in compensating for a lack of historical success and experience through a clever joining of their own resources to those of network partners (Sharma and Blomstermo 2003 refer to this as international learning through networking). The definition originally established from the U.S. perspective that born globals should achieve 25% of export in three years is, from the European perspective, only a small challenge. Gabrielsson et al. (2008) therefore expanded the framework of reference by strongly considering the potential in the domestic market, the product and the export market receptivity. Of particular emphasis is the importance of the initial commitment of the entrepreneur in connection with a global vision in the early phase of the internationalisation process.

Not only for "born globals" is internationalisation occurring in a much more "dynamic" manner than as postulated in the classic stage models (Zentes et al. 2004). In their studies, Shrader et al. (2000) have found an overall "accelerated internationalisation" of firms. The point of time in the lifecycle of a firm at which foreign business begins is earlier than it used to be, and this despite low experience levels of the management (Shrader et al. 2000; Berger 2006). But also firms which have been established for several years on the domestic market or firms after acquisitions or mergers can suddenly make a decision for (re-) internationalisation of their business and then move (depending on the strategy) incrementally like born globals; or they combine these strategies (Welch and Welch 2009; Hollensen 2007).

2.3.3 International entrepreneurship research

Entrepreneurs and their behaviour as managers play an important role in the internationalisation process (Jones and Coviello 2005; Kuemmerle 2005; Oviatt and McDougall 2005; Engelen et al. 2009). The resource-based view and the network perspective serve as primary explanatory models (Young et al. 2003). Young et al. (2003) emphasise the significance of resources, capabilities and competencies of firms and their actors in the initiation and implementation of internationalisation (Teece at al. 1997). The significance of the network is also emphasised. Particularly in the early phase of internationalisation, the network of the decision maker and his partners plays a substantial role in the success of the company's internationalisation (Link 1997).

Oviatt and McDougall (2005) describe international entrepreneurship as "a combination of innovative, proactive and risk-seeking behaviour that crosses national borders and is intended to create value in organisations". In particular, the perception of risk in the internationalisation process and control of the activities of the actors represents key areas of research (Benito et al. 2005). In their model of the entrepreneurial international process, Jones and Coviello (2005) emphasised the factors of "level of innovativeness", "level of risk tolerance" and "managerial competence" as main influencing areas for behaviour in the internationalisation process. The manager decisively influences the organisation through his/her actions and decisions. As a result of the behaviour, the company leaves a specific "fingerprint pattern" of the most important events, for example, the switch of an operation mode. In other words, as a sum of all events, a specific internationalisation profile results which, in its effects, is reflected in the performance of the internationalisation process. The two researchers assume a process of cyclical behaviour in the sense that success, know-how and experience influence the manager as a kind of feedback and thereby influence further decision-making processes. In current publications on the subject of international entrepreneurship research (Engelen et al. 2009), the influence of personal attitude and values is emphasised. Furthermore, it is pointed out that there are cultural differences depending upon origin and country which influence the behaviour of the manager and also the organisation as a whole in the internationalisation process. With regard to the characteristics of the entrepreneur and consequences for success in the foreign market, there is not total clarity. Frishammer and Andersson (2009) draw the conclusion that the influence of strategic orientation on internationalisation success is overestimated while Knight and Kim (2009) found that international orientation, international marketing skills, international innovativeness, and international market orientation represent the key competency basis for international success.

2.3.4 The Relationship School of the Network Perspective

An alternative view is provided by a more recent area of internationalisation research. It focuses on non-hierarchical systems in which firms invest in order to strengthen and monitor their position in international networks (Johanson and Mattsson 1992; Sharma et al. 2003). Referred to as the "Network Perspective", this research draws on the theories of social exchange and resource dependency, placing focus on a firm's behaviour in the context of a network of inter-organisational and interpersonal relationships (Chetty and Blankenburg Holm 2000; Li et al. 2004). Such relationships can involve customers, suppliers, competitors, private and public support agencies, family, friends and so on. Organisational boundaries thereby incorporate both business (formal) and social (informal) relationships. According to this school of thought, internationalisation depends more on an organisation's set of network relationships rather than a firm-specific advantage. Therefore, externalisation (rather than internalisation) occurs.

The Network Perspective offers a complementary view to the transaction cost theory, given that the latter does not account for the role and influence of social relationships in business transactions. In addition, internationalisation-related decisions and activities in the Network Perspective emerge as patterns of behaviour influenced by various network members, while the transaction-cost theory assumes rational strategic decision-making. Compared with the unilateral process suggested by the "stage" models, the Network Perspective introduces a "more multilateral element" to internationalisation (Johanson and Vahlne 1990). In this context, Johanson and Mattsson (1988) suggest that a firm's success in entering new international markets is more dependent on its relationships within current markets than on market-specific and cultural characteristics.

2.3.5 The configuration and "gestalt" - approach

In the GAINS approach (Gestalt-Oriented Approach of International Business Strategies) formulated by Macharzina and Engelhard (1991) takes a holistic view of dynamic internationalisation. Unlike the traditional stage models, this approach attempts to provide information on the dynamic processes of internationalisation through an analysis of the constellation of "environment-structure-strategy-process (management)" in the context of the three categories of Non-Exporter, Reactive Exporter and Active Exporter. In essence, firms experience certain spurts of development and take characteristic paths with regard to the three main configurations ("Gestalten") mentioned above. In the phase of transition, for example, realignment of the firm takes place through a switch of configuration ("Gestaltwechsel"). In the phase of relative stability, the "Gestalt" does not change. Internationalisation is therefore of process-oriented character and is an inherent part of corporate development. Over the course of time, revolutionary and incremental periods of change occur in alternation. This theory provides interesting indications of the sequences and the speed of internationalisation. For Macharzina and Engelhard (1991), continuous and incremental change may have the advantage that it, at first, seems to be more cost favourable and perhaps less risky than revolutionary change. The phase of transition, however, is a state between two optimal "Gestalt"-constellations, which can lead to disharmony and accompanying costs.

Building on the GAINS theory, Kutschker (1996) and Kutschker and Bäuerle (1997) have developed the "Three E's Model", which was further explained by others (Swoboda 2002; Zentes et al. 2004; Kutschker and Schmid 2006). For these researchers, the internationalisation process is characterised by a "muddling through" and by "trial and error". It takes place gradually and incrementally at various levels and there are evolutionary, episodic and epochal differences with regard to the intensity and the scope of organisational change (Swoboda 2002). Firms in foreign markets develop within an "ongoing" process (international evolution) and amidst epochal change (international epoch). In between, there are sporadic phases of greater changes in the degree of internationalisation (international episode). The term "evolution" stands for the numerous, small steps of internationalisation in the daily business of a firm which are either more or less conscious/intentional in nature but primarily incremental in their change of surface- or more fundamental organisational structures. Episodes, according to Kutschker, occur faster. They are revolutionary. Longer time periods of increased activity characterise this phase of internationalisation. Large parts of the company are affected and faced with new and complex challenges. Examples of this could be the establishment of a subsidiary or the takeover of a direct competitor in the foreign target market. Epochs comprise intensive change over a longer period of time, such as the implementation of a new internationalisation strategy. Within an epoch, there are various episodes of sporadic change, such as the integration of a takeover or the establishment of a subsidiary, followed by a phase of consolidation (evolution). An epoch always triggers fundamental change over a longer period of time. According to this model, there is always incremental internationalisation, while a revolutionary/discontinuous development is possible but does not necessarily have to take place. The far-reaching transformation tied to breaking out to a new epoch is seldom found. The international fingerprint changes intensely from epoch to epoch, and over the course of time. In the broadest sense, this interpretation also correlates to the "punctuated equilibrium theory" (PET) according to which firms evolve by experiencing enduring periods of stability (equilibrium) in their activities, punctuated by relatively short periods of more fundamental change (Gersick 1991). Accordingly, the foreign expansion can be considered "punctuation", and requisite changes to foreign management operation are necessary for the firm to respond appropriately to this punctuation. Katsikae et al. (2005) stated that in cases in which the punctuation is great, the corresponding organisational responses must also be great to return to an equilibrium state.

2.3.6 The three-level model by Swoboda

In the model for the internationalisation process by Swoboda (2002), three levels influence the international development of firms (Figure 2.2). The internal and external environmental factors act as stimuli and are interwoven in their context in the internationalisation. At the primary level, the basic orientation of the venture is determined based on decisions regarding the country portfolio, the operation mode and the transfer of value creation. These represent the guiding principle of the firm and form an internationalisation pathway. At the secondary or basis level, the changes follow in the areas of structure, process and culture. Depending upon the internationalisation pathway, firms leave characteristic structure-process-culture configurations behind them.

Figure 2.2 shows the three level model of internationalisation (Swoboda 2002) with stimuli of change, primary and secondary level of change.

Supplementary to the dynamic perspective of the GAINS model and the "Three E's", Swoboda reaches the conclusion that firms do not develop evenly with regard to the dimensions of process, structure and change. In his research, there were firms which entered various foreign markets but (within the time period analysed) did not change their operation modes. Other firms reacted to the low success of their foreign activities and withdrew from the markets either partially or entirely. Swoboda (2002) assumed that, with every "path", successful enterprises present different configurations ("Gestalten") than enterprises which are less or not at all successful.

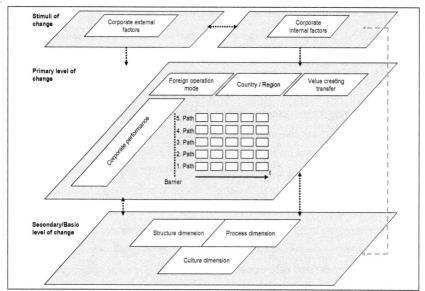

Figure 2.2: The level model of internationalisation (Swoboda, p. 433, 2002)

In summary, Swoboda draws the conclusion that firms can internationalise according to the three pathways of transaction-mode orientation, country orientation and speed/pace orientation.

This model, aside from Swoboda, has been tested in studies by Schwarz (2009) on internationalisation of trade companies and by Swoboda and Jager (2008) in a comparative study of the findings of Calof and Beamish (1995). Simon (2007) came to the conclusion that the level model not only portrays the traditional, market-oriented dimensions but also the internal company dimensions and thereby offers greater gained insights than previous models of internationalisation process research (Simon, p. 115, 2007). However, he critically views the strongly eclectic structure of the model. Due to the variety of applied theories and approaches, contradictions cannot be avoided.

2.3.7 Path dependency in internationalisation

Other behavioural internationalisation models find that learning with regard to internationalisation is a cumulative, path-dependent process in which each step adds to the firm's knowledge (Eriksson et al. 2000; Araujo and Rezende 2003; Hutzschenreuter et al. 2007). In other words, the knowledge accumulated in the past forms the trajectory for future international behaviour and shapes its ongoing evolution. In this sense, the path theory challenges the neoclassical assumption of long-term efficient market balances in that it defines the phenomenon of a lock-in – a situation in which, under certain circumstances, an inefficient and irreversible market result has established itself. The most prominent example of path research is the path dependency of the keyboard layout, QWERTY (David 1985). David explored the development of the QWERTY keyboard technology by demonstrating how an inferior (hence, inefficient) technological standard was established and why it is still maintained. David defined path-dependency as follows (David p. 333, 1985): "A path-dependent sequence of economic changes is one in which important influences on the eventual outcome can be exerted by temporally remote events, including happenings dominated by chance elements rather than systematic forces. Such stochastic processes do not converge automatically to a fixed-point distribution of outcomes and are referred to as non-ergodic" (David 1985).

With consideration to the current research on the dynamics of path dependency researchers such as Schreyögg and Sydow (2003), Holtmann (2008), Koch (2008) and Roedenbeck (2008) and Sydow (2009) observed paths as non-ergodic processes in which small events, in their sum, create stable behavioural- and thinking patterns, and continuously influence them. The concrete pattern, developed over time, is not predictable at the beginning of the process. It can finally lead to an inefficient situation. Increasing returns set the tracks for self-reinforcing processes and can then add to a solidifying of behaviour modes. A "lock-in" refers to the diminishing possibility of a return to decision-making freedom. It has a stabilising, self-reinforcing effect which, depending on the perspective of the decision-maker, can be positive or negative. Breaking the path or destabilising individual paths denotes a release from path dependency and the return to a starting point of assumed full freedom of decision. Schreyögg et al. (2003) continued the discussion of previous path research and added the sub-elements of "increasing selectivity", "positive feedback", "path-dependence" and "path breaking". The transitional conditions of "critical juncture", "lock-in" and "de-locking" form the connections between the path segments. Though few empirical works exist on this phase model, it persuades through its clarity in the operationalisation of the construct of path dependency (Dievernich 2007; Roedenbeck 2008; Koch 2008).

In his concept of lateral rigidity, Luostarinen (1989) provided important insights as to why companies are often limited in how they structure their internationalisation pathways. Companies behave "elastically" with regard to the further development of familiar alternatives and "non-elastically" with regard to new possibilities. Lateral rigidity is higher, the more sceptical a firm is of new and unfamiliar possibilities and thereby clings to existing pathways. The degree of lateral rigidity is determined by the degree of available knowledge. The more information and experience a firm has, the lower the lateral rigidity.

The research on Dynamic Capabilities (Teece et al. 1997; Zollo and Winter 2002; Winter 2003; Barreto 2010) treats the question of how firms deal with changed environment conditions. Teece et al. (1997, p. 516) defined dynamic capabilities as "the firm's ability to integrate, build, and reconfigurate internal and external competences to address a rapidly changing environment." This research theory builds on the resource-based view and extends it by the dimension of change capability of resources, abilities, operating routines (Eisenhardt and Martin 2000; Zollo and Winter 2002). In current studies, the decision-making process and the ability to recognise opportunities and risks is additionally considered (Barreto 2010). The historical development of firms plays a special role for the change capability. Teece et al. (1997, p. 522) remark on this: "Where a firm can go is a function of its current position and the paths ahead. Its current position is often shaped by the path it has travelled." Past successes or successful practices (core competencies) can easily become "core rigidities" that are very difficult to loosen (Leonard – Barton 1992) and thereby also influence the capability to change. For Zollo and Winter (2002), higher order capabilities are necessary for effecting a modification of operating routines.

From the perspective of mode research to date, Welch et al. (2007) assumed in their comprehensive studies on foreign mode switches that each new mode decision is influenced by previous experience in the countries in question: "Passage of time creates new influence which may lead to a perceived need for a mode change". To better understand mode decisions, Jones and Coviello (2005) advocated that the historical environment and development path of the company must be analysed.

Hutzschenreuter et al. (2007) differentiated between path-dependent and path-creating internationalisation. In the path-dependent perspective, scarce and firm-specific assets lead to a focused internationalisation trajectory with a limited capacity to change. Hutzschenreuter et al. (2007) argued that internationalisation paths are often seen as a "naïve" evolutionary journey disregarding strategic intent, entrepreneurship, or other aspects of managerial strategic decision. The path-creating perspective considers the firm's dynamic capabilities which represent latent abilities to renew its core competence over time. Managerial intention may be an important factor in influencing internationalisation.

Umbeck (2009) saw the main cause in a pursuance of competition rules, uncritical acceptance of previously successful behavioural patterns in the past, cognitive simplification of complex problems, dominating paradigms and distinct distortions with regard to the perception of information and risks/opportunities (Umbeck 2009).

This comparatively universal theoretical approach of path dependency has gained in significance in the past few years. From an international business theory point of view, it highlights the importance of understanding the temporal and spatial character of internationalisation processes as well as the multiple causes of events. It considers not only the influence of systematic forces but also that of contingencies. Contingencies play a role in explanation because systematic mechanisms are unable to completely account for how critical events, such as mode-switching, unfold and internationalisation processes take place in open systems subjected to a variety of conflicting influences (e.g. firm-based factors, host-country specific influences) (Araujo and Rezende 2003). By focusing on self-reinforcing socioeconomic mechanisms, this theory might provide a template for understanding the complex structural and cognitively entwined strategic patterns that guide the internationalisation process consciously or unconsciously and point it in a specific direction. It aids better understanding of how and why incumbent firms might lose their absorptive capacity and thus their scope of strategic choice (Cohen and Levinthal 1990).

The theory of path dependency concentrates on explaining stability and rigid behaviour and only contributes minimally to the mechanisms of the actual change in internationalisation (Werle 2007). Furthermore, the question of the opportunity to correct once-taken paths in internationalisation which have proved to be unsatisfactory remains open.

2.4 Significant influencing factors on Internationalisation

In the following, the discussion of internationalisation theory will be supplemented by a selection of significant influencing factors (Table 2.1). Through the integration of these factors, the author aims to achieve a change in perspective that will allow a closer look at the concept of integrated internationalisation. The selected factors are Time, Corporate Culture, Success Factors and Performance (Sachse 2002; Neubert 2006).

2.4.1 The role of time in the internationalisation process

The word "dynamic" indicates the aspect of time in international development. Only through the concept of time can the changes which take place within companies in the course of their internationalisation be portrayed. For Macharzina and Engelhard (1991), internationalisation is an inherent part of corporate development and takes place, gradually, over time. It is a process of increased expansion or reduction of foreign-market activity with corresponding consequences for corporate strategy and structure. For these researchers, internationalisation is therefore to be interpreted as a series of consequences of company-related decisions and not as a single, one-time act. With regard to the concept of the international value chain, dynamic internationalisation does not merely involve strategy and organisation, but also entire functional areas and their tasks. "At the right time", "a good time", "the duration of the project", "too late", "too soon", "too slow", "move quicker", "faster processes" and "shorter branch cycle" – these are all phrases often heard on executive management levels and which characterise daily business. Suddenly, "speed", "time" and "timing" belong to the buzz vocabulary of business news.

Despite its widely recognised importance (Swoboda 2002; Kutschker and Schmid 2006), it is only recently that a few research articles have appeared on this subject such as those by Ancona et al. (2001), Eriksson et al. (2001), Hurmerinta-Peltomäki (2003), Anderson and Mattsson (2004), Oviatt and McDougall (2005), Jones and Coviello (2005), Dibrell et al. (2005). Time is not perceived as having determinate characteristics, but plays a rather vague but complex role (Eriksson et al. 2001; Hurmerinta-Peltomäki 2003; Anderson and Mattson 2004). For Hurmerinta-Peltomäki (2003), time is an abstract relational concept for which specifically temporal relations need to be established. The researcher names this problem as a reason for low interest in this important topic. In order to achieve competitive advantages, the understanding of timing and its significance is vital for successful internationalisation (Jones and Coviello 2005). In their analysis of the U.S. pulp and paper industry, Dibrell et al. (2005) even come to the conclusion that the integration of a "time-based strategy" enables internationalising organisations to improve strategic position and enhance performance in the global marketplace.

2.4.2 The role of corporate culture in the internationalisation process

A firm's culture stems from the attitudes and behaviour of its employees. Conversely, however, the firm's need to differentiate itself within its market environment means that it, in effect, controls the patterns of expectation and behaviour of its management and employees (Swoboda 2002). Hofstede relates culture (in the sense of patterns of feeling, thinking, and acting) to mental programmes that constitute the "software of the mind" (2001). Culture, he claims, is the "collective programming of the mind which distinguishes the members of one group or category of people from another" (p. 5).

Corporate culture, on the other hand, is defined by Schein (1984) as "a pattern of basic assumptions that a given group has invented, discovered, or developed in learning to cope with its problems of external adaptation and internal integration. These assumptions have worked well enough to be considered valid and are therefore taught to new members as the correct way to perceive, think and feel in relation to those problems".

As an artefact comprised of routines and repertoires for organising and managing business activity, corporate culture is shaped by the national culture of the firm's founders and the national circumstances of the founding (Morosini et al. 1998). However, as Hofstede (1991) pointed out, the cultural element of corporate organisational structure and functioning does not mean that all differences between organisations can be traced back to culture. The structure and the function of organisations are not determined by a "universal rationality". In fact, Morosini et al. argues that firms which operate on an international scale may need to possess a diverse set of routines and repertoires in order to be competitive in a diverse world.

In their well-known articles, Hofstede (1980, 2001), Hall and Hall (1996) and Trompenaars (1994) also expounded on the wider significance of corporate culture for international management. These authors have significantly improved understanding by citing a variety of concepts and cultural dimensions to explain the differences between national cultures and to recommend courses of action.

From the perspective of internationalisation and the necessity to adapt for successful foreign business, the question of how company cultures change and are influenced is of interest. In the literature, there are the theories of culture as a variable (Miller 1984), culture as a metaphor (Greipel 1988) and culture as a dynamic construct (Heinen 1987). According to the variable theory, firms follow either a "fit-approach" (meaning the culture is aligned with the strategy, structures and systems) or a "follow-approach" (meaning the company culture must be designed out of the selected strategy, structure or systems – as with the motto "culture follows strategy, structure and systems"). The metaphor approach means, in essence, that firms do not have culture but are culture – implying that firms cannot easily change the company culture. With the third theory, firms both have and are a culture. For the management in an internationalisation process, this means that the process of evolutionary culture development can be influenced to a certain degree, however not within a short time period (Kutschker and Schmid 2006).

2.4.3 Key success factors in internationalisation

Strategic management research has long sought to identify general success factors of firms (Schmitt 1997). Success factors are the factors which are regarded as being essential for a firm's long-term success and the attainment of its long-term goals (Kutschker and Schmid 2006). Analysts of international management have endeavoured to find the key success factors for internationalisation and individual stages of the internationalisation process such as when to commence export trading, make acquisitions, or enter into partnerships (see Link 1997 and Weber 1997).

Although there has already been extensive research on putative success factors in existing literature, there does not yet seem to be a specific set of laws that, when adhered to, automatically lead to greater success. The literature does not include any generally applicable catalogue of factors that can ensure the success of export activities (Link 1997), joint ventures (Eisele 1995; Oesterle 1995), acquisitions or cross-border mergers (Kirchner 1991). Based on the various histories and a variety of decision-making situations which cannot be easily compared, the findings of success-factors research should be according to Becker (2005) viewed more critically. Attempts at a generalisation may hardly be expected as each factor has a different effect in a particular period and country or under particular market- or environmental conditions. Furthermore, each is in permanent interaction with a host of other influencing factors. Kutschker and Schmid (2006) therefore recommended the option of "thinking in success potentials". In this sense, success potentials represent control figures which generate competitive advantages and are given responsibility for the attainment of strategic business objectives. This approach enables a firm to establish, maintain and develop the internal and external resources, abilities and competencies of its international operations in a broad-ranging pool of success potentials (Kutschker and Schmid 2006). The skill is then to select and assess the relevant success potentials which, again, are specific to each firm and its particular geography, period and situation (Aharoni 1993). These success potentials must then be developed in line with the business objective of the internationalisation project.

2.4.4 Internationalisation and firm performance

The relationship between internationalisation and the performance of a corporation has triggered extensive interdisciplinary research throughout the last three decades (Krist 2009, Bausch and Krist 2007, Ramaswamy 1995, Sullivan 1994). Researchers have examined the link between performance and the degree of internationalisation, attempting to empirically prove the theoretical argument that international expansion is a precondition for superior financial success. Postulating only the benefits of internationalisation, early studies in the 1970's and 1980's hypothesised a linear relationship between the degree of internationalisation (DOI) and firm performance. The findings of these inquiries have been inconsistent and contradictory.

Recognising that internationalisation, like all other potential corporate strategies, can be subject to risk and failure, researchers in the 1990's acknowledged that internationalisation brought both benefits and costs, with costs exceeding benefits at high levels of internationalisation (Ramaswamy 1995; Gomes and Ramaswamy 1999). However, this prescription was soon questioned. Sullivan (1994, p. 166) argued that for multinationals the supposition of a "deterministic relationship between financial performance and internationalisation, seemingly irrespective of the type or strategy of the MNC, questions the premise of proactive management." He indicated with his statistical analyses that the internationalisation-performance relationship "is characterised by at least one, if not a series of, convergence, decline, reorientation and convergence cycles."

According to past studies, it is an oversimplification to conclude the existence of a linear relationship between internationalisation and performance. Assessment of the interplay between costs and benefits along a firm's internationalisation trajectory provides findings that are more useful. The essays of Gomes and Ramaswamy

(1999) and Johanson and Vahlne (1990) have provided valuable insights in this respect with their assumption of incremental internationalisation, as have Sullivan (1994) and Hitt (1997) with their conceptual bases on organisational learning theory. The first theoretical framework suggests that companies are not doomed to experience declining performance at a certain point on their expansion path, but that managers can proactively shape the internationalisation performance relationship by shifting existing thresholds or avoiding them altogether. In contrast, the second theoretical framework emphasises the dynamic nature of the internationalisation threshold itself and suggests that internationalisation creates the need for, and thus is accompanied by, internal change. A firm expands its existing structures, systems, and other internal settings in a continuous process and needs to re-orientate and re-configure periodically in order to maintain superior performance.

Success, in the context of value, is when a previously set goal has been achieved. It can therefore only be assessed ex post, based on the defined goals (Becker 2005, Lynch 2009). Goals thereby represent environmental conditions strived for by people and are dependent upon the "goal-setting authorities". With regard to the success of internationalisation, these goals must therefore be explored. Several objectives are viable in the context of the many interest groups; for example, stakeholders who (can) place demands on a company. In addition to the classic criteria for financial targets such as export turnover, export share, market share in the foreign market, profit in export, profit per foreign market – criteria are also employed to represent future potential such as new-customer acquisition, success in market launch, reputation, etc. In his meta-analysis for measuring internationalisation performance, Krist (2009) identified six major measuring criteria: return on assets, return on sales, return on equity, sales growth, market share and return on investment. Which criterion or combination of criteria is employed depends upon the individual understanding of the term "success" and thereby, as Simon (2007) pointed out on the goal-setting and influence of the various key groups in a company.

More and more companies are implementing the concept of value orientation (Malik 2009). In this, the internationalisation process is subject to the goal of adding value. In this sense, each step to internationalisation, including the mode switch, is to be analysed according to its ability to add value. Of significance are the effects on the firm and the management of major value drivers.

In recent studies (Bausch and Krist 2007; Krist 2009), reference has additionally been made to the importance of the individual context – this consists of R&D intensity, product diversification, country of origin, firm age and firm size and the effects from the relationship between internationalisation and performance. In this, the authors agree that a greater level of internationalisation only contributes positively to firm performance if there is sufficient absorptive capacity to cope with increasing complexity.

2.5 Research on foreign mode switch

On the second theoretical level to be considered (see Table 2.1), the current theoretical research on mode switching will be analysed.

As illustrated in Table 2.2 the first studies came in a period of global growth. Since more and more firms have become active in foreign markets, the number of studies on efficient organisation of the mode and switch of market-entry strategy has increased. As to content, the early works concentrate on an analysis of the decision-making process, in particular the reasons and motivations for the change. In his dissertation, Calof (1993, 1991) was one of the first to consider the decision to switch modes and thus created the basis for several later works, such as those by Benito et al. (2005, 2009), Pedersen et al. (2002), Petersen et al. (2000b, 2006) and Swoboda (2002). In particular, his concept of an "effective pre-mode-change-decision learning process" and the positive influence on mode performance in the internationalisation of business activity set a precedent. A further point of emphasis is the identification of determining factors of a switch. The work by Weiss/Anderson (1992) initially only makes reference to the U.S. market for electronic assembly parts and observes the switch from independent sales agent to direct sales force. With the concept of the perceived switching cost, however, the study supplied valuable findings on decision-making behaviour in management. Benito and Welch (1994) developed the concept of mode combination or mode package. In their research, they pointed out that mode decisions are made on the basis of previous experience and knowledge, and reciprocally influence each other. Clark et al. (1997) departed from the concept of an exclusively incremental internationalisation. Their findings show that firms combine modes to create a specific internationalisation path in a country. As major determinants for the switch, they differentiate between market-specific knowledge und generalised knowledge from operating internationally. From the view of these researchers, the mode switch is not only influenced by the individual context factors of the country but also by know-how, the network and the management capabilities of the persons in the organisation.

Starting in the year 2000, the research group with Bent Petersen produced a number of "switching papers" based on a longitudinal study of Danish exporters from 1992 to 1997. The number of publications on mode switching alone indicates an increase in research on international business. In content, it deals with derivation of reasons for but also against the mode switch. In later works, the research was focused on the reasons and motivation for the switch within or between certain mode structures. In summary, it may be said that these researchers, the majority of whom hail from Scandinavia, have greatly contributed to knowledge regarding foreign mode switches and have made both concept-based (Petersen at al 2002) and quantitative contributions that are valuable.

More knowledge was gained with Swoboda (2002) and the first data record on the mode switches of German companies. He observed mode switches within a timeframe of ten years, between the eighties and nineties. Swoboda developed various concepts for analysing behaviour in expansion but also for the reduction of commitment and reasons for a switch. For the first time, sequences of change after market entry were summarised into internationalisation paths and these "Gestalt"-paths were tested for their success (Figure 2.2). In contrast to the switching paper, this study examined the reasons for the diverging paths of internationalisation. In addition to considering the current status quo, it also made interesting findings regarding the reasons for increasing or reducing commitment. This provided an indication of the right time to change, the intensity and the duration of the transition process, and the sequence in which events occur (Swoboda 2002).

Kaufmann and Jentzsch (2006) analysed internationalisation strategies of automotive-parts suppliers to China. They observed the switch from the selected market-entry strategy with the aid of fifteen individual cases. In comparison to the other studies, a specific foreign market is given here and the development of the selected operation mode is observed. As a result, the strategy-mode combination for market entry, for the survey timeframe and five years in the future is presented. From this, four development paths could be identified, as well as reasons for the switch.

Asmussen et al. (2009) discussed mode switching from the perspective of a country portfolio and the interdependencies of the selected mode in the countries. The coordination of the selected modes in a company is derived as more of a decisive criterion than the contextual conditions of the country. On the basis of a mathematical configuration model, the researchers suggest decision-making criteria for the mode switch. This was done with consideration of path dependency and the net present value.

In presenting the internationalisation pathway of the multinational company Kone in Japan, Benito et al. (2009) discussed the mode choice and mode switch. As a conceptual result, they present a simplified model with the influencing factors tied to the mode decision and show options for acting with the aid of five levels of intensity of the mode switch. Interesting in this single-case study is that the researchers considered past experience and, in particular, mode experience, mode learning and mode competence as all bearing a strong influence on the decision-making behaviour tied to a future mode. With regard to future research, they support the demand for further longitudinal analyses of other research groups.

In summary, it can be established that determinants tied to motives and reasons for switching have been further analysed in the past few years and now represent a number of factors in the areas of environment, resources, attitude, perception, capability and organisation. The significance of the type and manner of foreign operation for internationalisation success has also been recognised. However, there continue to be gaps regarding the influence of management on the internationalisation process and the decision for a switch, the characterisation of more successful and less successful internationalisation paths, the influence of the mode switch used thus far and the timing of the switch.

From this, the following questions can be derived: How do companies develop over the course of a longer period of time – at the level of the country and the level of the mode? How does the mode strategy and the internationalisation path influence performance? Does the starting configuration influence the path structure over the course of time? What are the correlations between the determining factors (e.g. past success, aspects of the internal company environment) and the mode switch? What role does the attitude of the management play? When is the right time for a switch? How does mode switching influence performance?

Table 2.2: Overview of main mode switch research from 1992 to 2009

	Author(s)	Main research question	Methodology/Data content	Assumptions/Statements
1.	Weiss and Anderson 1992	Main focus: future behaviour when and why to switch, based on one sales district in USA for semiconductor industry – the role of perceived switching cost	258 manufacturers (district sales managers) with independent sales agents were interviewed (questionnaire) Switch from independent sales agent to own sales force was examined	1. Managers avoid switching from representatives to a direct sales force when they perceive high overall switching costs 2. Dissatisfied manufacturers are more likely to choose direct export than satisfied ones 3. Switching costs force managers to live with sub-optimal arrangements 4. Sense of switching costs is influenced more by setting up the new system (e.g. structure of new own sales force) than the obstacles to dismantling the old system (e.g. terminating contracts, negative reaction from rep network)
2.	Calof 1993	How do firms go about making mode-change and mode-choice decisions? How does this process affect mode performance?	38 Canadian-owned (Ontario-based), medium-sized companies with activities in developed countries between 1980 and 1990, 100 mode selection- and switch decisions between 1980 - 1990 Switches between Export, Sales Subsidiary, Joint Venture, Wholly Owned Product Subsidiary	Mode decisions depend on "gut feeling" (39%). Executives indicated that most mode choices arose because managers had an a priori belief about what mode was most appropriate for the market in question. Assessment was based on perceptions of the market's sales potential (benefit) and of various modes' sales potential and costs, subject to environmental and resource constraints. Increasing knowledge and experience over time influences mode decisions
3.	Benito and Welch 1994	Depiction and explanation of the choice of foreign market servicing modes	Conceptual paper on foreign operation mode choices Mode change in general, mode combination	Concept of mode package (mode combination) is developed Calling for exploratory research and in-depth longitudinal studies ("in-process investigation") "Mode decision are made in package context"
4.	Calof and Beamish 1995	Why modes are changed? What explains the pattern of mode change?	38 Canadian-owned (Ontario-based), medium-sized companies with mode changes in foreign countries between 1980 and 1990. In total, 76 executives were interviewed about 139 mode changes. Switches between Export, Sales Subsidiary, Joint Venture, Wholly Owned Product Subsidiary	Stimuli for mode change; Internationalisation pattern (One-Step, Multi-Step-Investment, De-Internationalisation) 1. The right attitude/mindset is the major determinant of the internationalisation path 2. Not only the strategy or the product must be appropriate, but also the attitudes of the firm's executives. Attitudes influence perception of benefit, costs and risk

Table 2.2: Overview of main mode switch research from 1992 to 2009 (cont.)

	Author(s)	Main research question	Methodology/Data Content	Assumptions/Statements
5.	Clark et al. 1997	Understanding mode of operating in specific foreign market under consideration of corporate level	In-depth interviews with senior management of 25 UK-based firms about what and how those companies switched 203 switches after market entry were reported; between-mode: 129 to FDI, 5 retrenchment; within-mode: 34; mixed-mode: 36 Switches between Export, Licensing, FDI (subsidiary, production, JV)	It is not the market per se which determines the institutional form of market operation. Rather, as firms operate they develop both knowledge of the process of internationalisation in addition to network arrangements. Past experiences, resulting from entry into other markets, feeds into current decisions relating to the form of foreign market servicing adopted in individual markets. Developed the concept of between mode shifts and within mode shifts
6.	Petersen et al. 2000a	Understanding the different options for international operations for and after market entry	3 short-cases and further company examples are used to explain the different options for international operations for and after market entry	Development of a four-field matrix as concept for foreign operation mode decisions: 1. Conceal – terminate, 2. Conceal – integrate, 3. Reveal – terminate, 4. Reveal – integrate Strategic flexibility (ability and preparedness to change international operations) as important factor to make international business operation mode decisions, so that the entrant firm is in a position to switch modes more readily to meet changing circumstances.
7.	Petersen et al. 2000b	What factors impel exporters to replace a foreign intermediary and what factors impede such actions?	Data collection at two points in time: 1992 (questionnaire)and 1997 (telephone interview) with 273 Danish exporters 74 had changed their foreign market servicing since 1992 (36 to an own sales organisation and 38 to a different intermediary)	Switching costs are important barrier to the replacement of foreign sales agent/distributor. Dissatisfaction with local intermediary does not appear as a determinant of replacement. Old relationship does not safeguard intermediaries against replacement.
8.	McNaughton 2001	Main focus: decision making at market entry vs. subsequent mode switches (type of decision process, decision period, use of formal study, external advice, alternative modes).	120 Canadian software exporters completed questionnaire 29 fast-growing firms had switched modes since market entry	The pattern of subsequent channel change is evidence of experimental learning. In accordance with stage models: movement between stages is a result of increased knowledge, as well as increased financial and other resources.

45

Table 2.2: Overview of main mode switch research from 1992 to 2009 (cont.)

	Author(s)	Main research question	Methodology/Data Content	Assumptions/Statements
9.	Petersen and Welch 2002	Examination of the issue of mode combination	Conceptual paper on mode classification	Mode combinations are not part of International Business literature yet, only limited knowledge exists on the subject. Foreign operation mode combination: Unrelated modes, Segmented modes, Mode complementarity, Mode competition. An intra-mode switch or the addition of a new strategy to the existing mode may be a more effective way of responding to changes in the market environment than the adoption of a completely new mode. Change within a mode or adding a new operation to existing mode may be a more effective way of responding to a change in market environment than a completely new mode switch.
10.	Pedersen et al. 2002	Main question: what and why the companies change foreign mode Focus on impetus for and motivation of single mode switch	276 Danish exporters, later reduced to 214. Out of these: 182 without a switch, 36 with a complete switch of operation mode, mainly from agent/distributor to companies' own sales forces/subsidiary Data collection at two points: 1992 and 1997	Switching costs as explanation for changing/not changing foreign management operations. Switching cost might be reduced through careful planning. The longer the exporters have been in the market, the more the propensity to switch increases (which is the opposite of Transaction cost approach – the longer a relationship, lasts, the more assets the parties will develop)
11.	Swoboda 2002	Main question: what, why and how companies change with consideration to internal and external factors	In total, 271 mode switches: 183 switches for further penetration, 88 switches for reduction Switches between end of 80's and end of 90's (within 10 year period)	Development of various concepts how to analyse mode structure and mode development. Three level model: stimuli of change, primary level and secondary level of change. Reasons and motivation for reduction and penetration differ. Success depends on willingness of management, capital employed, synergies, knowledge about internationalisation and product image.
12.	Benito et al. 2005	What are the effects of switch motivation/deterrents (e.g. contractual restriction, loss of sales revenue) on the choice of distribution channel?	260 Danish exporters in 1992 and 1997: 182 did not change foreign distribution, 42 replaced intermediary, 36 switched to in-house operation	The results suggest that the decision to carry out within-mode shifts (i.e. to replace an existing intermediary) is driven by a different set of factors than the decision to switch to another foreign operation mode (i.e. to in-house operations).

46

Table 2.2: Overview of main mode switch research from 1992 to 2009 (cont.)

	Author(s)	Main research question	Methodology/Data Content	Assumptions/Statements
13.	Fryges 2005	What triggers mode switch? How to predict mode switching?	Comparing sales mode for market entry, 1997 and 2003 for Germany and UK for software/services, ICT-hardware engineering, health/life sciences, other high-tech manufacturer 1997/1998: 362 completed questionnaires for UK, 232 questionnaires for Germany; 2003: 200 questionnaires for Germany; Total: 523 mode	Development of a model to predict mode switching. Ownership advantages (e.g., the firm's physical, financial, and intangible assets) and internalisation advantages (e.g., transaction-specific assets like the requirement of intense product customisation) are decisive for selecting the optimal sales mode, especially for predicting a sales mode change from exporting via an intermediary to direct exports.
14.	Petersen et al. 2006	Focus: performance of intermediary and development of incentives to address termination dilemma	258 Danish exporters: 183 had no major change, 40 replaced intermediary, 35 switched to in-house operation	Study examines incentives for stimulating foreign intermediaries and ensuring that foreign intermediaries are willing to commit resources. Results: both low and high performance increase, the risk of contract termination for the foreign intermediary (termination dilemma in foreign distribution). Recommendation on management export personal: Behaviour based compensation: own sales force; outcome-based compensation: agents/importer.
15.	Kaufmann and Jentsch 2006	1. Which internationalisation strategies? 2. Through which internationalization modes do companies realise strategies? 3. Which evolution paths can be observed? 4. Which parameters influence suppliers' choice of strategies and modes?	15 cases from automotive supply industry in China Mode time: Current mode and year when the new mode was established; intended mode in five years.	Comparable research approach in respect to how to analyse decision-making behaviour after market entry. Identification of four main evolution pathways over a certain period of time in China (for automotive sector): 1. Risk-averse early entrant, 2. Equity Joint Venture with non-Chinese partners or Chinese original equipment manufacturer, 3. Equity Joint Venture with Chinese suppliers, 4. Late-following wholly own foreign owned enterprise. Characterising and describing reasons of each pathway behaviour.
16.	Chetty and Agndal 2007	Influence of relationship related change scenarios on internationalisation process Main focus on what kind of mode change and why the mode changed	20 SMEs, 50 respondents interviewed, 53 mode switches identified (increased control mode: 34 cases; decreased control mode: 19 cases) Mainly Sweden and New Zealand	Identification of three groups with influence of social capital ("acquire resources from business network"): 1. Efficacy role, 2. Serendipity role, 3. Liability role and act as a trigger and enabler for mode change in internationalisation process. Social capital helps reduce transaction costs, such as relational and opportunity costs, develops knowledge and provides opportunities for change.

Table 2.2: Overview of main mode switch research from 1992 to 2009 (cont.)

	Author(s)	Main research question	Methodology/Data Content	Assumptions/Statements
17.	Swoboda and Jager 2008	Main focus: how and why companies change foreign mode including differentiation of expansion/reduction of engagement Comparison of these results with the observations of Calof/Beamish (1995)	265 German small to medium-sized companies reported 332 switches (219 penetration, 113 reduction; 93 companies described penetration and reduction of changes at the same time)	Experience and learning based models are still important for internationalisation research. Internationalisation development is based on a combination of evolutionary and revolutionary steps and not on single context factors such as corporate resources. Different reasons for penetration and reduction engagements. Internal factors (resources/strategy) play a dominant role in both studies Study applied evaluation framework from Swoboda (2002). Development of three-level model: stimuli/determinations of mode change, primary level of mode change, secondary level of mode change.
18.	Asmussen et al. 2009	Main focus: better understanding and explanation of foreign mode decisions What are interdependencies between foreign operation mode decisions across countries and over time? What might be managerial capacity to make these decisions?	Conceptual paper Descriptive model of foreign operation mode Discussion of dynamic configuration of foreign mode	Proposing a framework on how to configurate foreign operation modes. Looking at firm's foreign operation diversity, i.e. country-by-country variations of mode portfolio and foreign operation fluctuation, i.e. tendency to change mode over time.
19.	Benito et al. 2009	Main focus: What are foreign operation modes? What influences mode choice and the evolution of operation modes	Conceptual paper on mode choice and change Descriptive model of foreign operation mode Case example: Kone in Japan	Proposing a framework on how to choose and change modes. Past experience creates mode bias (mode inertia: tendency to use an existing mode) Asking for in-depth and longitudinal qualitative studies.

48

2.6 Critical evaluation of literature review on theory level 1 and 2

The numerous theoretical attempts to explain internationalisation (Malhotra et al. 2003; Zentes et al. 2004; Becker 2005; Kutschker and Schmid 2006; Leonidou et al. 2010) may not form one coherent picture, but they do give international companies sufficient pointers to enable them to develop a course of strategic management for their internationalisation process. It will not be the objective of this thesis to indicate which model is most or least suitable for the internationalisation of firms. This question shall remain open and there will be no attempt to argue for or against a particular theory. In the selection of theories, the author has selected models which have already shown to be of knowledge-gaining value with regard to the internationalisation process and mode switches. In their sum, they form the key theoretical framework for this thesis.

Coviello and McAuley (1999) regarded the process models as having the greatest influence on research on the internationalisation of medium-sized enterprises. They do, however, also refer to the results of other studies which leapfrog certain steps in the "establishment chain" and include periods of inactivity as well as periods of fast change or de-internationalisation in the form of increased import activities (Welch and Benito 1996; Turcan 2003). For Macharzina and Wolf (2005), the OLI-Paradigm by Dunning (1981, 2000) is the model which has had a particularly striking effect on the theoretical discussion in the last two decades (Kutschker and Schmid 2006). In this theory, company-specific advantages form the basis for determining which international market-entry and market-development strategies are to be selected and when they should be implemented. Although the Dunning theory offers a systematisation of international business activity, it assumes a rational key actor and thereby excludes behavioural aspects to a great extent.

An attempt to differentiate between the static, more traditional approaches and the dynamic process-oriented theoretical models will show that they cannot be strictly divided. With the behavioural school, for example, both the behaviour of key individuals at market entry but also the further process of internationalisation is taken into account. The knowledge gain is, however, generally far more comprehensive with dynamic theoretical approaches as they allow a more in-depth analysis of the research object and take time aspects into consideration. The GAINS-paradigm seems to be particularly useful in that it locates first significant development patterns and allows conclusions with regard to success and causal factors (Swoboba 2002; Macharzina and Wolf 2005; Kutschker and Schmid 2006). The model of the entrepreneurial internationalisation process by Jones and Coviello (2005) is excellently suited as an explanatory model for internationalisation behaviour regardless of whether it is a market-entry or more ex-post perspective (i.e. the mode switch). To a certain extent, the authors tie the elements of the "three E's" theory with the path theory and Gersick's punctuated equilibrium as a basis for change in the internationalisation (Jones and Coviello: "fingerprint pattern and profile"). The Three Level model (Swoboda 2002) is an integrated approach which shows the company-internal dimension of internationalisation in addition to the traditional, market-oriented perspective (Simon 2007). In this approach, the internationalisation process takes place within a continuum of evolutionary and revolutionary patterns.

Another interesting approach, particularly for explaining the course of internationalisation after market entry, is the previously mentioned construct of path dependency (Teece et al. 1997; Araujo and Rezende 2003; Hutzschenreuter et al. 2007). As presented, the path dependency limits conceivable internationalisation patterns and can – depending on the perspective – have a positive and stabilising effect (positive path dependency) or it can limit the international company development (negative path dependency). The path perspective places emphasis on the process, not the single decision. The unique character of the process determines the process result and its irreversible nature. This means that the path research considers historical components as development dramaturgy and integrates feedback loops from the behaviour during internationalisation. In this manner, the model by Jones and Coviello (2005) could be sensibly expanded.

A further aspect is the question of the reflective, ex-post orientation of most of the theories. Should internationalisation theory explain and rationalise behaviour of firms after the fact? Or should it rather be the goal to analyse actual, current behavioural patterns in order to derive possible future ones? Interestingly, the discussion of success factors and performance, which is necessary for this, has shown that a success-based analysis of a certain behaviour pattern tied to internationalisation is difficult to carry out but bears great knowledge value for describing and analysing the internationalisation of firms.

Although the models of the process-based theories (Uppsala- and Helsinki-School) presented first indications of time-related aspects of internationalisation, this subject has so far been widely neglected in the theoretical discussion (Hurmerinata-Peltomäki 2001; Zentes at al 2004). This particularly applies to the context of strategy and post-entry behaviour and decision making. Recently, however, this has begun to change and the subject of "timing" is growing in significance and in its bearing on corporate competitiveness (Vermeulen and Barkema 2002; Jones and Coviello 2005; Dibrell 2005). New studies on the subject present open questions and weak points. There is, for example, general confusion as to when activities should actually begin. How long is the optimal time period for a switch? What is the optimal speed/pace for a switch? What influence does the environment have on the definition of an opportune moment of change? What influence do changes in the environment have on the course of the process?

An analysis of timing in the context of internationalisation reveals the significance of the corporate past of firms and the dependency on context factors, such as the direct environment of the firm, the industry and the foreign market in question (Coviello and Jones 2005; Maitland et al. 2005; Kutschker and Schmid 2006). In summary, the factor of time and its influence on successful internationalisation has not been sufficiently considered in the research literature on this subject to date. As regards to the decision-making process, questions tied to changing the approach to developing export markets or a systematisation of the involved processes remains unanswered (Swoboda 2002).

In conclusion, research on the internationalisation process has become well established. However, research subjects revolving around a change of strategy after market entry are still rare (Benito et al. 2009) and only considered in due depth by a small number of top researchers (see Table 2.2). From the literature review, it can be established that the dynamic aspects of the management of foreign operations, switching modes and the observation of decision-making behaviour from the perspective of historical development have been overlooked in research. This is due to the manner and nature of the investigative methodology and surely also to the difficulty of gathering historical data regarding internationalisation behaviour.

After this interim conclusion regarding knowledge from internationalisation research to date, the following section will discuss the theoretical presentation with regard to decision-making behaviour tied to a switch of foreign operation mode. This section forms the core of the discussion of research results on the subject of mode switching.

The discussion to this point does not represent a comprehensive theoretical construct/explanatory approach. Rather, it has presented various partial approaches to internationalisation theory. To understand the concrete mechanisms at the micro-level of decision-making behaviour of the actors, additional assumptions/ considerations are necessary that are lacking at this point. For this reason, the inclusion of further, theoretical models on decision-making behaviour in the international management of foreign operations is necessary. In this case, first the terms tied to the mode switch will be clarified. Building on this, assumptions regarding decision-making behaviour in mode switching will then be derived from the literature. The subject and objective of the analysis following is therefore to formulate an economically-founded model that supplies indications of the content of the decision processes. The derived assumptions/expectations will then be presented in the form of hypotheses that are subsequently evaluated within the empirically operationalised design.

2.7 The decision making process of foreign mode switch

In this section, the theoretical levels of internationalisation (theory level 1) and research on mode switching (theory level 2) will be supplemented by the presentation of decision-making behaviour tied to mode switching (theory level 3). The aim is to achieve a holistic view of decision-making behaviour beginning with the start of internationalisation, market entry, and the preparation and implementation of the foreign mode switch. The results form the frame of reference for specification of the research questions and the derivation of proposition in the third chapter. Key terms will first be defined and the exact subject of investigation determined.

2.7.1 On the term "foreign operation mode"

The central term "foreign operation mode" denotes the manner and type of market operation of companies in foreign countries (Calof and Beamish 1995; Welch et al. 2007; Benito et al. 2009). Forms of operation or management methods could, for example, include: the use of agents, granting licences, setting up franchises, founding a subsidiary or acquiring firms (Kutschker and Schmid 2006). Contrary to the concept of market entry where these strategic options (export, licensing, subsidiary, etc.) are also used, the concept of market operation is more comprehensive. The firms have already entered the foreign market. This means that the decision about which country and the decision to enter a market have already been made and implemented. The market-operation strategy does not necessarily correspond with the strategy of market entry. Companies can, for example, enter a market with a sales representative, add a second representative after a certain amount of time and then gradually change this to another operation mode, such as a subsidiary. Or the representative may be combined with sales companies.

Foreign operation denotes the market servicing/management method which companies utilise to conduct activities in foreign markets after initial market entry (ex-post entry operation). That includes decisions on strategy, organisation and process of internationalisation (Calof and Beamish 1995). With the decision for a foreign operation mode, the understanding and content (e.g. organisational structure, personnel and coordination) are established from the perspective of the international management. From the view of international marketing, this decision affects, for example, control and viability of the price strategy or the success prospects of sales. In international business, the decision regarding an operation mode is a key decision with repercussions for the scope of expansion, diversification, differentiation and the application of resources (Welch et al. 2007).

The strategic switch from a previous mode of foreign operation to a new mode forms the central element of this research.

2.7.2 "Mode switch"

A mode switch occurs when
- a new operation mode replaces a previous one (e.g. sales company replaces importers) (Swoboda 2002; Benito et al. 2005; Fryges 2005; Welch et al. 2007)
- when a new mode supplements the previous mode of market operation (e.g. sales representative and sales company), (Petersen and Welch 2002; Welch et al. 2007)
- when an existing mode is expanded or reduced (e.g. a representative is supplemented by one or two further representatives or the number of agents employed is reduced from ten to eight), (Swoboda 2002; Petersen and Welch 2002; Fryges 2005; Welch et al. 2007)
- when significant changes are made within the selected mode of market operation (e.g. a change of manager or the exchange or replacement of a sales representative). (Benito et al. 2005; Welch et al. 2007)

In summary we refer to a mode switch when at the end of the change, a new type and manner of market operation is implemented and observable.

2.7.3 The theoretical construct of strategic decision making

Decisions in behavioural science are viewed in the context of a decision-making process comprised of several individual decision acts (Figure 2.3). After the analysis and establishment of the problem, information is gathered and analysed in the next step so that it may be subsequently evaluated. Various alternatives for solving the problem are generated. The alternatives are then assessed and, as a result of the decision-making process, a decision is made that must be accepted and implemented. The active structuring requires an occupation with the concepts and knowledge of current conditions which are usually gained in a decision-making process.

It can be argued that a decision-making process comprises the assessment of the current situation in the form of a status-quo analysis, the formulation of a target concept and the implementation of activities (Zentes et al. 2004).

Figure 2.3 shows a decision making model under consideration of the multi-level context of environment, actors and the process. It should be noted that this model represents an ideal-typical construct on the basis of which the individual steps of decision making can be discussed in a theoretical manner. Real decision-making processes are difficult to simplify; they overlap each other or may occur in opposite sequences. Some steps may even fall away completely. The ideal-typical process will be maintained here to serve as a framework of reference for further discussion of the theory on mode switching.

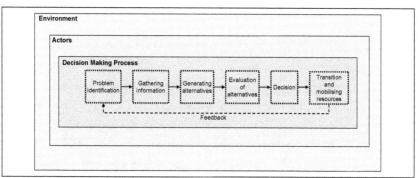

Figure 2.3: Multi-level model of "ideal" process and decision-making (adopted from Albaum and Duerr 2008, Ahlstrom and Bruton 2010)

In the context of the internationalisation process, this means that after market entry and a certain amount of time engaging in foreign market activity, a firm is inevitably faced with the question of how to optimise its foreign export organisation (Swoboda 2002). Based on the need to correct a perceived "misfit" between the foreign market environment and the current export strategy, the foreign operation mode is adjusted (Pauwels and Matthyssens 2004). The goal is to correct managerial misjudgement or to adapt to new circumstances (Welch et al. 2007). On these premises, certain possible measures and activities are discussed, evaluated, resolved, planned, modified and executed by the firm. According to the systems-theoretical perspective (Steiger and Lippmann 2003), the environment in which such activities are embedded, the structure of the corresponding process, and the behaviour of key actors involved in the process may all be observed as elements of the multi-level system shown in Figure 2.3.

The multi-level model represents a basis for understanding the decision-making process. The integration of the perspectives of Environment, Actors and Process allows a description of behavioural and decision-making aspects in the course of internationalisation and elucidates the relationships and interdependencies within and between these levels (Simon 2007; Albaum and Duerr 2008; Ahlstrom and Bruton 2010). The purely process-related view of internationalisation is thereby expanded to include influencing factors from the corporate environment and the behaviour of key decision makers with the aim of achieving a more comprehensive understanding of the challenges of internationalisation after actual market entry (Swoboda 2002).

At a superordinate level, the environment of the firm (with its market-relevant factors of sales organisation, demand development, customer behaviour, cultural distance etc.) forms the outer context for individual behaviour. Key actors in the internal and external environment represent the next level. Through their behaviour, they directly or indirectly influence decision processes within the firm. They form a complex system which interacts with other systems, such as the domestic or foreign sales organisation, or certain customers. Specific steps of development within structured time periods provide orientation for the actual transformational process (Jones and Coviello 2005). Areas on higher levels comprise the content of those below them. It is also assumed that the higher levels have a dominating influence on the levels below them. In this frame of reference, all structures and activities of all levels stand in causal connection to each other and may be interpreted in the context of the company and its social environment (Steiger and Lippmann 2003).

2.7.4 Dimensions of mode switching decisions – a theoretical analysis

In the following, the theoretical constructs of a general decision-making model are set in the context of a specific model for international management decisions. The aim of this section is to conceptualise the research subject on the basis of the corresponding theories and explanatory approaches. The research questions will then be formulated and the propositions constructed.

Figure 2.4 shows the conceptual model for the theoretical analysis on the main research focus of mode switching behaviour.

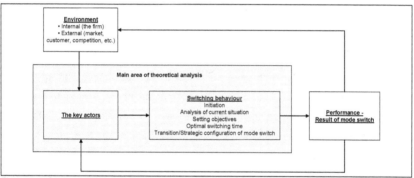

Figure 2.4: Conceptual model for theoretical analysis

For this purpose, and based on Jones and Coviello (2005) with consideration of the explanatory approaches of internationalisation theories discussed in Chapter 2, a specific set of constructs was identified which will serve as a theoretical framework in the proposed analysis.

2.7.4.1 Internal and external environment

As a social system, the national and international environment of a company is complex and dynamic (Steiger and Lippmann 2003). It is interrelated, reciprocally influencing factors are constantly changing and significantly affect the behaviour of key actors in the internationalisation process and their strategic options for action (Welch and Luostarinen 1993; Jones 1999; Li et al. 2004; Welch et al. 2007). Due to these changing conditions, management is limited in its ability to make a prognosis. There may be a completely different situation at the conclusion of the internationalisation process than there was at market entry. According to Nummela et al. (2004) depending on the level of international experience and the attitude/global mindset of the decision makers, environmental factors are perceived and evaluated differently in the main phases of decision process.

Environmental factors affect the timeframe of the new foreign operation and the degree of the successful achievement of targets. In business practice, reactions coming from the environment and directly or indirectly involving stakeholders are often not taken seriously enough (Sakhalin II 2005).

2.7.4.2 Key actors and their influence

Actors involved in the dynamic development of foreign operations can include the advisory board, top management, the export management or internationalisation team, the current (e.g. export managers, local sales or cooperation partners, direct customers) or future members of the foreign operation mode (e.g. new sales or cooperation partners). Other actors, such as investors, government representatives, shareholders or creditors may also participate in the opinion building. In the sense of a corporate international policy, these actors make individual or collective decisions regarding the further internationalisation or de-internationalisation of the firm in question (Kutschker and Schmid 2006). Today, such decisions are made by a team and no longer solely by a few individuals actively involved in the running of the organisation (McKenna and Martin-Smith 2005). A decision represents the resolution to take one specific action from a variety of possible alternatives (Rollinson 2005). It is influenced by perceptions of conditions in the foreign target market and of internal and external conditions in the home market. The status of past and present foreign operation modes also plays a role. Depending on the phase of the process, the key actors are the driving force, impulse-providers and context designers. They introduce methods, document and control (Chetty and Blankenburg Holm 2000; Müller-

Stewens and Lechner 2003). In making their decisions, they are influenced by internal stakeholders (e.g. middle management and employees in the various functional areas, e.g. service support, purchasing, logistics, R&D) and external stakeholders from the business environment of the firm (e.g. suppliers, investors, the government, customers). Naturally, competitive behaviour – "I guess we have to do it. Everybody is going there." (Aharoni 1966) – and other factors relevant to the corporate or general environment play an important role (see Chetty and Blankenburg Holm 2000; Sharma and Blomstermo 2003).

Decisions related to internationalisation are not (always) purely rational or the result of a conscious and intentional selection process. Benito and Welch (1994) and Johanson and Mattson (1988) even believe "that we no longer need to demonstrate that the rational models are inadequate descriptions of process". In correspondence with real deviations from a strict principle of rationality, the types of decision makers can be categorised within superordinate schools of thought in strategy research.

Mintzberg (1994) alone differentiated between "10 Schools of Thought". The fact that there is a bounded rationality of decision-making processes involved in internationalisation has been widely validated and is tied to intellectual, psychological, technical, contextual, process-related, political and historical limitations (Penrose 1956; Simon 1960; Cyert and March 1963; Vernon 1966; Aharoni 1966; Johanson and Wiedersheim-Paul 1975; Johanson and Vahlne 1977, 1990; McKenna and Martin-Smith 2005). Of particular significance for this are the factors effecting resistance to change, political pressure, power to execute, expectation of future development, trust in corporate capabilities, power struggles, global mindsets and "behaviour during phases of decision" (Ansoff and McDonnell 1990; Fletcher 2001; Swoboda 2002; Gupta and Govindarajan 2002; Nummela et al. 2004; Rollinson 2005). These factors influence (either individually or in combination) decision-making behaviours of key actors in corporate internationalisation and build the interaction platform.

Depending on the scale of the mode switch being planned, key stakeholders may demonstrate a strong resistance to change with regard to the decisions made by the top management. The resistance may delay the project, move it in a different direction to that originally planned (project deviation), increase the costs or bring it to a halt entirely (Ansoff and McDonnell 1990). Under certain circumstances, the top management may be pursuing different interests to the advisory board or other influential stakeholders. Resistance against planned changes arising from these decisions can influence the further strategic development of the foreign operation.

The more time actors have for the foreign mode switch, the lower the degree of resistance to change will be. In most cases, however, it is the specific environment of the company which will indirectly determine the right time for strategic changes (the windows of opportunity) and planned projects are then carried out in a phase of optimal balance between resistance to change and external time pressure. This phase is termed the "climate of change" (Ansoff and McDonnell 1990, Freidank 1994). In a situation of crisis, with its accompanying sense of urgency, the readiness to accept planned change can be increased with the result that implementation of measures and the change as a whole is accelerated (Ansoff and McDonnell 1990).

Political pressure coming from the top management or foreign mode management can reduce resistance and result in faster implementation. In some circumstances however, it also increases resistance and slow things down. The manner in which power is exerted can have a decisive influence on the opinions, emotions and actions of internal and external actors (Otto et al. 2007).

(Partial-) decisions are further influenced by the level of trust in the capabilities of company employees, the perception of the general and specific environment and the anticipated ramifications of the decisions (Child et al. 2005).

Behaviour during an internationalisation process is further affected by the international perspective (global mindset) of the actors. This refers, for example, to a manager's positive attitude towards international affairs, and also to his or her ability to adjust to different environments and cultures (Nummela et al. 2004). It refers to the actors' openness and awareness of cultural diversity and the ability to handle it (Fletcher 2001; Gupta and Govindarajan 2002). Actors also demonstrate an international perspective through a commitment to international markets, an international vision and proactive attitude, as well as customer orientation, responsiveness and marketing competence in a more general sense (Nummela et al. 2004). Actors also need the knowledge and the skills to maintain this international perspective. It must be cultivated and continuously revised through lessons learned and experience gathered in international markets (Fletcher 2001). The significance of the global mindset becomes apparent when certain decision-making situations are analysed. Different degrees of it can lead to differing perceptions of organisation, time, culture and country-market congruence – despite the same given stimuli – thereby leading to conflicting decisions (Swoboda 2002; Hinterhuber 2004; Rollinson 2005). Particularly when it is a question of the manner in which the foreign market is to be developed in the future (expectation of foreign market), a global mindset of the key actors plays an extremely important role. Factors such as previous international experience, the presence of an international vision, openness to foreign cultures, highly-developed customer orientation and the ability to continuously learn, influence the global mindset and assessment of risks and opportunities, and thereby all behaviour tied to the decision-making process (Swoboda 2002; Nummela et al. 2004).

From the heightened complexity, dynamics and discontinuity, higher demands on control and risk management result. A form of modern project management is the minimum requirement for this. Macharzina and Wolf (2005) noted that risk management has grown in importance due to the increasing number of international codes and regulations.

The importance of feedback-loops and ongoing communication of the actors in the internationalisation process is undisputed (Steiger and Lippmann 2003; Greif et al. 2004). Particularly "open" feedback in the course of the change process is part of a good management culture in internationalisation (Greif et al. 2004).

2.7.4.3 Initiating factors for foreign operation changes

In order to initiate an internationalisation process, triggering forces are necessary which prompt the firm and its key actors to change the current foreign operation strategy (Aharoni, 1966). According to Aharoni (1966), firms stick to behavioural patterns for as long as satisfactory results can be achieved through them. Although various studies have often observed a switch of modes after actual market entry, changes of, or adjustments to, initial market-entry strategies are seldom "planned ahead" and then carried out as a logical consequence (Petersen et al. 2000; Welch et al. 2007). Often the explanation for this lies in the assumption that switching the current mode will be difficult and expensive (Pedersen et al. 2002).

The initial impetus for a mode switch can originate from within the company itself (internal) or from the outside (external) (Pedersen et al. 2002; Welch et al. 2007). Internal triggers of a decision can, for example, come from the experiences which key actors have made in foreign countries through previous jobs or studies abroad. A strong affinity for a foreign market inevitably creates a strong interest which manifests itself in the initiation of the project. External triggers can come from pressure exerted by international customers or result from a fear of competitive disadvantages (Schoppe 1998). The fear that trade/import barriers may increase also has a motivating influence on key actors in an internationalisation process and can motivate an expansion of foreign activity (Aharoni 1966).

Depending on the perception filter of the internal and external conditions (and on the international perspective and specific targets), the actors involved may also vote against the internationalisation project. Here, individual objectives, aspiration levels, human relationships and even levels of authority or power among the key actors can play a major role (Jost 2000). This is demonstrated by the following examples given (Hammond et al., p. 2, 1998) of attitudes, beliefs and values held by management:

- "Do I have the full support of the executive and supervisory boards when it comes to the further internationalisation of our company, even if the process is more complicated and expensive than planned?"
- "If the internationalisation project fails, what will the consequences be for me?"

- "Do I have what it takes to be successful on an international scale?"
- "If I concentrate too much on export trade, might I not run the risk of missing opportunities elsewhere?"
- "The complexity of foreign markets is increasing. Is there not a danger that I'll lose my ability to influence and control operations?"
- "The risks are greater – am I putting my career on the line, needlessly?"
- "The time doesn't seem quite right to set up a sales subsidiary. Would it not be better to wait and trust market forces?"

Intuitive or irrational behaviour tied to vanity, envy, over-ambition, sympathy or antipathy, instability and foolishness, unsatisfied claims to power, social "baggage", concern only about own success, aversion or attraction to risk, yesterday's dispute, waking up on the wrong side of the bed, seasonal affective disorder, playing it by ear, blindness, temporary indecision or self-overestimation, can further influence the behaviour of key actors and prompt them to either accept or reject a decision in favour of internationalisation (Kappler 2003; Ahlstrom and Bruton 2010)

A major driver for a mode switch is the necessity of aligning the foreign operation to current conditions in the external environment (Ansoff and Sullivan 1990). Expansion or modification of the foreign operation is the result of continuous experimental learning about the foreign market in question (McNaughton, p. 18, 2001) with the accompanying perception of reduced risk. Perceived uncertainty regarding own behaviour and the future development of the foreign market is reduced by additional knowledge of the country in question (see e.g. Johanson and Wiedersheim-Paul 1975; Johanson and Vahlne 1977, 1990; Welch and Luostarinen 1988; Melin 1992). Anderson and Mattson (2004) argue that the development of foreign operation may be viewed as an ongoing, never-ending, reorganisation process within a dynamic network. In place of the variety of theoretical explanations as to why international strategies emerge, reference is made here to the eclectic theory of Dunning (1988b). Although his hypotheses only refers to direct investments, his approach reflects the major theoretical treatises on the strategic decision-making behaviour of companies in different phases of internationalisation (Swoboda 2002).

2.7.4.4 Evaluation of current situation

To identify the potential for future development or modification, the firm carries out an analysis of the current situation in the internal and external environment (Ansoff and McDonnel 1990). This initial assessment serves the definition of the current position in order to further determine which specific objectives are to be targeted and which measures will be necessary for this. As an aid, firms often employ the dimensions of market attractiveness and relative competitive position (Hinterhuber 2004). As criteria for determining market attractiveness, the factors of market volume, market growth, costs of market entry, intensity of competition, profitability and market barriers could be chosen. Examples of criteria for assessing the relative corporate competitive position could be reputation/image, product range/range of service, market share and market orientation. The aim is to have a solid assessment of the current situation as a foundation for discussing company-development potential in the selected target country markets. Depending on the abilities of the management/employees, and the selected strategy options, the results of this analysis can serve as a basis for further strategy development and structural organisation of export-market operations (Ansoff and McDonnel 1990; Hinterhuber 2004).

As Souchon et al. (2003) pointed out, critical in this phase is the gathering and evaluating of data about the international markets, customers, competitors, etc.. As this information is decisive for perceived uncertainty and risk, the major motive is to reduce uncertainty through an abundance of relevant details on the specific export environment. In the case of most enterprises, however, the limited absorptive capacity must be taken into consideration to avoid detrimental effects on decision processes Souchon et al. (2003) argued. According to him and further supported by Bazerman and Chugh (2006) the firm's ability to distribute such information effectively to different potential users and those users' ability to handle it in a way that enhances rather than hinders the decision-making process (in other words, the information is accessible and comprehensible, users have the right experience and knowledge for evaluation and anticipation) is critical in this phase (Teece et al. 1997). The interpretation and evaluation of information gathered can also depend on the objectives, attitudes and expectations of the management executive in question (Nummela et al. 2004). In the phase of information gathering and evaluation, the answer to the decision regarding internationalisation is often assumed in advance and the management seeks and accepts only information that confirms the pre-emptory decision (verdict-based information search as compared to evidence-based information search). With this phenomenon, referred to as "confirmation evidence bias", information and experiences tied to previously formulated assumptions or judgments are assessed more positively than information on options that are new and have not yet been considered (Ahlstrom and Bruton 2010). An export area sales manager who is stressed by foreign travel and whose leadership style is authoritarian will perceive, interpret and react to criticism expressed by colleagues differently than a manager who internationalises his/her company with a certain degree of ease and a high level of personal commitment (Steiger and Lippmann 2003). The subjective perception of the observer, the social network, education, health and his/her personality and style plays a major role here. Depending on whether the key internationalisation actors are tired, wide awake, angry or in a good mood, well- or insufficiently informed – this has an effect on how certain elements are received, rejected or just overlooked. Sometimes the decision makers are curious and open to new things in this phase of analysis, and sometimes they only skim over or even immediately dismiss new and interesting aspects (Bronner 2003).

The actual decision for (or selection of) the future strategic direction for international operations is prepared in the analysis of the current situation, with its extensive assessments and evaluations, and then officially made in the Future Concept phase.

2.7.4.5 Process of future business concept development

In the phase of Future Business Concept, the analyses carried out by the internationalisation team are evaluated and corresponding measures planned. Additionally, it is determined what kind of framework and resources are going to be necessary and how the project is to be managed (Ellebracht et al. 2002). The future or target business concept is based on the fundamental principle that successful internationalisation requires the development of a "match" (the concept of strategic congruence, Müller-Stewens and Lechner 2003; Kinkel and Lay 2004) between company strengths and future opportunities in the international environment

(Mintzberg et al. 1998; Sachse 2002; Swoboba 2002; Kinkel and Lay 2004; Kuemmerle 2005). As major elements of the future target concept for internationalisation, and with regard to strategic congruence, the corporate vision and the target system are determined (Niedereichholz 1996; Sachse 2002; Hinterhuber 2004).

The actual, final decision for further internationalisation is made in this planning phase. With this concrete decision, the key actors or internationalisation team reinforce their commitment to the project and the intention to internationalise (Hinterhuber 2004). The decision for a selected target concept is dependent upon the current company situation and the actors involved. The company utilises knowledge gained through the preparatory analyses in the Export Audit phase. The explicit (or, often just implicit) formulation of the corporate vision is the driving, motivating force for reaching new goals and gives the firm a sense of orientation throughout the internationalisation process (Hinterhuber 2004). The target system takes knowledge gained in the current analysis and determines objectives per area of activity and foreign market. The usual level of detail normally leaves the final, concrete targets for market development in the selected foreign markets open. An exact definition of all variables is viewed as being part of strategy development. Often, further specification work is delegated on to the international division or to decentralised management units in the foreign markets with the justification that they are closer to the markets and to potential customers. At this point, it is often observed that managers have a hard time anticipating future developments and then selecting the right option for action (Hammond et al. 1998; Bronner 2003). As Zaltmann and Moorman (p. 16, 1988) observed, "Essentially, the same information is available to competing firms at about the same time. As a consequence, competitive advantage is to be found increasingly in what is done with information, that is, how it is used or employed rather than in who does or does not possess it."

In the phase of strategic development, the internationalisation team wavers between the two extreme approaches of "strategic planning perspective" (e.g. Ansoff and McDonnel 1990) or "strategic incremental perspective" (e.g. Mintzberg 1994). In realising strategic behaviour, the actors need to balance between the conflicting demands for deliberate strategising and strategy emergence. The final decision depends on the individual case as De Wit and Meyer (2004) argued. Although all options for action can represent suitable approaches (strategy formulation), high communication costs and a limited information absorption capacity of the actors reduce the international strategy options to a few evaluation and decision criteria (Aharoni 1966; Schoppe 1998; Kutschker and Schmid 2006). Certain strategy options may be immediately ruled out at the beginning because information will be difficult to gather or because an implicit pre-selection has already taken place (e.g. "follow a key customer abroad to retain the business") (Li et al. 2004). In both the search for and the selection of suitable alternatives, the key actors normally look at that which is already familiar or "in the neighbourhood" (Cyert and March 1963; Schreyögg 2003). Such an implicit pre-selection can result when, for example, the top management is not truly open to possible decision-related variations or if there is the impression that unconventional decisions will not foster personal career success within the firm in question (Kutschker and Schmid 2006).

For the management of the later transformation process, operative sub-targets are derived from the target system and long-term corporate targets. These should serve all those involved as measure-relevant guidelines (Lynch 2009). Tarlatt (2001) recommended appointing a project manager, setting a fixed deadline for the end of the project and desired final result, determining indicators for measuring the degree of target achievement, selecting the most important key indicators, fixing frame conditions and operationalising with regard to time, scale and implementation of the project.

Viewed objectively, determination of the future strategic direction can take place at the same time as the initial market entry strategy is made. Although a switch of the mode of market entry is relatively common, an early planning of the next steps of market operations is rather seldom (Petersen et al. 2000). An example of this would be if an entrant firm had the intention of later replacing a local intermediary with a sales subsidiary as soon as sales in the foreign market reached a level that would justify the higher fixed costs of the switch.

Observations regarding actors' behaviour during initiation of the project may also be applied to their behaviour in the phase of Future Concept. In this phase, there are also conflicts, power struggles and different perceptions and expectations which influence the behaviour. The definition of the future concept or target system is being concluded at this stage with the result that arguments regarding availability and allocation of resources may even be intensified. Power, influence and tasks are explicitly stated in the future concept and target system and budget is allocated. It is at this point, at the latest, that different interests among the actors may arise and, in time, intensify.

Assessments and decisions are subjective, but they can be objectified with the right methods. The most common decision-making methods to evaluate strategies can be financially based (return on capital employed, net cash flow, discounted cash flow, break-even), shareholder value added and cost benefit analysis (Lynch 2009).

2.7.4.6 Determination of optimal decision time ("when?")

After the future or target concept is set one main question remains open: " when should the project begin?". The optimal decision time for a foreign mode switch is the result of a number of activities previously carried out by the key actors. As a milestone, the Optimal Decision Time is characterised by the factors of switching conditions (Pedersen et al. 2002; Swoboda 2002), switching barriers (Pedersen et al. 2002), switching motivators (Pedersen et al. 2002) and switching costs (Weiss and Anderson 1992; Pedersen et al. 2002).

Fulfilment of the switching conditions represents a first basis for the decision of when to begin the project. A differentiation between internal and external switching conditions must be made. Useful internal criteria have proven to be the following: level and availability of resources in the area of personnel (level of experience, global mindset), finances (profit, sales figures, results thus far, risk levels), the process (information flow, quality of information, number of new customers, length of foreign contacts) and organisation (dimensions of network, proximity to foreign market). Particularly important external criteria include the intensity of competition, market growth, and current and future demand development (Petersen et al. 2006). Depending on the degree of fulfilment of switching conditions (such as the actual achievement of a defined sales volume or planned market share) the decision regarding further development of the foreign export organisation is made. When certain conditions have been fulfilled, uncertainty (which has a decisive effect on commitment) is reduced and the probability of further development of the foreign operation is increased. If these conditions are not or only partially fulfilled, then this probability sinks or the timing for a decision is put off until the conditions have been fulfilled to a satisfactory level (Pedersen et al. 2002). Decision variables for these conditions cannot, however, be viewed as one absolute target value, as the example of termination dilemma in foreign distribution demonstrates (Petersen et al. 2006). If the foreign distributor is too good, he must fear replacement by a subsidiary. If his performance is too poor, there is the danger that he will be replaced by another distributor.

The decision is also influenced by switching barriers, such as an insufficient amount of information for a thorough analysis of a foreign market or differing individual perceptions of a business opportunity in a foreign market. According to Hymer (1976), who speaks of "barriers to international operations" (sometimes also referred to as "liability of foreignness"), firms must overcome certain barriers if they want to be successful in the international market. Depending on the weight and scale of these barriers, it can become a decision for or against a commitment, or alternatively the commitment is put off until later (Leonidou 2004). Analogous to market-entry barriers, the influence of these switching barriers varies according to the individual environment and company itself. In one case, gathering and analysing market data is the critical point and, in another, the assessment of consumer behaviour in the foreign market represents the greatest hurdle for a strategic change (Leonidou 2004). It must be expected that internal and external driving forces will also affect the optimal decision time. Particularly conflicts and power games between the actors involved within the organisation can represent a major barrier to change (Aharoni 1966; Kutschker and Schmid 2006). In most cases, the barriers to the evolution of the foreign management operation differ from the initial market entry barriers – not only in their manifestations but also in the criteria (Benito and Welch 1994).

According to Benito et al. (2009), previous experience, knowledge and competency tied to extant and new mode strategies represent major barriers. For these authors, extending knowledge about mode strategies is decisive for overcoming switching barriers.

The motivation of the different actors further influences decisions regarding a switch or alignment of foreign management operations to external environment conditions (such as increased know-how or experience, or necessary compensation for results achieved in the home market) (Pedersen et al. 2002). Switch motivators are factors that, to some extent, reduce perceived utility of continuing with the current set-up for foreign sales. They thereby increase the probability of alterations to the current organisation (Pedersen et al. 2002). For Benito et al. (2009), previous experience tied to internationalisation and the modes employed thus far play an important role in this context. They argue that past experience creates its own bias which may result in mode inertia and the tendency for an existing mode to be used rather than deciding on alternative ones. Calof and Beamish (1995) differentiate between attitude-based (e.g. increased commitment to foreign market), internal-environment-based (e.g. new export manager), external-environment-based (e.g. change of foreign market conditions) and performance-based (e.g. problems with distributor) stimuli for a mode change (Benito and Welch 1997). As with market entry motivators, proactive and reactive motives exist. For Hollensen (2007), proactive motives represent stimuli to attempt strategy change based on the firms' interest in exploiting unique competences or market possibilities (e.g. profit and growth, goals, managerial urge), and reactive motives indicate that the firm is reacting to pressure or threats in its home or foreign market and adjusts passively to them by changing its activities over time (e.g. competitive pressure, proximity to international customers/psychological distance). Depending on their intensity, these motives can have a decisive effect on the dynamic change of foreign management operations (Calof and Beamish 1995; Pedersen et al. 2002). What is certain is that these motives can differ from the motives for initial market entry (Benito and Welch 1994).

The concept of switching costs refers to difficulties – or costs – tied to changing the current mode of foreign operation (Pedersen et al. 2002). The typical cases are severance payment to a terminated foreign agent, the potential loss of local sales due to customers' loyalty residing with the distributor rather than the producer, the costs and revenue losses of setting up a new foreign operation mode (including expenses related to recruiting and training new personnel in connection with the establishment of a sales subsidiary) and foreign operation learning costs (Weiss and Anderson 1992, Pedersen et al. 2002, Welch 2007). According to Weiss and Anderson (1992), managers avoid switching from a sales representative to a direct sales force when high overall costs are perceived, even in the face of powerful incentives to change. It can often happen that the possible switching costs influence the decision maker to such a degree that sub-optimal conditions are simply accepted (Weiss and Anderson 1992). The logic of sunk costs ("throw good money after bad money") and the resulting behaviours with a tendency towards escalating commitments can, Bronner (2003) shared in this context, play a decisive role. It must also be taken into consideration that, depending on the mode switch, different determining factors apply as pointed out by Benito et al. (2003). The strategic transformation from a sales representative to an own sales subsidiary involves other measures and costs than the simple integration of additional sales representatives as a supplement to the existing one. A theoretical basis for the costs arising from a mode switch can be found in the "transaction cost theory" (Coase 1937, Williamson 1975, 1985). Depending on which costs are higher (an internal company solution or market-related activity), the more efficient transaction is then selected. As long as the costs of the market are lower, a market solution (for example, export or licences) is chosen. If costs for a market solution are higher, then the market is "brought home to the company" and internalised in the form of direct investments (e.g. Buckley and Casson 1991; Rugman 1997). With market solutions, one can differentiate between ex-ante transaction costs and ex-post transaction costs. Ex-ante transaction costs, meaning costs before conclusion of a contract, are, for example:

- the search (costs of identifying new and potential cooperation partners)
- the set up (costs of data aggregation) and
- the agreement (costs of negotiation).

Ex-post transaction costs involve:

- winding-up costs

- control and driving cost, and
- adjustments (corrections, modifications)

The sum of transaction costs is dependent upon the current level of uncertainty, the specific character of the investment and the frequency of transactions. The greater the uncertainty, the more specific and seldom the transaction – the higher the transaction costs are going to be (Kutschker and Schmid 2006).

Table 2.3 summarises the most important variables for optimal timing of mode switching with their significance and possible indicators for operationalisation.

Table 2.3: Contextual constructs relevant to optimal decision time of foreign mode switch

Variables	Meaning	Indicators/Examples
Switching conditions (Internal/ External)	Internal criteria as basis for decision regarding changes of foreign operation mode (decision criteria, priority, degree of fulfilment or threshold level decision)	Degree of performance (turnover, market share, reputation, image etc.): Drop in market share, loss of customer, profit loss, development of profit, reclamation rate, degree of customer satisfaction, age of the relationship (Weiss and Anderson, p. 102, 1992), risk, control, commitment.
	External criteria as basis for decision regarding changes of foreign operation mode (decision criteria, priority, degree of fulfilment or threshold level decision)	Quality of information, information flow, proximity to market/customer, marketing orientation, loyalty between agents and customers (Weiss and Anderson, p. 103, 1992), price increase/decrease
Switching barriers	Barriers/hurdles, which need to be overcome to switch mode	e.g. Sufficient information for analysing markets, perception of foreign business opportunity/risk, accessing export distribution channel, inadequate/untrained personnel for exporting, unfamiliar foreign business practices, limited financial resources, emotional/psychological factors (e.g. resistance to change), (Leonidou, p. 286, 2004).
		Verdict based vs. evidence based information search (Ahlstrom and Bruton 2010)
		Barriers within the organisation/corporate structure, complex systems, tight coupling (Roberto, 2002)
		Cultural distance
		Past experience, mode competence (Benito et al. 2009)
Switching motivators	Motivation for development of foreign operation. Switch motivators are factors which, to some extent, reduce perceived utility of continuing with the current set-up for foreign sales. They thereby increase the probability of alterations to the current organisation (Pedersen et al. 2002, Petersen et al. 2000b)	Calof and Beamish, (p. 121, 1995): Attitude based, internal-environment based, external-environment based, performance based
		Proactive motives: Export market growth (Benito et al. 2003; Calof and Beamish, p. 122, 1995), accumulation of market knowledge growth (export growth) of company, economies of scale, control difficulties, asset specificity, increase dissatisfaction/satisfaction with current intermediary (Weiss and Anderson 1992, Calof and Beamish p. 122, 1995)
		Reactive motives: competitive pressure, customer requirement (Calof and Beamish p. 122, 1995), proximity to international customers/psychological distance
		Management impression of the overall attractiveness of exporting, independently of particular contribution to own firm (Calof and Beamish p. 122, 1995)
		• International orientation – firms background/traditions/ attitude of top management to foreign business
		• Confidence in the firm's competitive advantage – Management perception of quality, price, products, financial, marketing etc.
		Past experience, mode competence (Benito et al. 2009)
Switching costs (switch deterrents)	Direct/Indirect Costs and Benefits, which evolve/do not evolve when mode is switched	Cost of setting up a new foreign operation: Extra training cost (Set-up cost), Extra recruiting cost/search cost (Set-up cost) Organisational cost (Pedersen et al. 2002)
		Take down costs incurred by dismantling existing foreign operations: Loss of local sales revenue due to customers' loyalty, Severance payment (right to compensation upon termination), Loss of reputation, Loss of performance (Pedersen et al. 2002)
	Switching deterrents/switching costs are the set of factors that make it difficult or costly to carry out mode switches (Pedersen et al. 2002, Petersen et al. 2000b)	Contractual restrictions on termination (Weiss and Anderson, p. 103, 1992)
		Magnitude of reps/partner reactions (Weiss and Anderson, p. 103, 1992)
		Reaction of rep/partner network (Weiss and Anderson, p. 103, 1992)

2.7.4.7 Behavioural issues before the decision

Over time, the variables of switching conditions, switching costs, switching barriers and switching motivators change. They influence each other and are closely interconnected (Pedersen et al. 2002). For an optimal decision time, at which point these factors are particularly favourable, there is a more or less unclear timeframe[3]. Key decision-making actors who are too early must wait with their decision until a more favourable time has come. Actors who are too late either wait until a more favourable time has come, change the strategy but execute it at a more favourable time, make no decision at all, or make a decision at an unfavourable point in time (Andersson and Mattson 2004; Oviatt and McDougall 2005). Andersson and Mattson (2004) reach the conclusion that the right assessment and behaviour at the "right" time depends on how companies learn to adjust to, compensate for and calibrate the immediate consequences of interconnected actions of the company and other actors in the international network. They place particular emphasis on timing: 1) if an activity negatively affects the usually already limited resources; 2) if an activity affects the resources of other actors; 3) if the activities will influence the overall effectiveness of the result; and 4) when it pertains to activities with irreversible effects on resources and competitiveness (Andersson and Mattson 2004). The management can display "proactive" behaviour and understand timing as a conscious choice (planning, decision-making, implementation) or as a situation determined by the environment which influences the company and forces it towards "reactive" behaviour (Andersson and Mattson 2004). According to the "real options theory" (Amran and Kulatilaka 1999; Copeland and Fufano 2004; Fisch 2004), an optimal decision time is when the net present value is higher than the value of the future option or an option at a later date. The decision maker has the choice between putting off an option until later, utilising part-options (partial and incomplete decisions), and completely taking on an option. Though often overlooked in research, the aspect of "serendipidity" (luck, coincidence, the unexpected discovery of a chance or opportunity) is also of major significance for the decision to internationalise (Meyer and Skak 2002; Svensson and Wood 2005). Still, many firms establish their first contacts by reacting to an initiative,

---

[3] *FAZ am Sonntag*, 15.1.2005, Interview with Jürgen Kluge, CEO McKinsey Germany: "When is Honda going to switch: In the world, whenever the GDP exceeds 1000 dollars then people change from bicycles to mopeds. And Honda immediately sets up a little motorcycle factory."

or by establishing contacts at trade fairs. Acting swiftly, they can realise new opportunities that open changes in the foreign network, initiatives by existing partners, or involve new entrants. Whether or not a key actor recognises a specific opportunity (the distorted perception effect) and when and how he/she reacts to it can sometimes affect success more than the overall management capabilities (Teece at al. 1997; Zollo and Winter 2002; Oviatt and McDougall 2005). The recognition of opportunities is the ability to identify a good idea and transform it into a business concept that adds value and generates revenues (Lichtenstein and Lumpkin 2005). Morris (2005) viewed an opportunity as being successful when it allows a firm to develop and implement a profitable strategy that takes the environment into consideration.

The current motivation level, but also the will and desire to change and move play an important role in this phase of the internationalisation process (Steiger and Lippmann 2003). Furthermore, the behaviour of key actors at the optimal decision time is influenced by the management or team's perception of the "right" time, the weight the decision carries for the key actors and for the firm, the decision style, the degree of uncertainty, the level of conflict and the complexity of the decision with regard to relationships and power struggles tied to the foreign operation (see Steiger and Lippmann 2003; Ahlstrom and Bruton 2010).

2.7.4.8 Action phase: Strategic configuration of mode switching

Once the decision to switch the mode is made by a firm and the timing for launching operations is determined, further decision aspects must then be taken into consideration (Swoboda 2002). The focus of these is on sub-processes involving initiation and implementation of major and subordinate targets, strategies, structural elements, systems, cultural aspects and behaviours of the actors (Gattermeyer and Al-Ani 2001).

As an important basic principle, it is assumed that the implementation of a strategy always triggers changes in the company on a structural, process-related and cultural level (Steiger and Lippmann 2003; Zentes et al. 2004; Lynch 2009).

The elements of the theoretical framework focus on strategic switching options which are presented and behaviour aspects of key actors involved. Not only the content of individual, optimal (part) decisions are analysed but also the entire spectrum of decision alternatives in their variety for the strategy configuration. The chosen degree of detail is based on the most important aspects for management and their significance for the transformation from status-quo (old mode) to the future concept (new mode).

2.7.4.8.1 Strategic issues of modes switching

During the transition process, a number of decisions are made regarding a new mode of foreign market operation (decision making process/decision timing). Kutschker (2003b) differentiated between the management of continuous or incremental evolution, the management of extreme/crisis situations (episodes) and the management of epochs with long-term organisational development (Swoboda 2002). The change of mode and all the decisions involved in this process correspond to the organisational change triggered by an extreme situation (episode). Episodic changes are built on a concept of structural development characterised by relatively seldom but volatile changes. According to Weick und Quinn (1999), these changes follow the classic Lewin three-phase model: (1) Unfreezing, (2) Change and (3) Refreezing as linear and targeted processes. Often, continuous changes with lower "amplitude" than revolutionary processes have been running parallel and long before the official decision to switch. These changes are based on the concept of self-organising systems as cyclical processes without a set end (Ellebracht et al. 2002; Steiger and Lippmann 2003). By consciously structuring the sub-steps and individual decisions, the efficiency of these episodes can be increased (Marcharzina and Engelhard 1991; Kutschker 1996). Depending on the path of company internationalisation development thus far, the decisions and actions taken by the key individuals involved will influence the dynamics and efficacy of the internationalisation process (Teece et al. 1997; Kutschker 2003b). In the following, the most important decisions relevant to a mode switch are presented (Ancona et al. 2001; Hurmerinta-Peltomäki 2003).

Firstly, there is a decision regarding the strategic direction of internationalisation. A vertical or horizontal direction can be differentiated. With the vertical strategic direction, the actors involved must decide if they would like to pursue a growth- or reduction strategy. The growth strategy is the kind of internationalisation process that points forward. It is accompanied by an increase in the current intensity of foreign market operations. The reduction strategy, or de-internationalisation, implies a backward-moving form of market operations, meaning a reduction of current commitment to market activities (Alajoutsijärvi et al. 2000; Turcan 2003; Pauwels and Matthyssens 2004; Benito et al. 2009). As Swoboda and Jager (2008) have established, the reasons for disinvestment in the mode switch may deviate. If a company maintains its current mode but changes partners (e.g. a new agent replaces the old), and this is done with the intention of optimising business, then this is normally classified as a growth strategy. There is no increase in intensity, but an improvement in results is strived for through the change in personnel. The current stage within the internationalisation process has, however, not been abandoned (Johanson and Wiedersheim-Paul 1975; Johanson and Vahlne 1977). That is why it is considered an internationalisation strategy with a horizontal strategic direction (Pedersen et al. refer to this form of mode switch as "intra-mode change" or "within mode shift"). In business practice, a sales agent is often replaced with the hope of achieving better results with the new one. It is, however, also common practice to employ further sales agents/representatives per foreign market in order to increase market coverage (Petersen and Welch 2002). It is possible to combine the different horizontal and vertical strategic directions mentioned above (direction combination) (Welch et al. 2007, Benito et al. 2009). According to Petersen and Welch (2002), four important groups can be identified: Unrelated Mode, Segmented Mode, Mode Complementarity and Mode Competition. Unrelated modes occur when a firm uses more than one mode, but without being connected to that market (e.g. a medium-sized enterprise with different product groups for a country market distributes its products through its own sales subsidiaries for each product). Direction combinations as segmented modes are used in the same industry to serve different segments. This means that large customers are served directly whereas all other customers are handled by an agent. Direction combinations are also used in a "combined" way. Within a country, production can be by contract with a local manufacturer but all marketing and sales activities can be made directly from their own domestic market. Competing modes may occur when firms target the same segment with the same product (e.g. direct sales and sales via wholesalers, focus on the same activities and the same segment, and are in direct competition) (Petersen and Welch 2002).

Depending on the results achieved through the usual mode of foreign operation, the future concept strategy is implemented either in an incremental order, always to the next stage (cf. Johanson and Wiedersheim-Paul 1975; Johanson and Vahlne 1977), or in a revolutionary order through a leap-frogging of stages until the planned foreign operation has been successfully institutionalised (cf. Calof and Beamish 1995). For an international growth strategy, firms can develop foreign business step-by-step either through indirect export via export trade companies or through the immediate establishment of subsidiaries. "Born globals" direct their value-creating activities towards international markets immediately on taking up business (Moen and Servais 2002; Chetty and Champell-Hunt 2004) and prefer a more discontinuous order of market development. These events do not necessarily have to correspond to our common understanding of a linear process with a beginning and end (Ancona et al. 2001). Hurmerinta-Peltomäki (2001) believe that events can also take place within a recurring time-based cycle (Jones and Coviello 2005; Ancona et al. 2001). The cycle is of a dynamic nature and can change. Furthermore, the cycle can take place in the present, the future or the past and, with regard to time, can constantly shift. If a linear time-based process of internationalisation is assumed, then the experience and the knowledge of actors in the past strongly influence current behaviours and future strategies. In business practice, there are then frequent repetitions of patterns for acting which were successful in the past (How did we do that back then? What was the reaction to our launch back then?). The following sequences (the "strategic pathway") are often found in international business (Swoboda 2002): 1. Independent agent to sales branch, 2. Importer to sales branch, 3. Sales branch to importer and 4. Sales branch to agent.

Table 2.4 shows the contextual variables relevant within the decision making period of mode switching.

Table 2.4: Variables of transition period within decision-making process

Variables	Meaning	Indicators/Examples
Duration of decision-making process (switch period 1)	Period/Time duration from the idea of a planned change of foreign operation until the actual execution	Time, t_0 to t_2 t_0 = time of first idea to change foreign operation t_2 = time new mode of foreign operation is implemented
Direction	As a matter of principle, the strategic force of the planned foreign operation: Forward or Backward • Forward: Expansion strategy (Internationalisation) • Backward: Reduction strategy (De-internationalisation, Mode deletion) (Swoboda 2002, Swoboda and Jager 2008)	Examples (capital transfer, level of commitment, level of resources involved) • Add new export sales reps, add new sales branch, enter new markets • Reduce reps, reduce number of agents, withdraw completely
	Other directions: • Vertical: change to a new stage (inter-mode change) – e.g. change of the current mode to a new mode • Horizontal: change of the current stage (intra-mode change) – e.g. maintain the existing form of foreign operation but with expanded/reduced resources (Welch et al. 2007, Benito et al. 2009)	Examples • From independent agent to sales branch • New agent as replacement of old agent
	Combinations of vertical and horizontal developments/changes (e.g. Petersen and Welch 2002)	Direct sales alongside sales via agents/importers, or OEM, or the awarding of additional franchise licences – dual distribution
Order	Order of activities/order in which events occur • Continous – following uniform time pattern vs. discontinous following non-uniform time pattern Incremental vs. revolutionary· • Incremental – step by step approach (e.g. Uppsala-Logic)· Revolutionary – appearance of event concentration (e.g. Born Global) Linear vs. cycle • Events with direction (future or past) · • Events without direction (Ancona et al. 2001; Hurmerinta-Peltomäki 2003; Jones and Coviello 2005)	Examples: 1. Indirect export, 2. Direct export, 3. Sales branch 1. Foreign sales cooperation (as result of export pool), 2. Direct set up of subsidiary
Timing	Event of time of activities (start of activities) within the change process Timing of single activities: favourable event of time, bad event of time, good times/bad times (Ancona et al. 2001; Hurmerinta-Peltomäki 2003; Andersson and Mattsson 2004)	Per day, week, month, year
Duration of transition period (switch period 2)	Period/Time duration from the decision to change mode until full execution (Timing of the switch between different modes) Remark: the author consciously concentrates on the time period between the decision and execution, meaning the implementation of the decision. It means that the author does not look at the decision time but at the time of the implementation process after the decision was made	Time, t_1 to t_2 T_1 = time of the decision to change the old mode t_2 = time the new mode of foreign operation is implemented

Table 2.4: Variables of transition period within decision-making process (cont.)

Variables	Meaning	Indicators/Examples
Intensity	Intensity (capital, resources, commitment) of selected form of future market activity (Kutschker and Schmid 2006)	• With/without capital transfer • Level of commitment • Level of resources involved • Etc.
Switch activities	Necessary activities of change process from original form of foreign operation to planned form of new foreign operation	Examples • Notification of importer/agent (notification of contract) • Training • Identification/Selection of new sales partner • Location of sales subsidiary
Speed/pace of change/switch	Speed of change/switch Level of pace: Constant pace, Irregular pace, Interval between activities (Hurmerinta-Peltomäki 2003; Amis et al. 2004)	Elapsed distance per time unit, measures per time unit
Sequence or strategic pathway (strategic pattern)	Type of selected strategic pathway / sequence Bundling of core decision pattern (basis sequences) Periodical behavioural pattern (Kaufmann and Jentzsch 2006; Chetty and Agndal 2007)	Examples • Independent agent to sales branch • Importer to sales branch • Sales branch to importer • Sales branch to agent
Coordination	Coordination of individual activities and decisions to reach objectives	• Number of meetings • Project management established • Internationalisation team involved/integrated

In the further course of mode configuration (Strategy Profile/Strategy Package/Strategic Configurator, Chip Programming), and independently of the target and actual export strategy of the project, the intensity must be defined (Swoboda 2002). The decision regarding the intensity is determined by the availability and scope of resources and the factors of capital investment, commitment, personnel, organisation, marketing budget etc. Two extreme forms can be differentiated here. With the incremental approach, there is low intensity of capital and resources. The progress of transition is disproportionally small. With the radical change approach, there is a high intensity of capital and resources and and progress can be disproportionally high (Tarlatt 2001). For a detailed configuration, the following criteria may be employed: informational (improve information for analysing markets, identify business opportunities), functional (more managerial time to deal with exports), marketing (meet product requirements, adjust export promotion), procedural (improve communication, increase support of overseas customers), governmental

80

(easier access to credits and subsidies) and environmental (knowledge of verbal/nonverbal language differences) (Leonidou 2004). But also other aspects can be important for selecting the "optimal" configuration" such as improved marketing, increased proximity to the market, better informational flows from the foreign market to the headquarters, better internal communication for an improved service quality, being nearer to customers, business (cost/profit relation) or legal aspects (liability, local content).

When switching activities have been defined, it is then a question of the implementation timing of these measures. The "right" time for carrying out decisions is a complex, elusive phenomenon and must be observed in its causal connections. Denbigh (1981) lists some terms for considering the concept of time: "the present", "earlier than", "simultaneous with" and "later than", "during", "event", "duration", "temporal interval", "moment", "instant", "temporal order", "transience", and the verbs "to be", "to occur", "to change", "to denote" and the tenses of these verbs. The optimal implementation time is directly affected by dynamics in the environment. The "right" time is important for the result because internal and external conditions change over time ("moving context" – Andersson and Mattsson 2004). For companies in a complex, international environment, this means that the result of strategic decisions greatly depends on the selected timeframe for actual implementation (Andersson and Mattsson 2004). Good or poor judgement regarding an optimal implementation time usually reflects the various internal and external influence factors with high importance of international (mode) experience and the knowledge of the foreign markets (Hollensen 2007, Benito et al. 2009). Companies with years of experience with international foreign operations are more likely to recognise a window of opportunity and use it to their advantage (Fletcher 2000, Sachse 2002; Nummela et al. 2004). The management is then required to carry out the planned project exactly within this time frame. Advantageous external conditions can mean that the planned measure may be more efficiently and effectively implemented because competition currently presents less of a hindrance or because there is an especially high demand. Naturally, there can also be unfavourable external conditions. The possible effects of the market entry of a new competitor or the delay of a planned norm can be negative for the project. Activities must then be carried out either in a different form or earlier/later than planned, or not at all.

The duration of the transition period is dependent upon the selected sequence, the strategic direction, the speed of implementation, the scale and the degree of fulfilment of the individual measures (Hurmerinta-Peltomäki 2003). Furthermore, the transformation period is also influenced by dynamics in the environment, such as availability of cooperation partners, location quality, duration of approval procedures, competitive behaviour, customer wants and needs, and so forth. It also often occurs that these factors influence each other. If a chosen cooperation partner fulfils their own company's criteria but, for whatever reason, not those of the customer (perhaps due to a poor reputation from past experiences), then additional time may be required to search and select an agent who is optimal for both the manufacturer and final customer.

Implementation speed refers to how quickly planned activities, e.g. for moving from one stage of internationalisation to the next, are carried out (Lynch 2009). It is the actual pace with which a company puts its (partial-) decisions into action. The majority of studies on the topic assume that there is better organisational performance through, e.g. accelerated organisational change or faster development of new products for internationalisation (Beamish and Jiang 2004; Dibrell et al. 2005). In other words, the faster an organisation aligns itself or the faster a product is developed, the better corporate performance in the context of internationalisation will be. The positive influence of a fast learning speed within an organisation seems to be widely accepted. Organisations which learn slowly from competitors, may find their international innovation performance rapidly deteriorating this is exemplified by Barkema et al. (2002). Studies by Vermeulen and Barkema (2002), however, showed that a fast pace negatively influences the expansion of foreign business because companies which rapidly internationalise (e.g. by founding several subsidiaries in a foreign market at the same time) have less time to analyse their experiences, learn from them and utilise this knowledge (Cohen and Levinthal 1990). Vermeulen and Barkema came to the conclusion that companies should follow a steadier path of growth, with even development patterns, in order to not overstretch their absorptive capacity (see Katsikea et al. 2005). This concept correlates to fundamental theories on behavioural perspectives of the firm (Cyert and March 1963). If the speed is too high, the firm may be confronted with the "speed trap" phenomenon (Barkema et al. 2002). The growing pressure to make decisions quickly can reduce the quality of these decisions. Recent studies made by Dibrell et al. (2005) with regard to a strategy of cycle-time reduction in the internationalisation process showed that the elimination of wastefulness and inefficiency across the international value chain can improve performance. For mode switching pace of implementation we assume that it is primarily determined by the resources applied and the main priorities. To accelerate implementation, tasks are carried out simultaneously and milestones achieved at a faster pace. A thorough controlling of the implementation process ensures efficiency and effectiveness.

Depending on the targets set and the previous status of the foreign operation, the firm and the key actors involved must carry out extensive switching activities. The implementation of the specific, necessary activities results in the actual transformation into a new foreign operation.

The end of implementation time has been reached either when the strategic (partial-) decisions have been institutionalised within the firm and become a regular part of the usual corporate business practice, or when the set time frame is at its end and (depending on the degree of target achievement) additional decisions regarding the further course are necessary.

Effectiveness of measures taken in the transition period is guaranteed through an optimal application of resources with regard to scale and timing. The coordination of all actors and measures for a project through the internationalisation team as main project authority, has a positive effect on success and secures target achievement.

2.7.4.8.2 Behavioural issues of mode switching

Once the final decision for a mode switch is made by a company, it must then be implemented (implementation decision/conduct decision).

The key actors apply the resources necessary for mode-switch implementation and, in doing this, also develop certain behaviours. The manifestation of their commitment shifts from the thinking- and decision-making processes of strategy search and formulation to the process of actually changing behaviours and actions (Jost 2000; Rogers 2003). The individuals (or groups) involved and the types of changes to be made stand in causal connection with corporate organisational structures, the transformational process, the specific status quo and context situation and the planned implementation activities (Ahlstrom and Bruton 2010). The chosen level of quality and acceptance may influence the effectiveness of the decision (Frey and Irle 2002). If a decision has far-reaching consequences and alternatives for action greatly differ, then the influencing factor of "quality" will be highly significant. If a decision is to be implemented by the actor in question, or if it has a bearing on their work motivation, then the influencing factor of "acceptance" will be particularly important. The decisions are interactively and interdependently tied to the different strategy elements and the behaviours of key actors. The course which the process takes and the contents of the transformation determine and influence each other (Kutschker 2003). Giddens (1988) commented that the measures which the actors have decided to take change given structures, and certain structures determine certain actions.

Depending on the content of the future concept and the objectives, key actors may experience a number of barriers and resistance in the transition phase. These barriers could have a direct influence on performance. Their primary source lies in the fact that fulfilment of specific interests and targets is assessed differently by all stakeholders involved in the transformation process. The different contributions made by stakeholders in this phase affect the structure of the operation and can trigger conflict situations.

Table 2.5 summarises the potential interests and influences on the different stakeholders and their different manifestations are also presented (Jost 1999).

Table 2.5: Potential interests of different stakeholders and their influence on foreign operation mode

Stakeholders	Interest	Influence
Owner	Increase of corporate value, future growth	Personal, strategy, allocation of resources
Investors	Return on capital invested	Strategy, operational decisions
Advisory board	Control and risk reduction	Increase/reduce control
Top management	Material/immaterial motivations	Structural/operational task
Member of existing foreign management operation network	Secure situation, back to normal, keeping the old situation, fear of loss	Spread gossip, influence image, purchasing behaviour
Member of new foreign management operation network	Secure situation, get the new organisation running	Informal communication ("spread gossip"), influence image, and purchasing behaviour
Other stakeholder	Specific interest of groups and/or individuals	Influence on other stakeholders
Competitor	Reduction of market share in its own favour	Lower price, better product
Customer	Quality of products, high profit, high service	Buy/No Buy
Supplier	Purchasing guarantee	Quality of product and service, negotiation after sales
Government/ Legislation	Tax income, reduction of unemployment rate	Legislation activities, infrastructure, tax, financial support
Internal stakeholder	Secure situation	Informal information, reduce/increase commitment

The decision-making authorities for these processes are recruited from the executive circle (i.e., the top management, the advisory board, the export manager, the director of the export department or the internationalisation team). Different interests among these individuals trigger resistance to certain elements of change accompanying the internationalisation process and thereby influence pace (fast/slow), sequence (process follows a certain order), and linearity (linear/non-linear change process) of implementation (Amis et al. 2004). Internal resistance presents the following characteristics:

1. Defending specific interests such as material advantages, prestige, power (for example, on the part of the previous branch director, importer or agent – "I'm losing my means of living")
2. Internal export departments and their employees experience apprehension with regard to future expectations (new procedures, new business partners)
   - What will happen with the current partners? (e.g. ending of relations vs. integration of old partner; concealed vs. revealed approach during initial

negotiation of the next foreign management operation) – (Petersen et al. 2000)

3. Insufficient data, different preferences or personal dissonance create conflict and resistance within the project team for internationalisation

For external resistance, the following symptoms are:

1. Contractual restrictions, such as termination clauses in the contract with the current foreign operation (Pedersen et al. 2002)

2. Lack of awareness/misunderstanding of the situation, frame conditions or objectives of the project can lead foreign customers to possibly freeze agreements ("the relationship with the sales agent has been excellent up to now, why would we as customers change that? Does the new partner even fulfil our requirements?")

3. Conflict situations with cooperation partners in the foreign market due to an overlap of interests ("this sales cooperation no longer meets our expectations")

There are alternative ways of dealing with the transitional mode-switch phase which foster cooperative interests. The different groups of stakeholders are all participating in the internationalisation process because they hope to add value in a joint effort. The value-adding process therefore represents a common interest of all stakeholders (Jost 1999). The change agents employed guarantee a controlling and risk reduction for the transition process and have the task of ensuring that, above all, internal stakeholders are highly motivated as this will foster a high degree of implementation activity.

A major factor for successful implementation is good communication in the course of the transitional process (Gattermeyer and Al-Ani 2001; Steiger and Lippmann, 2003). Through two levels of influence, "content" and "relationship", communication plays a major role in the interaction between those involved in the internationalisation project (Ellebracht et al. 2002). Implementation requires communicative measures for explaining the necessity of the mode switch and its elements and consequences. As an example the following measures identified by Gattermeyer and Al-Ani (2001) and Axley (2000) could be relevant to implementation:

Internal communication:

- Negotiation with current foreign operations regarding a termination or improved further cooperation
- Negotiation with new foreign operation regarding strategy of future cooperation
- Feedback, discussion and modifications with decision-making authorities from top management

External communication:

- Differentiated communication to external stakeholders in different phases of implementation of the mode switch
- Special communication to key accounts to explain the decision and show commitment to future cooperation.

The communication of strategy elements, solutions, intentions or concepts which are still abstract and not entirely clear (such as the question of exclusive cooperations, the location of the sales subsidiary or the scope of the product range) is often not undertaken by change agents or only in a watered-down fashion. There is often no final clarity and an official status has not been reached. Rather than making a continuous effort to keep up active communication, as should be the case in every successful mode-switch process, only "empty" and "uninteresting" statements are made (Gattermeyer and Al-Ani 2001). Gattermeyer and Al-Ani (2001) gave an example of this as the management is trying to avoid a problem through "*non-communication*".

Feedback in the form of specific behavioural patterns (and, in particular, those of the key actors during implementation of the measures) provides important information which may lead to an adjustment of the selected strategic direction. It can according to Gattermeyer and Al-Ani (2001) pertain to the following: the current foreign operation ("How will my business continue after contract termination?"; the new mode ("When can the first in-house training sessions begin?"); customers ("Will there be the same excellent service with the new partners?"); internal colleagues ("How will I get along with the new importer?"); and, of course, reactions from the competition

("Sudden charm-strategy directed at previous customers of the old foreign operation.").

The controlling of management behaviour during the mode switch consists of the Change Analysis, the Implementation Realisation, the Implementation Control and the Adjustment Analysis (Tarlatt 2001). In Change Analysis (Lynch 2009), changes to the strategic profile of the company and, possibly, of the organisational structure are analysed. It is followed by the definition of key actors and combined with a survey on attitudes towards a mode switch. Operational sub-targets can be formulated from this. For the Implementation Realisation, the most important objectives for implementation are first considered. Then guiding principles are set for the method of approach for implementation and its organisational basis. Finally, measures are defined for the areas of communication, organisation, motivation and other supporting areas. In Implementation Control, the process is monitored on the basis of progress- and result control. The Adjustment Analysis then comes into play when there are discrepancies between status-quo and target values. Reasons for possible discrepancies are analysed. Finally, adjustments are undertaken in the area of formal and informal organisational structure, processes and tasks to improve feedback and learning (Benito et al. 2009).

It is the task of the internationalisation team to ensure a "smooth switch" through ongoing controlling/monitoring of implementation actions and reactions from internal and external environments. Feedback provided by stakeholders, who to a certain extent function as "sensors", enables the key actors to continuously gather knowledge and adjust flexible sub-processes to gain new insights gained. Rollinson referred to this as closed-loop (feedback) control.

The continuous shifting of positions and perspectives (perception of switch context) of actors involved in the mode-switch process results in constantly changing perceptions of environmental conditions. Internal re-negotiations with accompanying adjustments or revisions of the original decision may follow from this (Schoppe 1998; Kutschker and Schmid 2006). The top management and the internationalisation team are therefore called upon to think ahead and anticipate all the different kinds of possible consequences of the mode-switch project. Otherwise, significant difficulties in implementation may be experienced. In this context, it is irrelevant whether it is the view of the top management that the selected strategy is not being optimally implemented ("the organisation has failed to implement the current export strategy properly") or whether the middle management believes that the strategy could not be optimally implemented because it was ill-suited to the target market ("managers (implicitly) pointed at more fundamental problems at the level of the overall export marketing strategy and the management of the entire export market portfolio") (Frey and Irle 2002; Pauwels and Matthyssens 2004).

Long-term success of the internationalisation process not only depends on conducting change processes successfully, but also on whether or not the final level of the transition can be maintained and is not reversed over time. Institutionalising the end-state means to "freeze" the desired level and prevent it from being altered or reversed again (Lewin 1948; Freidank 1994; Lynch 2009). The decision-making process therefore includes a control element for the phase after the new operation mode has been installed which monitors whether or not the organisational behaviour is following the new structure. Through institutionalisation, the significance of the international expansion is underlined. The consequences of implementation, such as new organisational or management units for international market development are observed and experienced in reality.

2.7.4.9 Institutionalisation of mode switch

The transition period ends when the new operation mode is institutionalised and, if applicable, the previous one dismantled. Targets are achieved and the mode is aligned with the new corporate internationalisation strategy. Ideally, the first sales and marketing activities have now already been launched for the selected expansion strategy. In the case of a reduction strategy, the new agent replacing an unprofitable sales subsidiary may, at this point, already receive his/her first training.

Successful internationalisation is be viewed as the achievement of a specific target system. But the exact path of transition from the previous status-quo to the desired target situation has shown to be "fuzzy" in the sense of being unclear and vague (Grünig and Kühn 2004; Kutschker and Schmid 2006). In real transitions, Grünig and Kühn (2004) argued that sub-processes can represent imprecise statements with contradictory content as regards strived-for targets (competitive statements). Jost (2000) therefore listed the conditions of thoroughness/completeness, operationality, segmentability, no redundancy and a minimum scale as indicators for achievement of target.

Once a firm has achieved its target in the form of a new mode, it then finds itself in a new state of internationalisation and foreign operation. The strategic decisions that were taken on this path of transition are discussed by members of the firm or key stakeholders in the foreign country with regard to the content of these decisions and how they were communicated. Bierhoff (2000) commented that sometimes difficulties arise in the foreign country, such as reactions of the competition (price wars or attacks based on possible breaches of law as with Microsoft/Google) or a drop in sales in the market which may lead to dissonance about the decision to switch. A thorough monitoring of final steps in the ex-post decision phase should keep the negative effects of those dissonances to a minimum (Rollinson 2005). Due to continuous, dynamic changes in environment conditions (spill-over effects of contract terminations involved in the new foreign operation, or the need for higher acceptance levels among specific customers to be achieved through a higher commitment – possibly including the founding of sales subsidiaries), additional ex-post decisions and activities may be expected and the company may follow different pathways towards a more mature stage of internationalisation.

The aim of Chapter 2 was to create a good understanding of the most important theories on the internationalisation of companies from the perspective of the research objectives. For this purpose, an overview of explanatory approaches and influencing factors of internationalisation was provided, the most important research on foreign mode switching was presented and decision-making behaviour tied to a mode switch was described based on a theory-supported model. Various theoretical concepts for variables and indicators tied to the most important aspects of the strategic switch of a foreign mode operation were introduced.

The aim of achieving further findings in this area has, however, not been thoroughly met at this point. First knowledge has been gained regarding the significance of the identified influencing factors, the correlations in the individual context of mode switching, the influence of actors and repercussions of the decision on performance. This knowledge has, however, not been solidified and orientation for taking action has most certainly not yet been derived. Furthermore, the strived-for holistic approach for solving current management problems tied to foreign operations remains to a great extent unfulfilled.

In the following chapter, these complex and unsolved problems will be made more concrete with the aid of specific research questions and propositions. Based on the fundamental assumption that companies demonstrate certain behaviour after market entry, propositions will be formulated regarding the mode switch, decision-making behaviour, the use of certain mode strategies, timing issues and the implications for performance. These propositions serve as the conceptual frame of reference for the empirical section and emphasise the focus of the study.

Chapter 3 Specifying the research questions and deriving the hypothetical points of emphasis

In the previous chapter, the literature review was undertaken with a focus on the three theoretical research levels: internationalisation, mode switching and decision-making behaviour tied to mode switching. Based on the literature review, a conceptual research model on decision making in foreign mode switching was developed (Chapter 2.7.3). This forms the foundation for formulation of the research questions and propositions in this chapter. Points of emphasis are mode switching and performance, factors influencing mode switching, the decision process, timing issues and aspects of mode strategy. First the detailed research questions will be presented. These refer to previous literature on the subject and the aspect of associations between individual factors, typologies and processes in the switch of foreign operation mode. Based on the assumption that internationally active firms present a certain number of efficient behavioural modes after market entry, further assumptions (propositions) will then be formulated for the sub-elements of the study subject. These propositions will then be more concretely defined based on the assessment of the qualitative results in Chapter 6.5 and transferred into research hypotheses.

3.1 Research questions – Internationalisation and mode switch

Based on the literature review in Chapter 2 and its emphasis on the study subject (Chapter 2.7.4), the following research questions are formulated:

1. Mode and performance: Which modes / mode strategies are most successful?

2. Mode profile and performance: Which combination of modes is most successful? Which combination/profile is used/most successful in which market?

3. Influence of firm-specific characteristics: How are firm-specific characteristics (firm specific characteristics: age, experience, risk perception, etc.) associated with mode profile and performance?

4. Mode switching: How is mode switching associated with performance? Are mode-switchers more successful than non-switchers? Why are modes not switched?

5. Mode switching decision: How do companies decide to switch? What are the main influence factors?

6. Timing of mode switch: When are modes switched and why? How long does it take to switch entry modes? How long does it take to reach specific modes?

7. Internationalisation process: Do the different paths of internationalisation depend on companies' characteristics?

In the next section, partial aspects of the research questions will be selected and formulated in propositions for further clarification. This establishes which aspects of mode switching are to be more closely examined.

3.2 Partial assessment and derivation of propositions for clarifying and structuring mode switching

The basic proposition and selected partial aspects of mode switching are summarised in the following. They form the first basis for the exploratory interview section (Chapter 5). Based on the qualitative results, they will then be formulated in statistical hypotheses to be assessed in Chapter 7 and Chapter 8.

Basic proposition
After foreign market entry, internationally active firms demonstrate a number of behavioural patterns which can be empirically identified in the internationalisation process.

3.2.1 Management of foreign modes and performance

It is established that objective determination of the success of internationalisation still presents a challenge, both in theoretical research and management practices (Krist 2009). The same applies to research results regarding the effect of the selected mode of foreign operation on internationalisation success (Calof 1993; Swoboda 2002; Welch et al. 2007).

Mode strategy and performance

According to Petersen and Welch (2002) mode combination is a common business practice. Instead of replacing one mode with another, firms add a new mode to an existing one (Welch et al. 2007). Combining modes are used to improve performance, to control activities, to reduce friction during strategic change or for other management reasons (Welch et al. 2007). For this work the following proposition is therefore to be explored:

Proposition 1: Mode combinations differ from single modes in their performance.

In the case of a non-country-specific perspective of operation modes, a firm only uses specific mode in all countries of operation and at any given time. That means a company prefers certain modes and combines those modes in a mode portfolio. The modes form a mode portfolio comprised of all the strategies for market operation.

Proposition 2: There is a relation between specific combinations within a mode portfolio and the probability of success in internationalisation.

Besides the foreign mode other corporate specific characteristics, such as experience, international marketing skills, innovativeness, resources, attitude toward risk or specific country and sector know-how are also critical for international success (Becker 2005, Kutschker and Schmid 2008; Krist 2009, Knight and Kim 2009). For this work the following proposition is therefore to be explored:

Proposition 3: Firm specific characteristics influence international success.

Mode switching and performance

In one of the first studies on the mode switch, Calof (1993) investigated the effect of the mode switch on performance three years after the switch and based on the selected indicators of turnover growth and perceived satisfaction. His results pertain to the question of how the decision-making process can be improved. He came to the conclusion that the use of formal studies, such as market analyses, the intensive informational exchange with experts and the duration or type/manner of the decision process can positively influence success.

The most comprehensive study on mode switching to date is by Swoboda (2002) who analysed the success of internationalisation with the aid of five various "Gestalten" of companies. He compares more and less successful companies to a "Gestalt" and ties the different success levels with the organisation of the country strategies, the internal structures and processes. In a total analysis of internationalisation behaviour, he particularly emphasised the high significance of the management characteristics and corporate culture. The strategy of market operation in this study only gave a low correlation to international success.

In their studies, Welch et al. (p. 452, 2007) even came to the conclusion that "the concept of optimal mode is meaningless given that so much of success in mode use is determined by the way in which the foreign operation is handled." They emphasised the importance of the right management of the foreign operation method as the decisive factor for success.

Existing literature on success research tied to internationalisation and mode switching can only help understanding here to a limited degree. There is a strong need for more research on this question.

Based on the research discussion of mode switching and internationalisation success thus far, the following proposition could be formulated:

Proposition 4: There is a relationship between mode switching and international success

Of note – it is highly probable that the mode-switching performance relationship depends upon the individual context. In this sense, an effect has results only under certain conditions. If this is the case then companies and their decision makers should not focus on the general associations between mode switching and performance but place more value on the identification of terminating factors which create variations in the relationship mode switching and performance.

3.2.2 Factors influencing the decision to switch or not to switch

A switch of mode is influenced by the internal and external conditions (Weiss and Anderson 1992), the perception of the switching cost (Calof and Beamish 1995; Pedersen et al. 2002), the switching barriers (Leonidou 2004; Welch et al. 2007) and the motivation of the management (Calof and Beamish 1995). Calof and Beamish (1995) emphasised four influencing areas in particular:

1. Stimuli of internationalisation change (e.g. opportunity, external/internal change, learning, performance)
2. Choice-based perception of modes (cost, risk, potential) and markets (cost, risk, potential)
3. Mediators (environment, resources/organisation, strategy)
4. The internationalisation pattern of the resulting mode.

For Swoboda and Jager (2008), it is predominantly a matter of the subjective perception of the management. In addition to the factors mentioned above, these authors place emphasis on the attitude of the management and point out possible interdependencies between environmental factors, success and the attitude of the management. In this, previous behaviour and experiences made in other markets can be a stimulus for switching modes in a particular country.

These considerations regarding factors influencing a decision lead to the following:

Proposition 5: The relationship of management-style pertaining to internationalisation is related to the probability of mode switching.

Proposition 6: The degree of satisfaction since market entry is related to the probability of a mode switch.

Proposition 7: There is a relationship between specific modes and the probability to switch.

3.2.3 Decision process

Literature on the decision-making process for internationalisation is primarily based on the process for reaching a rational decision, or the classic processes tied to strategy development. Beyond this, research theories are considered which, depending upon the rationality level of the theory and perspective, differentiate management decisions according to cost-profit considerations, as subjective and voluntary actions, as cognitive actions and political decision-making processes (Ahlstrom and Bruton 2010).

The decision-making process regarding the mode of operation is undertaken more from the perspective of marketing and sales strategies and less from the perspective of management orientation. Furthermore, it has been established that the theories to date in international decision-making focus either on firms at the beginning of internationalisation or firms which are already strongly active at the multinational level. The "transition phase" between these two poles has been somewhat neglected.

Under consideration of systematic strategy formulation and decision-making this leads to the following proposition:

Proposition 8: Systematic decision making regarding mode switching influences the success of firms.

The assumption is maintained that the influencing factors mentioned (internal and external environment, attitude of management toward internationalisation, switching cost and possible switching barriers) result in characteristic patterns of behaviour. The following proposition is therefore to be explored:

Proposition 9: In switching modes, successful firms follow specific decision typologies.

Strategic decisions in post-entry internationalisation focus on the past, primarily on the decision for the mode of foreign operation. However, more and more research studies show that this is an impermissible narrowing and simplification of the actual decision-making scope (Swoboda 2002, Jones and Coviello 2005, Welch et al. 2007, Benito et al. 2009) and that a broadening of the observation perspective tied to strategic aspects of mode switching is necessary.

To reduce complexity, firms often refer back to a familiar strategic profile. Mode-experience and knowledge of certain strategic options can raise the probability that modes employed thus far, or modes that are familiar, are taken:

Based on the results of the literature review (Chapter 2.7.4.8) the complexity and scope of the decision element of mode switching with various strategic options (Table 2.4), the following proposition will apply for this section:

Proposition 10: In switching modes, successful firms employ specific strategies (strategic profile)

3.2.4 Mode switching and timing

The influence of time-critical aspects has been long-known in management practice and is most certainly a critical factor.

In internationalisation research, questions revolving around timing have so far only been marginally treated (Zentes et al. 2004; Simon 2007). Only in recent publications (Calof 1993; Ancona 2001; Hurmerinta-Peltomöki 2003; Anderson and Madsson 2004; Jones and Coviello 2005; Dibrell 2005; Simon 2007) do time-dynamic questions pertaining to internationalisation form the focus.

In summary, three timing aspects are particularly interesting from the perspective of mode switching: 1. Speed/Pace of decision-making (duration of decision-making process), 2. Optimal timing for a switch and 3. Speed/Pace of implementation from the old mode to the new one. The optimal timing pertains to a relatively narrow timeframe. The speed of the decision making and implementation pertain to the activities undertaken within a timeframe.

Pace/speed of decision

It was Calof (1993) who concluded that the longer companies need to make a decision to switch modes, the more positive the influence on performance is. Intensive concentration on the situation and an increase in commitment and resources over a longer period of time improved performance in his sample group. The following proposition considers this:

Proposition 11: The decision time until modes are switched influences success.

Other researchers have found that fast decisions allow a competitive edge in the sense of the concept "early mover". The early decision results in less competitive intensity as not as many firms are present in the market, bearing a positive effect on company success.

In this study, a moderate/middle position will be taken which assumes that the necessary time requirement for a decision also represents a process of negotiation with the actors involved. Individuals may make the decision for a mode switch, but first the relationship structures must be understood and dismantled.

Timing of the switch (When to switch?)

The optimal timing for a switch is influenced by the decision-maker's perception of risk, barriers, costs and the prospects of profit (Welch et al. 2007). Fear of losses, pressure to justify and lack of knowledge may lead to distortion and rationality deficits with regard to the decision on the right timing for a switch and the timing of implementation activities (Becker 2005). In addition, key actors have different perceptions of time.

With the aid of the concept of "perceptual switching cost", first Weiss and Anderson (1992) then Petersen et al. (2000; 2002) and Pedersen et al. (2002) have analysed the influence of quantitative and qualitative criteria on the decision to switch modes. In this, the perception of the sum of switching costs influences the decision. Depending on the direction of the switch, take-down barriers (e.g. termination compensation, risk of career setbacks) or set-up barriers (e.g. training costs, loss of customer) influence the decision (Weiss and Anderson 1992). In the empirical studies by Petersen et al. (2000, 2002) and Pedersen et al. (2002), the probability of a switch increased with the duration of a relationship with a foreign partner. In other words, the longer a certain mode-constellation involving cooperation exists (from agent or importer as starting mode), the more likely a switch will take place. Pedersen et al. (2002) explained this with an increasing willingness, over time, to commit oneself and own resources in the foreign market. Welch et al. (2007) states that the switch takes place in a complex environment with the influencing factors of company conditions (resources, size, international experience, product/service, global strategy), the selected mode (control, risk, uncertainty, partner, profit, speed of foreign market entry) and external factors of the market (market volumes, growth, competition, inflation, currency differences, etc.).

Based on these influencing factors, no comprehensive statement could be derived so far regarding when a switch is particularly sensible, when a switch should not be undertaken and when negative repercussions can be expected. Many researchers such as Welch et al. (p. 452, 2007) found that it is illusory to try to calculate optimal timing of the switch. However, there is the possibility to at least approach the indicators for an optimal timeframe (Becker 2005). A first solution may be the real options theory and the discussion of a possible delay of a switch.

From the perspective of individual decision-makers and with consideration of internal and external conditions, the following proposition is made regarding optimal timing of the decision:

Proposition 12: There is an optimal time period for firms to switch modes

Pace/speed of the switch (How long should the switch take?)

The majority of studies on the topic assume that there is better organisational performance through, e.g., accelerated organisational change or faster development of new products for internationalisation (Beamish and Jiang 2004; Dibrell et al. 2005). In other words, the faster an organisation aligns itself or the faster a product is developed, the better company performance in the context of internationalisation will be. The positive influence of a fast learning speed within an organisation seems to be widely accepted. Organisations that learn slowly from competitors may find their international innovation performance rapidly deteriorating (Barkema et al. 2002). Studies by Vermeulen and Barkema (2002), however, show that a fast pace can negatively influence expansion of foreign business because companies which rapidly internationalise (e.g. by founding several subsidiaries in a foreign market all at once) have less time to analyse their experiences, to learn from them and utilise this knowledge (Cohen and Levinthal 1990). These researchers come to the conclusion that companies should follow a steady path of growth with even development patterns to avoid overstretching their absorptive capacity (Calof 1993; Vermeulen and Barkema, p. 642, 2002; Katsikea et al. 2005). If the speed is too high, the firm may be confronted with the "speed trap" phenomenon (Barkema et al. 2002): the growing pressure to make decisions quickly can reduce the quality of these decisions (Calof 1993).

Although no statements could be found in literature regarding the influence of the time duration of pace/speed of the switch, the following proposition is formulated based on empirical findings (Calof 1993; McNaughton 2001; Vermeulen and Barkema 2002; Welch et al. 2007) on the pace/speed of change and the demands of the internationalisation process.

Proposition 13: The perceived difference between starting mode and target mode, will have an influence on pace/speed of implementation.

3.2.5 Mode strategy and path dependency

Put simply, the theory of path dependency places focus on past experience and events as a foundation for future actions and behavioural patterns. A firm's development basically limits its management's current and future freedom to act. With regard to the subject of study, the path dependency can allow the formulation of a number of propositions which supplement previous theories.

The international development path of a firm is comprised of the theoretically derived dimensions of the decision to switch modes. It is the perspective of development intensity, a contextual variation and a time-based aspect (sequence, timing). The emphasis is therefore the configuration of the mode over the course of time.

Previous experiences, successes, failures, behavioural patterns and reactions to foreign business are assigned a major role (Luostarinen 1989, Hutzschenreuter et al. 2007). These factors are reflected in the manner in which the management continues to operate in the foreign market.

The configuration of the mode employed thus far – with its structure, profiles and strategies – influences the success of the firm's international operation. The success will be influenced by the totality of decisions regarding the modes employed thus far and their development over the course of time in the foreign market. The following proposition applies in this connection and is to be explored:

Proposition 14: Successful companies follow specific pathways in their internationalisation (entry mode, mode 1, mode 2, etc.) which differ from those of less successful firms.

This chapter concentrated on a formulation of research questions and the development of propositions with consideration of the literature review results. Based on the fundamental proposition that companies demonstrate certain behaviour after market entry, propositions were formulated regarding the mode switch, decision-making behaviour, the use of certain mode strategies and timing. These serve as a conceptual frame of orientation for the empirical section and present the subject of study.

The following chapter presents the methodological basis for the qualitative and quantitative analysis and the empirical evaluation of the propositions. First, the research process of this study will be presented and the research methods of previous studies on mode switching are discussed.

Chapter 4 Methodology

The preceding chapters reviewed the literature on the topic and developed a theoretical framework of mode switch decisions. Based on the literature review, research questions were identified and propositions about different aspects of foreign operation mode were derived to guide this research.

This chapter will concentrate on methodological issues in researching changes in foreign operation mode and describe the proposed research design and methods. First, the philosophical basis will be presented. Then the method of approach of existing research studies will be critically analysed. This should serve as one point of reference for defining a suitable research approach and for defining the research process. This chapter is completed by a presentation of the methods for data collection and analysis for the qualitative and quantitative study sections.

4.1 Philosophical foundation of the research

A "realistic" world view is the basic philosophy of this work and manifests itself in a position of scientific realism. In essence, this is the belief that the long-term success of a theory is to be viewed as an indicator for the actual existence of the units and structures to be found therein.

The question of which methods will allow scientific insights into reality is one of the central points of dispute in internationalisation research (Hurmerinta-Peltomäli and Nummela 2004). Those who adhere to the positivist research paradigm prefer a quantitative research approach. Followers of the constructive paradigm lean more toward a qualitative research method.

There cannot, however, be an a priori approach to accessing a definition of "reality" (Eisend, p. 31, 2007). This access is only ascertained through practical success from the resulting explanatory patterns for the reality. In this context, no extreme position will be taken here with the claim of sole representation for a certain paradigmatic research- or knowledge perspective – something found ever more rarely for complex research questions, such as this one (Bortz and Döring 2006).

With regard to the progress of knowledge on the study subject of foreign operation modes, the three aims of "explain", "understand" and "structure" (Gestalten) are of primary interest. "Understand" pertains to behaviour after market entry. This has not yet been analysed; there is no previous knowledge from which new insights could be derived or added to. Basic processes triggering a switch must be uncovered and understood. The aim of "explaining" is to explain the "reality" in a causal manner. Theories on mode switching are to be designed for this that can be empirically validated and that allow general, causal statements for the research subject. With the aid of methods and models, the aim of "structure" (gestalt) has the task of offering tools for decision making and reflections for scientific guidance and the management of foreign operations.

With regard to the function of the research process, focus is placed on the research problem or the problem of practicality (Chapter 1.2). This comprises the demand to formulate pragmatic statements regarding the effects on internationalisation and the management of foreign operations (Patton 2002). In the research process, this is reflected as a constructivist- and dialectic position with a bearing in an extensive analysis of discourses on reality (Guba and Lincoln 2005) and in the methodological synergy and process orientation (Schülein and Reitze 2005).

A consequence of this perspective, the research process presented in the following applies mixed research methods. The aim is to capture a complete, holistic picture of the subject matter with the objective of uncovering aspects of reality that might have been missed with a simpler, more rigid research design (Hurmerinta-Peltomäli and Nummela 2004; Flick 2005).

4.2 Research methods in previous studies and their limitations

To study internationalisation and post-market-entry mode switches, historical analyses are commonly carried out. Here, the development of internationalisation is either observed by the researcher as it actually occurs over a certain period of time, or it is reconstructed via a retrospective approach. The first variation is widely considered to be the "ideal" and most desirable approach (Swoboda, p. 298, 2002).

Short-term parallel studies are made over the course of a few years with a focus on one company or (in exceptions) with a small number of companies. Normally, however, circumstances related to the methodology or economic limitations stand in conflict with this approach. The second variation of historical analysis mentioned above reconstructs the development of a company based on secondary data, expert interviews and company surveys.

In Table 4.1 an overview of research methods for the study of mode switch for foreign operation is presented. In contrast to the overview in Chapter 2 and 3, the focus here lies not on a documentation of previous studies or identification of research gaps, but on a presentation of the methodologies, the selected sample, the type of switch examined and the identification of constraining factors.

Most large-scale studies on internationalisation and the mode switch are based on historical analysis. An example is the research group Pedersen (2002) and the switching papers (2000, 2002, 2004). Here, data was collected from the companies, first in 1992 and then again, five years later, in 1997 with a focus on what changed in the meantime. The central question was whether the companies interviewed had switched from their independent intermediary in the selected market, within these five years. In the study, switches to own sales representatives or to a subsidiary were observed. If a company changed by adding a further importer to an initial one only to then found a subsidiary and enter into a joint venture with a local supplier – then the model had to be abandoned. These steps went unassessed. Despite this problem, and although study reference is made to the same sample group of Danish exporters in 1992 and 1997, these publications represent an interesting methodology, in particular with regard to the perspective of a mode switch in a specific foreign market. The advantage of this focus – and the opportunity it presents to analyse several sequential mode switches – was not examined.

Although the more conceptually oriented studies provide few thoughts on empirical research methodology, the early work of Benito and Welch (1994) does challenge research on "mode choice" to progress by taking on more explorative methods. The two other more conceptual works, by Petersen et al. (2000) and Petersen and Welch

(2002), are based on Benito and Welch's research and experience and contain interesting approaches, such as a classification for a combination of foreign modes and a decision-making aid for strategic mode switching.

The work by Swoboda (2002) concentrated on the establishment of reasons for the switch and applies these to the strategic direction, the penetration or reduction of international commitment. For this, he developed a three-level model. In particular the primary level with the three dimensions of value-creation transfer, countries and activity modes provides statements about an organisational switch. As a method, Swoboda used a questionnaire-based quantitative analysis (346 questionnaires) which was supplemented by 47 personal interviews and secondary analyses. A later study (Swoboda and Jager 2008) with new data, uses the framework for analysis developed by Swoboda 2002 and compared the results with the findings of the study by Welch and Beamish (1995). This method of approach is interesting from the view of research methodology because the results of in-depth interviews with Canadian companies are set in relation to the findings of a quantitative survey of German companies. The objective is to compare the findings so as to derive or modify an internationalisation process model. Other important quantitative works on mode switching, are Weis and Anderson (1992) and McNaughton (2001) who concentrate their research emphasis on domestic business or view mode switching in general neglecting specific country conditions.

Fryges (2005) research paper, on the other hand, focuses on the switch of the sales mode from the perspective of 200 German and UK-based technology-oriented firms. The sales mode at market entry was compared to the situation in 1997 and 2003 for the three most important foreign markets of the companies surveyed. An econometric model for predicting the switch gave first results regarding the probability of direct export to export via a middleman and from export via a middleman to direct export.

In contrast to this are case-study analyses of the development of selected firms after market entry such as Chetty and Agndal (2007), Kaufman and Jentzsch (2006), Clark et al. (1997), Calof and Beamish (1995) and Calof (1993). In particular, the two recently published studies by Kaufmann and Jentzsch (2006) and Chetty and Agndal

(2007) showed, on the basis of 15 and 20 case studies respectively, how companies choose their foreign management operation for selected main markets, why they switched and what kind of role the environment played in this. Kaufmann and Jentzsch provided insights into development behaviour after market entry for a specific foreign market and over a longer period of time. Although this was the first study of this kind, one has to be careful. Difficulties tied to the case-study method include the question of general applicability and the relatively high level of abstraction given by the sample size. Nevertheless, qualitative methods such as case studies allowed analysis of the internationalisation process of companies and the organisational developments of international groups from a longitudinal perspective (Miles and Hubermann 1994; Zalan and Lewis, p. 512, 2004).

With regard to the methodology of data collection, historical analyses bear the problem of memory gaps, bias through selective perception and only limited or no access of the interviewee to information regarding past behaviour. This is a frequently observed problem in behavioural research (Söhnchen 2007). Depending on the perspective of the interviewee, the results can be subject to bias resulting from the individual characteristics, motives, perception, level of information and, in some cases, from a certain self-portraying effect of the interviewee. It is therefore important to ensure that the selected key informants possess the necessary information and competency so as to be in a position to assess the subjects questioned sufficiently well. For this work, this means paying particular attention to the quality of the interview partner with regard to export experience, export know-how and access to information.

In summary: the method to date for measuring internationalisation processes is historical analysis. Of its two variations, the approach of reconstruction dominates and is based on secondary data, expert interviews, large-scale surveys (Pedersen at al 2002; Swoboda 2002) and case-study analysis (Chetty and Agndal 2007; Kaufman and Jentzsch 2006). For statements pertaining to behaviour during a mode switch, most studies focus on the establishment of reasons and motives for the switch in the foreign markets. The concrete behaviour in a country market played no role. Aside from the qualitative work by Kaufman and Jentzsch (2006) and the "switching papers" of the Petersen researchers, the author is not aware of any work dealing with the switch at country level and the findings to be derived from this for internationalisation patterns and the timing of mode switches. In the methodological sense, a concentration on a foreign market and the tracking of past switching events in one market is necessary. Here, a country market is either given or the decision for the most important foreign market is established for the company surveyed. Which factors determine the significance (e.g. turnover, potential, access to information etc.) often remains open. A further limiting factor lies in the pre-selection of a country market and the contextual conditions tied to this. Aside from Swoboda – who carries out accompanying interviews in addition to the quantitative analysis, a single-case study and a survey – none of the reviewed studies used a mixed method approach. Furthermore, none of the studies, aside from Swoboda's, placed a large-scale survey as the focus of the switch analysis.

Table 4.1: Methodology used in mode-switch research from 1992 to 2009

No.	Author(s)	Research method	Sample	Mode switch	Comments on method employed and missing links
1	Weiss and Anderson 1992	Quantitative: Survey with questionnaire Main focus: future behaviour when and why to switch, based on one sales district in USA for semiconductor industry	258 manufacturers (district sales managers) with independent sales agents were interviewed (questionnaire)	Switch from independent sales agent to own sales force was examined	Domestic survey in the U.S. market (no foreign market focus), mainly electronic components Indented switches only Selection of one specific rep. organisation, acc. performance criteria (poor, mid-range or best-performing rep.) Analysis of one specific mode switch only (sales agent to sales man) Main focus: When and why will a manufacturer change from an independent sales agent to an employee sales force? ⇒ not looking at longitudinal data, therefore quite static view on one specific mode only
2	Calof 1993	Qualitative: Interviews and archive reviews	38 Canadian-owned (Ontario-based), medium-sized companies with activities in developed countries between 1980 and 1990, 100 mode selection- and switch decisions between 1980 – 1990	Switches between Export, Sales Subsidiary, Joint Venture, Wholly Owned Product Subsidiary	No direct consideration of foreign markets context General identification of mode switch decision process for specific switch-mode categories No consideration of former mode switch experience, no consideration of former country experience, no consideration of choice of entry mode, no consideration of timing
3	Benito and Welch 1994	Conceptual approach	No sample	Mode change in general, mode combination	- Asks for more conceptual and explorative work on mode switches
4	Calof and Beamish 1995	Qualitative: In-depth (Face to face) interview with open questions about why modes were changed	38 Canadian-owned (Ontario-based), medium-sized companies with mode changes in foreign countries between 1980 and 1990. In total, 76 executives were interviewed about 139 mode changes.	Switches between Export, Sales Subsidiary, Joint Venture, Wholly Owned Product Subsidiary	No direct consideration of foreign market context General identification of mode switching behaviour and decision making Specific switch-mode categories No consideration of former mode switch experience, no consideration of choice of entry mode, no consideration of international experience in general, no consideration of timing Identification of internationalisation path consisting of modes involved, but in general, not in respect to one specific country (in respect to the number of modes involved and mode combination) Identification of internationalisation pattern: de-investment, one-step, multi-step investment
5	Clark et al. 1997	Qualitative: In-depth interviews with senior management of 25 UK-based firms about what and how those companies switched	203 switches after market entry were reported; between-mode: 129 to FDI, 5 retrenchment; within-mode: 34; mixed-mode: 36	Switches between Export, Licensing, FDI (subsidiary, production, JV)	Mainly descriptive work documenting observed behaviour Routes and paths of internationalisation have been identified Identification of between- and within-mode switch and mode-switch combination But no consideration of time between mode switch No performance measures, or any statement about predictability

Table 4.1: Methodology used in mode-switch research from 1992 to 2009 (cont.)

No.	Author(s)	Research method	Sample	Mode switch	Comments on method employed and missing links
6	Petersen et al. 2000	Conceptual approach	3 short-cases and further company examples are used to explain the different options for international operations for and after market entry	No specific focus	Development of a four-field matrix as a tool for future foreign operation mode decisions (integration or termination of partner)
7	Petersen et al. 2000	Quantitative: Questionnaire survey and telephone interviews Main question: what and how the companies changed foreign distribution.	Data collection at two points in time: 1992 (questionnaire) and 1997 (telephone interview) with 273 Danish exporters 74 had changed their foreign market servicing since 1992 (36 to an own sales organisation and 38 to a different intermediary)	Replacement of foreign intermediaries between 1992 and 1997	- Selection of foreign market: 1. existence of an independent intermediary by minimum 1 year, 2. largest sales potential - Changes between five year period (1992-1997) were considered - No consideration of choice of entry mode and influence of subsequent mode - No consideration of time, pathway and routes
8	McNaughton 2001	Quantitative: Questionnaire survey Main focus: decision making at market entry vs. subsequent mode switches (type of decision process, decision period, use of formal study, external advice, alternative modes).	120 Canadian software exporters completed questionnaire 29 fast-growing firms had switched modes since market entry	Various mode switches, as well as multi-channel changes	- Mainly descriptive work documenting observed mode decision behaviour - No foreign market focus - No consideration of former mode-switch experience - No consideration of former country experience - No consideration of time, pathway and routes
9	Petersen and Welch 2002	Conceptual paper	No sample	Foreign operation mode combination: Unrelated modes Segmented modes Mode complementarity Mode competition	- Theoretical examination of mode combination in foreign operation - Development of conceptual framework to analyse the nature of mode combinations ⇒ Not tested concept
10.	Pedersen et al. 2002	Quantitative: Questionnaire survey and telephone interviews Main question: what and why the companies changed foreign mode	276 Danish exporters, later reduced to 214. Out of which: 182 without a switch, 36 with a complete switch of operation mode, mainly from agent/distributor to companies' own sales forces/subsidiary Data collection at two points: 1992 and 1997	Switch from agent/distributor to companies' own sales forces (sales subsidiary, local sales office, home-based sales force)	- Focus on impetus for and motivation of single mode switch - Selection of foreign market: 1. existence of an independent intermediary by minimum 1 year, 2. largest sales potential - Changes between five year period (1992-1997) were considered - No consideration of choice of entry mode and influence of subsequent mode - No consideration of time, pathway and routes

Table 4.1: Methodology used in mode-switch research from 1992 to 2009 (cont.)

No.	Author(s)	Research method	Sample	Mode switch	Comments on method employed and missing links
11.	Swoboda 2002	Quantitative: Survey (questionnaires) Main question: what, why and how companies changed with consideration to internal and external factors	In total, 271 mode switches: 183 switches for further penetration, 88 switches for reduction Switches between end of 80's and end of 90's (10 year period)	Indirect export, direct export, licensing, contract manufacturing, JV, sales subsidiary, production	- Most comprehensive study on dynamic internationalisation to date - Changes within ten year period (end 80's until end 90's) were considered - No direct consideration of performance development before/after mode switch in one specific country or mode switching pattern. Swoboda concentrates more on reasons and motivation for switching and takes care of performance from corporate objectives point of view. - No consideration of former country experience. No consideration of choice of entry mode and influence of subsequent mode 1, mode 2, mode 3, etc. - No consideration of switching and decision time between mode 1, mode 2, mode 3, etc.
12.	Benito et al. 2005	Quantitative: Questionnaire survey and telephone interviews	260 Danish exporters in 1992 and 1997: 182 did not change foreign distribution, 42 replaced intermediary, 36 switched to in-house operation	Switch from agent/distributor to companies' own sales forces (sales subsidiary, local sales office, home-based sales force)	Decision to undertake within-mode switches are driven by control difficulties and knowledge accumulation, whereas the decision to switch to another foreign operation mode is more driven by contractual restrictions. - Concentration on one switch only, no consideration of former mode-switch experience, no consideration of choice of entry mode and influence of subsequent mode 1, mode 2, mode 3, etc. - No consideration of switching time between mode 1, mode 2, mode 3, etc.
13.	Fryges 2005	Quantitative: Questionnaire survey (1997/98) and computer aided telephone interviews (2003) Comparing sales mode for market entry	1997/1998: 362 completed questionnaires for UK, 232 questionnaires for Germany 2003: 200 technology oriented firms Total: 523 mode 1997 and 2003 for Germany and UK	Sales modes analysed direct exporting, agents, distributors, sales joint venture, wholly-owned subsidiary and licensing	- Concentration on changes of exporting (direct export to intermediary (130 observations) and intermediary to direct export (242 observations) - Concentration on probability of switching on changes of direct export to intermediary and intermediary to direct export – Interesting model on how to measure probability of switching - The sample consists mainly of high-tech service firms which differ from manufacturing goods especially in distribution requirements. - Switches between 1997 and 2003 are not considered, only to specific point in time such as 1997/1998 and 2003
14.	Petersen et al. 2006	Quantitative: Questionnaire survey and telephone interviews	258 Danish exporters in 1992 and 1997: 183 had no major change, 40 replaced intermediary, 35 switched to in-house operation	Switch from agent/distributor to companies' own sales forces (sales subsidiary, local sales office, home-based sales force)	- Looking at Danish exporting firms and their relation to foreign intermediaries over a 5 year period - Measuring exporters' perception of the intermediares' performance: market growth measured with GDP seems to be not specific enough - Restricted empirical context

113

Table 4.1: Methodology used in mode-switch research from 1992 to 2009 (cont.)

No.	Author(s)	Research method	Sample	Mode switch	Comments on method employed and missing links
15.	Kaufmann and Jertzsch 2006	Qualitative: Explorative (15 cases) approach, Case study. Main focal points: Timing and mode for market entry. Current mode and year when the new mode was established. Intended mode in five years.	15 cases from automotive supply industry into China	Involved foreign modes: equity joint venture, greenfield/ acquisition, export partnering, licensing, foreign subcontracting	- Concentration on one specific market only (China) - Identification of four main evolution pathways over a certain period of time into China (for automotive sector); Exact position of company mode in the model not empirically determined (more by intuitive logic), accuracy of discrimination of used model - High level of abstraction by considering future mode switch and developing pathway - Explorative and mainly descriptive work based on 15 cases only
16.	Chetty and Agndal 2007	Qualitative: Explorative (20 SMEs) approach, Case study. Focus on the direction of change control. Main focus on reasons for what kind of mode change and why the mode changed.	20 SMEs, 50 respondents interviewed, 53 mode switches identified (increased control mode: 34 cases; decreased control mode: 19 cases). Mainly Sweden and New Zealand	Direct export, distributor, agent, licensing, subsidiary, joint venture	- Identification of three groups which influence of social capital ("acquire resources from business network") - Explorative and mainly descriptive work based on 20 SMEs with less than 250 employees only - Categorising circumstances surrounding mode change are not fully transparent - Concentration on one switch only, no consideration of former mode-switch experience, no consideration of choice of entry mode and influence of subsequent mode 1, mode 2, mode 3, etc. - No consideration of switching time between mode 1, mode 2, mode 3, etc. - Selection and comparison of the Sweden and New Zealand
17.	Swoboda and Jager 2008	Quantitative: Survey. Main focus: what and why companies changed foreign mode and comparison of those results with the observations of Calof and Beamish (1995)	265 German small and medium-sized companies reported 332 switches (219 penetration, 113 reduction; 93 companies described penetration and reduction of changes at the same time)	Indirect export, direct export, licensing, contract manufacturing, JV, sales subsidiary, production	- This study builds on Swoboda (2002) and uses its main concepts how to analyse switching behaviour concentrating on mode strategy and reasons for switching with new data from a survey about the last five years mode switching behaviour. - Confirmation of results of Calof and Beamish (1995) in main aspects such as direction of switch and intensity of switch - Strong influence about individual perception of decision maker / manager about past results influence survey results strongly - No consideration of mode development from market entry to current mode and consideration of mode switching on performance
18.	Bentio et al. 2009	Qualitative approach: one case analysis. How the Finnish MNE Kone penetrated the Japanese market	Finnish MNE Kone	Cooperation (R&D, purchasing), Licencing, Export, Management contract	- Development of a conceptual model explaining mode choice and change - Focussing influence of mode experience, mode learning, mode competence - No consideration of timing aspect and performance - Asking for longitudinal research

4.3 Research method adopted

The level of knowledge available in the selected research area determines the type of research question. The question then, in turn, determines the nature of the research and the research method to be applied (Riesenhuber 2007). In this context, and to develop a theory that is individually of value and that can also be validated – several steps will be taken. In the first step, a uniform understanding of the subject of study, the terms of reference and concepts is created. Familiarity with these concepts, and the ability to describe and define them, is necessary for the next step of describing the manifestations of the real phenomenon of mode switching to be studied. Building on this, a subsequent step of theory formation examines the reasons how the various manifestations came about. It thereby delivers a past-related explanation of the real phenomenon. Based on the explanations of the previous step, prognoses for future developments are derived and tested. In the fifth theory-creation step, practical recommendations for action or behaviour are derived from the prognoses or confirmed variable-correlations.

In view of the complexity of the research questions and the objective to observe mode switching behaviour, qualitative and quantitative research were combined and applied as a "mixed method". Both methods are employed, complementary to one another, in a previously defined sequence following Hurmerinta-Peltomäki and Nummela (2004) and Flick (2005). First the qualitative research section was carried out through interviews with managers with the aim of identifying characteristic processes, behaviours, motives, reasons, reactions and their consequences. The explorative interviews focused on the questions of "How?" and "Why?" with regard to the switch of foreign operation mode. Statements made in the interviews were then analysed, interpreted and compared. Behaviour patterns and typologies were determined. Hypotheses were formulated. The quantitative survey then followed with the questions of "What?" and "How often?" – typologies and categories were then set in relation to each other. Hypotheses were tested; prognoses for future developments derived, tested and formulated as recommendations for action (Riesenhuber 2007). Data collection and analysis were carried out step-by-step, in sequence, with time gaps reserved for interpretation of the data (Hurmerinta-Peltomäki and Nummela

2004). Neither method is viewed as superior or preliminary; rather, the results of qualitative and quantitative research are tied with the aim of better addressing the complex problem of mode switching.

4.4 Justification of the method

Qualitative research

The central strength of qualitative methods in the context of the study subject is that they allow the researcher to explore relations in a company's developmental path since market entry. This is particularly the case when management decisions are increasingly affected by a complex environment. Research strategies are required that allow a precise and comprehensive picture of real business activity in a foreign market (Daniels and Cannice 2004).

The internationalisation of companies is a longitudinal and iterative process. This requires a process-oriented research approach that records, documents and discusses behaviours, decisions, motives and reactions after market entry with the aid of biographically relevant descriptions (Hurmerinta-Peltomäki and Nummela 2004, Flick 2005). Unlike the quantitative research, the focus lies on the exploration and reconstruction of the problem as an individual case to allow a basic understanding of the subject of study.

The selected study approach is a retrospective-historical analysis of the company biography up until the current study time. The historical perspective allows a certain distance to the events whereby the overall view of the internationalisation process and the switch of foreign operation mode gains in concision (Schuh 2009).

With the aid of the selected qualitative method, both expected and unexpected causal connections can be discovered and made plausible. As new explanations arise for changes in the internationalisation process, there is the opportunity to continuously supplement gained insights with further knowledge by posing additional questions (Flick 2005). The questionnaire developed for the interviews (Chapter 4.7.2) and the Critical Incident Technique form the methodological basis.

Insights gained from the explorative interviews build the central basis for the formulation of hypotheses (Chapter 6.5). Further, they serve the preparation of the standardised survey (see Annex) on the subject of mode switches. Perspectives and contexts gathered from the explorative interviews greatly supported the formulation of the survey questions.

Quantitative research

This approach serves to generate quantifiable and reliable data that will allow a numerical generalisation of identified patterns and typologies of internationalisation behaviour (Hurmerinta-Peltomäki and Nummela 2004).

For the study subject, emphasis is placed on the frequency, intensity, probability and assessments of foreign mode switches. Of particular importance here is the derivation of hypotheses, their evaluation with regard to the validity of the reference model developed and the theory underlying this. From this the research project's empirical confirmation (or rejection) of its theories on mode switching results and a contribution is made to the knowledge of a little understood real phenomenon (Benito et al. 2009). The use of quantitative methods allows a closer and more precise definition of the explanatory theories and prognoses on the subject study thus far (Bortz and Döring 2006).

Denzin and Lincoln (1994) posited that the greatest weakness of the quantitative approach lies in the fact that it de-contextualises human behaviour in such a way that it removes the research object from its real-world setting and ignores the effect of variables that have not been included in the resultant model.

Nevertheless, an important aim of this study is to evaluate the significance and characteristics of the assumed relationships and effects with the aid of a larger sample. With regard to the caveats of Denzin and Lincoln (1994), the standardised survey was carried out after the qualitative research and a mixed-method approach was applied. In this way, false assumptions based on a generalisation of the survey results were avoided (Pettigrew 1990).

Mixed methods

Flick (2005) also draws the conclusion that the use of a mixed method approach allows knowledge to be gained that could not be achieved with the use of one single method. Reciprocal supplementation of the two methods is fundamentally assumed. In the qualitative section, a basis for broad understanding of the study subject is created while in the quantitative section, the significance of the identified phenomena is derived. The concrete connection of the two methods occurs in their sequential structure through derivation of the hypotheses from the qualitative section and their assessment in the quantitative section, and also through the connection between the results from the qualitative and quantitative section. The aim of this combination of method is to gain a more comprehensive knowledge than would be achieved with just one method (Hurmerinta-Peltomäki and Nummela 2004). Care must be taken, however, to ensure that the two-way perspective of mode switching does not verify or falsify the results through complementary triangulation but solely creates broader understanding of the subject (Flick 2005, Diekmann 2009). Viewed in sum, a mixed method approach allows for consideration of multifarious aspects of one phenomenon – the mode switch.

4.5 Retrospective-processual approach

Decisive for choosing a design for assessment was the requirement to obtain relevant information for describing the decision-making behaviour and for testing hypotheses. This study reconstructs internationalisation behaviour through a retrospective-processual approach and examines changes of foreign operation mode over time. The change of foreign operation is set in relation to the company's performance in this time frame of analysis. Benito et al. (p. 1463, 2009) argue more history, context and process-oriented research is needed to create a better understanding of foreign operation mode behaviour of firms.

The primary focus is the identification of events in the participants' past tied to the switch of foreign operation mode. The following questions give an indication of what retrospective studies consider:

- What increases or emerges over time?
- What is cumulative over time?
- What kinds of surges/epiphanies occur over time?
- What decreases or ceases over time?
- What remains constant or consistent over time?
- What is idiosyncratic over time?
- What is missing over time?

(Saldana 2003)

In simplified terms: the companies are asked to choose a foreign market and to describe their developments and behaviour in this market since entry. For the selection of a foreign market, its significance for the company was defined (Pedersen et al., p. 333, 2002). They focused on the criterion of turnover achieved on the market. Beginning with market entry ("How did it all start?") and the market-entry strategy, the foreign operation mode was examined in the context of time ("How did things develop?"). Completing the circle was what came at the end of this development ("What was the result of it all?") and the strategy for future operations ("What's next?"). With regard to the country selection, this work follows the approach by Pedersen et al. (2000, 2002) and Fryges (2005) in which companies surveyed were asked about their most important foreign market.

The identification and assessment of the context conditions plays a large role in evaluating internationalisation over a certain period of time (Hollensen 2007; Albaum and Duerr 2008). Information on the company, experiences, motives, justifications and attitudes together with background information on the interview partners forms the company context conditions. All other context conditions, in particular from the external environment, are exclusively considered in the qualitative section.

4.6 Description of the research process

The sequence of the empirical study can be broken down into four main phases: 1. Exploration, 2. Conceptualisation, 3. Data collection, presentation and analysis, and 4. Interpretation and finalisation.

The main phases of the research process are displayed in Figure 4.1.

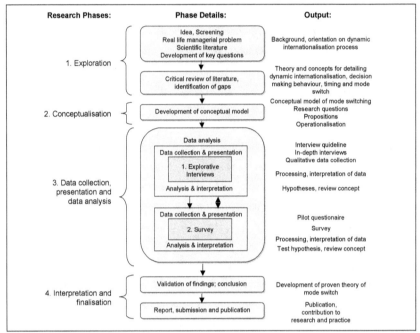

Figure 4.1: Main phases of research process

1. Phase of exploration

In the first phase of the research process, existing theories from the subject literature and previously established and empirically supported causal connections are identified and analysed. The aim is to create a broad understanding of the internationalisation process of firms, the contextual factors influencing mode decision, the behaviour of decision makers when it comes to a change of foreign operation, the decision-making behaviour itself and the switch of mode (Chapter 2.2. - 2.6.)

2. Phase of conceptualisation

This phase serves the development of a conceptual model (Chapter 2.7) and the formulation of detailed research questions pertaining to mode switching decisions, influence of firm-specific characteristics, timing aspects, performance issues and mode strategies. With consideration of the results of the literature review, propositions are developed and serves as a basis for the empirical part in the next phase.

3. Data collection and analysis

Data collection and analysis are undertaken within a multi-phase process. With the aid of a guideline, in-depth interviews are carried out and the results are analysed and interpreted (Chapter 5 and Chapter 6). The original developed propositions are transferred into hypotheses. On the basis of these results the questionnaire attained its focus on the switch of foreign operation mode in a specific foreign market. The knowledge gained from the preliminary qualitative interviews shaped the survey questionnaire. The questionnaire was tested several times, focused and reduced in scope. The data basis was provided by member firms of German Chambers of Commerce. From a total number of approx. 3 million companies, a sample group of 5,400 production-oriented companies with export activities was identified. A major requirement on the sample was that the companies are active in international business and thereby have made a market-entry decision in the past. The analysis, discussion and interpretation of the information collected refers to the individual research questions and the hypotheses derived from the qualitative section (Chapter 7 and 8).

Neither the preliminary analysis nor the quantitative survey that followed adhered to a purely linear research process. Iterative partial-steps were taken that guaranteed continuous revision, validation, construction and reconstruction.

4. Interpretation and finalisation

In the concluding phase, the individual results are interpreted in the context of the internationalisation of the firm. The phase comprises the final results on foreign mode switching, the validation of the theoretical model and comparision to literature. In the discussion of the findings, a critical position is taken which considers limitations regarding interpretation and representativeness of the results. In conclusion, recommendations are provided (Chapter 9).

4.7 Data collection and data analysis – 1. Explorative interviews

4.7.1 Introduction to research process

To develop a basic understanding of the process of changes of foreign operation, personal interviews were first conducted with managers in leading positions. Point of reference in this was the individual case and the reconstruction of interpretation patterns, orientation for action-taking and levels of knowledge.

The selected analysis design is a retrospective-historical description of the company´s biography leading up to the current point in time of evaluation. It focuses on change processes in foreign operations from the perspective of the participating managers (Bortz and Göring, p. 315, 2006). The combination of historical analysis with the current case analysis considers the fact that current phenomena (as the current mode) are often only explainable through past events (Schuh 2009).

The aim here is to analyse experiences, knowledge and actions revolving around mode switching and in the specific context of the internationalisation of firms.

The method of approach comprises the preparation and development of the interview guideline for the explorative interviews, the conduct of the interviews including the visualisation of the internationalisation process in a Critical Incident Chart, the analysis of the transcript, coding and category building, data reduction, analysis and interpretation.

Figure 4.2 illustrates an overview of the method of approach for collection and analysis of data from the explorative interviews.

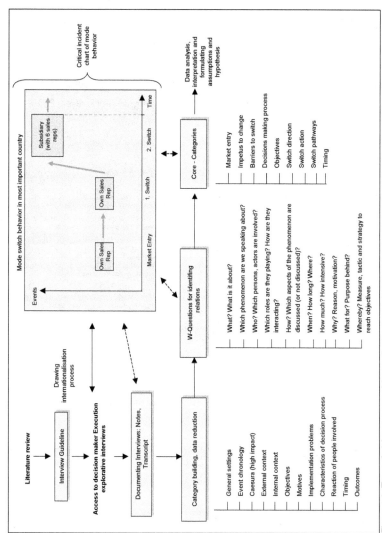

Figure 4.2: The underlying process of the qualitative research approach

4.7.2 Question development for interviews

Of importance here was a clear concept of how questions pertaining to the development or switch of foreign operation mode (impetus, processes, consequences, strategies) should be formulated so as to elicit useful information and still allow the researcher to remain open for new insights (Flick et al. 2005). Hence, the following questions shown in Table 4.2 were formulated.

Table 4.2: Guiding questions for the explorative interviews

Question	Variable/ Construct	Indicators/Examples
How did the foreign management operation change over time?	Strategy/ Behaviour	Define old mode / new mode, define time, define critical events/explain/describe ⇒ Draw diagram (foreign operation status vs. time), retrospective processual analysis
Primary objectives for the venture?	Strategy/ Behaviour	Explicit/Implicit targets. Serendipity role? Indented?
What made you think of changing/switching? Most important factors, why did you want to switch? Why are you staying where you are?	Conditions to switch	Loss of market share, loss of customers, quality of information, development of profit
What made you switch? Primary factors considered	Motivation to switch	Market growth, accumulation of market knowledge, increasing dissatisfaction, competitive pressure, management perception
Describe decision process (Who decided? What criteria? How long did it take? Did you follow a certain procedure/certain rules? Content of decision milestones)	Decision process/ Organisational culture	Formal/informal, people involved, communication network, task characteristics, delays, scope of negotiation, sources of information, etc.
Describe reaction/behaviour of important stakeholders (e.g. reaction/behaviour of existing foreign operation/new foreign operation)	Influencing factors	Political factors, shareholder view vs. stakeholder view, stakeholder dialogue
Major obstacles during the decision process? (internal/external)	Influencing factors	Organisational, personal, financial, etc.
Major obstacles/challenges during transformation/switch? (surprises, expectations, learning, satisfaction, performance)	Influencing factors	Context variables
How did you overcome these obstacles/challenges?	Behaviour/ culture/ mind-set	Skills, capabilities, mind-set
How did you judge performance/success? What is good/bad performance? How do you reward good performance/ success?	Behaviour/ culture/ mind-set	Emotional aspects
How did you consider potential risk? What did you do to reduce risk? What happens in the case of failure?	Behaviour/ culture/ mind-set	Control/Risk perception
Typical aspect that was true for most of the switching decisions?	Process	Individual perception, experience
What role does time plays in switching foreign management operations? (optimal switching time, decision time, transition/switching time)	Time	Speed/pace, duration/length of time, dynamic
What have been some of the most important things you have learned in your experience in switching foreign management operations? What would you recommend to "switchers" ?	Learning/ behaviour/ mind-set	Success factors, factor priorities

124

4.7.3 Selection process of companies and interview partners

Case companies were selected who, according to experts in the international department of the German Chamber of Commerce, had demonstrated distinctive developments in their foreign operations after market entry. These experts prepared a pre-selection on the basis criteria of "successful exporter", "experience in international business", "growth rate above average" and "successful in international business". In essence, it is a purposeful sample based on assumed intensity of certain characteristics, processes and experiences (Miles and Huberman 1994).

The provision was made that the Chamber of Commerce experts not only know the companies, their CEOs and their export management personally, but also that their contact with the companies enable them to provide a general assessment of the companies' business development on the foreign market and of the quality of the management. Through this approach, companies with high relevance for the subject could be located with a saving of time and resources. A feedback loop regarding detailed results with the Chamber of Commerce did not take place because the researcher was obliged to maintain confidentiality. There was, however, a feedback discussion with the contact partners after completion of the interviews regarding the procedure, the atmosphere of the interviews and the content quality of the contributions. This provided an additional opportunity to gather further information about the business performance of the companies and to also validate the most important statements.

4.7.4 Execution of Interviews

The scope of social processes and influencing factors is too wide to be directly observable or documented in the form of an interaction. For this reason, an interview guideline was chosen from a number of possible variations with pre-formulated questions intended to ensure a certain degree of control in the interviews. With the guideline, a conscious effort was made to shift back and forth between a purely question and answer oriented scheme for asking about decision-making behaviour and questions intended to elicit a general discussion of developments since market entry (Flick et al. 2005).

Altogether, 15 companies were interviewed and 17 development (evolution) pathways were identified. The average interview duration was approx. 110 min.. The longest interview was 150 minutes, while the shortest interview took 85 minutes. The selected firms represent an interesting cross-section of German industry across all important sectors and a good distribution of turnover- and employee classifications with highly varying contextual- and country-related conditions (for detailed sample description see Chapter 4.8.2).

The subject of interest was introduced via a targeted question regarding actual behaviour in a specific foreign market. As a criterion for selecting a foreign market to discuss, the interview partners were asked to consider the significance for the company (in terms of turnover, growth or future potential). The market selected should, however, also be representative and reflect the company's behaviour in other foreign markets as well. The direct answering of this question led to a transition into a more narrative interview, supplemented by qualitative statements on performance. The interview partner tried to recall the past levels of development, to changes and influencing factors in the selected foreign market. From there, situations leading up to the present were discussed from the current perspective. The focus of the interview was therefore not on the company itself, but on the description of events, behaviours and influencing factors by the interview partner.

The historical analysis bears the inherent problem of memory gaps, selective perception and biased information assessment by the interview partner. To counteract these effects and aid completeness and time-related classification, the most important actions, conditions and characteristics were made visual on a flipchart. At the end of the interview, there was joint evaluation of the completeness and sequence of the critical events; memories were critically questioned. In three cases, a further manager took part in the interview. In two cases, an employee who had worked at the company for several years was consulted at short notice. This served to supplement the most important activities in the past and, if necessary, reclassify them.

4.7.5 Analytical approach: From text to theory

Before the data collected could be interpreted, it had to documented and processed. The two major steps for the interview were the recording of the spoken word by digital voice recorder and the written documentation thereof. From 15 interviews, 80 DIN A4 pages of text resulted. Eleven interviews were digitally recorded. In addition to the recordings, field notes were made on the semi-standardised interview guideline.

The following categories were derived from analysis of the interviews. The identified categories and a brief explanation are shown in Table 4.3.

As a methodological basis for analysis of the development (evolution) pathways in the country markets selected, the Critical Incident Technique (CIT) was chosen. This method was originally developed by the U.S. Air Force in the 1940's for differentiating between effective and ineffective working behaviour (Flanagan 1954; Gelbrich 2009). Today, CIT is often employed as a method for analysing difficulties and problems in international firms (De Geer et al. 2004).

In correspondence with the Critical Incident Technique – situations, conditions, events, actions, strategies and behaviours viewed as being either problematic or successful/success-bringing were gathered in this study with the aim of solving practical problems and making a contribution to the development and promotion of the competencies necessary for further developing the foreign operation mode in the country. In this, a situation is "problematic" when negative consequences have arisen from it either for the company or for the individuals involved. "Successful" situations are those with highly positive consequences. Through an analysis of critical situations or events, insights are gained into the company's and its individuals' strategies for solving and handling such situations. Events bearing a strong influence on the activity of the internationalisation process are illuminated (Miles and Huberman 1994; Patton 2002). The status of the foreign operation mode for the individual company and the changes in the internal and external environment formed the focus of analysis for this study. It became clear in which form activities were tied to the environment and influenced by it. From this, causal connections could be reconstructed which co-constituted the social environment during the switch of foreign management operation.

Table 4.3: Definition of selected categories - Switch dynamics

Categories	Explanation
General settings	General information on the environment in which the case is embedded, placing the study in a larger context.
Event chronology – foreign management operation	Sequence, strategy, organisation, structure of market entry and the subsequent modes of operation.
Caesura (high impact)	Strong breaks between two time episodes or epochs, resulting in decisive changes in the internationalisation process.
External context	Factors, changes, or activities in the external environment of the company and on the part of decision makers with a direct or indirect influence on behaviour in the foreign market (sudden death of cooperation partner, market entry of a new competitor, a change of norms or standards, etc.).
Internal context	Factors, changes, or activities in the external environment of the company and on the part of decision makers with a direct or indirect influence on behaviour in the foreign market (new product innovations, takeovers, change in management, etc.).
Objectives	Setting formal and informal targets tied to the switch of operation mode.
Motives	Official and unofficial motives and justifications for the switch in mode.
Implementation problems	Difficulties, challenges, barriers tied to implementation.
Characteristics of decision process	Ways of decision making, activities, behaviour, turning point
Reaction of people involved	Reaction, formal and informal behaviour before, during and after the decision and implementation process in the context of the mode switch.
Timing	Timing and duration of decisions, activities, measures tied to the mode switch.
Outcomes	Positive and negative experiences.

In a next step, the categories were further refined and differentiated (Flick et al. 2005). Strauss and Corbin (p. 78, 1990/1996) recommend the use of a coding paradigm for clarifying relationships between a phenomenon, its causes and consequences, its context and strategies (Flick et al. 2005). The following "W" questions provide orientation for the process of setting the categories into "relation" (Straus and Corbin 1994):

- What? What is this about? Which phenomenon is being discussed?
- Who? Which individuals/key actors are involved? What role do they play? How do they interact with each other?
- How? Which aspects of the phenomenon are being discussed (or not discussed)?
- When? For how long? Where? Time, course and place;

- How much? How strongly? Intensity aspects;
- Why? What motivational factors were given or may be inferred?
- What for? With what intention? For what purpose?
- What with? Means, tactics and strategies for achieving the goal.

The subsequent step, made at a higher level of abstraction, involves a further development to the "core categories" (market entry, impetus to change, barriers to switch, decision-making process, objectives, switch direction, switch action, switch pathways and timing) and the central phenomena in the developmental history of the company in its foreign market. Based on these relationships between the core categories – the phase model for decision-making behaviour during the switch, the Switch-Mode Profile (as a framework of orientation for the options of switching) and the typologies (characteristic behaviour patterns after market entry and the resulting pathway dependency) were derived for the formulation of the theoretical assumption.

4.7.6 Quality criteria

According to Miles and Hubermann (1994), the quality criteria of objectivity/validability, reliability, internal validity/credibility, external validity/representativeness/suitability and usage/application/orientation for action have continued to be useful. Flick (2005) however criticizes that there is still no satisfying answer to the question of validity justification with regard to qualitative research criteria (Flick, p. 343, 2005). Considering this argument, a system of criteria was set which covers as many aspects of evaluation as possible: general applicability, objectivity, validity and reliability (Miles and Huberman 1994; Steinke 2005; Flick 2005; Bortz and Göring 2006).

For assessing general applicability, it needs to be analysed under which conditions (context, events and situations) the results apply. It goes without saying that particularly the context conditions in the foreign markets and the sector conditions are individual and therefore they exclude the possibility of generalisation. A numerical generalisation is not the aim here; rather, new insights and theories are to be developed. For Flick (2005), the focus lies on the relevance of the cases investigated in the context of the research problem. In this study, the cases were carefully selected both with regard to the composition of the sample group and (pertaining to the interviews) with regard to the subject of mode switching and the questions posed.

As the intercultural context bears such high significance in internationalisation research, generalisation is always a challenge to achieve and usually impossible to realise. A "typology" is therefore employed to allow a generalisation of the results. The typology comprises the identification and theoretical explanation of case-internal characteristics. In this research work, the inner logic of the typology is of primary interest, independently of the frequency of its occurrence (statistical representation). In this study, a typology was made with the development of the Phase Model for decision-making behaviour, with the Switch Mode Profile as a framework for orientation for switch options and the typologies of characteristic behaviour patterns after market entry.

Objectivity is lost when, e.g., a researcher only refers to his "long-year experience" in carrying out interviews without being able to state exactly how he is proceeding in his research (Bortz and Göring 2006). In this study, great emphasis was therefore placed on a transparent research process with documentation of the assessment method, the context of the assessment, the data and interpretation (Table 4.3, Table 2.5 and Table 4.1)

An approach for determining validity of the interviews is the assessment of whether or not the strived-for level of authenticity has been achieved. The interview situation for this study was analysed for such distortions of truth or deceit. In all cases, credibility of the statements is supported by detailed information on context conditions and further material, such as turnover lists, brochures, plans and product descriptions supplied by the interviewees.

It was also analysed as to whether a "working bond" had materialised between the researcher and the interview partner. Here, openness, trust and work ethics play a strong role. All interview partners declared their availability for further questions even after the interview appointment. This signalised trust and a collegial relationship with the researcher.

As one form of validation during the research process, the evolution pathways in the selected foreign market were made visual during the interview. By visually following the pathway on the flipchart, the interview partner could directly see, correct and make additions to important statements, characteristics, influencing factors and strategies. This allowed for a high degree of correspondence between what was verbally expressed by the interviewee and how the interviewer comprehended this.

An especially important criterion for the validation of qualitative data is the interpersonal consensus building (Bortz and Göring, p. 328, 2006). If several people can agree on the credibility and relevance of the material, then this indicates the material's validity (Bortz and Göring 2006). In this study, consensus can be assumed between the researcher and interview partner (communicative validation) and the interview partner and company colleagues (argumentative validation) who, in many cases, were included in the interview.

According to Yin (1994), reliability of qualitative research increases through comprehensive documentation of the research process and the data collection. At a later stage, a researcher following the same procedure should be able to come up with the same results. Steinke (2005), however, comes to the conclusion that the replication of a study due to the often limited standardisation in qualitative research is hardly possible. Nevertheless, both the research process (phases, time plan) and data collection (recordings, notes, research diary, calendar, category tables, results and interpretations) were meticulously and comprehensively documented.

4.8 Data collection and data analysis – 2. Quantitative survey

After the qualitative analysis of the internationalisation process undertaken thus far, the design of the quantitative analysis is presented in the following. The methodology used in this quantitative research section to test hypotheses will be discussed in terms of research target, research approach, data collection, sample, measurement instrument/variable coding and analytical approach.

4.8.1 Objectives of quantitative research

The research objective for the quantitative section is a comprehensive gathering of quantitative data pertaining to the behaviour of companies in the development process of internationalisation – in particular beginning at market entry and the mode switches in the foreign market with consideration of company-specific frame conditions. For the research subject, the questions of frequency, intensity, probability and evaluations for switching foreign operation modes form the emphasis. Of particular importance is the testing of hypotheses, their validation with regard to the model framework developed and the overall generalisability of the underlying theory.

The following questions provide an overview and give orientation:
- Are there preferred modes of market operation and how do these change over time?
- What company-specific conditions influence the switch of foreign market mode?
- What reasons dominate for switching or non-switching?
- Are switchers more successful in the foreign country than non-switchers?
- How long does the decision-making process for the switch take?
- When is the market-entry mode switched? When is the second or third switch?
- Are there certain patterns of behaviour in the switch process?
- What influence do duration, frequency and speed/pace of the switch bear on performance?
- How does performance develop with consideration to the foreign mode switch?
- Are some modes more successful than others?
- What factors influence the probability of the switch?

Following this is an empirical evaluation of the relations tied to switching behaviour is made. The basis for the development of these causal connections is the already existing theoretical concepts on management of foreign operation and the empirical findings of the qualitative interviews.

There are a number of conceptual and qualitative studies on this study subject (Table 4.1). The research questions and hypotheses, however, remain to a great extent unvalidated. Reasons for this could lie in low interest of researchers and the difficulty of obtaining relevant information from senior management.

4.8.2 Data collection and sampling

The analysis is based on a sample of members of the German Chamber of Commerce. Detailed information about the sample is shown in Table 4.4. The German Chamber of Commerce receives its addresses from the Trade Supervisory Centre where German companies register. This is the most comprehensive database of industrial German companies. In the German economy, the industrial sector continues to represent a central area – even if its significance has been somewhat reduced in past years due to other business areas. Its contribution to added gross value in Germany in 2005 was approximately 23.4 % according to the Federal Statistical Office.

Table 4.4: Information on sample

Segment description	Size	Sources, Remarks
Firms in Germany	3,036,758	Federal Statistical Office: "value added tax/Umsatzsteuerstatistik 2005", Wiesbaden 2007
Production-oriented companies with export activities	79,065	Federal Statistical Office: " value added tax Umsatzsteuerstatistik 2005", Wiesbaden 2007, Calculation of "Institut für Mittelstandsforschung Bonn"
Survey population: Production-oriented companies with export activities	5,400	German Chamber of Commerce, IHK/DIHT 2007
Data set	192	Relevant sample

The selection of the sample involved three steps. In the first step, the existing list of addresses was cleared of companies predominantly active in the service sector. This was to ensure that exclusively production-oriented companies would be included. In the next step, all companies which did not do business in export were eliminated. Additionally, the segment of processing trade – which by definition also belongs to the production industry – was eliminated in this pre-selection. Finally, companies with fewer than 50 employees were removed from the sample. These measures were intended to ensure that sample companies possessed export experience and had a certain capacity of employees for internationalisation at their disposal. The final sample included the target group of 5,400 German companies with international sales and represented a wide variety of production.

Mailing by post was undertaken in two parts based on postal codes and evenly distributed throughout Germany in the summer of 2007.

The number of usable and mostly thoroughly filled-out questionnaires (to a great extent due to the author's initiated conversations, phoning and emails) was 192. The corresponding response rate was 3.5%. In light of the special requirements, such as questions on turnover and success, strategic alignment, details on organisational structures and management abilities, the feedback lies within the expected spectrum. The reason for this response rate could well lie in the generally low willingness of firms to discuss and openly present strategic behaviour and success-related data with regard to their foreign business (Bachmann 2007). A further reason may lie in the non-personalised addresses of the sample group. Furthermore, a sample-study follow up showed that some companies never take part in surveys on principle because it is too time-consuming for the managers.

Altogether, as one of the few internationally available data records, the sample contains current information about the relationship between firm-specific characteristics and internationalisation behaviour.

4.8.3 Structure, Pilot Study and Questionnaire design

The questionnaire was developed on the basis of results from the explorative interviews. In contrast to the qualitative phase of this study, the frequency of identified patterns and the characterisation of these typologies are of central interest.

In simplified terms, companies were asked to provide information on all changes of foreign operation mode by answering specific, mostly closed, questions.

In order to increase the reliability, validity, and usability of the survey, piloting a survey is recommended (Newmann and McNeil 1998; Berenkoven et al. 2006). Piloting took place in two steps. First the questionnaire was sent by mail to 6 experts. After the questionnaire had been answered, there was an interview by telephone with the interview partner regarding comprehensibility, time required, practicability and recommendations for optimisation. After the correction and revision, the questionnaire was tested by 15 internationalisation experts as part of a management seminar. After a further revision of the questionnaire, a discussion with the experts followed regarding structure, content and readability. Written comments and recommendations for improvement were also added to the filled-out questionnaires. As a result, comprehensibility problems were removed, the reply options for justifying the switch and measuring performance were modified and the introductory instructions for completion were adjusted.

The following methodical problems arose from the development and the testing of the questionnaire (Saldana 2003; Berenkoven et al. 2006):

- First, a period of 15 years was to be taken as a timeframe for companies to reflect on mode switches. The explorative interviews, however, indicated a necessity for a substantially longer period of time. To be able to "carry" timeframes of 20 years and more, the initially selected table form of presentation had to be abandoned for a sequential form. Visualisation of the development behaviour in a diagram was sacrificed for comprehensive inclusion of all mode switches in a foreign market.

- Based on the feedback provided by the internationalisation experts and the explorative results, the questionnaire was significantly reduced in its scope. The initially-added questions regarding influencing factors, decision-making criteria and barriers to mode switches were removed to shorten the time needed for completing the survey, thereby increasing the willingness to participate, without detracting from the quality of the results. The questionnaire's scope was more focused and the process time was reduced by 30%.

- The aim of the study was to obtain a sufficient number of relevant events tied to the switch of foreign operation mode ("non-switcher" vs. "switcher") to promote general applicability of the results. The questionnaire was to be structured in such a manner that companies which had switched modes after market entry as well as companies which had not switched after market entry could be included. The aim of this approach was to compare the company success of both groups. The pre-test of the questionnaire with experts provided valuable recommendations here for fulfilment of this requirement.

- With the objective of obtaining a comprehensive picture of the company's behaviour on a market, there was the difficulty that some interview partners no longer remembered certain events clearly or no longer possessed information on past behaviour in the market. It was for this reason that the survey focused on a single foreign market and the most important one, as it was assumed that for a foreign market with high relevance for the company, there would still be enough information and knowledge about changes of foreign operation.

- A further problem lay in the description of market entry and the identification and description of changes in foreign operation. It took several tests and correction to identify a format which was easy to read, easy to understand and not too time consuming for the respondent to answer.

- Written surveys carry the problems of low response level, uncontrolled assessment situation, no control of the response process, low motivation of participants and a relatively long timeframe requirement (Berenkoven et al. 2006). To reduce the problem of the uncontrolled assessment situation, in particular with regard to the non-personified addresses, the attempt was made to at least address the survey to the managing director for foreign business or the export manager. It was hoped that the survey would be placed in the "right" hands. The questions were organised in such a way that they supplemented each other and followed a certain sequence designed to hold the participant's interest.

Based on the feedback during piloting, several additional revisions were made to the original questionnaire. Each change was followed up by further piloting with experts and pre-testing where necessary until the final version for the survey on mode switching was agreed. The final questionnaire is displayed in the Appendix.

4.8.4 Non-respondents

The problem of the non-response, or non-participation or non-reaction to the survey is a frequently observed phenomenon in retrospective studies (Swoboda 2002). Individuals who cannot remember the internationalisation history may also not take part in the survey because they do not believe they have information to supply. Also, more recent employees may not possess the requisite knowledge of past foreign activities.

Further reasons for the non-response include the time required to fill out the questionnaire, approximately 30 minutes. The presentation of past switching events and the assessment of reasons and effects of the switch was particularly time intensive – rather than the high number of closed questions.

It should also be taken into consideration that for people with more of a short-term-oriented and operative understanding of management – a strategy-oriented, long-term-based survey with reconstruction of international developments is sometimes of little interest.

Another reason might be that management is highly reluctant to share information, experience and knowledge about successful or unsuccessful results.

To reduce the non-response rate, a raffle with award was offered and the questionnaire was continuously optimised and tested for its structure and content over the duration of several months. The survey was addressed exclusively to the management or the management of foreign business because a high level of interest was assumed here. The assessment of the mode switching was intentionally limited to the most important foreign market (with regard to sales or potential). It was assumed that a critical event, such as a mode switch, would have to be of high importance for the company, meaning the company would have exact knowledge regarding performance development or motives for past developments. The concentration on one foreign market also reduced the required time for filling out the questionnaire, thereby increasing willingness to complete it.

What continues to be problematic is the effect of non-respondents on the quality of the survey results. In particular, when the behaviour of companies which have not responded varies from the companies which have responded – results can be distorted (Bortz and Göring 2006). In general, it can be established that it is precisely the various structures, country priorities, context conditions and diverse strategies in the form of modes that are characteristic for internationalisation. It can therefore be assumed, with regard to the most important categories and influencing factors, that the significance of a non-response bias is negligible. An exception could be the analysis of company success, as it is to be expected that unsuccessful firms for example, will not be interested in making their poor results known. This aspect is considered in the generalisation of the results.

Realistically, every researcher depends on the goodwill of the company and of its managers. In the preliminary studies, however, it was noted that the subject and its high relevance for foreign business met with a great amount of interest on the part of respondents and that they were also highly interested in the results of the survey.

4.8.5 Analytical approach

The assessment and evaluation of the survey was done by means of SPSS 16 and EXCEL 2003 using of various analytical methods. The statistical methods used are shown in Table 4.5.

Table 4.5:Application of statistical methods used

Application	Methods used	Tool
Descriptive univariante statistic	Distribution, Frequency, Exploratory data analysis	Microsoft Excel
Test of hypothesis	Analysis of variance	
	Correlation analysis	
Structure-assessing statistics	Regression analysis	SPSS 16
	Classification results	PASW Statistic 18
Structure-exploring statistics	Factor analysis, Cluster analysis	
	Survival or Failure analysis	
Time related analysis	Logistic regression	
	Time series analysis	

First, the characteristics of the companies is given (e.g. number of employees, turnover, sector, age of the company and number of years in foreign business). Then the characteristics of the interview partners is provided (position, time working at the company and experience in foreign markets). From the statistical-methodological perspective – description, analysis, modelling of frequency distribution and analysis of mean values form the focus.

The management style is analysed with the use of a semantic differential and information provided on bipolar attitudes and behaviourisms in the internationalisation process. The ten contrary characteristics-variables were taken from the preceding exploratory interviews. The evaluation is made through the assessment of the discrimination values of the management style, their mean values and standard variances.

To examine the influencing factors and relation effects in the internationalisation process, the independent variables are identified with the use of factor analysis. In this manner, it is possible to test a number of characteristics and to extract factors which are actually relevant for behaviour during the foreign operation mode switch. Information regarding to what extent the sample is suitable for factor analysis or to what degree the starting variables correlate with the description of the management style is provided by the Kaiser-Meyer-Olkin-(KMO-)criterion and the Bartlett test of sphericity. The Bartlett test asks the significance of the χ^2-value. The KMO criterion allows an evaluation of the correlation matrix and individual variables. As a method for factor derivation, an orthogonal (square) rotation according to Varimax with Kaiser normalisation is employed. The derived factor loadings are summarised in the factor-loading matrix and show the correlations. The identified factors of growth, risk, specialist and mode form the basis for the subsequent cluster analysis.

The starting problem to be solved with the aid of the cluster analysis is the analysis of a heterogeneous totality of various modes of operation with the aim of identifying homogenous partial quantities of single modes and mode combinations. For this, the degree of similarity is first determined, then the groups are summarised. Finally, the number of clusters is determined with consideration of the target conflict between manageability (low number of clusters) and homogeneity requirement (large number of clusters).

To assess whether the identified clusters hold validity beyond the identified clusters, standard errors and 95% confidence intervals are determined for the expected values.

Analysis of timing aspects with regard to the preparation and implementation of a switch of foreign operations is undertaken through the use of cross tabulation and contingency analysis. In addition to the duration of the individual decision-making phases, it is of interest whether a correlation can be assumed between the duration of the decision and success of the company. The evaluation of statistical independence is undertaken through the χ^2-Test.

For analysis of the internationalisation strategy and behaviour of the companies after market entry, observed changes in the market-entry strategy are presented in the form of frequency tables and cross tabulations. As mentioned, the information on internationalisation behaviour pertains, individually, to one foreign market. The companies surveyed were to take the foreign market they deemed most important. This was to reduce gaps in memory to the best extent possible. The emphasis is on the mode of operation, the switch or non-switch, the reasons for the switch, timing aspects of the switch and the employed mode over the course of time. From the methodological-statistical perspective, the analysis of mean values for the individual subject of analysis and the measurement of the intensity and direction of correlations forms the focus.

Of particular interest in this work is the question of whether influence can be detected between the operation mode and the company's success. Though internationalisation success has been widely covered in the literature, only a few studies so far have taken the success into the context of the mode switch (Swoboda 2002; Calof 1993). The analysis is made from the perspective of the currently employed mode of operation. Whether the market-entry strategy was switched or not in order to achieve this mode is, at this point, of no relevance. In addition to individual modes of operation, mode combinations are also analysed. To measure the success of the company, four measurement indicators are employed which refer to the objective success measurement of changes in turnover and personal satisfaction as a subjective success indicator – both for the individually most important foreign market. The selected mode of analysis has the advantage that both immediate and long-term effects of the switch on company success can be identified.

With the use of the survival analysis as a non-parametric approach, the question of which kind of probability mode switching will occur over time is addressed (Foster et al. 2006). The event observed here is the mode switch with consideration of individual countries, sector and specific modes. Using the survival analysis, the probability with which a switch was not yet made up to a certain period in time or also up to which time period can be established, e.g., half of the companies had switched. The reliability was tested using the Kaplan-Meier estimator. In this work, it is of particular interest whether it may be assumed that certain modes are more quickly switched after market entry than others and what kind of influencing factors could contribute to explaining this phenomenon. With the regression analysis following Cox, it is examined how the covariates influence the survival probability (in other words, the non-switching). To evaluate the quality of the model, the quality criteria are taken on the basis of the log-likelihood function, chi-square distribution and Wald statistics.

In addition, the hazard function is used in this work. The complement of the survival curve is the hazard function or curve, which reflects the risk of mode switch. It gives the rate with which, to a certain time ("t"), companies "survived" without a switch to then experience a change of the status quo ("momentary tendency to change status quo") and a switch of mode.

To evaluate the selected hypotheses, the relationships between dependent variables and independent variables are analysed in order to quantitatively present and explain the observed correlations and to predict the values of the dependent variables. For this, regression analysis is one of the most flexible and most frequently used statistical analysis approaches (Backhaus et al. 2006). The primary area of application in this work is the examination of causal relationships with regard to the study subject, the switch of foreign operation mode.

4.8.6 Research Variables

Included in this section are the dependent and independent variables used to measure the hypotheses presented in Chapter 3. All variables employed are presented in the Appendix. In the following section the most important measures are described:

Performance

The dependent variable in this study is performance. For operationalisation of the company's success and the assessment of the effect of a switch in the most important foreign market, four approaches as shown in Table 4.6 are analysed.

Table 4.6: Performance measurements of mode switching in most important country

Performance indicator	Time related effects	Measurements
Objective Performance		
Immediate turnover growth	Short-term	Ratio of turnover three years after the switch to the turnover one year before the switch $((T_3-T_{-1})/T_{-1}$, assessed if growth ratio is $>1)$
Long-term turnover growth by year	Long-term	Ratio of turnover in 2006 to the turnover one year before the switch. This was also computed by dividing this ratio by the number of years since the switch $((T_{2006}-T_{-1})/T_{-1}/$number of years)
Subjective Performance		
Immediate satisfaction improvement	Short-term	The difference between satisfaction with performance in the country three years after the switch and satisfaction one year before the switch on a scale from 1 (highly satisfied) to 5 (not satisfied)
Long-term satisfaction improvement	Long-term	The difference between satisfaction with performance in the country in 2006 and satisfaction one year before the switch on a scale from 1 (highly satisfied) to 5 (not satisfied)

In addition to the measurement criteria for changes caused by the switch of mode which has dynamic character, current satisfaction with the success of market operations thus far and the turnover share of the foreign market are collected. A satisfaction survey additionally provides indications of success in foreign business for the company in general.

Management style

To characterise management behaviour and attitudes toward internationalisation and the management of foreign operations, a total of ten management attributes were derived from the literature review and exploratory interviews (Chapter 6.2). The individual statements regarding risk perception, strategic planning, direction (reduction or growth) and process of internationalisation, intensity, speed/pace of switch and mode strategy are presented in Table 4.7.

Table 4.7: Sample questions for assessing managerial style of foreign management operation

Strategic Planning		
Our success is the result of a consciously chosen strategy.	- 3 to + 3, with zero as neutral position	To be honest, our success has had a lot to do with luck, chance and the taking of unexpected opportunities.

Attitude towards risk		
We are more careful in the foreign market and only take very low risks.	- 3 to + 3, with zero as neutral position	We're willing to take risks, as long as there's the corresponding profit.

Standardised vs. Differentiated approach		
For foreign market operations, we always follow the same concept, which looks the same for all countries-	- 3 to + 3, with zero as neutral position	We decide on an individual case-by-case basis what the best foreign market operation would be.

Direction: Reduction vs. Growth		
We have reduced our number of foreign activities in the last five years.	- 3 to + 3, with zero as neutral position	We have expanded our foreign activities in the last five years.

Process: Incremental vs. Ad -hoc		
We prefer a policy of a small step-by-step approach, such as 1. Agent, 2. Own sales rep, 3. Sales office	- 3 to + 3, with zero as neutral position	We prefer a policy of larger steps in foreign operation, e.g. direct foundation of a branch or acquisition of a company.

Rhythm of international activities: regular vs. irregular		
A switch of foreign operation is undertaken normally at the same, regular time intervals.	- 3 to + 3, with zero as neutral position	The switch of mode takes place irregularly, sometimes at shorter, sometimes at longer time intervals.

Speed: very slow vs. very rapid		
The number of foreign activities develops very slowly, e.g. a new agent/distributor in five years.	- 3 to + 3, with zero as neutral position	The number of foreign activities is growing very rapidly. Every 6 months or so there is at least one new agent/distributor in the foreign market.

Intensity: within mode switch vs. between mode switch		
We always switch at the same level of intensity, e.g. the agent is replaced by a new agent.	- 3 to + 3, with zero as neutral position	When we switch modes, we jump from one level of intensity to another, for example, an importer is replaced by a sales subsidiary.

Number of modes: Single mode vs. multi mode per country		
We only use one mode per country, for example with an agent.	- 3 to + 3, with zero as neutral position	We combine several modes per country, for example, importer and sales subsidiary simultaneously.

Mode strategy: single mode strategy vs. multi mode strategy		
We always use the same mode for all countries (e.g. exclusively agents).	- 3 to + 3, with zero as neutral position	We always use different modes for our country markets, e.g. agent in country A, sales subsidiary in country B, Importer in Country C.

Company and Interview partner characteristics

The characteristics of company size, number of employees, age of company, how long the company has been in the foreign market and the domestic and foreign turnover are measured. For characterising the sample, it was also necessary to ask the interview partner about his or her position, tenure at the company and the extent of personal international experience in years.

Country and Sector Context

Sector classification was made into six groups, based on the classification of the business sectors for the German production industry. The classification of the sectors is presented in Table 4.8:

Table 4.8: Sector of respondents

1.	Building, Furniture, Household
2.	Chemical Industry, Plastic Industry
3.	Metal, mechanical engineering
4.	Electronics, Electrical engineering (EDV, Electricity, Control, Medical instruments, Optic)
5.	Automotive Industry (cars, lorries, supplier of parts)
6.	Others (paper, packaging; print; food; cigarettes; textile/clothing; energy)

The country classification is made from a marketing-oriented perspective following Johansson (p. 229, 2005) and is presented based on the economic environment and purchasing behaviour of a country. Classification of the countries for which the internationalisation behaviour is traced is shown in Table 4.9:

Table 4.9: Country groups

1.	Mature markets	Western-Europe, North America, Japan, Australia, New Zealand
2.	Newly industrialized markets	Eastern Europe (e.g. Poland, Czech Republic, Romania), South Corea, Singapore, Mexico, Malaysia, Middle Eastern Countries, South Africa
3.	Emerging markets	China, Russia, India, Pakistan (and all newly democratized post communist nations: Kazakhstan, etc.) and Vietnam

Mode characteristics, mode portfolio

The potential mode strategies are divided into a total of 13 groups (Table 4.10). Especially important in this was the subdivision of export strategies into indirect and direct, as well as the further subdivision according to the commercial position of the

145

middleman. In contrast to the widely found categorisation of strategy in exporting, contractual and investment mode (Welch at al. 2007), the conditions of the German market with regard to particular strategy preferences are considered. International project operations, contracting and management contracts, however, are not individually listed as low significance was expected[4].

Table 4.10: Mode strategy classification

1.	Internet, E-Commerce
2.	Indirect Export, with Exporter located in domestic market
3.	Direct Export, without intermediare
4.	Direct Export, wit own sales person
5.	Export Service Consultant
6.	Direct Export, Commercial Agent
7.	Direct Export, Importer
8.	Strategic alliances, partnering
9.	Franchising. Licensing
10.	Joint Venture
11.	Subsidiaries, Affiliates, Branch
12.	Acquisition
13.	Others

To determine the strategy in the context of the modes employed in foreign markets in total, the percentage significance of the modes employed against the foreign turnover and the degree of satisfaction (Scale 1 highly satisfied to 5 not satisfied) were asked per mode.

Mode-switching decision

To determine the decision-making behaviour (duration of decision), the individual duration for opinion building and the implementation of mode decisions was also determined. The question was posed for foreign business in general, without direct reference to individual modes.

---

[4] Going Global 2007, p. 23: of all strategic options for market operation, 88% of German companies employ an "export strategy" for international market operations (multiple answers were possible).

Timing

The problem of timing of the mode switch, to be examined using the quantitative analysis, refers to the dwelling time after market entry up until a switch was made. For this, the market-entry strategy and mode after the switch were determined. In this work, the three time dimensions of "average time until entry mode is switched", "average time until the first new mode is reached" and "average time (duration) between market-entry mode until new mode" are analysed for the most frequent switching pattern.

Other influencing factors

Dimensions of the external environment, such as competitive conditions, norms and standards, political- and technological developments or cultural aspects were not considered in the quantitative survey. These influencing factors were part of the qualitative analysis.

4.8.7 Measurements and accuracy criteria

After a decision has been made as to which research design is suitable for the proposed research and once the measurement criteria have been established, the demands on the quality criteria must be defined. The central demands, or requirements, are objectivity, representativeness, reliability and validation. Such requirements must be practical, economic and useful (Raithel 2008).

Objectivity

The degree of objectivity expresses to what extent the findings are independent of the individual researcher applying the quantitative method. Objectivity must be guaranteed in the interviewing, the evaluation of results and their interpretation. With standardised quantitative methods, such as are used here, a high level of objectivity can be assumed (Bortz and Göring 2006; Raithel 2008).

Representativeness

Representativeness of the sample must be measurable based on the question of whether the sample, in its composition, is comparable with most companies. A reliable comparison of the sample demography with demographic characteristics of the production industry is only possible to a very limited degree as reliable sector information related to international activities is either not available or is incomplete. Figures tied to foreign activities, based on the German sales tax statistics,[5] provide a first indication of turnover, number of employees and export ratio – but these are not divided according to a sector key. It is therefore a question of the general population whose distributions of characteristics allow conclusions to be made. What can be established here is that the most important sectors of automotive, chemical industry, construction and engineering are highly represented in the sample and that the participating companies lie above the German average for SMEs in terms of their export ratio (approx. 40%).[6] Of decisive importance for evaluating the adequacy of the sample is the question of whether a suitable contact person in the company was found. In this study – managers, sales directors and marketing directors dominate with approximately 85 percent of the respondents. Here it is clear that the objective to survey managers who are familiar with decentralised decisions of international company management was achieved.

The analysis of the sample and its composition is presented in Chapter 7. Detailed information regarding data collection and sampling is presented in Chapter 4.8.2.

Reliability

A study is reliable when the measurements are precise and stable – that means, repeated measurements have to produce the same results.

---

[5] Statistisches Bundesamt (Federal Statistical Office): Sonderauswertung der Umsatzsteuerstatistik 2004, by commission of IfM Bonn, Wiesbaden 2006.

[6] At the time of the survey in 2007, approx. three-fourths of all companies in the SME panel of the BDI (results of online SME survey spring 2008, p. 24) could increase their export sales. The export ratio (export turnover share of total turnover) in 2007 was, on average, approx. 40%.[6]

For this reason, there must be systematic control of every single phase of the survey from its first concept to its mailing and the response (Roth et al. 1999). In the development of the questionnaire, great care was taken to ensure that measure and measurements sufficiently portray the study subject and that they are clear, comprehensible, differentiable and do not overlap (Böhler 2004). The question items used in the questionnaire were tested for their reliability and stability in a pilot study. Two survey waves were conducted with the same survey instruments, first with the aid of six internationalisation experts in single interviews and finally in a group discussion with 15 participants. Each provided detailed feedback to the questionnaire. The concluding evaluation confirmed the reliability and stability of the selected question items for measuring behaviour tied to a switch of foreign operation.

The quantification of the measurement precision or reliability of a test is undertaken in the description and interpretation of the results in Chapter 7 and Chapter 8.

Validity

Validation refers to the conceptional accuracy of the measurement instrument and thereby to the degree to which the selected measurement instrument actually measures the characteristics of the construct to be analysed (Bortz and Göring 2006; Raithel 2008). In the literature, four forms of validation are identified (Bortz and Göring 2006; Diekmann 2006; Raithel 2008):

External validity is given when a selection of characteristics portrays the property to be measured to a high degree. Addressing external validity means answering the question: "To what extent can we generalise from the research sample and setting to the populations and settings specified in the research hypotheses?" For this reason, a large-scale survey was selected in order to achieve general applicability of the results.

Furthermore, there is the question of the significance of the findings for potential beneficiaries. To ensure this, the employed questions, instruments and scales were developed from the following sources:

- Managers experienced in the internationalisation of companies and experts in market research were consulted regarding relevant assessment dimensions and these findings were taken into consideration.

- Existing questionnaires on organisational change and the mode switch were evaluated and relevant items were adopted or adapted (Calof 1993, Freidank 1994; McNaughton 2001; Swoboda 2002; Pedersen et al. 2002)

- Literature on the conduction of surveys in general and, in particular, for international business was considered with their concepts for the preparation of the questionnaire (Saunders et al. 2003; Marschan-Piekkari and Welch 2004; Berekoven et al. 2006).

Internal (content) validity concerns the extent to which one can draw conclusions regarding the causal effects of one variable on another. It addresses the question of: "To what extent does the research design permit us to research casual conclusions about the effect of the variable on the dependent variable?" This work strives to achieve content validity through a precise division in content between the selected constructs on mode switching and other constructs, as well as through recourse to previously employed constructs and their partially validated operationalisation.

The criterion-related validity shows to what degree the results achieved with a measurement instrument empirically correlate to other relevant characteristics (external criteria). Here, the often non-uniform measurement- and evaluation procedures for assessing company success represented a major challenge with regard to criterion validity (Bachmann 2007; Krist 2009). In this work, objective and subjective measurement approaches are combined as a supplementary operationalisation in the same measuring model. From the conceptual perspective, it must therefore be ensured that no variations in the definition and aggregation problems contribute to an observed event. This requirement was tested in a pilot study and the assessment format was adjusted based on the test results.

Construct validity demands that the construct assessed by a measurement instrument stands in as many theoretically-grounded causal connections with other variables as possible, and that hypotheses may be derived from this which can hold up under empirical assessment (Raithel 2008). Construct validity strives to address the question of to what extent the constructs of theoretical interest are successfully operationalised in the research. High construct validity means that all constructs being studied have been successfully represented by the specific variable the author selected. The suitability of the various measuring instruments was examined during the expert tests and in the pilot study and adjustments made before the actual survey.

In this work, construct validity is also tested through the use of extensive, statistical testing programmes pertaining to the formulated hypotheses and the theoretical model on mode switching (Chapter 3 and 8).

4.9 Limitations

The focus of the survey falls in a period of strongly increased international trade and direct foreign investment. Goods transportation without barriers, the reduction of customs restrictions and China's WTO contribution caused the global economy to boom. In Germany, export continuously developed from 1950 with 4.2 billion Euros, 1970 with 64 billion Euros, 1990 with 348 billion Euros and 2007 with 965 billion.[7] The gross domestic product in Germany has grown continuously since the 50's, however with regressive growth rates in decade comparisons.[8] The economic frame conditions mentioned above represent important exogenous influencing factors. To what extent this influenced the switch of foreign mode can only be answered on an individual basis. It is, however, clear that despite diverse economic downturns at global level, the timeframe of the study falls in a general phase of booming economic development.

---

[7] Außenhandelsstatistik (Foreign trade statistics), Statistische Bundesamt (Federal Statistics Office), Fachserie 7, Reihe 1, January 2009, p. 18.

[8] GDP Germany acc. Statistische Bundesamt (Federal Statistics Office): 1960 – 1970 +4.4%, 1970 – 1980 +2.9%, 1981 – 1991 +2.6%, 1991 – 2000 +1.7%

As with most studies that take past developments as a subject, the fundamental question of available knowledge of past events related to the mode switch is relevant. The availability of detailed information regarding the conditions of the switch must be critically considered. Both with the explorative interviews and the survey it was necessary that the interview partners remember the mode switch or that information on the subject be available and accessible in the company. Changes in the organisation, personnel changes and other changes resulting from company acquisitions and sales render the necessary transparency difficult to achieve and can influence the level of detail and assessment of past activities. As previously mentioned, the author will therefore focus on the most important foreign market for the company in the qualitative and quantitative sections. The author made the assumption that the high significance of the foreign market would mean that corresponding information and knowledge would be available. In addition, only individuals at management levels were interviewed for both the qualitative and quantitative sections. It was assumed that the longer the interview partner had been at the company, the higher his or her position in the hierarchy and the more internationalisation experience they had at the individual level – the better would be the assessment of the problem-subject of mode switching.

A further problem with retrospective-processual studies and the retrospective assessment of influencing factors on the mode switch is the tendency of the interviewee to rationalise developments after the fact which were initially of little intention. This aspect can be partially objectified through the quantitative statements on the significance and success of internalisation and the switch.

Although the information here was collected from only one person from each respondent company, a decision-making unit usually consists of more than one individual (Leonidou 1998). Bias may result from diverse ways of defining and operationalising manager's attitude (e.g. systematic planning, risk taking, standardised strategy, incremental development, or speed) resulting in semantic confusion or from the subjectivity of self-reported managerial characteristics.

The measurement of the company's success is based on objective and subjective criteria. The literature showed inconsistent results regarding the correlation of objective and subjective success-measurement criteria with the result that subjective information is viewed as additional information in the case of lacking objective information (Bachmann 2007). Subjective success measurements are subject to bias and selection of human perception and therefore do not always correspond to objective data. Causes of this include psychological processes, such as positive illusions, the striving for cognitive consistency, or projections. At the same time, subjective success measurements are accompanied by intuitive consideration of experience, knowledge and motivation. They are therefore richer in content because a greater area of performance is covered (Bachmann, p. 97, 2007).

The assessment of satisfaction is thereby to be viewed as a supplementary and supporting measurement criteria for evaluating the effects of switches of foreign operation modes. Variations in perception, the ability to judge and mental models, however, result in a rationality deficit in the assessment of satisfaction.

Dimensions of the external environment, such as competitive conditions, supplier conditions, norms and standards, political- and technological developments or cultural aspects were not considered in the quantitative survey on mode switching. Also dimensions of competitive strategy, such as cost- or price leadership in general or in the selected important countries were not an element of the study. The reasons for this lie in the higher complexity of the survey which would have been involved and a longer survey time requirement. In the qualitative part of this work, these factors were, however, comprehensively addressed whenever they bear direct influence on internationalisation pathways and the switch of the foreign operation mode.

This chapter presented the research methodology for analysing switches of foreign operation modes. In addition to the philosophical foundation, the research method for addressing the research questions and propositions are presented with consideration of research methods of the existing research. A further point of emphasis is the presentation of the procedure of qualitative and quantitative data gathering and evaluation. The chapter closes with an assessment of the limiting factors of the method of approach selected.

In the following chapters, the empirical analysis for the switch of foreign operation modes will be presented. First, the sample of in-depth interviews is shown along with the qualitative results. Then the sample of participating companies in the large-scale survey is characterised. Finally, the comprehensive results are presented and discussed.

Chapter 5 Presentation and analysis of qualitative data on mode switching behaviour

In the previous chapter, it was shown with which research methodology the problem of the foreign mode switch can be explored. The reason behind the decision for a quantitative and qualitative method mix was explained and approaches of other researchers with regard to the study subject were discussed. This allows transparency of the research sections, the most important measurement criteria, the measurement apparatus and possible limiting factors.

In this chapter, the data gathered from the in-depth interviews are presented. Emphasis is placed on presenting descriptive profiles of the study sample companies based on their number of employees, sector, turnover, export share, year of founding, experience in the specific foreign market and behaviour at and after market entry. The results are interpreted in Chapter 6.

5.1 Characteristics of the sample companies

All 15 participants are from different German manufacturing companies which also primarily produce in Germany. They include medium-sized businesses with 100 to 3000 employees. Turnovers ranged from 25 million to 900 million Euros. As may be inferred from the list of founding years below, these are all traditional businesses with long histories and with extensive experience in the individual sector. The "youngest" company was founded 36 years ago, the oldest company is 250 years old. Most of the companies entered the selected foreign market in the mid-90's. The duration of activity in the selected foreign market ranged from 7 to 45 years. The companies represent various sectors ranging from automobile supply, to the production, installation and operation of air conditioners, to installation systems for building management. Predominantly represented are companies from the chemicals-, engineering- and electrical engineering sectors (exceptions: Firm No. 12 is a trading company for gardening products, Firm No. 14 is a medical technology company). Companies from the service sector (e.g. financial services or IT-services) are not represented in the sample. Also not included in the sample are "born globals", companies which immediately internationalised after founding.

Table 5.1 shows the sample of participants who were interviewed and the related company characteristics.

The sample analysed comprised of internationally successful companies from the most important sectors of the production industry in Germany. The broad spectrum of companies with regard to structure, number of employees, turnover and performance characteristics has been consciously selected so that various behaviours and reactions of key actors can be identified and learned from (Chapter 4.7.3). The patterns and mechanisms identified are thereby of interest and relevance for companies planning a switch of mode after market entry.

Table 5.1: Characteristics of the sample companies

No.	Interview partner	Industry sector	Year of founding	Sales Turnover	Employees	Export Ratio	Selected Country	Country Experience
1	Director International Sales Industries and Trade	Fixing components, clips, plastic joints	1949	250 m. Euro	1600	63%	USA	> 25 years
2	1. CEO, 2. Director	1.Industrial gates, 2. RFID	1970	25 m. Euro	130	42% (2001: 14%)	USA	> 7 years
3	Managing Director	Air Conditioning	1956	60 m. Euro	320	15%	Russia	> 25 years
4	Director International Sales and Board Member	Sanitary and Heating Systems	1899	800 to 900 m. Euro	2500	45% (+15%/a)	Czech Republic	13 years
5	Export Manager	Lighting concepts, lamps	1947	45-50 m. Euro	350	40% (1996: 23%)	Poland	14 years
6	Managing Director	Vacuum pumps	1890	170 m. Euro	690	70%	China	11 years
7	CEO	High resistance coating/ painting	1890	744 m. Euro	740	50-60%	China	11 years
8	1. CEO, 2. Export Manager	Composite elements	1815	50 m. Euro	200	54 % (2002: 33%)	Poland	15 years
9	President and CEO	Carbon brushes	1913	700 m. Euro	3000	60%	China	15 years
10	1. CEO; 2. Export Director	Fine wire	1889	100 m. Euro	550	75%	China, USA	15 years, 20 years
11	CEO	Current resistor elements	1827	60 m. Euro	430	16%	Japan	16 years
12	Managing Director	Home and garden decoration	1872	30 m. Euro	168	28%	Poland, Switzerland	13 years, 10 years
13	Export Manager	Shop equipment and presentation systems	1951	40 m. Euro	200	60-70%	Poland	12 years
14	Managing Director	Dental, impression materials for dental use	1944	25 m. Euro	140	60-70%	France	> 30 years
15	President and CEO	Folding bellows for bus and rail	1946	150 m. Euro	1350	60%	China	13 years

157

Characteristic patterns of switching behaviour

From the 15 company interviews, 17 characteristic patterns of how companies act in 8 different countries could be established. The individual switches and characteristic patterns comprise in a total of 41 mode switches. In addition to the initial market-entry strategy, the time of market entry, the switch from the initially selected foreign operation mode and the length of time between the old and the new mode are presented with the aim of illustrating the company´s development. The term "switch" in the tables refers to a change from a previous operation mode in a foreign market to a new mode of operation (Chapter 2.7.2).

For the participants in the interviews, the country market they selected represented a typical example of their company's foreign operation management, with the characteristic decisions and behaviours (Chapter 4.7.4).

A prime example with regard to the theoretical findings (Chapter 2.7) is Case No. 3 involving Russia. Here, the initially selected market-entry strategy of "piggy-back" was changed into the strategy of "importer" after ten years. After ten more years, this importer was then replaced by an own subsidiary. There were therefore two switches after market entry. Further mode switches are currently not planned (Table 5.2). Table 5.2 and Table 5.3 show the different strategies for market entry and the changes made in foreign operation.

The identification of position, processes and pathways provides comprehensive information on the management of foreign operations. This will be analysed under consideration of the research method defined in Chapter 4.7 in the following section.

Table 5.2: Cases 1-9 with characteristic switch behaviour

Case -No.	Market Entry	Time of Market Entry	1. Switch	Time period until 1. switch	2. Switch	Time period between 1. and 2. switch	3. Switch	Time period between 2. and 3. switch	4. Switch	Time period between 3. and 4. switch	Future switch
1	Importer (joint cooperation of five German companies)	Mid 80's	Importer - Sales Subsidiary	15 years	Closing production	6 years	No switch	/	No switch	/	No switch planned
2	1. Piggy Back, 2. Importer	1. 1999, 2. 2001	1. Piggy back - Importer, 2. No switch	1 year	1. No switch, 2. Export Service Agency (planned)	(7 years)	No switch	/	No switch	/	2. Export Agency as intermediate step to prepare own sales subsidiary (sales subsidiary officially announced Jan 2007)
3	Piggy Back	Mid 80's	Piggy Back - Importer	10 years	Importer - Subsidiary	10 years	No switch	/	No switch	/	No switch planned
4	Own Sales Person	1993	1 Sales Person - 2 Sales Person (support from export service agency)	2 years	2 Sales Person -3 Sales Person (support from export service agency)	2 years	3 Sales Person - 4 Sales Person (support from export service agency)	2 years	Sales Person - Subsidiary (support from export agency)	3 years	No switch planned
5	Importer	1992	1 Importer - 2 Importer	3 years	2 Importer - 3 Importer	1 year	Importer - Sales Person	10 years	No switch	/	No switch planned
6	Importer	1995	Importer - Sales Subsidiary	11 years	No switch		No switch	/	No switch	/	No switch planned
7	Sales Office	1995	Sales Office - Joint Venture Marketing & Sales	11 years	JV - Licence Production	6 years	JV - JV production	/	No switch	/	No switch planned
8	Indirect Export	1991	Indirect export - Agent	6 years	Agent (old) - Agent (new)	5 years	(Cooperation with local producer planned)	1 year (2007)	No switch	/	Cooperation with local producer planned and either additional agent or own sales person
9	Export Area Manager	Early 90's	Direct Export - JV Sales Office Hong Kong	unclear	Sales Office Hong Kong - Affiliate Sales & Production	unclear	No switch	/	No switch	/	No switch planned

Table 5.3: Cases 10 - 17 with characteristic switch behaviour

Case-No.	Market Entry	Time of Market Entry	1. Switch	Time period until 1. switch	2. Switch	Time period between 1. and 2. switch	3. Switch	Time period between 2. and 3. switch	4. Switch	Time period between 3. and 4. switch	Future switch
10	Importer	Beginning 90's	Importer - Affiliate (Sales & Production)	15 years	No switch	/	No switch	/	No switch	/	Expanding Sales Office by building sales structure with own sales persons
11	Importer	Beginning 80's	Importer - Own sales person	20 years	Own sales person - sales subsidiary	5 years	No switch	/	No switch	/	Step by step reduction of importer involvement
12	Importer	1989	Importer (old) - Importer (new)	10 years	1 Importer - 2 Importer	5 years	Importer - Export Area Manager Asia (focus on Japan)	2 years (2006)	No switch	/	Sales Person or Sales Subsidiary with own warehouse and training facilities
13	Agent	1993	Local agent - Importer	3 years	Importer - Subsidiary	3 years	Sales subsidiary (old MD) - sales subsidiary (new MD)	4 years	Downsizing sales subsidiary (closing warehouse)	/	Profit Centre to Cost Centre, with key account management as main function
14	Importer	1996	Importer - Importer	6 years	Importer - Sales Person	3 years	No switch	/	No switch	/	No switch planned
15	Piggy Back	1994/1995	Piggy Back - Sales Person	7 years	Sales Person - Project Consultant	2 years	Project Consultant - Importer	2 years	(Service subsidiary planned)	1 year (2007)	Service subsidiary for detailed planning of presentation displays
16	Direct Export	Beginning 60's	Direct Export - Direct export with export manager	20 years	Direct Export - Own sales persons (support from export service agency)	15 years	Own sales persons - subsidiary	10 years	No switch	/	No switch planned
17	Importer	1993	Importer - Affiliate (Sales & Production)	6 years	1 Subsidiary - 2 Affiliate plus JV Production	2 years	No switch	/	No switch	/	No switch planned

5.2   Analysis of management behaviour during mode switching

The information gathered from the exploratory field interviews is analysed with an emphasis on the behaviour of the sample-group companies and their key decision-makers in the context of a switch of foreign operation mode (Chapter 4.7). The analysis will first present the interview results for one country from market entry and then, step-by-step, discuss the most important aspects tied to each mode switch from the perspective of these companies. The method of approach, conceptual points of emphasis and assessments follow the research design presented in Chapter 4.7.

Citations from the interviews support the arguments of the individual categories (Table 4.3). The statements are translations as the interviews were predominantly carried out in German. The stated sources pertain to fieldnotes and transcripts. Transcripts are the original recorded interviews in writing; field notes are notes taken during the interview. The specific behaviour patterns refer to the companies (Company No., Table 5.1) and the individual case with specific behaviour after market entry (Case No., Table 5.2 and Table 5.3). It is necessary to differentiate between the two reference levels of company (Company No.) and internationalisation behaviour (Case No.) so that the conditions of the switch can be presented and discussed based on structures, experiences, resources and performance (see Chapter 2.4).

This process-oriented approach (Chapter 4.5) is to allow a comprehensive analysis of the impetus for the switch, barriers, decision-making behaviour, objectives of the switch, actual changes in foreign operation mode (categorised according to their number and manifestations) for the sample companies, switch direction, switch pathway, timing issues and the reactions of significant parties to the switch.

Under consideration of the problem statement and research questions this analysis strives to locate and define significant context-factors and actions (in a similar manner as Pettigrew 1990) influencing or involved in a switch of foreign operation mode.

5.2.1 The market entry

With the exception of one company (No. 15), market entry for the firms interviewed took place between 1980 and 1996, and took the form of a direct or indirect export strategy. This market-entry strategy is typical for medium-sized businesses in Germany which are to a large extent export-oriented (German Chamber of Commerce 2007). The strategy of "export" was chosen by these decision-makers because it involves only a low investment of resources and low risk.

The general motives for market entry varied greatly in the sample group and were largely dependent upon aspects related to the specific foreign market selected. No other particular tendency is apparent.

With regard to decision-making behaviour at market entry, the sample cases could be mainly characterised in total as having taken a "systematically unsystematic approach". Most of the companies had only a faint idea at the time of entry what was ahead of them in the foreign market.

> "Our market entry was definitely not marked by strategic analysis or extensive market research." (Company 1, Field Notes, p. 1)

As a result, sales partners (agents/importers) were taken as suppliers of important market information (Company 1, 2, 5, 6, 7, 8, 12, 15). The decision for export trade was made consciously without any kind of systematic consideration of other possible strategy options. Most interview partners expressed that their main concern at market entry had been to minimise risk and keep resource investment low. This is why they chose corresponding market-entry strategies. This is supported by the following interview statement:

> "Why should I work with consultants? We used to spend lots of money on that. Today we prefer to try things out ourselves and limit the risk. With a new agent, our sales director usually visits the market first, then a cooperation develops, step-by-step, and we gradually get to know the market. Customers are visited and our marketing manager is sent over to support the agent. That way we can get to know the market best ourselves and can plan the next steps better." (Company 6, Transcript, p. 11)

Alternatively possible modes of foreign management operation were not considered and played only a subordinate role in the decision-making process for market entry. Strategies were chosen cautiously, as reflected in the low investment of resources that would not pose a risk to the company or limit its flexibility. The interviewees were, as a majority, of the opinion that modes had been chosen that would leave future options open and not limit company development.

> "After all, we can change this strategy any time we choose." (Company 6, Transcript, p. 8)

There were, with the exception of one case (Company 4), only small indications given in the interviews that – at the time of market entry – decision-makers had thought ahead and planned the next two or three steps of foreign operation or anticipated the pathway of its development. This could be due to a lack of experience or knowledge necessary for a prognosis of likely developments in the environment, which would then have allowed planning of subsequent strategies. Only after a certain degree of knowledge and experience of the foreign market had actually been gained, did switch considerations come into play and interim steps leading up to the actual configuration of the target begin were planned (Company 2, 8, 11, 13).

That some analogies are made and behaviour from strategies with other countries either consciously or unconsciously transferred to the new market is further illustrated by the following statement:

> "Every company uses certain mechanisms, be they good or bad. As a medium-sized business, we just perceive the conditions and adapt to them. We don't necessarily think in terms of strategic change..." (Company 8, Transcript, p. 26)

An exception was Company 4, a company with extensive foreign experience. Market entry into the Czech Republic was made via a company representative (an experienced sales engineer), who was sent to the country. After approximately two years of successfully working in the market, more sales persons were gradually sent (four) and, finally, a subsidiary was founded. On the basis of previous experience gained from founding subsidiaries in other countries, the decision-maker in Company 4 was able to draw analogies and apply them to the Czech market. The interview question regarding at what threshold the founding of a subsidiary becomes worth it revealed that a decision for a foreign management operation had actually already been made at the point of market entry.

> "My threshold lies at 3-4 salespersons. That's only a rule of thumb, but it's always worked – all through my career at the company, and my career has been thirty years." (Company 4, Field Notes, p. 1)

In summary, it may be established for the sample group that market entry was characterised by a "classic export strategy" that was then (in most of the cases) switched over the course of time. There was a relatively low level of planning for market entry. Decision-makers chose direct or indirect export as a means of gaining knowledge of the foreign market whilst maintaining low risk and low resource investment. Exceptions to this were companies which had previous experience with other foreign markets. These companies used existing know how and experience and transferred their knowledge to the market under observation. At market entry, they therefore already had plans for later operation modes.

5.2.2 Impetus for the mode switch

It is self explanatory that any foreign operation mode selected at entry is not necessarily the best choice for all time. When conditions change, the mode often needs to change as well (see Chapter 2.7.4). The factors leading to such a need for adaptation and the impetus for a mode switch will be analysed for the sample group. The various factors gathered from the interviews can be organised into the four main categories of Internal Change, Change in Environment, Performance, and Expectation (Chapter 2.7.4.3 and 2.7.4.6).

The internal factors in the category "internal change" are tied to the company itself and its organisation, resources, processes, culture and strategy. The decision maker can almost always at least partially influence these internal factors.

The category "environmental change" represents external influences which have a more or less direct effect on the company and are determined by "outer" forces, over which the company has no control.

The category of "performance" refers to the results achieved with the current mode. It is a critical assessment of the mode that may present both positive and negative findings.

"Expectation" comprises of the hopes, expectations, wishes and visions of the management with regard to a mode switch. The cognition and the attitude of the key decision-maker(s) play a central role here. This category, too, can be of positive and negative character. Each category contributes to the explanation of why the sample-group companies interviewed switched modes.

Provided in Table 5.4 is an indicative overview of the influencing factors, stimuli/reasons and motivations for a switch stated in the interviews and based on these four categories:

Table 5.4: Impetus for mode switch per case

Categories/Cases	1	2a	2b	3	4	5	6	7	8	9	10	11	12	13	14	15	16	17
Internal change	√		√	√	√		√	√		√	√	√	√	√	√	√	√	
Environmental change		√	√	√	√	√	√	√	√		√	√			√	√		√
Performance	√		√	√	√	√	√	√		√	√	√	√	√	√			√
Expectation	√	√	√	√	√		√	√	√	√	√	√		√			√	√

An analysis of the individual cases shows that there are normally several factors, or, a combination of factors presenting the reason or the motivation for a switch of foreign operation mode. Single criteria are normally not sufficient for triggering a switch (an exception is Case 9: sudden death of a current sales partner).

The detailed analysis of the categories is to illuminate what kind of criteria and specific factors motivated the switch for these companies is presented in the next subchapter.

5.2.2.1 Internal change

Internal influencing factors comprise criteria which, to a great extent, are within the decision-makers' control. Listed in Table 5.5 are some key statements made by the interview partners on this subject:

Table 5.5: Impetus to switch – Internal change

Impetus for mode switch	Statements	Case-No.
Internal change	- "New product innovation", "product improvement/modification"	1, 2b, 4, 10, 16
	- "New ownership"	10, 11, 13
	- "New CEO", "new export manager", "problems with CEO"	3, 9, 10, 13
	- "Lack of resources", "Internal capacity"	12
	- "Lack of capabilities"	9, 12
	- "Customer proximity"	4, 7, 15, 16
	- "More", "better" information	10, 4
	- "Improvement of market knowledge"	3
	- "Increasing fear of losing know-how"	6

For the companies interviewed, it was a change in resource investment that particularly influenced the motivation for a mode switch. This involved new products or product modifications (Cases 1, 2b, 4, 10, 16) requiring a new sales structure, or changes in personnel structures (Cases 3, 10, 13) – such as, for example, a new sales management. In three cases (10, 11, 13), a change of owner strongly influenced the company internationalisation strategy and the question of a mode switch. A further motivation was to be "closer to the customer" (Cases 4, 7, 15, 16), entailing greater commitment to the foreign market ("We are serious about our commitment."). Finally, the desire to either improve knowledge/know-how (Cases 3, 4, 10) or to protect own knowledge/know-how prompted the idea to switch (Case 6).

5.2.2.2 Business environmental change

In contrast to the internal influencing factors mentioned above, there were changes in the external business environment prompting the switch over which there was no control.

The statements listed in Table 5.6 illustrate the influence of external factors on the decision to switch modes:

Table 5.6: Impetus to switch – Business environmental change

Impetus for mode switch	Statements	Case-No.
Business environmental change	- Increase of intensity of competition ("Stronger competition over time", "Importer started his own production", "Ex-partner works together with direct competitor")	5, 8, 14, 17
	- Market development ("very strong market growth", "steady", "volatile", etc.)	2a, 2b, 4, 5, 6, 7, 8, 10, 11, 14
	- "Strong growth of key customer"	15
	- "Sudden death of sales partner"	8
	- National requirement given by government ("local content", "obligation to build JV with Chinese partner")	17
	- "High degree of corruption/bribery"	3

The analysis of the statements showed that, for the decision-makers, the factors of market development (Cases 5, 8, 14, 17) and intensity of competition (Cases 2a, 2b, 4, 5, 6, 7, 8, 10, 11, 14) were of the highest significance for a mode switch. Further motivating factors included strong growth of a major customer (Case 15), bribery and corruption in the foreign market (Case 3) and national laws or regulations (Case 17).

Of note is the importance of the individuals' perception of signals in the environment and their influence on the motivation to switch. In some cases, market development deemed enormously positive lead directly to discussions as to whether a switch should be made from importer to own subsidiary (Cases 11, 17). In another case, there was the same perception but also the sense that experience for founding a subsidiary was lacking (Case 12) or that founding a subsidiary did not fit the current "philosophy" of how foreign markets should be developed (Case 5). These examples illustrate how the influence the subjective interpretation of aspects in the outer environment can bear on the motivation to switch.

5.2.2.3 Performance

This category comprises motives and reasons which are directly or indirectly tied to the performance of the current mode of foreign operation thus far.

Presented in Table 5.7 are some of the key statements made in this context in the interviews:

Table 5.7: Impetus to switch – Performance

Impetus for mode switch	Statements	Case-No.
Performance	- Dissatisfaction with performance of partner ("Dissatisfaction with performance of the cooperation", "Importer doesn't know how to develop a market")	1, 2b, 6, 10, 11, 12, 17
	- "Too little information transfer", "Not open enough since they produce their own products"	3, 5
	- "Our core problem with our importer: profitability was not good enough"	14
	- "Sales so far prompt us to change"	4, 13
	- "We were running under full capacity, we needed to expand"	7
	- "The behaviour of our CEO was not acceptable anymore"	9

The major factor mentioned was dissatisfaction with the results of the previous foreign operation mode. This was expressed with regard to low profit or poor information transfer. Some selected statements illustrate this:

"We were not satisfied with our results in the USA, particularly in comparison to other countries where our product had been successfully launched." (Case 1, Field Notes, p. 2)

"We were lacking not technical information but market-relevant information. Furthermore, we needed to get more systematic, more organised, and enter into a real dialogue with the market." (Case 3, Field Notes, p. 2)

The following two statements show dissatisfaction with the low level of appreciation, priority and attention:

"Our partner has so many other products. We're not receiving the kind of attention and priority we need." (Case 6, Transcript, p. 10)

"The importer's spectrum was just too wide. We weren't getting ahead fast enough. That's why we couldn't continue." (Case 6, Field Notes, p. 2)

Overall, dissatisfaction dominated as a negative assessment of the previous market mode motivating a switch. Exceptions, however, were found with Case 4 and 7 in the sample group. With these cases, it was very good performance that motivated a switch. In the first case (4), the sales team was gradually expanded, leading up to the founding of a subsidiary. With Case 7, positive performance led to an expansion of licensing and an increase of production capacity through a joint venture.

5.2.2.4 Expectations

For analysis, statements made in the interviews regarding "expectations" were categorised. These are displayed in Table 5.8.

Table 5.8: Impetus to switch - Expectations

Impetus for mode switch	Statements	Case-No.
Expectations	- "Promising outlook and trust in positive development"	1, 2b, 4, 6, 7, 9, 10, 15
		3
	- "For long-term development, we need to be there."	6
	- "With the right preparation, the orders will follow."	7, 9
	- "We have a good feeling about how the markets will develop in future, therefore we need more commitment."	6
	- "We don't believe that we can have success there in the market if we go against our partner's interests."	7
	- "We don't always have to do everything to 100% ourselves."	
	- "If the Polish producer keeps developing so positively, I'll be able to imagine cooperation."	8
	- "Stagnating development is expected."	13

Many of the reasons for a switch were based on high expectations (or perceived development potential) of foreign markets (Cases 1, 2b, 4, 6, 7, 9, 10, 15). On closer observation, the influence that sales volume and expected market growth had on the decision becomes clear. Despite a high level of uncertainty and substantial risks, eight of the companies interviewed (Cases 1, 2b, 4, 6, 7, 9, 10, 15) stated that a solid belief and trust in the positive development of sales in the market had triggered the switch.

Strongly apparent in this category was the positive attitude of the interview partners towards internationalisation of their companies and their hopes to achieve positive effects for their companies through a mode switch. It becomes clear that the revealed reasons and motivations for a switch are a reflection of a company's objectives and

169

the strategy it has selected for them. The management designs the strategy to achieve these objectives. The objectives therefore contain the expectations, hopes, wishes and visions of the management. Perceptions and attitudes of the key decision-makers come into play. It also becomes clear that the categories of "external change" and "expectation" overlap. Both reflect decision-makers' perceptions of risks and opportunities, and how these are interpreted with regard to the foreign business.

5.2.2.5 Further issues influencing mode switch

Further influencing factors regarding mode switching could also be identified and will be discussed in the following:

Adjustment to dynamic of environment

Over the course of time, as the results indicate, the company continuously adapts and realigns itself to changing external conditions in the environment. This occurs first in that the company perceives the changes then assesses their significance for future decisions. In certain cases, measures are taken to counteract the external development or its negative effects. Most of the firms interviewed claimed that they react to certain environmental circumstances and readjust their behaviour and actions to them (Cases 2b, 4, 5, 10, 11, 12, 13, 14, 15). The following statements stands as an example for this:

> "Due to price drops of 10-15 percent by the competition, we are now under pressure to act. We have to do something. Next week I'm travelling to the U.S. to visit the most important fair for our sector and will check out our options." (Case 11, Transcript, p. 55)

It is, however, not always clear whether it is more the internal or external factors which trigger decisions and future actions. In one case, access to the attractive automotive-sector was only possible through the launch of a new product series, and this then demanded a mode switch (Case 11), as the following statement expresses:

> "As the new battery-management system became available in 2003, we suddenly became interesting for the Japanese customers. That opened the

170

door to the Japanese automobile industry we had been looking for." (Case 11, Transcript, p. 50)

In another case (No. 10), the belief in a continued strong growth rate, the positive market research results and the requirements of the Chinese customer all led to the necessity of a stronger presence in the country – reason enough for a mode switch, as the following statement shows:

> "The results of our market research showed us that there was a high demand for our products in China. We also strongly believe in the Asian market. We believe we can get a good toehold there. No agent would be sufficient for that." (Case 10, Transcript, p. 40)

In the interviews, it became clear that the situation in the sector and current dynamics strongly influence decision-making behaviour for a switch. Managers from the more globally-oriented automobile supply industry (Case 12) or the strongly internationalised food industry (Case 15) seem to have little chance to influence their own internationalisation process according to their own wishes. If a customer builds a new factory in Japan or new outlets in Poland then, sooner or later, the company is going to have to follow with a subsidiary or sales person. Otherwise, the customer will be lost, the competition will grow or no new orders will be placed. Such companies only require a limited number of instruments for their foreign strategies. The following statements support these assumptions:

> "PLUS9 our biggest customer sets the pace, either we keep up or we're out..." – (Case 13, Transcript, p. 69)

> "We supply a producer of wind power stations in Europe. It goes without saying that we want to continue to supply him at his new production location in China. For purely logistical reasons, this requires our moving with him." – (Case 7, Field Notes, p. 2)

Factors influencing switching decision

---

[9] PLUS achieved a turnover of 9.6 billion euros in 2006 and was bought from Tengelmann by Edeka (Germany's largest supermarket chain) at the end of 2007, Welt-Online, 16. Nov., 2007.

The internal and external conditions for a company in a foreign market are constantly shifting and changing (all cases). One would think that a switch of foreign operation in response to these new conditions caused by changes in the external environment would be inevitable and undertaken relatively often. This is not the case, as the following statement shows:

> "When all of our importers in Poland started producing lamps and lights themselves, we knew we had to take some kind of action. We installed one of our own sales persons there, parallel to the importers we had. This sales person was primarily responsible for project business. Naturally we could have switched at an earlier point but I wanted to first see how things develop... Importers just are the more economic solution for us." (Case 5, Transcript, p.6)

Interview statements showed that companies often hesitate and take some time before they switch even when changed circumstances would make it advisable to do so – when internal or external variables render the initial strategy no longer optimal:

The following comment shows that further alignment of a company's foreign operation mode is often necessary but is not always undertaken because company-political reasons speak against it:

> "Up to recently we were not able to change our strategy in the U.S. We were always tied to policies that did not allow us an own subsidiary. There was nothing logical about our behaviour, we should have founded the subsidiary 10 years ago." (Case 10, Transcript, p. 47)

Switching influence by specific event

The decision to switch was often accelerated by some kind of acute circumstance or sudden occurrence. In one case, an interested cooperation partner just happened to contact the company right in a phase during which it happened to be intensively considering changing foreign distributors. The company took the occasion as a welcome opportunity to switch (faster than expected) to a sales subsidiary (Case 1). In another case (Case 12), there had already been latent dissatisfaction with the previous partner. When this importer breached his contract by starting with parallel imports "that was the straw that broke the camel's back and action had to be taken."

According to the interviewees, the "influence of serendipity" also played a significant role. It did not necessarily trigger the switch alone, but it decisively affected the decision in that an unexpected possibility suddenly arose, or a "happy coincidence" came along (Case 5, Case 7).

Non-switching behaviour

Only in a couple of cases was the decision to *not* switch modes discussed. In one case (Case 2a) there was (as a result of stagnating demand) no hope of achieving positive change through a mode switch. In another case, the company first wanted to "wait and see how things develop" before making further decisions (Case 2b). In the last case (Case 5), the proposed future mode did not correspond to the company's "usual strategy" for foreign market operations and was therefore rejected.

The low number of non-switchers in the sample group might be explained by the age of the companies and their long time in business. Interviewing born globals or companies with short business history would have presented more non-switching situations.

5.2.2.6 Summary of impetuses

On the whole, the interviewees in the sample group all confirmed the high degree of influence that changing conditions in the internal or external environment can have on the decision to switch modes. The general impression gained was that there is a certain rigidity with regard to mode switches. This reluctance to change, or, "status quo bias", seems strong with the result that the old method is adhered to even in the face of drastic changes in the environment – changes that might call for a switch from the perspective of the decision makers. Although the decision maker is aware that the current mode needs to be aligned, the switch isn't made or is postponed. Whether this has a directly negative or positive effect on the foreign business activity is an open question. It appears that the sample group for this analysis predominantly consisted of companies which are highly adverse to change. These are companies which hesitate (Cases 3, 5, 8, 11, 12, 13, 14). The decision-makers seem to believe that they can better control the development of foreign business activity by *not* taking advantage of arising opportunities. Whether it is a case of unjustified risk aversion ("threat bias") remains open.

The often-attempted strict division between influencing factors, motives and actual reasons is not supported by this analysis and the interview results. Influencing factors often gradually grew into solid reasons over time. Some relatively insignificant factors became significant factors in the subjective eyes of the individual decision-maker – elevating them to decision-making criteria. In the course of the decision-making process, some criteria are intensified leading to a prioritisation. On the basis of the interview results, it is therefore not possible to strictly divide between these categories. They overlap. In particular, it often cannot be ascertained as to which factors were of mere influencing character and which were actual reasons for the switch.

It is clear that only in a few cases is a switch carried out on the basis of a few criteria alone. There is normally a complex mix of the factors of "internal change", "environmental change", "performance" and "expectation" leading up to it.

5.2.3 Barriers to a switch

When a company begins to consider a mode switch, a number of barriers, blockades and other problems can arise in both the internal and external environment, and in all phases of the decision-making process. In addition to the common barriers frequently encountered in foreign business (cultural, legal, financial, political or language-related), some factors will be discussed here that were mentioned by the sample group as aspects bearing an influence on the decision-making process for the mode switch. The following table presents the barriers identified for the sample companies, categorised into "Capabilities", "Management capacity", "Mental barriers" and "Switching costs":

Table 5.9: Barriers to a switch

Categories	Details	Company No.
Capabilities	Country know-how	1, 2, 3
	Market studies and market information is lacking	2, 3, 10
	Difficult and complex nature of the switch	4
	Project management skills to coordinate and organise the switch	2, 3, 7, 9, 10
	Strategy evaluation, alternative evaluation	1
Management capacity	Lacking availability of the right personal	1, 2, 6, 7, 9, 10
Mental barriers	Resistance of internal organisation	3, 8
	Personal preference and attitudes (e.g. dominating logic)	3, 5, 11
	Possible failure and consequences thereof	3, 13
	Perception of cultural differences	1, 2, 6, 11
Switching costs	Compensation in the case of contract cancellations	3, 12
	Switching costs with current and new customers	4, 12, 15
	Costs of training, recruitment, etc.	5, 11
	Resources already invested in the area of sales of marketing (sunk costs)	6, 7, 8, 9, 10, 15

Capabilities

As anticipated, several companies interviewed admitted that they simply did not have the necessary capabilities, knowledge or experience to carry out a mode switch. Often the ability to evaluate possible strategies in the planning phase was lacking, or the know-how required for founding a subsidiary. One interview partner formulated it as follows:

"I don't even know who in our company – besides the two CEOs – would have the capabilities needed to found a subsidiary in a foreign market!?" (Company 12, Transcript, p. 55)

Management capacity

According to the interviewees opinion in general, there was not only a lack of capabilities necessary for the systematic planning of a mode switch, but also of management capacity. The following quote indicates this limiting factor for internationalisation:

"Our problem is management capacity. We are always short on the right people. Sometimes we block ourselves. That's why we concentrate on the really important steps; we don't want to neglect our actual business amidst all the globalisation efforts. The core question is: When there are several opportunities, which one should we take?" (Company 7, Field Notes, p.3)

Mental and psychological barriers

Anticipated resistance in the internal organisation, possible loss of reputation in the case of failure and perceived cultural differences all represent mental or psychological barriers for the interview partners. These may either individually or in their sum represent severely limiting barriers to a switch. To what degree such "mental blockades" can bear influence is illustrated by the following statement:

"Way back in 1993, we wanted to enter into a joint venture with a trader in Japan. This would have been sensational for our company but first, of course, all the problems were highlighted, loss of know-how, we can do it on our own, problems with profit distribution. And so it never came to a cooperation. Not in Japan, and not elsewhere." (Company 11, Transcript, p. 49)

How experiences from the past, attitudes and personal preferences can affect behaviour and become barriers is shown by the following comment:

"We learn from other countries and then apply that concept to our target market. Market entry is made by sending over one sales person first. If demand is good we then send a second sales person. Then a third. When four representatives have been sent over, we consider founding a subsidiary. This approach almost always works ... although, okay, when I think about Spain or Great Britain, where we also applied this principle ... we urgently need a solution for our problems there." (Company 4, Field Notes, p. 3)

A further example of how lack of knowledge and low levels of experience can become mental barriers to taking action is the following comment:

"We have a kind of mental block when it comes to some kinds of operation modes ... like entering a partnership or founding a subsidiary. I guess we just lack experience here. Despite the major changes in the market and our sector, which certainly call for some kind of action." (Company 11, Transcript, p. 55)

The following example shows the complexity of influencing mechanisms on opinion-building and the perception of possible barriers with regard to a switch of mode.

> "The classic export strategy is a shot-gun approach. My predecessor tried to push internationalisation this way, in almost all countries, lots of agents and importers, hardly any risk. As a result, lots of traffic, but little substance. Expectations were raised and brought into the planning, personnel were stocked and costs increased, but the turnover never came. There were huge problems. This kind of internationalisation is bad for our business." (Company 3, Field Notes, p. 5)

Switching costs

As a further and significant barrier-aspect, the interviewees mentioned additional costs for the switching process and the new mode. Switching costs were defined as compensation payment to importers or agents, listing fees, advertising costs, travel costs, contract costs, logistical costs and costs, and hiring of new personnel (Chapter 2.7.4.6). Already invested resources for advertising, fairs, brochures etc. presented a barrier in the form of "sunk costs". What significance the perception of switching costs have and how this perception can be influenced is illustrated in the following example regarding one company and its importer in Russia (Company 3):

> "The importer knows that we would actually prefer to have our own company there. That's why he portrays the Russian market as being so difficult. The actual conditions are exaggerated in the negative sense. Bribery and corruption run rampant, without political contacts you can forget it, the competition is growing, etc., etc. The importer won't let you look at his cards. He tries to steer things in such a way that no subsidiary is founded because it is all so 'difficult' and 'complicated'. At the same time, he has to make sure that he is good enough that we don't seek another importer in his place." (Company 3, Field Notes, p. 3)

The companies indicated what kind of barriers had to be overcome for a mode switch, but it was not made completely clear as to what degree these barriers influenced decision-making. The impression was gained, however, that decision-making anomalies resulting from deficits in the areas of capability, knowledge and motivation bear a significant influence on the perception of barriers. This would explain the desire to hold on to old modes.

5.2.4 Decision-making process of the mode switch

Most of the companies interviewed characterised their decision-making process as being gradual with slow opinion-building over a longer period of time (ranging from several months to one year) (Company 1,2, 4, 5, 6, 7, 8, 11, 12, 13, 14).

The scope of systematic planning seemed to have been influenced by the previous experience of the decision makers. Subjective perceptions of conditions in the environment and how they will affect business played a key role. The selected statements below give a good indication of attitudes and reasons regarding decisions on international business issues:

> "We've never developed strategies like in a complex corporation. It's more a process of perception and understanding, good benchmarking, criteria management and budget planning give a certain amount of transparency. This gives us good navigation in most cases. I guess I could have told you something smart and show-off just now, but that is really what we do, no mystery to it, just the tools of the business." (Company 8, Transcript, p. 26)

5.2.4.1 Strategic planning procedure

Firms carry out a minimum scope of business analyses which provide them with greater transparency of causal connections in foreign markets. In the final phase of decision-making, personal preferences and emotional aspects dominate:

> "In other markets, we carried out profitability- or break-even analyses and option assessments of alternatives – the whole programme. Usually, the results of customer satisfaction analyses are integrated too. But in the end it's always a slow opinion-building process often leading to an emotional decision. Therefore it can be the case that there is actually nothing solid backing the decision." (Company 4, Field Notes, p. 3)

For a few interview partners, the significance of strategic planning (e.g. efficiency analysis; customer satisfaction analysis) in the internationalisation process is a given:

> "...in the old days, an opinion-building process went over the period of about one year, unsystematic, no milestones. A profitability analysis followed in its basic forms. Today is mandatory for all large projects, although comparative

indicators may also be formed on the basis of analogies from other countries." (Company 1, Field Notes, p. 3)

When there is a high investment of resources, as in the case of a subsidiary or joint venture, intensive preparation accompanies the decision-making process. The greatest effort flows into the preparations of the CEO and the advisory board (Company 9, Transcript, p. 33). The vital due diligence assesses the situation in the location and represents an important aid for the decision-making process (Company 9, 10, 15). The founding of a subsidiary or possible holdings in the foreign country requires particular care (Company 6, 7, 9, 10, 14, 15). In cases where there was direct foreign investment, the interviewed companies used planning aids (market research, business plan, systematic analysis) and profitability analyses (Pathways 1, 4, 6, 7, 9, 10, 14, 15).

The following quote indicates that there are differences in the type and nature of planning intensity and resource commitment in the planning phase, depending on the significance of the country:

"We don't have any task forces of people working for us. We prefer pragmatic country planning, an expanded export structure, primarily with importers, in 70 countries. We concentrate on 2-3 core markets per year and think about how we want to proceed. Finally, the experience made by the key decision makers plays a major role. I don't know any company which works totally systematically. It's always trial and error." (Company 5, Transcript, p. 6)

5.2.4.2 Decision criteria

Management problems, insufficient marketing knowledge, problems with product launches and the challenges of separating are only some of the disadvantages decision makers weigh in their minds. The advantages of a switch (use of market knowledge, networks, proximity to the culture and better understanding of the situation) are often only implicitly weighted. A decision is made for the "lesser evil". The following statement illustrates the dilemma of the decision for "export with the help of middlemen":

"You're always in the passenger's seat. You don't know the people. You have to proceed carefully. It's the subtle undertones that cause a local customer to make a deal or not. We think we understand it, but we don't. The local partners receive guidelines, but we can't do more than that. A switch is not possible without arousing the resistance of partners and customers." (Company 6, Transcript, p. 12)

In a lot of cases on the other hand, the decision maker trusts a "perceived profitability" based on general business experience and sales development. This perception may lead to a decision for sub-optimal switches, such as joining up with an agent or a franchised dealer in the foreign country (Company 2, 3, 6, 11, 15).

"Naturally we know that the agency is not an optimal solution. Usually they don't do any marketing and they're just after the money. But only with a certain size is it useful to do everything yourself." (Company 6, Transcript p. 10).

5.2.4.3 Market entry vs. mode switch decisions

In accordance with the research problem, emphasis has so far been placed on decision-making behaviour during a switch of foreign operation mode. Though not an element of the study subject, there is the additional and interesting question of differences in behaviour between market entry and mode switching. The impression was gained that there is a higher level of knowledge/know-how at the point of the mode switch rather than at market entry. Correspondingly, a higher investment of resources than at entry was also required. Further, it was noted that the companies proceeded far more systematically with their mode switch than at market entry. The higher the planned investment of resources is, the more the aspects of market research, sector development, competition, legal parameters and customer potential were taken into consideration (Company 4, 6, 7, 9, 10, 14, 15).

5.2.4.4 Influence of the decision maker

For the companies interviewed, the question of who the decision maker should be depended largely on the overall significance of the switch, and the volume of resources to be invested in it. In the cases with direct and indirect export, it was the country manager or manager of the international department who normally made the decision (Company 5, 8, 12, 14, 15). This changed, however, when the decision involved the hiring or dismissal of employees in the foreign market. Here, the CEO or Managing director decided or at least significantly influenced the decision – the impulse for which usually came from the international department. This was also the case when a pro-forma organisation was created through cooperation with a trust company in order to, for example, fulfil labour-law related requirements of the foreign country. Such export service agencies often represent the mid-step between "export" to an own "subsidiary" (Company 4, 14). Decisions involving a high investment of resources (e.g. a subsidiary or a joint venture) were made by the CEO and the advisory board of the companies.

Interestingly, the interview results indicate that the composition of the advisory board can bear a decisive influence on perception and assessment of opportunities and risks for foreign operations. The interview results of two companies from the same sector (Company 10, 11) showed that the question of who is on the board can also affect the decision-making process and the overall speed of internationalisation. There was an internationally experienced advisory board and an advisory board comprised of German family members with only management experience in the domestic market. In the first case (Company 10), the company (which had just reorganised and changed ownership) underwent a systematic decision-making process for moving from an exclusive export orientation in the direction of "international business transfer" with a foreign subsidiary and production facilities in China. In the second case (Company 11), foreign business was primarily export-oriented and there was very little experience with the founding and management of international subsidiaries. The statements below illustrate the significance of the advisory board and the influence its composition can have on decision making:

The following comment reflects the opinion regarding the influence of financial investors as part of the advisory board:

> "In addition to the many other advantages (of financial investors) for securing the viability of SMEs, they are of extraordinary importance for the professionalisation of strategic decisions. Sure, they also want lots of money

and returns for this but they also strongly professionalise decisions. Facts are gathered, ... there is no sacred cow. In family businesses, local aspects often play a role: ...I want to stay in the village, my great-grandfather was born here, or the company's got to have a certain name,...even if no one can pronounce it, I've got to have it on my bronze plaque. And in corporations, there are totally different motivations that are not always rational. Financial investors have one concern, and one concern only – to make the company as large and rich as possible. Then everything else will fall into place. You're successful when you're professional, ... and lucky. That's an attitude I really appreciate." (Company 10, Transcript, p. 43)

The significance of the composition of the advisory board and the tied effects on certain operation modes is shown in this comment:

"Our advisory board is primarily comprised of family members, a tax consultant from the region and the previous CEO. We've created 150 new jobs in the last eight years and have doubled our turnover. I think it's safe to say we are a success. In regards to internationalisation though, we are lacking experience in the advisory board and the management capacity (for example, for the founding of a sales subsidiary. That's why we do not yet have one. Our foreign organisation consists to 50% of agents and 50% of importers." (Company 11, Transcript, p. 55, 56)

The following statement illustrates the involved actors in the advisory board with international decisions pertaining to capital transfer:

"If a decision needs to be made regarding foreign direct investment, then the project is discussed in the CEO's circle ... an ROI is prepared and discussed and decided on by the advisory board. Luckily our board is a successful formation: the two owner families, ...the previous CEO, a Stuttgart lawyer and the Fraunhofer Institute." (Company 15, Transcript, p. 87)

5.2.4.5 Matrix – Summary of decision making behaviour

The results of the interviews so far can be divided according to the main actors of the decision process and the degree of strategic planning as shown in Table 5.10.

Type 1: Companies in this group possess a great deal of experience in the foreign market. For market operation, they employ low-control export strategies. They know the special challenges of the search, selection and management of representatives and distributors for their foreign markets. They follow certain behavioural patterns which they have learned over the course of the years and employ these patterns again and again. In this manner, they reduce perceived uncertainty even in new, previously unknown markets. They trust in their partners and the existing network. The local partner serves as a key informant. There is no own active market research for opinion-building regarding the mode switch and there is generally a low-level of knowledge regarding international business opportunities.

Table 5.10: Matrix of four types of decision making behaviour in international mode switching

Decision maker	Unsystematic/unplanned	Systematic/planned
Export department, Export function, Sales team, Business development manager	1. Experienced in low control export (low level of resources), no clear strategy, but pattern of activities Process of perception and understanding, Informal evaluation/assessment of situation, rely on network and relationship Trail & Error Reactive	2. Experienced in low control export (low level of resources), implicit export strategy exists Implicit export targets, benchmarking, budget planning, cost-/benefit-analysis
	Company 8, 13	Company 2, 3, 5, (8), 12, 14
General management, Advisory board, CEO, MD	3. Low degree of international experience, low level of global mind-set of decision maker Difficulties with management capacity No clear export strategy budget planning cost-/benefit-analysis only for large projects	4. High degree of international experience (all levels of resources), high level of global mindset of decision maker Business plan, customer satisfaction analysis, building analogies from other countries, profitability analysis, market research, marketing strategy Proactive
	Company (3), 11	Company 1, 4, 6, 7, 9, 10, (14), 15

Type 2: Companies in this group plan more systematically than those in type 1. In the planning process and in matters related to the mode switch, they employ tools such as competition comparisons, aids for budget and efficiency analyses. These companies also possess extensive experience with representatives and distributors as sales agents. However, these companies rely more on systematically developed strategies and less on trial-and-error experiments.

Type 3: Decision makers for the internationalisation process are no longer the export department or export manager but the CEO or executive board. Internationalisation experience is limited. There is not yet a clear export strategy and a current lack of resources. The "global mindset" is limited but there is the intention to further extend foreign business. The decision-making behaviour is non-systematic. Business evaluation procedures are available.

Type 4: The companies possess a high level of international experience and extensive resources. The global mindset is strongly developed. The decision-making behaviour is proactively managed and driven forward. The mode switch is part of the internationalisation process. Business methods, such as the customer satisfaction analysis, market research, profitability analysis, marketing strategy and business planning are part of the daily work of decision makers in the executive board, advisory board and management.

5.2.5 Objectives of a switch

For the main objectives of a mode switch, the following three categories were identified for the sample companies interviewed: "Expansion", "Consolidation", and "Reduction". These are presented in Table 5.11.

Table 5.11: Objectives of a switch

Switching objectives	Company-No.
Expansion (increase resources)	1, 2a, 3, 4, 5, 6, 7, 8, 9, 10, 11, 12, 13, 14, 15
Consolidation (no change in resources)	2b, 8, 11, 12, 13
Reduction (reduce resources)	12, 13

In most of the sample cases, the objective of the mode switch was international expansion. To achieve this, the interviewed companies increased their resources and activity by, for example, sending additional salespersonnel into the foreign market (Company 4), founding a subsidiary as a supplement to an importer (Company 6), or by combining several different modes (Company 5, 6, 7, 10, 12, 14 and 15). For

184

realisation of the objective, either single configurations or combinations of modes were employed.

Companies with the objective of "consolidation" kept to the old foreign operation mode. In these cases, no mode switch was undertaken (Company 2b). The current mode was merely optimised by, for example, replacing the management of an already existing subsidiary (Company 13) or by replacing one importer by another (Company 12, 13). A consolidation of the current mode of foreign operation was strived for here, without drastic change in the level of resource investment.

The sample cases of "reduction" illustrated that companies can also intentionally withdraw from a foreign market and "de-invest". Here, subsidiaries were closed (Company 13) or commitment was reduced by installing a sales agent rather than an own employee (Company 12). These companies followed the necessity of investing limited resources as efficiently as possible. A "reduction" suggests, in this context, also a withdrawal of resources from one foreign market, in order to be more competitive on another market where the resources can generate greater profit.

The objective of the switch is normally formulated with reference to the individual foreign market in question. Which role other foreign markets play could not be detected by this research.

5.2.6 Switch direction

The analysis of characteristic action and behaviour patterns tied to the mode switches of the sample group revealed four predominant directions in which a switch is made (Chapter 2.7.4.8).

A within-mode switch ("intra-mode" switch) is a change of mode within the same level or configuration. Examples of this could be when an importer is replaced or supplemented by a new one (Case 4, 5, 12), or when the current sales organisation is optimised (Case 13).

With a between-mode direction ("inter-mode" switch), the current foreign operation mode is replaced by a new, different one. For example, an importer is replaced by a subsidiary (Case 1, 3, 6) or a direct export strategy is replaced by a joint venture (Case 9). A switch is made between modes, and a new level of intensity, a new configuration, is entered.

In a third case, the companies interviewed combined their strategies, making a switch from a single mode (mono-mode) in a foreign market to several, parallel forms (multi-mode). Some companies combined importers and a salesperson (Case 5), or importers and a subsidiary (Case 6). An interesting special case was a combination of a salesperson with export-service agents (Case 4, 16). In these pathways, the employment of the agent was temporary and served tax- and labour-law interests. It enabled the companies to use their own salespersonnel without founding a foreign subsidiary.

In the fourth "direction", no mode switch was made; the current configuration was maintained (Case 2b).

The results of switch direction are shown in Table 5.12.

Table 5.12: Switch directions

Switch direction	Switch actions	Type/Cases
Within-mode switch/intra-mode change	Agent to agent, importer to importer, salesperson to salesperson, optimising organisation	4, 5, 8, 12, 13
	JV marketing & sales to JV production	7
Between-mode switch/inter-mode change	Piggy back[10] to importer/agent	2a, 3, 8
	Piggy back to salesperson	15
	Salesperson to agent	15
	Agent to importer	15
	Importer to own salesperson	5, 11, 14
	Importer to sales subsidiary	1, 3, 6
	Importer to affiliate for production and sales	10
	Direct export to JV sales office	9
	Own salesperson to sales subsidiary	4, 11, 16
	Sales subsidiary to JV production	9, 17
	Sales office to affiliate	10
	Sales office to JV marketing sales	7
	JV marketing sales to licence production	7
Mode combination	Importer to importer and own salesperson	5
	Importer to importer and sales subsidiary	6
	JV/licence to JV/licence and JV production	7
	Importer and salesperson to importer and sales subsidiary	11
	Affiliate to JV production and affiliate	17
	Salesperson and export service organisation to sales subsidiary	4, 16
No mode change	No switch	2b

5.2.7 Mode strategy and frequency of switching

Following the analysis of market entry and the behaviour preceding a change of foreign operation mode provided above, the actual action (or implementation) of a mode and the switch of mode will now be discussed. A total of seventeen foreign

---

[10] In piggybacking the rather inexperienced company ("the rider") deals with a larger company ("the carrier") which already operates in the potential target market and is willing to act on behalf of the rider that wishes to export in this country (Hollensen, p. 316, 2007).

markets were selected by the interview partners for their companies. The development of the foreign operation is presented based on the type of mode, the number of switches, and their sequence. Starting with market entry the developmental pathways based on the four strategic mode categories of direct/indirect export, licensing, joint venture, subsidiaries & affiliates are shown in Table 5.13.

Table 5.13: Mode strategy categories and switch frequency

Switch action		Export	Licensing	Joint Venture	Subsidiaries & Affiliates
Market entry mode	Case-No.	1, 2a, 2b, 3, 4, 5, 6, 8, 9, 10, 11, 12, 13, 14, 15, 16, 17	/	/	7
	Σ	17	/	/	1
1. Mode switch	Case-No.	2a, 2b, 3, 4, 5, 8, 11, 12, 13, 14, 15, 16	/	7, 9	1, 6, 10, 17
	Σ	12	/	2	4
2. Mode switch	Case-No.	(3), 4, 5, 8, 12, 14, 15, 16 (16)	7	/	3, 9, 11, 13, 17
	Σ	9	1	/	5
3. Mode switch	Case-No.	4, 5, 12, 15, 16	/	7	13
	Σ	5	/	1	1
4. Mode switch	Case-No.	/	/	/	4
	Σ	/	/	/	1
Current mode	Case-No.	2a, 2b, 5, 5, 6, 8, 11, 12, 12, 14, 15	7	7	1, 3, 4, 6, 9, 10, 11, 13, 16, 17, 17
	Σ	11	1	1	11

From the table it is suggested that the strategic mode selected at market entry is normally of a transitory nature and, sooner or later, is switched. For all countries observed, there was at least one strategic switch after market entry. In fifteen cases, there were two switches; in seven cases, there were three; and, in one case, the mode was switched four times. A total of forty-one mode switches were documented for the sample companies. It can be emphasized that the foreign operation modes of direct and indirect export were represented in the sample by over 80%. Market entry

188

via the strategy of "export" was characteristic for most companies interviewed. With one exception (Case 7), all of them chose direct- or indirect export for market entry. Other modes, such as franchising, holdings or the takeover of existing companies did not play a role for this sample group.

This changes, however, when it comes to the first mode switch. In six cases, the market-entry strategy of export was replaced or supplemented by a joint venture (case 7, 9) or a subsidiary/affiliate (Case 1, 6, 10, 17). This behaviour continued into the second and even third mode switch. The sample companies seemed to prefer gradual changes of mode. Over time, the importance of subsidiaries and affiliates has increased to the extent that, currently, they are just as important as the strategy of export for foreign operation. Companies equally favour changes within the export strategy and the founding of subsidiaries and affiliates – possibly also in combination with other strategies. With regard to frequency, the options of licensing and joint venture played only a subordinate role. These configurations were, however, employed in China as a particularly dynamic market (Case 7, 9).

A more detailed display of the individual switch actions within the main configuration categories of Export, Licensing, Joint Venture and Subsidiaries and the specific pathway after market entry is presented in Table 5.14.

Table 5.14: Individual mode strategy and switch frequency

Switch action		Indirect Export	Agents (Direct Export)	Importer (Direct Export)	Direct Export (Without Intermediary)	Export Service Consultant	Salesperson (Direct Export)	Licensing	Joint Venture	Subsidiary	Affiliate	Total number
Start (Market Entry)	Case - No.	2a, 3, 8, 15	13	1, 2b, 5, 6, 10, 11, 12, 14, 17	16, 9	-	4	-	-	7	-	18*
	Σ	4	1	9	2	0	1	0	0	1	-	
1. Mode switch	Case - No.	-	8	2a, 3, 5, 12, 13, 14	16	(4)	4, 11, 15	-	7, 9	1, 6	10, 17	18
	Σ	0	1	6	1	1	3	0	2	2	2	
2. Mode switch	Case - No.		8, 15	5, 12		(16)	(3), 4, 14, 16	7		3, 11, 13	9, 17	15
	Σ	0	2	2	-	1	4	1	0	3	2	
3. Mode switch	Case - No.	-	-	15	-	-	4, 5, 12, 16	-	7	13	-	7
	Σ	0	0	1	0	0	4	0	1	1	0	
4. Mode switch	Case - No.	-	-	-	-	-	-	-	-	4	-	1
	Σ	0	0	0	0	0	-	0	0	1	0	
Current Situation	Case - No.	-	8	2a, 2b, 5, 6, 11, 12, 15	-	-	5, 12, 14	7	7	1, 3, 4, 6, 11, 13, 16, 17	9, 10, 17	
	Σ	0	1	7	0	0	3	1	1	8	3	
Future switch planned	Case - No.	-	-	-	-	2b	12	-	8	13, 15	-	1
	Σ	0	0	0	0	1	1	0	1	1	0	

190

As mentioned above, all the sample companies – with the exception of one company – selected the strategy of "export" as the mode for market entry. For this sample group, it is clearly the "importer" which enjoys particular interest as a sales intermediary. This also does not change with the first mode switch, which continues to revolve around the importer (in six out of eighteen cases). With the second switch, sending salespersonnel and founding a subsidiary played the major role. If a third switch was undertaken, this involved own personnel and an optimisation of the sales organisation. Unlike at the point of market entry for these companies, foreign operation mode today is generally characterised by importers and own subsidiaries. Foreign operation via own employees, possibly in the form of a branch with production- and sales function, is also increasingly of interest. Other foreign operation modes (e.g. licensing, joint venture) were considered by several of the sample companies, but actually implemented by only a few.

If one observes how the sample-group companies carry out their foreign operations today, it becomes apparent that with some evolutionary cases (5, 6, 7, 11, 17), several modes are employed simultaneously. In contrast to the point of market entry with only one mode, combinations of modes have become common over the course of the companies' process of penetrating a country. For this sample group, the combination of importer and subsidiary (Case 5, 6, 11) was of greatest practical relevance.

From the analysis of the modes employed for foreign operation, a characteristic developmental or evolutionary process can be derived for each individual company which will be analysed in the next section.

5.2.8 Switch pathway per country

In the following, the behaviour (switch actions) of the sample group will be presented in the evolutionary form of their development (pathways). These pathways of development – these strategic configurations – represent manifestations of internationalisation resulting from specific contextual factors. The sequence of the pathway marks the modes employed thus far and reflects the dynamic evolution. It leaves a chain of configurations, a strategic fingerprint that defines the company's activity in the foreign market (Chapter 2.3). The analysis of the evolutionary pathway takes into consideration the various modes, which were employed along the way, their position, their sequence and their development over time (Chapter 2.5).

In Table 5.1, the individual configurations of foreign operation modes for each pathway are presented. The numbers of the evolutionary pathways refer to the sample-group case numbers. Altogether, seventeen different pathways were identified, each pathway consisting of mode types and their changes over a specific period of time. For orientation and better understanding, the company (company no.) and the process in a country (case no.) are also stated in Table 5.15. The corresponding information on the company and the selected mode strategies are presented in sections 5.1 and 0 and summarised in Table 5.2 and Table 5.3.

To identify the individual patterns of action, classic export trade was divided into indirect export (e.g. piggy back, exporter) and direct export (without intermediaries and with agents, importers, export service consultants or a salesperson). Further modes included licensing, joint ventures, subsidiaries and affiliates. The subsidiaries were focused on sales and the affiliates on production and sales functions. A differentiation based on the degree of involvement in cooperations and joint ventures was not possible due to a lack of transparency and the interviewees' requests for confidentiality.

The developments after market entry are presented in Table 5.15 as a chain of modes. With Pathway 6, for example, the company entered the Chinese market with an importer and then founded a subsidiary. Today, the company uses both modes parallel for the market. The company has been active in China for a total of eleven years.

Table 5.15: Mode-switching pathway per country

Pathways	Case-No.	Company No.	Market entry strategy and modes used over time	Country
Pathway 1	1	1	importer (joint cooperation of five German companies) – sales subsidiary	USA
Pathway 2 (a, b)	2	2	1. Piggy back – importer 2. Importer – no switch (export service organisation planned)	USA
Pathway 3	3	3	piggy pack – importer – subsidiary (supported by export service organisation)	Russia
Pathway 4	4	4	salesperson – second salesperson – third salesperson – fourth salesperson – subsidiary (supported by export service organisation)	Czech Republic
Pathway 5	5	5	importer – second importer – third importer –salesperson (parallel)	Poland
Pathway 6	6	6	importer – subsidiary (Parallel)	China
Pathway 7	7	7	sales office – JV marketing sales – licence production – JV production	China
Pathway 8	8	8	exporting (indirect) – agent – new agent -	Poland
Pathway 9	9	9	export area manager – JV sales office – affiliate	China
Pathway 10	10	10	Importer – affiliate	China
Pathway 11	11	10	importer – own salesperson – sales subsidiary	USA
Pathway 12	12	11	importer – new importer – second importer – export area sales manager	Japan
Pathway 13	13	12	agent – importer – sales subsidiary – sales subsidiary (new MD) – (sales subsidiary, closing warehouse)	Poland
Pathway 14	14	12	importer – new importer – salesperson	Switzerland
Pathway 15	15	13	piggy back – salesperson – project consultant/agent – importer	Poland
Pathway 16	16	14	direct export – export manager – salesperson – subsidiary	France
Pathway 17	17	15	importer – affiliate – subsidiary – affiliate plus JV production	China

5.2.9 Time-related issues on mode-switching decision making

The switch of a foreign operation mode raises the question of the influence on "timing". In this context, the sample interview partners were asked to relay some of their thoughts on the significance of "time" and "timing" in the internationalisation process and for the mode switch.

Table 5.16 contains selected statements made in the interviews relating to the categories of "duration of decision-making", "optimal decision time" and "pace of implementation".

Table 5.16: Time-related categories of mode switching

Category	Statement	Company No.
Duration of decision-making	• "It took us two years before we knew what we should do in Japan and how we should do it. Then it took two years more until we had persuaded our partner."	6
	• "When structures break down (e.g. through insolvency) we have to act quickly and create bridges to the customers."	14
	• "We take our time with human resource matters. We take whatever time it takes until we have found the right person for our business abroad."	14
	• "Competition speeds up timing. If we're too slow, then our decision may no longer be the right one by the time it is made."	7, 14
Optimal timing for a decision or an action	• "For me, good timing means waiting for an opportune moment."	8, 11
	• "The importance of timing depends on the frame conditions. If they don't change (is seldom), then timing is irrelevant."	14
	• "Timing is critical for acquisitions and joint ventures, less so with greenfield investment."	9
	• "In our business, season plays the biggest role. A switch of foreign operation can only take place between October and December. Any other time would bring losses."	12
	• "When offer meets demand, it's time to take action. If, in the case of foreign investments, you then have to wait for the advisory board, this can be deadly. This situation must be avoided."	3
Pace of implementation	• "When a decision has been made, implementation should theoretically follow quickly. But this is not always possible in reality."	4, 6
	• "Unlike in Europe, [in China] speed goes before thoroughness. We wanted to produce the first wire in December."	10

5.2.9.1 Duration of mode-switching decision

It remains unclear as to whether a longer decision timeframe with thorough preparation has a more positive effect on success. It equally cannot be claimed with certainty that quick decisions to switch (made necessary, for example, by some sudden, high priority) set successful firms apart from the less successful ones. Both fast decisions taken in of a few days or weeks (Company 9, 10, 15) and slower decisions extending across several years and involving in-depth data collection and a slow opinion-building process (Company 6, 9, 10, 11) were mentioned in the interviews.

Of note is that the length of time taken for the decision was influenced by the current internationalisation phase of the company and its current management. With Company 10, for example, there had long been a need to switch modes for the U.S. market. The process of information gathering and opinion-building had already taken five years and the country managers agreed that it was time for a switch. Due to the management of the group to which the company belonged, however, the founding of a subsidiary was not possible. This changed when there was a change of owners. After a phase of cost reduction and consolidation, the company was newly aligned for international expansion. There was a brief status-quo analysis and within a matter of weeks, the decision to found a subsidiary in the U.S. was made (Company 10, Transcript, p. 47).

The owner of a family company with a long tradition in foreign business (export share 60%) stated the following opinion on human-resource related decisions:

> "Any decisions tied to human resources must be made very carefully ... for finding the right person, time cannot be an issue ... the farther away the market is, the more important the partner becomes. We give ourselves sufficient time for this." (Company 14, Transcript p. 81)

5.2.9.2 Ideal time for switching

All companies interviewed were aware of the importance of the "opportune moment" for the decision to switch modes and the implementation of this decision.

"We already knew years ago what we need to do in China in order to have success. We just didn't know when, how, and with whom ... then the new management came and now we're pursuing a growth programme with full power." (Company 10, Transcript p. 44)

There was, however, no consensus regarding the degree to which time is important. This varied depending upon the objectives of the switch and the internal/external conditions of influence. In one case, a direct competitor suddenly and unexpectedly went bankrupt (Company 14), becoming available for acquisition. In another case, the sudden death of a salesperson prompted the change and the need to make a decision within a limited time frame (Company 8). In both of these cases, the significance of the opportune moment was extremely high – the new situation caused by changes in the external environment of the companies presented their decision-makers with new opportunities and options for the development of the foreign business. Companies which assessed the significance of the opportune moment as being relatively low were mostly of the opinion that their behaviour was little influenced by time-factors and that, with previous mode switches, there had been no imminent pressure to act or make a decision (Company 1, 11), as the following comment shows:

"Even if everything takes a bit longer in Japan and we just have to have more patience – I think after over 80 enquiries now we should be finally beginning the first pilot project." (Company 11, Transcript p. 52)

When the selected foreign market is observed, the impression is further conveyed that the significance of the opportune moment is tied to the current dynamics in that market (Company 3, 6, 7, 9, 10, 13, 15). If dynamics are high in the market, then it is more important for decision-makers to wait for an opportune moment, rather than in a market with low dynamics. The following statement for the Polish retail market underlines this:

"The dynamics in the Polish market are so high at the moment that we can barely keep up with deliveries. That wasn't always the case; the intensive tying of Kaufland and Plus was profitable for us. We're profiting now from the positive development of our customers in Poland and will be hiring our first employees there soon." (Company 13, Transcript p. 71)

5.2.9.3 Pace of implementation

The interview partners mostly agreed that the duration of implementation should be kept as short as possible. They also emphasised, however, that while the speed of implementation is important and a quick speed desirable, this is simply not always possible. Key actors in the implementation process do not always have control over the speed.

The following comment reflects the influence of resources as a limiting factor:

> "We have problems with our internal capacity; we can't be everywhere all at once." (Company 1; Field Notes p. 4)

The following statement is a positive example for optimal resources and the influence for timing aspects:

> For implementation, we were supported by external people [China-consultant, lawyer from China, foreign chamber of commerce] with the result that we were able to begin production and sales as planned, despite limited capacities." (Company 10, Transcript p. 42)

Reactions to the proposed mode switch in the internal or external environment can reduce or increase the length of time needed for implementation. The following statement comments on the spectrum of problems when modes are switched and its effect on implementation speed:

> "We can't always put ourselves in the shoes of the customer. When a change is announced it often comes to a conflict, which affects the speed of implementation. A logical consequence. Nevertheless, the customer has to be protected when there is confrontation. We achieve this by being strongly present in the country and by involving everyone in the change process." (Company 6, 7; Field Notes p. 4)

On the whole, the interview partners agreed that timing is a major success factor on the pathway of international development. Some claimed that as long as decision-makers "hit" the right timing, the decision will find approval (Company 5, 9, 10). Being too late, or too early, can negatively affect further steps of the internationalisation process (Company 9, 10).

5.2.9.4 Evolutionary pathways and switching duration

On closer study of the evolutionary development pathways of the sample companies, the influence of timing-issues on mode switching becomes apparent. In the following tables (Table 5.17 to Table 5.21) an overview of the respective duration between selected modes, or, for how long a mode was actually employed is provided.

The duration taken for a mode switch decreases with the length of time spent in the market (Table 5.17). The average length of time before making the first switch was 9.1 years. For the second switch, it was 4.9 years. Therefore it may be concluded for the sample group that the second switch took place faster than the first switch (or, the other way around, the first switch after market entry was made after a longer period of time than as with the second switch). For the third switch, the length of time then slightly increases again or remains the same as the second switch.

The interviewed companies switched faster when resource investment was to remain at the same level: resource perspective (a switch within the mode was faster than a switch between the modes) (Table 5.18, Table 5.19). This suggests that companies are more willing to switch modes when the new mode involves the same level of resource allocation as the previous one. In other words, large discrepancies in resource levels reduce the probability of a switch.

The exchange or replacement of personnel resources (Table 5.20) with the first switch was made on average after a relatively long period of time (10 years) with two importers (case 12); after six years (case 14), replacement was made after five years with a new agent (second switch) (case 8). After four years, there was a new managing director for a subsidiary (third switch) (case 13). Whether there were particularly rigid structures or whether the pathway (or other influences) played a role must remain unanswered here.

Less time was taken to switch in cases in which (human) resources were merely extended within an existing configuration rather than as with an exchange of (human) resources (Table 5.21).

Table 5.17 shows the duration in years for the specific mode swiches.

Table 5.17: Duration (years) between modes

Initial mode / Target mode	Duration until 1. Switch (years)	Duration until 2.Switch (years)	Duration until 3.Switch (years)	Duration until 4. Switch (years)
Direct export - Export area manager	20			
Direct Export - Salesperson		15		
Direct Export - Joint Venture Sales Subsidiary	unclear			
Piggy Back - Importer	1, 10			
Piggy Back - Salesperson	7			
Indirect Export - Agent	6			
Importer (old) - Importer (new)	10, 6			
Importer - Importer (additional)	3	1, 5		
Importer - Salesperson	20	3	10	
Importer - Subsidiary	15, 11	10, 3		
Importer - Affiliate	15, 6			
Agent (old) - Agent (new)		5		
Agent - Importer	3		2	
Salesperson - Agent		2		
Salesperson - Salesperson (additional)	2	2	2	
Salesperson - Subsidiary		5	10	3
Sales Subsidiary - Joint venture	11			
Subsidiary - Affiliate		2		
Subsidiary - Subsidiary			4	
Joint Venture - Licence Production		6		
Average Switch Time	146/16 = 9.1 years	59/12 = 4.9 years	28/5 = 5.6 years	3 years

199

Table 5.18 shows the duration in years for within-mode switches.

Table 5.18: Duration (years) between "within-mode" switches

Within-mode switches	Duration until 1. Switch (years)	Duration until 2. Switch (years)	Duration until 3. Switch (years)	Duration until 4. Switch (years)
Direct export - Export area manager	20			
Importer (old) - Importer (new)	10, 6			
Importer - Importer (additional)	3	1, 5		
Agent (old) - Agent (new)		5		
Agent - Importer	3		2	
Salesperson - Salesperson (additional)	2	2	2	
Subsidiary - Subsidiary			4	
Average Switch Time	44/6 = 7.33 years	13/4 = 3.2 years	8/3 = 2.6 years	

Table 5.19 shows the duration in years for between-mode switches.

Table 5.19: Duration (years) between "between-mode" switches

Between-mode switches	Duration until 1. Switch (years)	Duration until 2. Switch (years)	Duration until 3. Switch (years)	Duration until 4. Switch (years)
Direct Export - Salesperson		15		
Piggy Back - Importer	1, 10			
Piggy Back - Salesperson	7			
Indirect Export - Agent	6			
Importer -Salesperson	20	3	10	
Importer - Subsidiary	15, 11	10, 3		
Importer - Affiliate	15, 6			
Salesperson - Agent		2		
Salesperson - Subsidiary		5	10	3
Sales Subsidiary - Joint venture	11			
Subsidiary - Affiliate		2		
Joint Venture - Licence Production		6		
Average Switch Time	102/10 = 10.2 years	46/ = 5.7 years	20/2 = 10 years	3 years

200

Table 5.20 shows the duration in years for the replacement of ressoruces for between modes switches.

Table 5.20: Duration (years) between modes for replacement of resources

Replacement	Duration until 1. Switch (years)	Duration until 2. Switch (years)	Duration until 3. Switch (years)	Duration until 4. Switch (years)
Importer (old) – Importer (new)	10, 6			
Agent (old) – Agent (new)		5		
Subsidiary (old) – Subsidiary (new)			4	
Average Switch Time	16/2 = 8 years	5 years	4 years	

Table 5.21 shows the duration in years for between modes switches for additional ressoruces.

Table 5.21: Duration (years) between modes for additional resources

Additional	Duration until 1. Switch (years)	Duration until 2. Switch (years)	Duration until 3. Switch (years)	Duration until 4. Switch (years)
Importer – Importer (additional)	3	1, 5		
Salesperson – Salesperson (additional)	2	2	2	
Average Switch Time	5/2 = 2.5 years	8/3 = 2.66 years	2 years	

The aspect of timing was considered by all interviewees as carrying high significance for the internationalisation process. The right timing can positively affect a switch (because conditions are particularly advantageous at that moment), or negatively affect it (or make it utterly impossible) due to reactions in the internal or external environment.

What may be established from the analysis is that not only optimal switching timing is significant for the switch but also the different time related issues such as decision and implementation duration, time between the first, second and third switches, and the length of time for expansion investments (e.g. additional importers) in contrast to replacement investments (e.g. replacement of current importer with new one).

5.2.10 Reactions to a switch

The sample companies reported that after a decision to switch had been made, there were relatively strong reactions from partners in the foreign country (Company 10, 12, 15).

> "There is always resistance. It's the nature of group dynamics that there are automatically reactions and counter-reactions. That's why determination and solidity are so important." (Company 8, Transcript p. 28)

In particular, the switch from importer to subsidiary and to salesperson presented a delicate case for these "internationalisers". Actions had to be carefully thought through so as to not threaten the future business relationship. The following statement tells about a separation that did not go smoothly:

> "If I had known before what the separation would mean for the Swiss market, I would have tried to extend contracts with our customers before leaving the importer. I would also have made greater efforts to negotiate with the importer and try to reach a solution. At the end of the day, the fast break cost us a lot of money and we have gotten ourselves a new competitor with our importer with lots of specialised knowledge which is most likely going to cost us more than we have made up to now." (Company 12, Transcript p. 64)

In another case (Company 10) a more cooperative approach was chosen and intensively negotiated with the importer in the attempt to reduce his resentment over the new subsidiary:

> "It took over five years for us to finally make the decision to found our own subsidiary. Our importer was constantly in the defense. He had no interest in us founding a subsidiary in the U.S.. Some really hard threats were made about what would happen if we could found one. We were therefore more or less forced to think about how we could accommodate him." (Company 10, Transcript p. 47)

In a further case, the advantages of a parallel market operation had to be first presented in order to minimise feared reactions:

> "The previous partner had to first be convinced of the benefits of a parallel subsidiary. This took a long time." (Company 6, Transcript p. 13)

Reactions to the switch of mode can also take the form of maintaining certain behavioural habits, as shown in this comment:

> "After opening the branch, our customers in Italy continued to call Germany for over two years to ask their questions and receive advice." (Company 4, Field Notes p. 4)

Naturally, new competitive conditions can arise as a reaction to a separation from partners. The previous partner can become a hard competitor:

> "Right after we separated from our importer, he began working with our direct competitor. If I had known that was going to happen, I would have handled the situation differently." (Company 12, Transcript p. 64)

Such reactions of key stakeholders, be they from within the company or the external business environment, show what kind of challenges a mode switch can entail and how important professional management is in the transition phase. If the switch is going to take away a partner's means of living, then it is only natural that reactions will be strong. Professional management of this phase can help keep the "damage" to a minimum and reduce the intensity of negative reactions. The following statements show possible approaches taken by the companies interviewed.

> "Separation is a question of compensation, or 'investment'. The structures for the new mode should actually already be in place before the separation. Then you have to stick to them. Time heals all wounds." (Company 3, Field Notes p. 4)

> "Separations must be prepared for. This includes meetings with important customers and possibly also contract adjustments before the actual separation to limit possible losses to the partner." (Company 13, Transcript p. 68)

The following positive comments indicated that it is worth preparing and implementing a mode switch carefully:

> "The importer remained very friendly after the separation. The new management was very motivated and committed." (Company 1, Field Notes p. 4)

"The founding of our subsidiary in France was very positively accepted by our French business partners." (Company 14, Transcript p. 78)

Overall, the sample interviewees demonstrated a high level of knowledge and experience with regard to the question of negative reactions to a switch of foreign operation mode – in particularly regarding the switch from importer to sales person.

This chapter presented the information taken from the in-depth interviews regarding the behaviour of companies after market entry. In addition to the most important influencing factors for the mode switch, such as internal and external frame work conditions, expected value and company success, various strategic aspects, processes and pathways of the companies have been shown. A four-field matrix provides indications of the decision-making behaviour of decision makers in consideration of the scope of systematic planning. Time-critical results and reactions to a switch complete this section.

In sum, it may be concluded from the detailed results on mode switching presented thus far, that determining influencing factors for understanding the behaviour of managers, as well as internal and external influencing factors have been successfully identified. The original objective of creating better understanding through the preceding qualitative analysis can be considered achieved.

As discussed in Chapter 3, the findings from the qualitative approach will provide the basis for formulation of the statistical hypotheses to be evaluated in Chapter 7 and Chapter 8. As a next evaluation step, the following interpretation will more closely differentiate between specific behaviour patterns, revise the theoretical analysis framework thus far and more firmly establish the major research objectives by transforming the propositions into hypotheses.

Chapter 6 Interpretation of qualitative data analysis on mode switching behaviour

In the last chapter, the results of the exploratory interviews were given. In addition to the most important influencing factors, the characteristic behavioural and decision-making processes were documented and discussed. These results create the foundation for the following discussion, typologisation and systematisation of the identified characteristics tied to mode switching. First the decision process is developed and structured on the basis of the results in Chapter 5.2.. Then the various decision-making- and development possibilities are brought into a strategic context with consideration of the qualitative results and the theoretical status quo analysis (Chapter 2.7.4.8). From this, a strategic profile of the foreign mode switch is derived. The identified behaviour patterns are then typologised into seven groups of characteristic decision-making patterns and management styles. Finally, the assessed mode strategies and aspects from Chapter 5.2.7 and 5.2.8 are integrated in a conceptual organisation framework of reference. The resulting pathways are discussed. The chapter closes with the formulation of hypotheses which will be subject of the quantitative analysis in the following chapter.

6.1 Four decision phases of mode switching

Based on the results thus far, the decision-making behaviour can be divided into five developmental phases: 1. Market entry, 2. Impetus to switch, 3. Decision to switch, 4. Transition and 5. New mode.

Phase 1: In the first phase, the company selects a market-entry strategy and enters the foreign market. The selected market-entry strategy forms the institutional platform for future changes. Entry modes are predominantly low-resource strategies, such as indirect and direct export. As shown in Chapter 5.2.1, the market entry is usually planned independently of possible subsequent steps for penetrating the market. Uncertainty with regard to market conditions, loss aversion and risk aversion and, at the same time, expectation of and hope for a positive sales turnover development characterise the first decision phase. Experience made in other markets and the transferral of this experience through analogies reduces perceived information deficit and the uncertainty tied to it.

Phase 2: In the second phase, changed conditions in the internal or external environment – such as the market entry of a new competitor, new laws, new products, changes in customer requirements or low performance – create the impulse to switch (Chapter 5.2.2). Over time, the signals for opportunities and risks grow stronger and are more or less systematically followed and observed by the decision makers. Information is gathered for opinion building, then assessed and weighted until a decision is finally made (Chapter 5.2.2.5).

Phase 3: In the third phase, a decision is made as to whether a switch should be made or not, or whether the decision should be made at a later point in time (for example one wants to wait and see how things develop, or information is not fully available). The decision takes the "popular opinion" of formal and informal networks into consideration, corporate objectives, as well as the analysis of the current situation. Under consideration of the barriers to switch (Chapter 5.2.3), the knowledge level and problem solving capacities of the decision makers, an assessment of opportunities and risks is made. A systematic assessment of alternatives took place only rarely in the sample group (Chapter 5.2.4.5 and Table 5.10). For direct foreign investment such as Subsidiaries, however, this is increasingly becoming the rule. The beginning of the switch does not immediately follow the decision. Mostly, the decision maker uses the time after the decision to then decide "what should be switched", "how should we switch", and "when should we switch" and negotiate with key involved parties and coordinate interests.

Phase 4: The fourth phase comprises the start of the change process and implementation leading up to the new mode (Chapter 5.2.9.2 and 5.2.9.3). This phase is based on a comprehensive process of opinion building and decision making. The right timing of the switch is influenced by the duration of the decision-making behaviour, the assessment of the optimal timing for the switch and the speed of implementation (Chapter 5.2.9). The qualitative results also show that the reaction of the environment to the decision and the type of future mode can positively or negatively influence the duration and results of the transformation (Chapter 5.2.10).

Phase 5: The fifth phase comprises the successful completion of the transformation; the new mode of foreign operation is institutionalised. Ideally, the management determines timing, possible transition timeframes, resource capacity, target formulation and strategy. The current mode may be fully replaced or supplemented (Chapter 5.2.9.4). The decision-making process is concluded with the implementation and institutionalisation of the new foreign operation.

Figure 6.1 shows the different phases of decision making and the time-related mode switching issues.

This decision process visualised in Figure 6.1 is based on the assumption that the entire process must be followed from the beginning and that, beginning and end points (and the sub-processes between them) can be determined. In reality, however, the beginning and end points of decisions can not be determined with complete certainty. While implementation can be more clearly defined as to its start and its end, the phase of collecting ideas is much more difficult to frame. Within the implementation phase, it can come to an abrupt break of the relationships to potential sales or cooperation partners and, therefore, the entire project. This is fundamentally a result of the fact that the sub-processes of a mode switch are embedded in the context of the company development and are subject to a number of influences and interests.

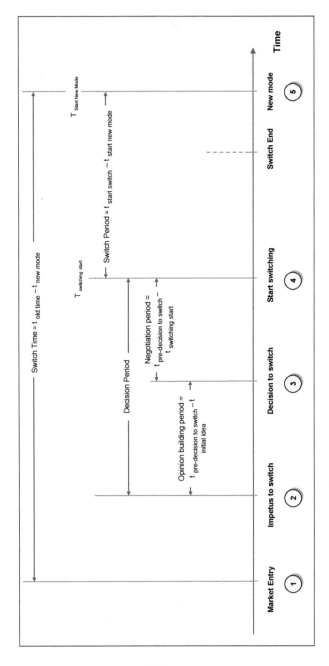

Figure 6.1: Decision process of the switch of foreign modes

6.2 Development of mode-switching profiles

The analysis and assessment of characteristic patterns of action and behaviour of the sample indicates that companies take on a mode switch within a framework of decisions. With consideration of the literature review (Chapter 2.7.4.8.1) the results thus far from Chapter 5.2 can be integrated in the following strategic decision framework: 1. Objectives, 2. Direction, 3. Order, 4. Intensity, 5. Speed and pace, 6. Duration of the decision making, 7. Duration of the transition (switch period) and 8. Sequence or the pathway of internationalisation. From these eight dimensions or strategy elements, the switch mode profile is formed as a static configuration of a certain status. Together, the individual statuses form the dynamic pathway of development of internationalisation in a country. The strategy elements are, in their individual manifestations, part of this decision framework and are generally characterised in Figure 6.2. In the following section, the different strategy elements and their manifestations will be discussed and interpreted:

Strategic objectives

The internationalisation of activities normally take the form of an expansion – in other words, a forward-moving extension of current activities in the foreign market. Under certain circumstances (stagnating or falling market/segment), the maintaining of current foreign operation (stagnation) or even the reduction (de-internationalisation) of commitment can be wise.

Direction

In the case of a within-mode switch, the current foreign operation is replaced or supplemented by additional strategies/individuals that are similar. The importer is replaced with a new importer, for example. With a between-mode switch, the foreign operation mode is replaced by a new strategy (for example, the importer is replaced by a sales subsidiary)). If there are several channel arrangements in a foreign market, then a combination of both kinds of switches is possible. This could mean, for example, that a subsidiary is founded but the importer maintained with only a change of contract that involves a reduction of tasks (mode combination).

209

Order

The order of strategic steps involved in a switch of foreign mode operation can take the form of a gradual increase of allocated resources and commitments, within a continuous process of change. By taking on a new status, be it from indirect export to importer or importer to own subsidiary – the company enters into an incremental process of learning and increases its knowledge and know-how.

Intensity

The intensity with which a mode switch is undertaken is tied to the allocation of resources (mostly financial resources or human resources) or to the level of commitment given to the achievement of the future form of foreign operation. Direct and indirect export modes have a low intensity while the establishment of a sales office or the founding of a subsidiary or a joint venture involves a high level of commitment.

Speed/pace of switch

The pace of the switch and the speed of transformation from the old mode to the new depend upon the individual problem solution and the internal and external influencing factors in the environment. Two forms of pacing have been discovered, one "time-based", with reorientations initiated at temporal milestones, the other "event-based", with actions initiated when the right event occurred.

Duration of decision making

The duration of decision making (meaning the time needed from the first concept to the conclusion of the decision regarding how and when a switch should occur) is also a part of the company´s switch profile. Companies take their time to discuss, negotiate or assess strategic options. Mentioned as an important additional condition for successful implementation was the duration of decision-making within a "favourable" timeframe.

Duration of the transition

The duration of implementation or the time length of the transition period from the old to the new mode indicates how long it takes a company to move from one state of relative balance to a new state of relative balance. For this duration, the search, selection and contractual agreement with a new sales partner is often the decisive element. The shorter the time period is, the sooner a firm can begin with the new strategy. In business practice, there is seldom total control over the duration or the time which needs to be invested in the transition.

Pathway (sequence)

In summary, the market-entry strategy and the previous mode of foreign operation characterise the past and current activity in the foreign market. All past decisions and occurrences can affect and also limit future business development. Mode switches represent pivotal turning points in the internationalisation process and are recorded as significant, encoded strategic elements in the form of sequences. These patterns form a chain of events in certain, biographical intervals. Examples are the following typical sequences from the explorative interviews:

- Market entry: piggy back procedure → 1. Switch: Importer → 2. Switch: Sales subsidiary
- Market entry: Salesperson→ 1. Switch: Stocking up on own personnel/export service agency → 2. Switch: Subsidiary
- Market entry: Importer → 1. Switch: Subsidiary
- Market entry: Subsidiary → 1. Switch: Joint venture→ 2. Switch: Production and sales subsidiary/office
- Market entry: Importer → 1. Switch: Salesperson

In the described strategic elements, a characteristic switch profile (Figure 6.2) for every single enterprise appears. The decision maker configures the overall strategy by selecting single strategic elements which form, in total, a switch profile.

Dimensions	Mode switching options		
Strategic options	Expansion	Consolidation	Reduction
Direction	No mode change	Within mode change	Between mode change	Mode change combination
Order	Sequential		Discontinuous
Intensity	Low	←————————→ High	
Speed/Pace	Low	←————————→ High	
Duration of decision making	Short	←————————→ Long	
Duration of transition	Short	←————————→ Long	
Pathway	Type of selected foreign management operations, including market entry mode		

Figure 6.2: Options of strategic mode switch profile

In consideration of the actual behaviour of a selected company (Case 8), the decision behaviour regarding the structuring of the mode can be interpreted as follows (Figure 6.3):

Example (case 8): After a total of eight years of successful market operation in Poland and partnership with an agent on a commission basis, the export management was surprised with the sudden death of this agent. Within a short period of time, the company had to solve the situation for the benefit of the customers (→ Switch objective: consolidation) and replace the previous partner with a new one (→ Switch direction: within-mode change). The previous activities in the foreign market were interrupted by this unexpected event. The export manager had to temporarily (→ Order: discontinuous) and intensively care for the Polish customers of the company in order to compensate for the lack of the local contact partner. Previous experience in Poland through the partnership with an exporter and an agent had been characterised by a gradual approach and low level of resources in order to limit possible risks (Pathway: exporter-agent). Extensive efforts had to be made for the location- and selection process of potential candidates. The back-office additionally increased its telephone service and held direct contact with the customers (Intensity: increased level of invested resources). In the phase of the search process, a new manager began with international experience. For this case the importance of the company's international expansion was immediately clear.

Luckily, an export employee of a trade customer could be won as future agent and relatively quickly persuaded to enter the partnership. After only a short induction phase, the new sales partner took up the successful market operation as agent (→ Duration of decision making: relatively short).

Source: Company 8, Transcript p. 18

Figure 6.3 shows the application of the switch profile for one specific company (Company 8, Case 8)

Dimensions	Mode switching options			
Strategic options	Expansion	Consolidation		Reduction
Direction	No mode change	Within mode change	Between mode change	Mode change combination
Order	Sequential			Discontinuous
Intensity	Low			High
Speed/Pace	Low			High
Duration of decision making	Short			Long
Duration of transition	Short			Long
Pathway	Exporter - Agent			

Figure 6.3: Strategic mode switch-profile for case 8

6.3 Pathway Patterns

6.3.1 Typologies of internationalisation behaviour and mode switching

Based on the selected mode strategy, and in consideration of various decisions and environmental conditions, specific behavioural patterns result for the companies surveyed. These typologies are presented and described on the basis of characteristic differentiating features derived from the previous analysis of the interview results. These comprise the selected mode of operation, the strategic force, target setting, decision-making behaviour, country emphasis, timing factors, and internal and external conditions. When these individual patterns are viewed closely, a characteristic style of internationalisation and management behaviour can be established. The individual management style will be described in the following for the seven typologies as apparent to the author after the interviews and analysis ("perceived management style"). The cases reference is stated in parentheses.

Table 6.1 shows the different typologies of internationalisation behaviour and management style in respect to the management of foreign operation.

After a summarising presentation of the characteristic behavioural patterns, the development pathway will also be illustrated with consideration to the contextual conditions over the course of time. The most important activities, events, decisions and influencing factors are shown in the individual context. The individual strategy employed is structured based on the scope of resources and over the course of time. For each typology, one case out of the sample was selected as an example.

Table 6.1: Typologies of internationalisation behaviour and management of foreign operation

Typology	1. Risk averse optimiser	2. Strategic optimiser	3. Cooperative strategist	4. Pragmatic opportunity seeker	5. Relationship and control driven	6. Systematic risk taker	7. Flexible risk taker
Cases	(2a), 8, 12, 15	5, 14	6, 11	1, (2b), 3, 13	4,16	9, 10	7, 17
Preferred switch pathway (Beginning/End)	Optimising indirect/direct export	Importer to Own Salespersons	Importer, Subsidiary (parallel)	Direct export to Sales Subsidiary	Own salesperson to Sales Subsidiary	Direct Export to Affiliate	JV to Affiliate/WOFE
Involved operation modes	Indirect Export, Importer/Agent	Importer, Salespersons	Importer, Subsidiary (parallel)	Importer, Agent, Sales Subsidiary	Own salespersons, Sales Subsidiary	Importer/Agent, Affiliate for production and sales	JV, Licence, Subsidiary, Affiliate
Strategic outlook	Export Orientation	Export Orientation	Export Orientation	Export Orientation	Export Orientation	International Business Transfer	International Business Transfer
Direction	Within mode switch	Between mode switch	Combination	Between mode switch	Between mode switch	Combination	Combination
Countries	USA, Poland, Japan	Poland, Switzerland	China, USA	USA, Russia, Poland	Czech Republic, France	China	China
Industry dynamics	Stable market	Stable market	Market growth	Market growth	Market growth	Very high market growth	Very high market growth
Internal conditions	Incremental improvement of market knowledge	High profitability	High potential expected	New product innovation	Incremental improvement of market knowledge	Change of ownership	International experience and export knowledge on high level
Motivation	Unexpected event, higher service level required, access to new sector needed	Unsatisfied with results, client followership/ customer proximity	Higher control of service (loss of know how), stronger participating on market growth	Unsatisfied results, fear to lose know-how; larger proximity to customer (client followership)	Promising market development, threshold reached, proximity to customer needed (client followership)	Participating on large demand, unhappy with results so far, "committed" management	New production capacity needed, pre-condition for public tender, "committed" management
Key decision maker	Director sales	CEO, Director Export	Advisory Board, CEO	CEO, Director Export	CEO, Director Export	Advisory Board, CEO	Advisory Board, CEO
Decision process	Gradual opinion building, pragmatic, ad-hoc decisions, event-based, mainly reactive; aversion to risk taking	Gradual opinion building, pragmatic, event-based, mainly reactive, but long-term oriented	Gradual opinion building, structured, negotiation, cooperative, time-based, mainly pro-active	Gradual opinion building, sometimes systematic, ad-hoc and opportunistic decisions, event-based, exploit new networks	Gradual opinion building, systematic process, event-based, pro-active	Highly systematic, time-based, build and acquired global network	Systematic, negotiation, time-based, build network
	Market oriented	Market oriented, efficiency oriented	Market oriented, Efficiency oriented	Market oriented	Market oriented, Efficiency oriented	Resources oriented	Market-, Efficiency-, Resources oriented
Objectives	Improvement of sales	Position and margin improvement	Sales and margin improvement, control of former importer, further use of know-how existing importer	Improvement of sales, gaining market share, better information about target market	Improvement of knowledge and know-how, better understanding of customer, improvement of service competence	Firm growth, competitive advantage, compensation of weak domestic market	Firm growth, competitive advantage, high control
Pace of evolution (after market entry)	low pace	low pace	medium pace	fast pace	medium pace	fast pace	fast pace
Decision time for master switch	Medium	Long	Medium/Long	Medium	Medium/Long	Medium	Medium
Implementation time	Short/Medium	Medium	Medium	Medium	Medium/Long	Short or Long	Medium

215

1. Risk-averse optimiser (Pathway (2a), 8, 12, 15)

The preferred action and behavioural patterns of this pathway focus on an optimisation of the current foreign management operation. Current partners or structures are supplemented by additional ones. There are no combinations of various modes. The switch is made with a low investment of resources, commitment and risk. There is a stable and/or saturated market with only low growth rates. The main interest of the decision makers is that foreign business is improved via a low-risk plan at the level of direct and indirect export and without sending their own employees to the foreign country on a regular basis. The decisions are mostly reactions to the influences of the external environment and are only made when a necessity has become apparent (right timing). For the future, the decision makers desire a development and implementation of reward and incentive models in order to increase the efficiency of partners in the foreign market.

Figure 6.4: Risk-averse optimiser (using the example of pathway 8) shows the behaviour of risk-averse optimisier (using the example of pathway 8).

2. Strategic optimiser (Pathway (5, 4), 14)

Companies which follow this pattern of action approach foreign operations via their own employees who will gather as much information as possible about the local market. They are less concerned with purely turnover-related considerations than with the overall profitability of the foreign engagement. The business environment is stable with slow growth. For market operation, there are no combinations of various modes but one specific configuration. Either dissatisfaction with the results achieved by the sales partner or higher customer proximity leads the decision makers to invest their own employees and a higher degree of resources into the foreign operation. This action is taken when a certain level of dissatisfaction or a turnover threshold is reached. The opinion building takes place less through analyses and more through observation, discussions and informational exchange with experts in the corporate environment. The decision is made on the basis of the current development but, contrary to the "risk-averse optimiser", with a longer planning horizon. The decision maker trusts in his/her experience and network contacts.

Figure 6.5 shows the behaviour of a strategic optimiser (using the example of pathway 14).

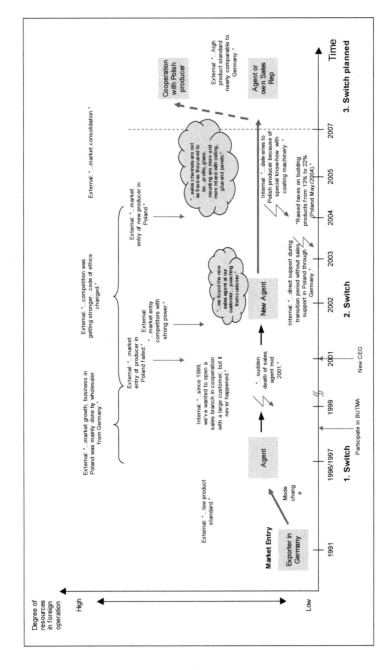

Figure 6.4: Risk-averse optimiser (using the example of pathway 8)

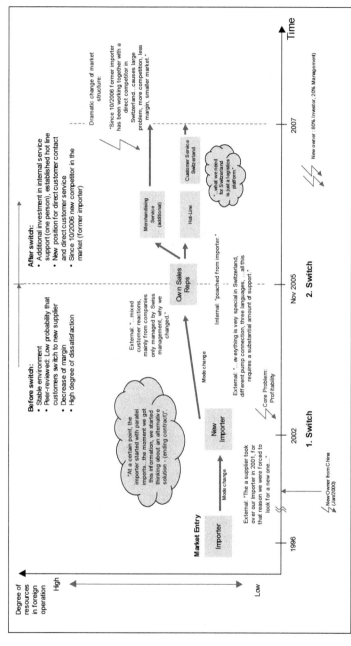

Figure 6.5: Strategic optimiser (using the example of pathway 14)

3. Cooperative strategist (Pathway 6, 11)

In this pathway the decision is systematically prepared with consideration of the previous experiences of the employees on site in the country. There is Experience exists with the founding and management of sales companies and subsidiaries. For these companies, control of foreign activities is important in additional to successful market development. No decisions, however, are made against local partners. The decision-making behaviour is characterised by a cooperative management of foreign operations and cooperative development and implementation of the strategy with old and new sales partners. The speed of the switch is relatively slow because the selection of the new mode takes place in agreement or "negotiation" with the previous sales partners and can demand a long period of time – even several years.

The old foreign operation is maintained. Parallel to this, decisions are decentralised and subsidiary or sales company are quickly founded for the growing foreign market. Two modes exist simultaneously and complement each other. The reasons for such a decision often lie in fears of negative reactions of the foreign sales partner and the decision maker's experience with switching from direct export (in this case, importer) to a sales company or subsidiary. Particularly if the previous sales agent possesses an extraordinary position in the market and thereby a high amount of power and influence, then "multi-modes" are employed. To avoid conflicts in the market operation in the long-term there is an intention to reduce the influence of the simultaneously employed sales agent or to align the sales strategy to the effect that no channel conflicts result. There are normally good prospects for the future segment development in the foreign market.

With regard to this strategy, Case 14's comment comes to mind:

> "If I had known how much trouble our importer would make, I'd have never separated from him but, instead, searched for a more cooperative solution."

Figure 6.6 shows the behaviour of a cooperative strategist (using the example of pathway 6).

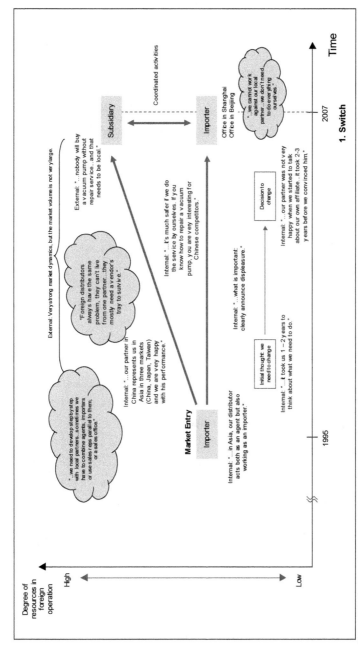

Figure 6.6: Cooperative strategist (using the example of pathway 6)

221

4. Pragmatic opportunity seeker (Pathway 1, (2b), 3, 13)

In this pathway the focus is placed on the benefit from market growth though a switch of the current strategy of direct export to an own sales subsidiary. The intention is (for example) to be closer to customers and to reinforce product innovation in the initial phase. A reason for the change can also lie in dissatisfaction with the previous partner. The decision is rarely made in a systematic fashion, but (unlike with the low resource investment – Type 1, Type 2), the CEO is actively involved in the process. There is pragmatism and the desire to take advantage of opportunities in the foreign market. The environment grows and offers exciting development options. Characteristic for this pattern are the relatively frequent intermediate steps and modifications, together with an incremental opinion-building process leading up to the actual decision to invest. The previous sales partner (sales agent or importer) has provided an accumulated knowledge of the market over the years which is then used as an experience basis for switching to a subsidiary.

Figure 6.7 shows the behaviour of an pragmatic opportunity seeker (using the example of pathway 1).

5. Relationship and control driven (Pathway 4, 16)

For companies using this pathway, the step-by-step development of relationships through proximity to customers (first through employees, later through a sales subsidiary) is the most important aspect. At the core, it is a matter of optimising relationship management with cooperation partners in the foreign market. The goal is to continuously improve market knowledge and know-how. After a certain threshold is achieved (a certain number of employees or a specific turnover amount), a switch is made to an own sales branch or subsidiary. As preparation for the decision, information is systematically gathered and assessed. Decisive for the switch is the opinion of the "locals". The local foreign network plays an important factor.

Figure 6.8 shows the behaviour with strong emphasis on relationship and control (using the example of pathway 4)

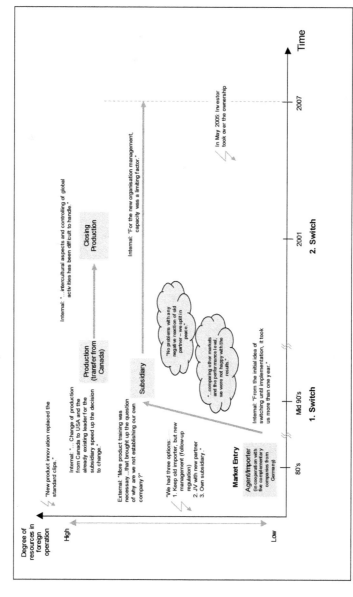

Figure 6.7: Pragmatic opportunity seeker (using the example of pathway 1)

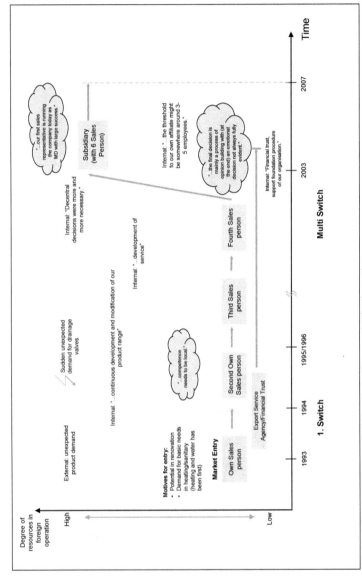

Figure 6.8: Relationship- and control driven (using the example of pathway 4)

224

6. Systematic risk taker (Pathway 9, 10)

In this pathway the action and behavioural pattern is characterised by a highly systematic preparation and implementation of decisions. The selected foreign market grows at an above-average rate. The company takes advantage of this growth via the transfer of single business units in order to benefit from high demand in the region. Different modes may be combined here. The CEO and advisory board make the decision. As an aid, the whole repertoire of professional planning is used. Allocation of resources and control over the foreign market play an important role. In many cases, this has the result that implementation is left up to the "big boss" (the CEO), who does, however, take the "locals'" opinions for this.

Figure 6.9 shows the behaviour of a systematic risk taker (using the example of pathway 10).

7. Flexible risk taker (Pathway 7, 17)

The focus of this pathway is the transfer of value-adding units – in particular, production – to the foreign country. Negotiations with key individuals and the implementation of the strategy are carried out according to a strongly systematic plan. Market growth is above average. Major motives are cost reduction and increase of efficiency. The CEO and advisory board make the decisions. Previous experience (with subsidiaries, joint ventures or affiliates) is used as a resource for intensifying foreign operations. The CEO and advisory board carefully prepare the decision but also leave it somewhat flexible so that it may be adapted (for example, to country regulations on JVs). Engagement (commitment, resource allocation) is extremely high.

Figure 6.10 shows the behaviour of a flexible risk taker (using the example of pathway 17).

In summary, the typologies discussed serve as characterisation of various behavioural patterns of firms after market entry. As a criterion, the preferred switch mode provides a clear convention for differentiating between the typologies. The results gathered from the interviews show that, in the process of internationalisation, firms are often confronted with shifting conditions and radical change (particularly with regard to foreign operation). The typologies can provide a first orientation aid for effective organisation of internationalisation. This possibility must now be explored and assessed through quantitative research and then be further developed.

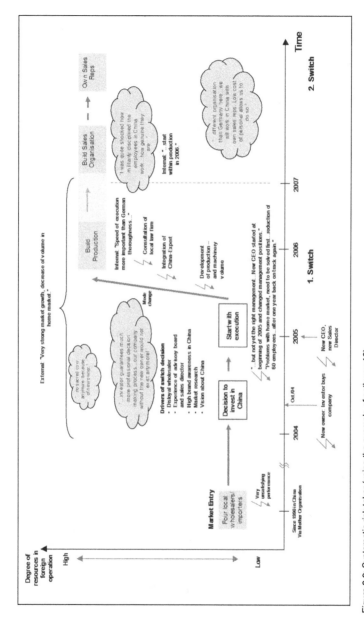

Figure 6.9: Systematic risk taker (using the example of pathway 10)

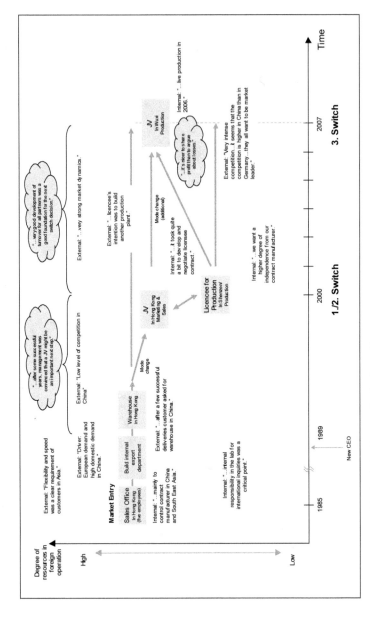

Figure 6.10: Flexible risk taker (using the example of pathway 17

228

6.3.2 Mode-switching pathways of sample companies

Now that the general decision-making behaviour and the individual characteristic management styles have been analysed, the dynamics of the development pathways will be observed and compared based on individual cases and the specific behaviour of the company in one country. The mode employed and the development of the mode strategy will also be observed. The aim is to identify the differences between the evolutionary pathways and the reasons for the formation of pathways.

The methodological basis is the isolation of the positions with regard to the selected form of market operation. In this, the individual cases from 1 to 17 are presented with their individual modes at the time of market entry and the further course leading up to the current mode strategy (Chapter 5.2.7 and 5.2.8). A division into Export, Contractual and Foreign Investment serves as an organisational framework. In Figure 6.11, the theoretical organisational framework with the individual sub-categories is presented. For the category of Export, the three categories of "indirect export", "direct export via agents and importers" and "direct export with and without company-own sales person" are used. The category of Contractual comprises franchising and licensing as well as partnerships (JV and strategic alliances). The category of Foreign Investment comprises, in particular, sales companies, branch offices and acquisitions.

In Figure 6.11, the position of the cases is presented starting from market entry, over interim steps, leading up to the current situation (Chapter 5.2.7 until 5.2.9).

The evolutionary pathways are illustrated in Figure 6.12 and were discussed in the subchapter 5.2.8.

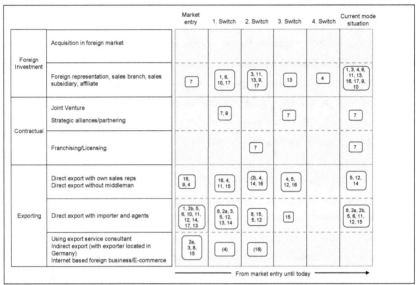

Figure 6.11: Position of selected mode strategy

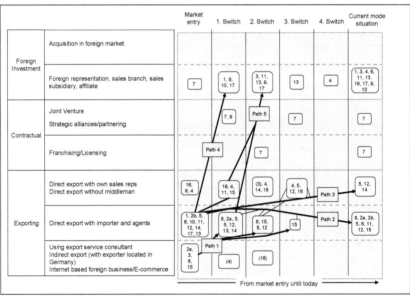

Figure 6.12: Pathway of mode switching

230

Path 1 represents companies which would like to participate in foreign business but which only possess a very low level of knowledge of the requirements. They use their network of German customers abroad and export, to a certain extent, "on the shoulders" of the German partners. Piggy Back as an indirect export strategy involves low risk and requires little investment. However, this low-risk position is only temporary. Changes in the internal and external environment are consistently used by the company to align its mode position and switch to importer or agent. Through the newly installed partner, the company has more direct contact to the foreign market. The temporary market-entry strategy of indirect export is replaced by direct export. Through the partners on site in the foreign market, the company now has direct contact. Know-how and knowledge-building regarding market demands and management of the foreign partner are developed step-by-step.

Path 2 represents companies which work with importers and agents and which concentrate on the management of this partnership. Market-entry is made with an agent or an importer. Over the further course of time, these partners are exchanged or expanded on depending on the intensity of the environmental dynamics. It can be derived from the interview results that this path is primarily selected by companies in special niche markets with limited potential for development and only few of their own resources.

Path 3 represents companies which first begin with an importer or an agent in a foreign market and then, after a period of partnership, either have these activities carried out by their own employees or add own employees as support to the previous partners. The reasons can lie either in better use of potential because there is a lack of satisfaction with the result of market operation or they can lie in a higher level of control over the market-operation activities. Implicitly, it is assumed that their own employees are better in market operations and information transfer than the previous (external) partners and thereby promise more success.

Path 4 represents companies which initially entered the foreign market with importers and agents and who, over the course of time, applied resources and commitment in the form of their own branch office or subsidiary. Similarly to Path 3, the reasons lie in better exploitation of potential, a higher degree of control and greater proximity to the market and customers. From the interviews, it became apparent that Path 4 was preferred for overcoming cultural distance (e.g. China, USA).

Path 5 represents companies which strive for their own branch office or subsidiary but which achieve this via various market-entry strategies and subsequent temporary modes. Path 5 represents companies which enter a country via agents or importers and then undertake changes and alignments within this mode, e.g. the partner is replaced or further partners are installed for expansion of sales territories. After this step foreign direct investments are undertaken. The interim steps reduce uncertainty regarding market conditions and increase the basis of knowledge.

From the perspective of the current mode strategy, Path 4 and Path 5 are employed for achieving branch offices and subsidiaries. This means that companies begin with importers/agents and test the market. When there is sufficient profit potential, the mode of branch office or subsidiary is chosen (Path 4). In Path 5, importers/agents are employed and then replaced or supplemented by their own employees and then a branch office or subsidiary is founded. In Path 2, importers are multiply changed, exchanged or supplemented. The management and continuous optimisation of these partners is characteristic for Path 2 and manifests itself in the high number of switches. Path 3 also relies on importers/agents who are then replaced or supplemented by own employees. Path 1 is a temporary entry path. Market entry is made with the lowest level of resources and risk. In particular, Path 2 and Path 5 can then be followed with a gradual increase of resources and risk.

Certain market-entry strategies which immediately result in capital transfer, e.g. the holding in a company or acquisition, are not considered in these pathways. Furthermore, no evolutionary pathways were identified with market entry relying on a franchising strategy or "electronic modes". Due to the low number of cases, it cannot be ascertained to what extent this reflects the reality of firms in Germany. What may be concluded, however, is that a gradual development of the operation mode is a characteristic process and what the managers interviewed thought was of high importance.

6.4 Summary of main findings of the qualitative mode switching analysis

1. The analysis of the various behavioural patterns in internationalisation and of the management style shows that mode switching is a strategic option, quite common and integrative, for the internationalisation of a company. Depending upon the perceived change dynamics and individual reasons, motives and interests companies adjust their behaviour, targets, strategies and organisational structure while considering a mode switch.

   The practical relevance renders the study subject an appropriate choice, particularly in light of the low level of knowledge regarding the subject (Chapter 2)

2. The analysis showed that companies take various lengths of time after market entry until a mode switch is made. It is therefore assumed that specific modes are more rigid and thereby more difficult to switch than other modes. This is an interesting finding and will be evaluated with a larger sample group. Of particular interest is the question of the factors influencing the probability of a switch.

3. The results show that specific management- and company characteristics are of high importance for success in the foreign country and that these characteristics influence the behaviour of the management of foreign operations and thereby the success of the operation. But which exact factors are responsible for success in the management of foreign operations is an open question and is to be analysed based on a larger sample group (Chapter 7 and Chapter 8).

4. The results show that companies do not apply a uniform mode strategy for managing foreign operations, but prefer various approaches. In this context, there is the question of the influence of certain mode strategies on the company's success and performance in the foreign country.

It is also an important finding that mode strategies influence success and this confirms the basic assumptions thus far (Chapter 3.2). In what kind of scope and in what manner they do so is to be evaluated using a larger sample group.

5. A mode switch is undertaken with the aim of increasing success in the foreign market. The key influencing factors identified are internationalisation experience and performance to date. To what extent they have influence needs to be analysed using a larger sample group.

6. The impression emerges that companies surveyed have a lot of experience in export business and are also very successful, but when it comes to a necessary intensification of internationalisation, they find themselves standing before a "decision hurdle" between a purely export-oriented strategy and a "direct investment" approach. The detailed definition of the barriers, how to overcome those hurdles and how to manage specific mode switches seems to be of particular interest. The literature provides comprehensive knowledge regarding market entry and entry barriers (Kutschker and Schmid 2006). But how specific modes of foreign operation can be successfully carried out, often remains open (Chapter 2.5).

7. The way in which companies achieve their current operation mode is not uniform. After market entry, companies pursue different evolutionary pathways. The importer and agent plays a particularly large role and is used in many cases for market entry as a starting point or an interim station on the way to the ideal mode. If one follows the theory of Vermeulen and Barkema (2002) that pathway dependency (Chapter 2.3.7) explains different performance levels, then its significance as a success factor in the internationalisation process becomes apparent. In this context, it becomes a question of identifying certain post-entry process patterns which present the most effective levels for a certain group of companies.

8. In the implementation phase of the decision to switch a foreign operation mode, the significance of the reactions from external actors becomes highly

apparent. Conscious management and negotiations with previous partners and consideration of their interests seems to represent a factor for successful mode switching (Chapter 2.7). The course of the negotiations and agreements regarding compensation and balancing of interests influences the duration of the implementation phase and the initial success of the new mode. In this context, the question arises as to how management can influence successful implementation of the new foreign mode.

9. For reducing uncertainty regarding opportunity and risk in foreign markets, knowledge of the market and its customers is of great importance. The establishment and expansion of international market research as an opposite pole to the knowledge of the export partner may not be a new demand, but gains new significance in the question of whether or not a switch should be undertaken.

10. The phenomenon of the mode combination is significant in the literature (Meissner and Gerber 1980, Petersen and Welch, p. 158, 2002, Welch et al. 2007). The results of this study, show that firms combine modes to specific profiles for their switches. Single strategies are used just as often as strategy combinations. This reduces the risk of the switch and potential problems tied to it.

11. The analysis of the qualitatively gathered data clarifies the significance of the actors and their individual attitudes toward internationalisation (Chapter 2.3.3). Beginning with the decision to internationalise, to enter a market or switch a mode, it is always a matter of the motivation, interests and targets of the actors from export, the international division, the management, the executive board or the advisory board. If several managers or hierarchy levels are concerned, target conflicts can influence the decision and its implementation. As a consequence, the demand for a transparent decision-making process remains, which is comprehensible, which communicates targets and motivation, and which documents the basis for the decision.

With regard to the applicability of the results, it may be established that the assumption that mode management and mode switching are strategic tools has been confirmed. This finding corresponds with the pre-existing opinion in the literature. The innovation of this research lies in terms of the comprehensive significance and influence for firms. An interesting finding is that modes seemingly vary as to how easy or difficult it is to switch them. Of high importance for the future management of foreign operations is the question of which factors influence the probability of a mode switch and which do not. This is to be established based on a larger sample group. The assumption that mode strategies affect a company's success has been confirmed. Now, it is to be determined to what extent and in what manner they do so, based on the sample group. This is formulated in section 6.5 as concrete research hypotheses for the quantitative study part.

6.5   Specific research hypothesis

Based on the propositions formulated in Chapter 3 and the results of the qualitative analysis of the exploratory interviews from Chapter 5 and Chapter 6 the assumptions and theories are made more concrete and shall be evaluated using a large-scale sample study and quantitative methods. Specific research hypotheses result from this which are presented in the following as hypothesis-pairs.

Basis Hypotheses:

H_{B01}: There is no relationship between mode switching behaviour and international success.

H_{B1}: There is a relationship between mode switching behaviour and international success.

Hypotheses for management of foreign operation and mode switching:

H_{01}: Satisfaction about market entry strategy is not correlated to the probability of a mode switch.

H_1: Satisfaction about market entry strategy is correlated to the probability of a mode switch.

H_{02}: There is no specific mode that is more successful than others.

H_2: Specific modes are more successful than others.

H_{03}: Systematic decision-making to switch modes has no influence on international success.

H_3: Systematic decision-making to switch modes has a positive influence on international success.

H_{04}: Firm-specific characteristics are not associated with international performance.

H_4: Firm-specific characteristics are associated with international performance.

H_{05}: Companies switching to single modes in one country are not more successful then those switching to combination of modes.

H_5: Companies switching to single modes in one country are more successful then those switching to combination of modes.

H_{06}: The length of the mode switching decision process has no influence on the outcome.

H_6: The longer the mode switching decision process takes, the more positive the outcome is.

H_{07}: The duration/time after market entry has no influence on the probability to switch.

H_7: The longer the duration/time after market entry the higher the probability to switch.

H_{08}: Specific management-styles pertaining to internationalisation are not related to the probability of mode switching.

H_8: Specific management-styles pertaining to internationalisation are related to the probability of mode switching.

H_{09}: There are no specific modes which influence the switching probability more than other modes.

H_9: There are specific modes which influence the switching probability more than other modes.

This chapter focused on the interpretation of results from the exploratory interviews for the study subject. The relevant decision-making phases from the initial idea up to implementation are presented, the strategic decision options for mode switching are shown, the observed behaviour is typologised and finally characteristic pathways after market entry are identified and discussed. The end of the chapter summarises the most important findings and transforms previous assumptions into concrete research hypotheses.

The presentation of the results is to allow deeper understanding of the influencing mechanisms, factors and context conditions of the management of foreign operations – thereby fulfilling the initial objectives. The concepts derived regarding decision-making behaviour, typologies and pathways are now to be evaluated regarding their significance, frequency and probability of occurrence on the basis of a large-scale study sample. The approach required for this is shown in Chapter 4. The questionnaire can be found in the Annex.

In the following chapters 7 and 8, the results thus far will be evaluated based on a large-scale sample group of German companies and their behaviour in the management of foreign operations. Chapter 7 presents the characterisation of the companies with regard to strategy, structure and performance. Various typologies of internationalisation behaviour are identified and evaluated. With a comprehensive look at the most important timing aspects and indications of effective performance characteristics, clarity and transparency of the composition and content is to be achieved. In Chapter 8 follows the evaluation and the addressing of the research hypotheses.

Chapter 7 Presentation of quantitative research data – Exploration of survey

In the previous two chapters, the results and interpretation of the explorative interviews on foreign-operation management are presented. With consideration of the qualitative findings, the hypotheses were derived (see Chapter: 6.5) as a basis for the theoretical explanatory model. To evaluate them, comprehensive information has been gathered with the use of a questionnaire pertaining to the behaviour of firms in the management of foreign operations. This information can now be presented, discussed and interpreted.

In this chapter, the results obtained from the quantitative survey on internationalisation behaviour are presented. First, the sample companies surveyed will be characterised based on their demographic aspects, such as position, international experience, turnover, number of employees and sector. The respondents' own assessments of their company's management style with regard to foreign activity and operation modes will be discussed. This will include strategy and risk perception, level of standardisation vs. adaptation, strategic force, switching order, speed/pace of switch, intensity of switch and direction of switch. The significance of these factors will be assessed. Analysis of the types of foreign operation mode allows an overview of their significance and creates the basis for the formation of five mode clusters, each with a basic strategic alignment and a characteristic portfolio of mode strategies. The relationship between switchers and non-switchers, and the probability of a switch within identified clusters or sector-structures will be discussed. In the next step, performance of the sample companies and their development of foreign operations will be presented based on sector and the mode cluster. A concluding summary of the most significant findings will then set the basis for further analysis of switching behaviour in Chapter 8.

7.1 Characteristics of company and business sector

The survey by mail elicited 198 responses from internationalised companies with their main corporate headquarters in Germany. The sample was chosen based on the criteria and methods selected in Chapter 4.8.2.

After analysis of the scope and pattern of missing data, the sample group comprises 192 usable questionnaires.

The companies surveyed belong to the manufacturing industry in Germany. With regard to turnover achieved in Germany, the production-oriented industry (26%) represents the most important sector after trade (32.3%) and before business-related services (11.7%) (Bundesministerium für Wirtschaft und Technologie, p. 19, 2007).

The positions held by the respondents are displayed in Figure 7.1.

Figure 7.1: Job classification of interview partners

In the survey, some 85% of respondents were positioned at director level and accordingly experienced in developing and setting up strategies. In light of the survey respondents' executive positions in their respective companies, it may be assumed that they possessed adequate access to all relevant information about the company's internationalisation behaviour. As the respondents have been working at their companies for a number of years and have also occupied their senior positions for a comparably long time, it is assumed that they present intensive knowledge of their companies' internationalisation activity in foreign markets. The high quality of the sample group is apparent from the extensive international experience of the respondents (Figure 7.1).

The industry sectors of the respondents companies were first individually assessed based on their major product and then categorised into six more or less homogenous sector groups based on the sector groups corresponding to the German industry statistics.

Table 7.1: Respondent characteristics by industry sector (mean)

Industry	N	Percent	Number of years in this position	Number of years in the company	Number of years in international business
Building, Furniture, Household	32	16.7%	7.1	9.3	15.1
Chemical Industry, Plastic Industry	24	12.5%	9.0	14.7	16.8
Metal, Mechanical engineering	51	26.6%	9.3	13.8	15.0
Electronics, Electrical engineering	40	20.8%	6.7	10.8	14.5
Automotive industry	14	7.3%	8.0	10.4	14.5
Others	31	16.1%	6.2	9.5	14.7
Total / Average			7.7	11.6	15.1
Standard Deviation			0,53	0,76	0,73
Minimum			0	0,2	0
Maximum			47	60	51

From Figure 7.1 and Figure 7.2 it is apparent that the respondents are very experienced with an average of 15 years in international business and 7.7 of these years in their current positions. In terms of employment with company the respondents in the different sectors are fairly consistent.

Table 7.1 and Table 7.2 show a summary of the companies to which the respondents belonged.

Table 7.2: Corporate characteristics by industry sector (mean)

Industry sector	N	Number of employees (average)	Turnover in 2006 (in Mio Euros)	Export Turnover in 2006 (in Mio. Euro)[11]	Export ratio (Export turnover/ Total Turnover)	Export turnover per employee (in Mio. Euro)
Building. Furniture, Household	31	413.61	91.3	30.6	0.35	0.06
Chemical Industry, Plastic Industry	23	233.87	73.8	35.2	0.39	0.08
Metal. mechanical engineering	50	223.98	64.3	37.96	0.54	0.14
Electronics. Electrical engineering	38	282.03	70.3	26.96	0.48	0.07
Automotive Industry	13	429.85	71.8	32.4	0.43	0.05
Others	31	248.6	80.7	33.4	0.33	0.69
Total / Average		287.7	74.25	33.0	0.44	0.86
Standard Deviation		24.82	8.6	4.4	0.43	0.01
Minimum		7	1.3	0.2	0.02	0
Maximum		2000	700	300	1.67	1,5

From the table above, one can observe that – in comparison to the general export level in Germany, which is approximately 40% – the export ratio in the sample is high. Equally noteworthy is that the companies are highly established with an average age of 68 years, 35 years of international experience and recent turnover of 96 million euros (Figure 7.2). This gives reassurance that the sample is indeed well-suited for investigating aspects of internationalisation.

---

[11] German foreign trade statistics include no company-specific data; the question as to how many medium-sized companies export or import cannot be answered, nor can it be clarified as to how many medium-sized companies participate in the dynamic development (BMWI, p. 19, 2007). For this reason, and for orientation, data is provided here from the BDI-"Mittelstandspanel" from spring of 2006. In this study, the export ratios of the German companies surveyed had an average of approximately 40% in 2007. Although the data strongly varies depending upon company and industrial sector, it can be established that foreign trade is an important pillar for German industry (Chamber of Commerce, Going International, p. 28, 2007).

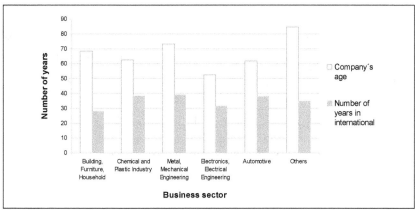

Figure 7.2: Number of years in international business and company's age per sector

The usefulness of the sample is reinforced by the fact that over 65% of the respondent companies have been operating simultaneously in more than eleven countries. This is illustrated in Figure 7.3.

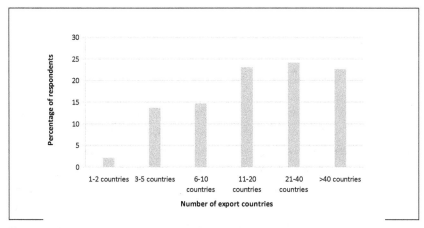

Figure 7.3: Number of export countries companies operating in

7.2 Types of modes employed

The popularity of different modes is displayed in percentages in Figure 7.4. The individual modes of foreign operation are presented based on the absolute frequency of use by the sample group.

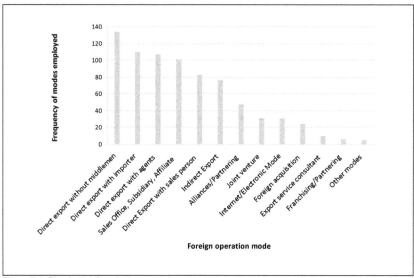

Figure 7.4: Popularity of modes

In general, all of the modes mentioned in the survey were actually employed with varying degrees of frequency. Most frequently employed is the use of direct export without a middleman (N=133), followed by export with intermediaries (importer N=109; agent N=107, total N= 216) and foreign subsidiaries/sales offices (N=101). Infrequently used are an export service consultant (10) and franchising or licensing strategies (N=6).

How modes are related to turnover and the satisfaction with these modes is displayed in Table 7.3.

Table 7.3: Turnover and satisfaction related to mode

Mode Strategy	Mode used in percent (mean)* N=181	Mode weighted by export turnover (mean)** N=165	Degree of satisfaction (mean) 1 very good - 5 bad	Degree of satisfaction (standard deviation)
Internet/Electronic mode	1.12	0.4	3.14	0.237
Indirect export	4.42	1.0	2.76	0.125
Direct export without middleman	20.37	3.8	2.09	0.073
Direct export with own salesperson	10.84	3.4	2.08	0.111
Export service consultant	0.29	0.2	3.56	0.338
Direct export with agents	13.28	2.9	2.62	0.097
Direct export with importer	22.75	8.5	2.30	0.97
Alliances/Partnering	3.95	1.3	2.30	0.128
Franchising/Partnering	0.33	0.3	2.67	0.211
Joint venture	1.61	1.6	2.52	0.195
Sales office, Subsidiary, Affiliate	18.72	11.6	1.96	0.098
Foreign acquisition	2.14	2.1	2.55	0.171
Other modes	0.18	0.4	2.00	1.0

Notes:
a) * Mode used in %: The mean represents the average percentage of the respective mode for all the companies. It does not take into consideration the turnover.
b) ** Mode share of total turnover in %: The mean represents the average of the percentage of the respective mode for each company, weighted with the respective turnover.

Companies use various forms of operation modes and combine them to a mode-portfolio. Depending upon the perspective, frequency (in percent) or weighted turnover, the modes take on varying levels of emphasis. With regard to the "frequency" of use, direct export dominates – with importers (22%) and without middlemen (20%). With regard to "turnover", subsidiaries/affiliates dominate strongly over the remaining modes. Interestingly, high turnover is coupled with a high degree of satisfaction, followed by export with own sales representatives and direct export without middlemen. The most common form of direct export, with importers, falls behind subsidiary/affiliate with regard to turnover.

7.3 Management style by modes of operation

The second part of the questionnaire was composed of questions aimed at allowing identification of the management styles of the respondents. In Figure 7.5, a profile of the responses to these questions is presented in thematic groups. Corresponding terms are used for this which pertain to internationalisation behaviour and the development of foreign operation mode. Ten corresponding terms were derived from the results of the qualitative interviews and serve as attributes for describing the characteristic management styles for internationalisation of the companies surveyed. The detailed presentation of the bipolar stated factors is taken from the description of the quantitative research approach in the section research design (Chapter 4.8.5). In Figure 7.5, the mean values of the sample are given on a scale of -2 to +2. The more the mean values extend to the left or the right, the stronger the agreement is for the individual quality characterising the management style.

The sample group reflects companies which have strongly pushed international expansion in recent years and which attribute their success to a consciously selected strategy. Luck or coincidence played no significant role for the companies surveyed. The respondents stated that they manoeuvre rather cautiously in their foreign markets, selecting activities with low risk. They can therefore be characterised as rather "risk-averse" than "risk-taking".

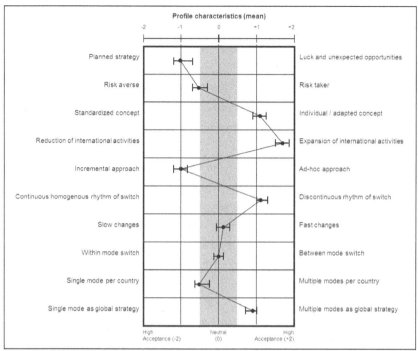

Figure 7.5: Profile characterics of management style
Notes:
a) Average value and standard devisation of management perception (N=180) for selected attitudes to describe internationalisation behaviour
b) Scale: Increase towards the stated factors, with neutral position in the middle: -2=high acceptance, -1=acceptance, 0=neutral, 1=acceptance, 2=high acceptance.

All of the companies surveyed had expanded their foreign-market activity in the past few years. No sample company had de-internationalisation on its agenda. The modes of foreign operation gradually increased in their scope with regard to resources and level of commitment. According to the respondents, immediate market entry with direct foreign investment was extremely rare. A switch in foreign operation mode was made at irregular intervals and did not follow any specific time-pattern. In the sample, the scope of foreign activities and their intensity developed with highly individual speed and without the presence of any particularly dominant internationalisation behaviour. With regard to the use of various strategies for market cultivation in one country, the sample group showed a preference for one single mode – for example, an agent or a subsidiary – rather than a combination of modes. As regards their entire country portfolios, however, the companies employed a number of different operation modes and did not solely concentrate on any one form.

Further interesting findings can be established when the management styles of switchers and non-switchers are compared. Figure 7.6 shows the assessments of management style using contrary reference pairs on a scale of –3 to +3.

Significant differences, identified from independent sample t test, can be found for the characteristics of strategic planning (p=0.035), international growth (p=0.029), speed of the switch (p=0.031) and intensity of the switch (p=0.026). Here, it can be established that switchers have a greater tendency to assign their foreign business success to comprehensive and systematic planning. Switchers are thereby more growth-oriented than non-switchers and maintain a high speed of further development of their foreign business. Switchers are more willing to switch between modes and to take leaps in the context of resource allocation. Often, the selected mode is maintained and personnel are merely exchanged; or changes are made within export strategies (e.g. further importers are added to an exclusive importer). For all other attributes pertaining to management style, no significant differences could be found.

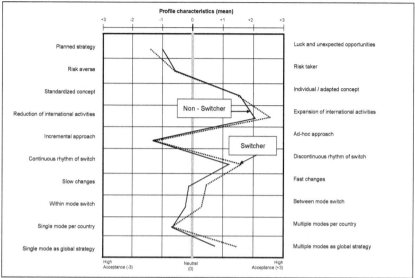

Figure 7.6: Profile characterics of management style for Switcher and Non - Switcher

Notes:
a) Average value of management perception for selected attitudes to describe internationalisation behaviour for switcher ((N=83) and non-switcher (N=96)
b) Scale: Increase towards the stated factors, with neutral position in the middle: -3=high acceptance, 0 = neutral, 3 = high acceptance.

7.4   Basic strategic alignment

The assessment of the basic strategic alignment of the foreign operation is made based on self-classification with the mentioned management-style factors, the characteristic company details and the mode strategy.

To further investigate capabilities and competences, factor analysis with varimax rotation[12] was used to reduce the ten questions to key variables representing management style. When Cronbach's Alpha was applied, it indicated that the first question representing a dimension of planning to a more opportunistic approach was not consistent with the other questions (excluding this item raised Cronbach's Alpha

---

[12] Orthogonal Rotation in which the number of variables with high factor loading is minimised.

from 0.556 to 0.635). Consequently, the first question was not incorporated into the factor analysis. This performed adequately with a Kaiser-Meyer-Olkin Measure of Sampling Adequacy of 0.655 and Bartlett's Test of Sphericity being significant at less than the 1% level. Four factors were generated which accounted for over 64% of the original variation. The rotated factor loadings are displayed in Table 7.4 with the factors of growth, risk, specialist and mode.

Table 7.4: Rotated component matrix

Variables to characterise management style	Component			
	Growth	Risk	Specialist	Mode
Reduction of international activities vs. Expansion of international activities	.815			
Slow vs. fast changes	.814			
Incremental approach vs. ad-hoc approach		.807		
Risk-averse vs. Risk-taker		.730		
Within-mode switch vs. between-mode switch	.342	.474		.451
Continuous homogenous rhythm vs. discontinuous rhythm of switch			.749	
Standardised concept vs. individual concept			.741	
Single mode vs. multi mode per country				.839
Single-mode strategy vs. multi-mode strategy			.484	.616
Variance accounted for (%)	16.7	16.5	15.6	15.5

Notes:
a) N=178 (92.7%), Variance explained = 64.286 %
b) Extraction Method: Principal Component Analysis
c) Rotation Method: Varimax with Kaiser Normalisation, Rotation converged in 5 interactions
d) Bartlett Test of Sphericity: approx. Chi-Square = 195.653, Sig. = 000
Factor Loadings on the dimension of managerial style
The relationships of the factors to the individual variables are derived from Table 7.4 and were given appropriate names.

The large factor loadings indicate a high significance of the two observed variables for the factors growth, risk, specialist and mode.[13]

---

[13] The factor "growth" was composed of the degree of expansion of international activities and the degree of the speed of change. "Risk" was primarily composed of responses to two questions which showed the degree to which approaches were ad-hoc and the degree to which the company was a risk-taker. The "specialist" factor involved questions ascertaining the lack of homogeneity in change and the greater degree of individuality. Finally

The factor Growth is to a great extent influenced by whether the companies have expanded or reduced international expansion in the last five years and with the degree of speed with which they have developed their foreign operations.

The factor Risk is determined by the attitudes of the decision makers with regard to the taking of risks. The factor loadings indicate risk-averse behaviour. Whether the foreign business is expanded ad hoc or incrementally also influences the factor of risk. The step-by-step transfer of resources to a foreign country over the course of several years is naturally less risky (in terms of losses) than direct capital- and know-how transfer to a foreign country after a short period of time.

The timing of the mode switch and degree of standardisation in the level of international marketing characterises the factor Specialist. This factor shows to what extent the management adjusts foreign organisation to the local conditions in the country. In this regard, the managers surveyed are of the opinion that they individually decide how the best mode of foreign operation is characterised. This is also reflected in the change of foreign organisation which occurs more irregularly – sometimes after long intervals, sometimes after short intervals – depending on necessity and not according to a fixed and regular rhythm.

Considered in the factor Mode is the scope of various individual strategies for developing business in a market and the importance of these strategies in the mode portfolio of the company. This factor shows the strong influence on the design of the internationalisation strategy as a tool for market operations in individual countries.

The identified factor values and the original variables are presented in Table 7.5.

---

the "mode" factor was chiefly composed of the extent to which the company employed a multi-mode operation and strategy.

Table 7.5: Factors and original variable

Factor	Original variables	Meaning
Growth	Reduction of international activities vs. Expansion of international activities	Scope of international activities
	Slow vs. fast changes	Pace of internationalisation process
Risk	Incremental approach vs. ad-hoc approach	Scope of transfer of resources and commitment at specific point
	Risk-averse vs. risk-taker	Risk perception in foreign countries
Specialist	Continuous homogenous rhythm vs. discontinuous rhythm of switch	Timing of change of foreign management operation
	Standardised concept vs. individual concept	Level of standardization in international marketing
Mode	Single mode vs. multi-mode per country	Number of modes per country
	Single mode strategy vs. multi-mode strategy	Mode portfolio

One-way analysis of variance was used to assess whether the factors varied significantly with the management-style variables between the industry sectors. No significant differences were found.

To better understand the composition of the various mode strategies of the firms in the sample, a hierarchical cluster analysis was carried out with the aid of the derived factors of growth, risk, specialist and mode. Using the Ward-approach (Backhaus et al. 2008), groups were formed via the closest distance measures and reduced, step-by-step, to five homogenous clusters.

The factors which are identified as separating measures are presented with their mean values in Table 7.6.

The signed consider the factor loadings with regard to management style. The relative measures of the analysis of variance statistics (ANOVA) show the significant differences between the groups. The assessment of statistical independence presents a high confidence-probability of 99% for the covariates "growth factor" and "risk factor" and 95% for the covariant "specialist factor".

Table 7.6: Mean value for covariates and clusters

Five clusters	Growth factor		Mode factor		Risk factor		Specialist factor	
1	0.302		0.182		0.478		0.054	
2	-0.352		-0.054		-0.177		-0.022	
3	-0.109		0.003		0.110		0.358	
4	0.031		-0.066		-0.251		0.005	
5	0.096		-0.099		-0.216		-0.095	
Total	0.002		-0.011		-0.026		0.048	
ANOVA	F=6.424	P=0.002	F=0.443	P=0.643	F=4.806	P=0.009	F=0.943	P=0.0391

Based on the variance analysis and the results thus far, clusters can be described as follows:

Cluster 1 represents firms which prefer fast international expansion and make ad hoc decisions based on specific necessities in the foreign market. They consciously take higher risks if the profit prospects are in accordance. Compared to other groups, they tend to employ several modes of market operation rather than one single mode.

Cluster 2 represents firms for whom internationalisation is not of particular importance. The pace is slow or does not play a significant role. A step-by-step approach dominates with consideration of specific risks.

Cluster 3 represents firms which predominantly prefer an individual approach and adapt concepts depending on the country requirements. If interesting opportunities arise in the foreign market, the management decides ad hoc and consciously takes risks.

Cluster 4 represents particularly risk-averse firms which sequentially develop their foreign countries further and compared to other groups, they tend to employ several modes rather rather than one single mode.

Cluster 5 represents firms which gradually expand business activity in the foreign country. They do this with the aid of standardised concepts and behave in a risk-averse way. The management concentrates on single modes and not on mode combinations.

To understand how modes are distributed across companies, K-means cluster analysis was used, using the percentage mode share for each company. This yielded five clusters. The percentage-distribution of modes in these clusters is displayed in Table 7.7. This refers to the entire international business of the respective companies and is not country-specific.

Table 7.7: Percentage of mode utilisation by mode cluster (mean percentage)

Internationalisation mode	Cluster				
	1 (N=26)	2 (N=38)	3 (N=40)	4 (N=53)	5 (N=22)
Internet/Electronic mode	0.3	1.1	2.4	1.2	0.9
Indirect export	3.5	5.1	4.8	6.2	2.6
Direct export without middleman	5.6	65.4	13.8	13.1	6.4
Direct export with own salesperson	3.3	3.0	47.4	5.0	2.9
Export service consultant	0.1	0.3	0.8	0.1	0.3
Direct export with agents	6.1	4.3	7.9	40.1	4.8
Direct export with importer	11.3	6.4	8.5	11.1	69.8
Alliances/Partnering	3.1	3.7	3.5	7.9	1.3
Franchising/Partnering	0.4	0.0	0.3	0.6	0.2
Joint venture	2.0	1.7	0.2	2.9	0.9
Sales office, Subsidiary, Affiliate	62.5	7.8	5.4	8.3	9.2
Foreign acquisition	1.0	1.2	4.8	3.5	0.6

The first mode cluster is composed of 63% "Subsidiaries / Affiliates" and 11%, "Direct export with importer". This group of companies achieved the highest export turnover and allotted the most personnel to foreign business.

The second cluster relies mainly on direct export without a middleman (65%). This group presents the lowest export turnover and lowest number of years in foreign business.

In the third mode-cluster group, direct export with own salespeople (47%) is combined with direct export without middlemen (14%), export with importers (8%) and export with agents (9%). Companies in this group have the lowest number of employees in foreign countries and have been in the market the longest.

The fourth cluster is also a combination of direct export modes, mostly relying on agents (40%), no middleman (13%) and importers (11%). This group has the lowest dominance of a certain mode and achieves the highest export rate.

The fifth group is comprised of companies which place their primary focus on direct export with importers (70%). Otherwise, there are no specifically conclusive quantitative tendencies. This group does, however, have a comparatively lower number of employees in the foreign market and achieves a comparatively high export rate.

How these clusters are related to attributes of the respondents is presented in Table 7.8.

Table 7.8: Respondent characteristics by cluster – mean values

Cluster	Company in international business (in years)	Experience of interview-partner in international business (in years)	Employees in international business	Export Turnover in 2006	Export-turnover ratio	Foundation of company (average year of foundation)
1	36	14	517	73.8	46%	1941
2	30	14	153	11.5	30%	1945
3	37	12	111	27.6	43%	1926
4	38	17	174	35.1	52%	1942
5	32	18	115	39.7	50%	1936
Total	35	15	214	37.4	44%	1938

Cluster 1 comprises companies with the highest foreign turnover of all clusters and the most employees in the foreign market. For the management, internationalisation is of high importance. This is expressed in an intentional promotion of international expansion. In doing so, these companies take higher risks than those in other clusters.

Cluster 2 comprises companies with the least amount of international experience, the lowest foreign turnover and the smallest export ratio. For the companies in this cluster, internationalisation is yet of little importance.

Companies in Cluster 3 have the longest company histories of all clusters. They allocate the lowest number of employees in the foreign market. For international operations, the management relies in particular on individual strategies for fulfilling the requirements of the specific country. The cluster thereby differentiates itself from the others, whose readiness to adapt is less manifested.

Companies in Cluster 4 possess the most international experience and have the highest export ratio. Their export turnover is average. In the foreign market, these companies manoeuvre particularly carefully and only take risks to a limited degree.

Companies in Cluster 5 also have a high export ratio, however they send fewer employees to the foreign market than companies in Cluster 4. The management mainly prefers standardised concepts for international market operation and behaves in a risk-averse way.

The analysis of satisfaction (from 1 "highly satisfied" to 5 "not satisfied") regarding results in the foreign market thus far did not show any significant differences between the five identified clusters. The observation showed a slightly higher average degree of satisfaction with the foreign business with companies in Cluster 1 (2.91) and Cluster 5 (2.93). Companies in Cluster 3 and 4 rated their satisfaction at 3.14. The lowest satisfaction was to be found among the companies in Cluster 2 (3.34).

With regard to further characterising qualities, such as turnover-per-employee and export turnover for the identified clusters, apart from cluster 2 which shows significantly lower values for both measures. All other clusters showed no significant differences as can be seen in Figure 7.7 and Figure 7.8.

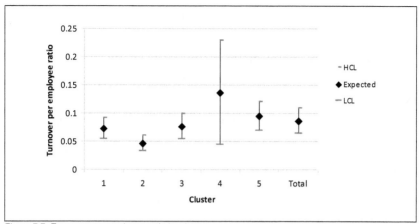

Figure 7.7: Turnover per employee ratio by cluster

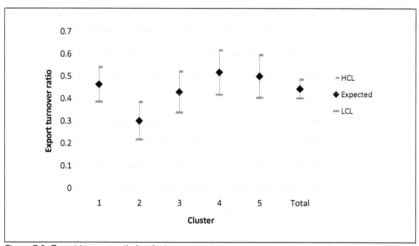

Figure 7.8: Export turnover ratio by cluster

7.5 Timing of mode decision

The third part of the questionnaire pertained to the question of the structure and duration of the decision-making process for a mode switch.

From the analysis of the questionnaire it was found that approximately 35% of the surveyed companies undertook a change of the originally selected operation mode for market entry after three years of market entry. Six years after market entry a total of 75% had changed their mode.

From the perspective of the five dominating industry sectors, no differing decision-making behaviour could be observed.

For the various mode clusters it can be established that Cluster 1 requires the longest time before switching the market-entry strategy while Cluster 3 changed fastest after market entry. Cluster 2, 4 and 5 lie in the middle, with their decision time frame of an average of 4 – 6 years.

The decision-making process revolving around whether a mode switch should be undertaken or not, and in which form, occurred in several phases. These phases varied in their duration and content (
Figure 7.9).

Most of the companies (71%) made a decision as to whether or not an operation mode should be changed or not in less than 12 months. Yet, approximately 30 % needed more than 1 year to make their decision. The majority of the companies (61%), "negotiated" within 6 months with the actors concerned (sales partners, customers, suppliers and employees). After this decision, there is, for the majority, a timely implementation of the mode switch to the strategy selected and severance from the initially selected market-entry strategy. Implementation can involve contract terminations, entering into new partnerships, search for ideal locations and the building of new facilities. For the majority of the companies surveyed (68%) the time required for implementation of the new mode is at least 12 months.

258

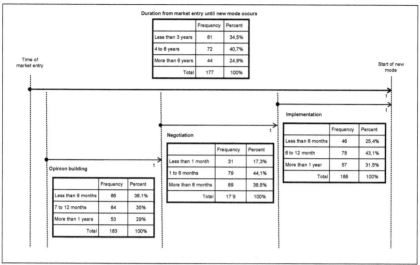

Figure 7.9: Decision process and timing for first mode switch

A strict time definition of the identified decision-making phases is not possible because some decisions for market strategy and major aspects of implementation are made at a very early stage while other details regarding how the switch will actually be implemented may not evolve until actual implementation is underway. For example, the target mode of subsidiary may already be settled very early in the opinion-building phase because the advisory board has decided on this. However, how and when communication of the switch from importer to the most important customers should take place is something that can be decided on an ad hoc basis at a later point in the implementation process. In this regard, the decision-making behaviour is more of an iterative process with feedback loops.

Figure 7.10 shows the distribution for these three categories of decision-making paces.

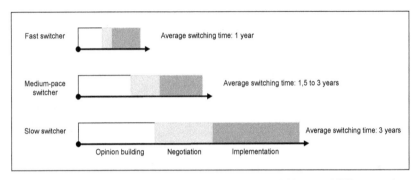

Figure 7.10: Differences between switcher types with regard to switching speed (Differences of pace categories)

Based on the above duration structure (Figure 7.10), three major types of pace categories can be identified: fast switchers, medium switchers and slow switchers. The category of "fast switchers" mostly needs up to 6 months to form their opinion regarding the necessity of a switch, up to another one month for negotiation, and up to 6 months for actual implementation. In sum, a maximum decision-making and implementation duration of little more than one year can be assumed.

The category of "medium switchers" takes between 7 and 12 months for the opinion-building period, more than 1 month (often around 1 year) for negotiation, and more than 6 months (frequently also over one year) for the implementation of the decision. On average, the total process from the initial idea to implementation thereby takes between 1.5 and 3 years.

The category of "slow switchers" requires more than 1 year for opinion-building, always more than 6 months for negotiation, and more than 1 year for actual implementation. In total, they require more than 2.5 years, often more than 3 years for the decision and implementation regarding a first switch.

In Table 7.9, the distribution of satisfaction with foreign business is indicated in relation to the three paces of decision-making behaviour.

Table 7.9: Distribution of overall satisfaction with the international business for the three categories of decision-making pace

Pace of switching decision making		Overall satisfaction			Total	Satis- faction (Mean)	SD of mean
		Good	Ok	Poor			
quick	N	13	23	12	48	2.0	0.105
	% of row	27%	48%	25%	100%		
medium	N	18	18	10	46	1.8	0.113
	% of row	39%	39%	22%	100%		
slow	N	7	7	8	22	2.1	0.179
	% of row	32%	32%	36%	100%		
Total	N	38	48	30	116	1.9	0.071
	% of Total	32.8	41.4	25.9	100%		

Notes: the original scale of overall satisfaction from 1 (highly satisfied) to 5 (not satisfied) is reduced to Good (1+2), Ok (3+4) and Poor (5); SD: Standard error of mean

It can be established that no particular frequencies with regard to the level of satisfaction can be observed for the various decision-making phases. Furthermore there is no statistical evidence to suggest that a faster or a slower pace in the decision making process concerning the switching behaviour would lead to higher overall satisfaction in international business.

From the observations, it may be established that it is not necessarily a matter of fast or slow decision-making behaviour for the decision makers but more a question of efficiently using available time for opinion building and negotiating with actors concerned.

The observed behaviour may give a first indication that the speed of decisions has practical relevance but to what extent it affects success in the foreign market must remain open. Based on these results, success can be achieved with both fast and slow decision-making behaviour.

Furthermore, the indicators and measurement categories only give orientation of the actual time duration. Particularly the beginning and end value of the decision phase is problematic. It is surely very difficult for the participating managers to define exactly when the opinion-building process regarding a mode switch began or when the first negotiations were started. Does an action begin with deliberations on it, with the first small measures or with a big announcement to employees? A similar problem applies to the end of a phase. When has implementation been completed? What was the legal founding of a subsidiary? Was this the first turnovers or first contact with international customers with the new mode? In this respect, statistically valuable information regarding the exact timing or time periods could not really be achieved through this quantitative survey.

7.6 International mode-switching activity

The analysis of behaviour after market entry represents another important element of the survey. In the sample, the respondents were asked about their mode strategy and whether they had switched the original selected market entry strategy in the most important foreign market. The sample contains a nearly equal number of switching and non switching behaviour (Table 7.10). Of note is the significant difference between the levels of satisfaction with the originally selected market-entry strategy: those seeking new modes are less happy with their first choice; or, in other words, non-switchers are significantly happier than switchers.[14]

Table 7.10: Share of switcher / non-switcher in the sample

Switcher vs. Non Switcher	Frequency	Percentage	Entry mode satisfaction	Standard Deviation	Standard Error Mean
Non Switcher	94	48.96	1.65	0.791	0.087
Switcher	98	51.04	2.44	1.127	0.114
Total / Average	192	100.00	2.08		
Levene's Test for Equality of Variances			F=16.247	p=0.000	

Notes: Valuation of satisfaction of entry mode was based on the following scale: 1 (highly satisfied) to 5 (not satisfied).

---

[14] The analysis of the reasons for not switching the market-entry mode in Chapter 8.3 confirms (from today's perspective) a high level of satisfaction with the selected market-entry mode as the main reason for not switching. Further important reasons for not switching were an unclear business benefit of the switch, and the opinion of decision makers that business development thus far does not justify a change. Uncertainty about possible consequences of a switch or lack of management capabilities played, according to the survey respondents, the smallest role.

It was found that 51% of the sample had switched mode at least once. Of those which did switch, 80% switched once and 18% switched twice. The maximum number of switches was 4.

In terms of the probability of switching, the companies in the automotive industry seem to switch with a significantly higher probability than other industry sectors as shown in Figure 7.11. For the identified cluster, the probability of switching shows no significant differences (Figure 7.12).

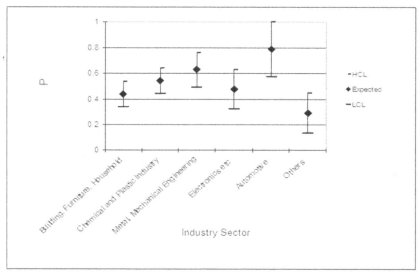

Figure 7.11: Probability of switching, by industry sector

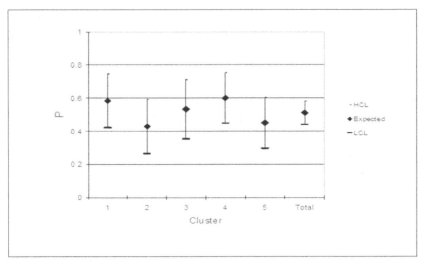

Figure 7.12: Probability of switching, by cluster

From the analysed sectors it could be observed that there is a significantly greater probability in the automotive sector that a market entry strategy will be switched. Whether this is due to the well-known particularly high dynamics of this sector and the accompanying necessity to adjust remains an open question. Through the obviously high number of influencing factors and the very heterogeneous environmental conditions within the sectors and their partial segments, significant results had not been expected beforehand.

The analysis of the influence of the clusters on the probability of a switch also did not produce significant results. A possible prognosis as to whether a switch will occur or not therefore depends on other factors that lie beyond the configuration of the mode portfolio and the cluster-related company characteristics.

7.7 Overall satisfaction

On average, the respondents' satisfaction with their international business scored 3.086 based on a scale of 1 (highly satisfied) to 5 (not satisfied) and with a 95% confidence interval of plus or minus 0.144. This indicates a statistically significant degree of dissatisfaction.

The variation in satisfaction between industry sector and cluster are shown in

Figure 7.13 and Figure 7.14.

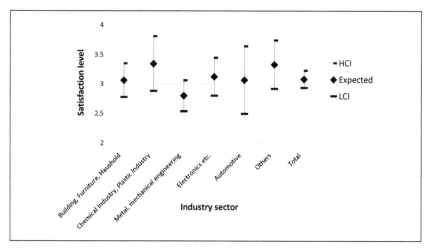

Figure 7.13: Satisfaction level by business sector

Highest satisfaction with foreign business was to be found in the engineering sector. Companies in the chemical industry were least satisfied with their foreign business compared with the other sectors.

The two clusters, Cluster 1 (subsidiary) and 5 (importer), showed the highest satisfaction while in Cluster 2 (without middlemen) the companies were least satisfied.

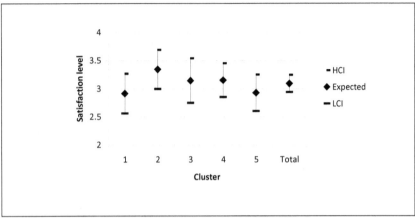

Figure 7.14: Satisfaction level by respondent cluster by mode of operation

The reason for the high level of satisfaction in Cluster 1 could well lie in the better knowledge of the market resulting from closer proximity to the customer. This reduces uncertainty and the foreign market is more transparent with regard to market participants, price levels, buying behaviour, market growth, quality and so forth. Altogether, the strong dominance of the subsidiary in the mode portfolio results in better knowledge of the requirements of foreign customers.

In Cluster 5, the high level of satisfaction of the companies with the dominating mode of importer may be explained by the low level of resources required for this mode. Although less know-how is transferred via the foreign market to the home market, the company can economically participate in developments on the foreign market through the importer. The usually low market shares are consciously accepted with the knowledge that more resources and possibly capital transfer to the foreign country also means higher risk – risk the decision makers do not want to take. Therefore, it can be said, that the higher degree of satisfaction is a consequence of lower expectations.

The low level of satisfaction in Cluster 2 is most likely due to the low level of knowledge of market requirements. There is still a great deal of uncertainty with regard to the most significant demands in the foreign market and this uncertainty manifests itself in a level of dissatisfaction that is higher than in any of the other clusters.

Observing the reasons behind the level of satisfaction within the identified clusters makes it apparent that the information processing of the decision makers as well as the perception and interpretation of opportunities and risks are important influencing factors.

7.8 Summary of sample characteristics

The findings presented are mostly based on information provided by the top management of the companies surveyed (85% were at director level and accordingly experienced in developing and implementing international strategies). The sample group presents a cross-section of German industrial companies, with a relatively high average export share of 44%. These are companies with extensive experience in foreign markets (15 years), and which have been highly successful in these markets. This is apparent in the high number of foreign markets being simultaneously operated in (65% of the companies are active in more than 11 countries).

The results clearly show that companies do not solely employ one form of market operation, but combine various modes to form a mode portfolio. Frequently found were strategies with low investment risk, such as direct export without middlemen, importers and export with the help of sales representatives or commercial agents. With regard to turnover for the individual operation modes, subsidiaries and affiliates take a major place in the mode portfolio, followed by direct export through importers. Satisfaction with the own mode was highest for subsidiary/affiliate, followed by direct export without a middleman and with own salesman.

Overall, the companies assessed the development of their foreign market activity as being unsatisfactory with clear potential for improvement.

Mode switching is often viewed as a strategic option for optimising internationalisation. The sample group comprises 98 (51%) switchers and 94 (49%) non-switchers. Of the switchers, another 18% switched their mode of foreign business operation a second time – independently of sector or the characteristic mode strategies.

In its internationalisation, every company possesses a characteristic structure or combination of mode types. For the sample respondents, five groups with homogenous behaviour could be identified in which either single modes or mode combinations dominated.

The clusters are to be interpreted as follows:

Cluster 1 comprises companies whose primary strategy for operation on their international markets is made with a subsidiary. These are large companies which are operating in a high number of foreign markets simultaneously. For the management of these companies, internationalisation is of high importance. This is manifested in consciously strived-for international expansion. Companies in this cluster are willing to take greater risks than the companies in the other clusters. They also tend to be more prepared to react in an ad hoc way to country requirements. In comparison to all other clusters, these firms combine modes with particular intensity. Their management demonstrates an above-average level of satisfaction with the international market operation. Fast implementation of international mode switches is characteristic of these companies.

Cluster 2 includes companies which mainly employ direct export without middlemen as their strategy for foreign markets. These are smaller companies with fewer resources and comparatively little experience in internationalisation. In this cluster, internationalisation is of low importance.

Cluster 3 includes companies that predominantly prefer own salespeople or direct export without middlemen. The companies are older and switch quicker.

For international operations, the management of these companies relies, in particular, on individual strategies to fulfil the demands of a specific country. They thereby sets themselfes apart from the management of the companies in other clusters where readiness to adapt is less marked.

Cluster 4 comprises companies that employ several modes and also combine them. Of particular note is a simultaneous use of agents, importers and direct export without middlemen. These companies possess years of experience in internationalisation and need somewhat more time for implementation of a switch. They manouever carefully on the international stage and only take risks to a limited extent. Incremental international expansion is their preferred management approach.

Cluster 5 companies primarily concentrate on market operations via an importer. They are strongly internationalisation-oriented and show a high level of satisfaction with internationalisation thus far. Implementation of new operation modes is slower. The management mostly prefers standardised concepts for international market operation and demonstrates risk aversion.

In their summary, the clusters are to be interpreted from the perspective of the mode portfolio and the accompanying character of its management style for internationalisation.

In Table 7.11 the identified clusters are described by their preferred mode, company characteristics on decision behaviour and managerial style.

Table 7.11: Cluster characteristics on mode and decision behaviour

Cluster	Preferred mode	Behaviour	Company characteristics
1	Subsidiary	Domination	Strong dominance of subsidiaries, only in a few markets importer (not important, high cultural distance importer), active in a large number of countries, larger companies in terms of turnover and employees, risk taker, high degree of satisfaction with mode used, quick execution of new switch
2	No middleman	Low resources	Mostly direct export without middleman is used, smaller companies, low resources available, low level of experience, quick execution of new switch, internationalisation is not yet of high importance
3	Salesmen	Control	Mainly salesmen are used in combination with direct export (agents, importers and direct without middleman), prefers individual/adapted concepts, Quick switchers (< 3 y), older companies
4	Mixed direct export	Balanced	Mainly agents are used in combination of importers and direct export with no middleman, long experience, risk averse, incremental internationalisation, longer execution for new switch
5	Importers	Selective	Mainly concentrating on importer only, very international, prefers standardised concepts, risk avers, very happy with results, longer execution of switch

This chapter focused on the description, characterisation of the sample and analysis of management issues tied to foreign operations. A presentation of the frequency of the employed modes and their significance with regard to company success reveal the internationalisation strategies of the companies surveyed. The description and analysis of management styles in foreign business clarifies the difference between switchers and non-switchers. As observed in the qualitative section (see Chapter 5 and Chapter 6), groups of homogeneous behaviour are shown and described in relation to their mode strategy, decision-making behaviour, timing aspects and company and management characteristics. As a result, the sample can be divided into the basic orientations of "Domination", "Low Resources", "Control", "Balanced" and "Selective". The description of the sample thereby allows deeper understanding of influencing company-related conditions.

The introductory hypothesis (H_{B1}), stating that there is a relationship between foreign mode switching behaviour and the company's success in a foreign market, can be confirmed at least partially.

H_{B1}: There is a relationship between mode switching behaviour and international success

This fundamental hypothesis is comprised of many individual hypotheses. Therefore, further evidence is needed to explain the influencing factors on switching behaviour and success as presented in Chapter 8.

In the following chapter, the sample will be analysed with regard to its behaviour in one specific foreign market. The mode switch is descriptively analysed beginning with the market-entry strategy, reasons for market entry, decision for country and timing of entry. Then the results of the reasons for switching or not switching, and selected performance characteristics are presented. The effects of the switch are analysed and timing aspects of the mode switch are discussed.

Chapter 8 Survey Results on Mode Switching

In the previous chapter, the sample firms were comprehensively described with regard to their strategy and the management of their foreign business. The five clusters which are identified show the preferences in decision-making behaviour, the strategy of market operation and the turnover significance. This creates sufficient transparency of the sample's structure.

What mode strategy is most successful? What kind of switching behaviour is characteristic for the companies surveyed? What factors influence mode switching? How critical are timing aspects? These questions are answered in the section to follow, based on the individual companies' most important foreign markets. Other countries beyond the most important foreign market are not considered in the analysis of the internationalisation behaviour. Therefore this section can be seen as single country analysis on strategic behaviour. For this the actual switching behaviour is shown beginning with the market entry. Switches are presented first according to country group and region. The reasons for switching will be identified and compared with reasons for non-switching. The company success is observed from the perspective of the selected mode strategy and the company-specific and management-specific influencing factors. The target mode as a preliminary "final" interim entity is determined. Following this, the effects of the switches will be discussed. Five performance criteria under consideration of turnover and satisfaction are used for this and both long and short-term effects of the switch on company performance are shown.

Then the timing of the switch will be set in relation to the initial mode and presented for countries in various categories of economic development. The analysis of the revealed path after market entry shows the modes employed over time. The result of time to switch will be investigated and discussed with regard to the degree of probability and the main influencing factors. Finally an attempt will be made to develop an exploratory model which explains the complex subject of mode switching under consideration of the assumed relationships and results. A statement on the research hypotheses formulated in Chapter 6.5 follows after each section.

8.1 Entry mode strategy: Distribution and Reasons

For the surveyed companies, the decision for the market entry strategy represents the starting point for internationalisation. In Table 8.1 the five most important market entry strategies for their chosen most important foreign market are presented with reference to frequency and level of satisfaction.

Employed often as a market-entry strategy were importers (27%), direct export without middlemen (19%) and agents (16.5%). With the exception of "subsidiary", all of the market entry strategies belong to the category of export strategy. These are characterised by a very low level of resource allocation and are particularly attractive for this very reason.

Table 8.1: Most important entry modes

Entry mode	Frequency	Percent	Degree of satisfaction (entry mode)[1]	Standard error of mean
Importer	47	26.4	2.17	0.159
Direct Export, without middlemen	34	19.1	2.12	0.192
Agents	39	21.9	1.93	0.164
Sales office/Affiliate/Subsidiary	19	10.7	1.55	0.143
Direct Export, with own salesperson	19	10.7	2.11	0.241
Others	27	15.2	2.41	0.246
Total / Average	178	100%	2.07	0,08

Notes: [1]Valuation of satisfaction with the results of the mode was based on the following scale: 1 (highly satisfied) to 5 (not satisfied).

In assessing the selected market entry strategy on a scale from 1 (highly satisfied) to 5 (not satisfied) from the current perspective, the sequence is as follows: subsidiary (1.55), agents (1.93) and direct export with own sales representatives (2.11).

The stated reasons for the selection of the market entry strategy are presented in Table 8.2.

Table 8.2: Most important entry modes and the respective reasons based on frequency

Entry mode Reasons (N=154)	Importer	Direct export, Without middleman	Agent	Subsidiary	Direct export, Own sales person	Others	Total
Customer oriented & opportunity	9	18	5	6	5	5	48
	18.8%	37.5%	10.4%	12.5%	10.4%	10.4%	31.2%
Low effort	4	4	5	1	2	4	20
	20.0%	20.0%	25.0%	5.0%	10.0%	20.0%	13.0%
Low cost	5	1	7	0	2	1	16
	31.3%	6.3%	43.8%	0%	12.5%	6.3%	10.4%
Previous experience	7	0	5	1	0	2	15
	46.7%	0%	33.3%	6.7%	0.0%	13.3%	9.7%
Competence and capabilities	3	0	3	2	2	2	12
	25.0%	0%	25.0%	16.7%	16.7%	16.7%	7.8%
Low risk	5	1	0	1	0	0	7
	71.4%	14.3%	0%	14.3%	0%	0%	4.5%
Control	0	1	0	4	1	0	6
	0%	16.7%	0%	66.7%	16.7%	0%	3.9%
External influence	0	1	0	0	1	2	4
	0%	25.0%	0%	0%	25.0%	50.0%	2.6%
Others	8	1	1	5	3	8	26
	30.8%	3.8%	3.8%	19.2%	11.5%	30.8%	16.9%
Total	41	27	26	20	16	24	154
	26.6%	17.5%	16.9%	13.0%	10.4%	15.6%	100%

The reasons of "customer-oriented & opportunity" (31%), "low effort" (13%), "low cost" (10%) and "previous experience" (10%) are, from the view of the sample, the most important factors for the selection of the market entry strategy.

The most frequent market entry strategy, "importer", was selected by the companies surveyed mainly because there was the wish to take advantage of the distribution network and contacts of the importer. In many cases, this strategy presented itself as a good opportunity from first information gathering for possible market operation.

Direct export without middlemen was also primarily selected because it allowed direct contact with customers and thereby a good opportunity for first foreign business transactions. In some cases, however, the business model requires direct contact to the customers (particularly in the case of high consultation intensity).

Companies which chose an agent primarily did so because this option represents a cost-favourable means of market entry. The agent is normally paid based on commission which only falls due when sales have been achieved.

The main reasons for a subsidiary were a high level of customer orientation from the start and the wish to control activities in the foreign market.

Own sales representatives were also employed in order to achieve close customer contact from the beginning.

The reasons for the selected market-entry strategy show further interesting patterns. If low costs and low effort dominate the decision making then agents (and to a lower extent, importers) are selected. Risk-aversion leads to market entry with importers. If the decision-maker is mostly concerned with exercising control then a subsidiary is chosen. Previous experience with a mode leads to the further usage of those familiar strategies. In the sample group, this particularly applies to agents and importer strategies.

Other reasons which could not be assigned directly to the main groups included fast implementation speed, conflict potential, internal reasons, cultural proximity, strategic focus and market significance.

8.2 Market entry and mode switch by countries

The nature of the most recent mode switch was investigated by asking the respondents about their operations in the foreign country which is most important to their organisation. The distribution of the most important regions classified by market type and region are presented in Table 8.3.

Table 8.3: Number of mode switches clustered by market type and regions

Market category[1]	Number of mode switches	Percentage	Country share of total export turnover
Mature market	72	73.5%	25
Newly industrialised economy	9	9.2%	18.9
Emerging market	17	17.4%	22.9
Total	98	100%	24.03

[1] Country categories according to the country development index introduced in Chapter: 4.8.6.
Number of mode switches includes all respondents who switched once in the respective group of markets.

As presented a total of 98 switches was identified. Nearly three-quarters (72) of the companies' mode switches were made in mature markets. Most mode switches undertaken by the respondents (approx. 50% of all cases) were made in Western Europe. The respondents undertook the least changes of initially selected market entry in newly industrialised countries. These countries presented the lowest turnover share of an average of 19% of export turnover.

The geographical emphasis of the identified switches reflects the market activity of the surveyed companies in Germany. Based on the German domestic market, the internationalisation of business activity took place first in the predominantly saturated markets in Europe and the U.S. Mode switches were most frequently made in these countries. Only after market entry in these markets and a certain period of market activity there was expansion to rapidly growing countries, such as in Eastern Europe or Asia.

In Figure 8.1 the time of market entry and of the switch is shown in relation to the economic development status of the country in question.

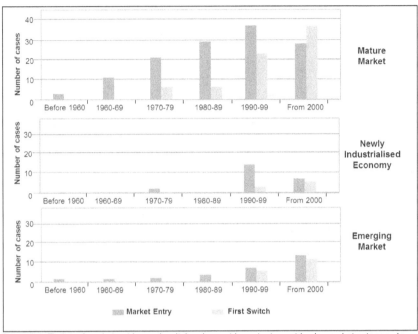

Figure 8.1: Timing of market entries and switches in most important countries by market category, in absolute figures.

It should first be noted that these companies have an average of 35 years of foreign business experience. This means that the majority of the companies surveyed which have switched modes in a foreign market entered their most important market back in the 60's or 70's. These companies began switching modes in the 70's. Between 1990 and 2000, the number of switches tripled, and in the years 2000 to 2006, there was a further increase of 50% in foreign operation mode switches. In Western-Europe, there was, for a long time, no need to change the selected market-entry strategy. The companies developed positively along with the markets. It was only after a certain threshold value had been achieved that modes were switched at the beginning of the 90's, with a further increase since 2000 (due to positive demand, increase in competitive intensity, dissatisfaction with results, general experience and knowledge gained). These adjustments of strategy took place in an increasingly dynamic international environment with the introduction of the Eurozone, the East expansion of the EU, the opening of China, the German reunification and the general increase in world trade.

Market entry in countries of the newly industrialised economies occurred mostly at the beginning of the 90's. First adjustments of the market-entry strategy were made only in a few cases with a slight increase in the recent past. The significance of emerging markets has gradually increased. In particular, since the 90's this group of countries has developed into important foreign markets for German companies. Alignments of strategy in the form of mode switches were undertaken from the 90's onward. China, India and Russia only opened to foreign markets in the middle or even at the end of 90's. Up to that point, they had not been very attractive for German companies. The same applies for markets in Eastern Europe, which may explain the late market entries.

It can be established that both the frequency and the timing of the mode switch depends on the context of the country market in question (Chapter 8.12). Most switches are undertaken in the geographically close markets of Western Europe and the culturally similar markets in North America. In these markets, switches were mostly made in the past twenty years. In the younger markets of Eastern Europe and Asia, market entry and the timing of the mode switch are much closer together. In addition it can be assumed that the overall increased dynamics caused faster switches in all markets.

8.3 Reasons for switching or non-switching

8.3.1 Reasons for non-switching

In the following, the reasons why some of the companies surveyed did not switch their market entry strategy are analysed. The reasons are given in relation to the most important market entry modes, based on their importance. Contrary to the open question for switching, the respondents were asked to give their judgment for given reasons and to prioritise. These are displayed in Table 8.4

Table 8.4: Reasons for non-switching based on the five most important entry modes

Reasons not to switch	Reason for non-switching (average of degree of importance)					
	Importer	No middle-men	Agent	Subsidiary	Own sales person	Average of all modes
Uncertain about consequences	2.4	1.8	1.9	1.8	2.7	2.1
High cost	3.0	2.4	2.4	1.5	2.5	2.3
Not enough resources	2.6	2.2	2.4	2.1	2.3	2.2
Not the right moment	2.1	2.3	2.6	2.0	1.9	2.2
Economic development in foreign market does not justify changes	2.7	2.6	3.5	2.8	3.8	3.1
Lack of management capabilities	1.8	2.1	2.3	1.9	2.4	2.1
Not economic enough	3.6	3.2	3.2	3.1	2.5	3.1
Happy with current situation	4.1	4.0	4.0	4.3	3.6	4
No experience with other modes	2.0	2.3	2.8	1.6	2.6	2.3
Mean	**2.7**	**2.5**	**2.8**	**2.3**	**2.7**	**2.2**
Mean number of respondent	26.3	16.5	15.4	7.5	5.9	

Notes:
a) Degree of Importance on a scale from 1 (less important) to 5 (most important)
b) Method: The respondents were asked to prioritise a given list of reasons for non-switching; more than one answer was possible.

The most important reasons for not switching were a high level of satisfaction with the current situation (4.0), an unclear business-benefit from the switch (3.1), and the opinion of decision-makers that business development thus far does not justify a switch (3.1). Uncertainty about possible consequences of a switch (2.1) or lack of management capabilities (2.1) played, according to the survey respondents, the smallest role.

With the exception of the option of direct export with own salesperson, for all other modes a high level of satisfaction with the status quo is an important reason not to switch. Own salespeople are not switched mainly due to low future economic expectations and the opinion that business development thus far does not justify a switch.

The initially selected market-entry mode of "agents" is mainly not switched due to satisfaction with the current situation. Stated as a further reason, an assessment of business development does not render a switch sensible in the view of the respondent. This justification indicates that the switch from an agent is only "worth it" when a certain turnover or profit threshold is exceeded. Below this threshold value, the switch is not perceived as economical.

It is a similar case with "direct export without a middleman". Here there is high satisfaction with the status quo as well. In addition, however, there is the opinion that a switch will not be economic.

Thus the survey respondents mostly decide against a mode switch because they are satisfied with the status quo. The status quo is valued higher than the potential of a new operation mode. There is the implicit logic that a switch is not made because the potential benefit is expected to be smaller than the potentially arising "costs". This becomes evident in the frequent reasoning of "not economical enough" in the context of a switch. Some of the mentioned reasons for non-switching, such as not economical enough and high cost, could also be interpreted as business risks. These make the switch appear to be too "risky".

8.3.2 Reasons for switching

In this section the reasons leading to a switch of market-entry strategy will be examined. The most important reasons for a first switch and the new mode of foreign operation are presented. The survey respondents were asked to settle on one major reason as to why they wanted to change their market-entry strategy. These are presented in Table 8.5. This table also includes the frequency of the new mode of operation and whether this new mode replaced the old strategy or was employed in additional to it.

Table 8.5: Reasons for the switch in relation to the selected mode

Reasons for the first switch	Most important five first switch modes												Total		
	Subsidiary		Importer		Own sales-person		Agents		JV		Others		Total		
	r.	a.	r.	a.	r.	a.	r.	a.	r.	a.	r.	a.	r.	a.	total
Customer oriented & growth	5	9	3	4	3	4	3	1	4	2	1	6	19	26	45
Unhappy with partner	8	0	3	0	2	0	4	0	0	0	0	0	17	0	17
External factors	5	1	2	0	1	0	0	0	0	0	1	1	9	2	11
Control	2	2	1	1	0	2	0	1	0	0	0	1	3	7	10
Improvement	0	0	1	0	1	0	0	1	1	0	1	1	4	2	6
Others	1	0	0	1	0	0	0	0	2	0	1	0	4	1	5
Total	21	12	10	6	7	6	7	3	7	2	4	9	56	38	94

Notes:
a) Answer: Only one answer was possible.
b) r=replacement - the old mode was replaced with the same or a new mode, i.e. agent replaced by subsidiary or old agent replaced by a new agent; a=additional - the new mode was used in addition to the old mode, i.e. importer and own salesperson

The criterion of "customer orientation and growth" was the most frequently cited reason to switch from the initially selected market entry strategy. In this context, the new mode selected was employed to achieve greater closeness to the customer, improved customer orientation and international growth targets in the foreign market. "Dissatisfaction with partner" was the most important reason for switching in 17 cases. "External factors", such as the fulfilment of a specific market demand, the termination of a partner's contract or loss of a partner, or certain behaviour on the part of a competitor influenced the decision in 11 cases and meant, in the majority of the cases, a replacement of the previous mode of market operation. Finally, 10 companies surveyed switched their previous form of operation mode in order to achieve a higher level of "control" in their most important foreign market. In the majority of cases, this was strived for via intensification and additional resource transfer in the form of an additional subsidiary, further distributors and own sales personnel.

In 60% (56 cases) of the switch cases, the market-entry strategy was replaced by a new one. A previous partner was exchanged for a new partner, a new manager was installed, the previous importer was exchanged for a subsidiary or an own sales representative was employed rather than an agent. In 40% (38 cases) of the cases, the market-entry strategy was kept and supplemented by a division of territory, more partners for market operation, a subsidiary or own salespeople.

If a switch was made with the motivation of "customer orientation and growth" then this usually meant adding a further mode to the existing one (26 cases). In particular subsidiaries (9 cases) were added to an existing strategy. If, however, there was dissatisfaction with the result of the partnership thus far then the mode was replaced without exception (17 cases). In these cases a subsidiary was also the predominant choice (8 cases). If external factors were of significance for a switch then the previous mode was replaced; here, too, in the most cases by subsidiaries.

If the reasons for market operation with a single mode in comparison to operation with mode combinations are observed it becomes clear that the motivation "customer orientation and growth" and "control" lead more to the use of mode combinations. It can, for example, be that importer was selected as a market-entry strategy and this was then supported by own sales personnel. All other motivations would increasingly lead to a replacement of the selected market-entry strategy, to market operation with a single mode.

Most frequently, the selected market-entry strategy was replaced (21 cases) or supplemented (33 cases) by subsidiaries. This was followed by importers (in total, 16 cases) and own sales personnel (13 cases).

The reasons for the replacement or exchange of a current mode strategy indicate the particular demands on partner identification and partner selection in international business. Active partner management, partner design, training and trust-building measures are further important aspects which can be referred to as starting points for optimisation in the discussion of unsatisfactory partnerships.

The reasons for supplementing a mode strategy with further modes indicate that decision makers tie further growth to mode combinations. It could, however, also indicate the difficulty of releasing themselves from existing partnerships. Only through mode combinations can the transition be gradually made.

Overall, the survey participants explain the switch of foreign operation mode with their attitude towards the business in their most important foreign market. Expanding business, gaining stronger customer orientation, improving cooperation with a foreign sales partner or having more control, all point to a vision that is eager to meet the challenge of internationalisation. Proactive attitudes seem to dominate; there is a positive attitude towards the potential need for adjustment. The added value achieved by a mode switch is deemed as being higher than potential costs arising through the switch. It is feasible that this is the case with companies possessing extensive experience in internationalisation, a vast network and know-how.

Figure 8.2 shows a conceptual drawing on the degree of satisfaction as the main reason for mode switching.

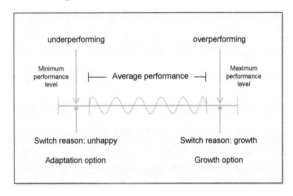

Figure 8.2: Reasons for switching – Degree of satisfaction

With regard to the dominating reasons for switching or not switching according to the reasons thus far, the level of satisfaction seems to be of importance. From the perspective of the companies surveyed, this can mean that if performance in the foreign market lies over the average expectations (over-performing), a switch will take place. Here, the main driver for a mode switch is the aim to take further advantage of potential through future growth. Performance may also lie below expectation (under-performing). In these cases, a high level of dissatisfaction with the results thus far is what creates a strong desire to switch.

In reference to the initial proposition (see Chapter 3), it can be assumed that satisfaction with performance thus far bears a decisive influence on the probability of a switch.

Additionally, non-switchers are retrospectively more satisfied with the selected mode of market entry (1.65 as opposed to 2.47, $p > 0.001$) than companies which have switched (Table 7.10). Therefore, and based on the results of Chapter 7.6, a partial alternative research hypothesis (H_1) can be given:

H_1: *Satisfaction about market entry strategy is correlated to the probability of a mode switch.*

Nevertheless further evidence is needed to explain the influencing factors on switch probability, as presented in Chapter 8.4, 8.5 and 8.12.

8.4 Mode Strategy and Performance

Performance of non-switcher vs. switcher

With regard to mode switches, the question of whether mode switching influences performance is of interest and whether mode-switchers are more successful than non-switchers.

As main indicators, satisfaction with market entry, satisfaction with the foreign market today and the turnover achieved in this country in comparison to the foreign business turnover were analysed in respect to the individual mode strategy for non-switchers and for switchers.

For measuring performance, the following three measures have been used: degree of satisfaction with entry mode (1=very good, 5=bad), degree of satisfaction with performance in the selected foreign market (1=very good, 5=bad) and share of turnover in the foreign country in % of overall export turnover.

Table 8.6 shows the differences between perceived performance by the interview partners and the share of turnover as percentage of export turnover for the current mode for switchers and non switchers.

The results show no significant differences on the performance measures between the different mode strategies and non-switcher vs. switcher.

Table 8.6: Mode strategy and performance: non switcher vs. switcher

Mode strategy		Satisfaction at market entry (1 very good, 5 bad)		Satisfaction with foreign market (1 very good, 5 bad)		Country Turnover in 2006 (in % of export turnover)	
Non switcher (market entry strategy = current mode)							
Direct Export with own sales person	Mean	1.61		2.72		5.38	
	SD of Mean	.216		.211		1.75	
Direct Export without middleman	Mean	1.88		2.38		8.74	
	SD of Mean	.125		.420		3.58	
Agents	Mean	1.42		2.17		2.61	
	SD of Mean	.193		.322		.715	
Importer	Mean	1.59		2.33		13.16	
	SD of Mean	.170		.214		8.05	
Joint Venture	Mean	1.00		2.00		/	
	SD of Mean	/		/		/	
Subsidiary	Mean	1.50		2.64		53.15	
	SD of Mean	.139		.289		32.33	
Acquisition	Mean	3.50		2.00		46.50	
	SD of Mean	1.500		.000		13.50	
Others	Mean	2.00		2.80		4.02	
	SD of Mean	.000		.374		1.90	
Total	Mean	1.65		2.46		16.60	
	SD of Mean	.087		.110		6.10	
Anova		F=2.390	P=0.029	F=0.592	P=0.760	F=1.522	P=0.187
Switcher (current mode)							
Direct Export without middleman	Mean	2.44		3.00		3.22	
	SD of Mean	.412		.408		.81	
Agents	Mean	3.00		2.75		2.03	
	SD of Mean	.408		.479		1.32	
Importer	Mean	2.11		2.11		7.62	
	SD of Mean	.261		.200		4.92	
Joint Venture	Mean	2.75		3.00		1.80	
	SD of Mean	.629		.577		.95	
Subsidiary	Mean	2.64		2.11		9.33	
	SD of Mean	.201		.157		2.88	
Acquisition	Mean	2.33		3.00		4.36	
	SD of Mean	.882		1.000		.95	
Multimode, without subsidiaries	Mean	2.18		2.47		5.55	
	SD of Mean	.287		.229		2.44	
Multimode, with subsidiaries	Mean	2.15		2.69		9.39	
	SD of Mean	.373		.208		3.22	
Others	Mean	3.75		3.00		8.10	
	SD of Mean	.479		.000		4.43	
Total	Mean	2.47		2.48		6.99	
	SD of Mean	.120		.098		1.22	
Anova		F=1.240	P=0.286	F=1.736	P=0.102	F=0.546	P=0.818

Note: SD of Mean: Standard Error of Mean

From the perspective of the performance today, however, non-switchers and switchers barely differ in their perception (2.46/2.48). Today, non-switchers present markedly higher dissatisfaction with the operation mode than as at market entry. No differences between modes could be observed. With the exception of acquisition, satisfaction with all modes of non-switchers had declined. From the perspective of the switchers, no uniform picture was observed. Satisfaction with market operation with agents and subsidiaries improved in comparison with the previously employed mode, while satisfaction with all other modes declined or remained the same.

These observations could give first indications that non-switchers already found the "right" strategy for market entry at the beginning. Over the course of time, this high, initial satisfaction changes negatively without any mode switch. Switchers, on the other hand, set the entry strategy but switch from it when the conditions change or when targets are not being reached.

For the two most frequently employed market-entry strategies of importer and direct export with own salesman, an interesting picture of the development of satisfaction becomes apparent. Firms which had first been highly satisfied with the market-entry strategy of direct export with own sales person are markedly less satisfied with the then-selected mode. The same applies for the importer. With this mode also, the satisfaction of non-switchers has significantly decreased.

In their strategies for market operations, switchers and non-switchers seem to markedly differ. Switchers employ mode combinations; non-switchers concentrate on single modes. Possible reasons for this could lie in the difficulty of separating from partnerships and the accompanying necessity to temporarily integrate new modes in existing structures in the case of a switch. The observed combination of importer with the operation mode of subsidiary is to compensate for possible problems resulting from the change of strategy. Further reasons for the combination of mode strategies are the use of various developments in the dominating sales channels of the country. On the other hand, and in particular at market entry, unclear market conditions, low volumes and the not-yet clearly recognisable sales structures do not justify the use of multiple mode strategies with the result that only single modes are employed.

Switchers are also characterised by a high share of subsidiaries and mode combinations. Non-switchers prefer importers and export with own sales personnel (more integrated/show more commitment).

A further interesting observation is that countries in which no switch has been made will have higher significance in the export share than countries in which the foreign operation mode was switched after market entry (16.6% export share, as compared to 7%). Non-switchers achieve the highest turnovers with export, either with own sales personnel or through direct export without middlemen. Switchers, on the other hand, achieve the highest turnover through mode combinations with subsidiaries.

For assessing the success measurements, it must be considered that country satisfaction and turnover share are influenced not only by the mode but by a plethora of other factors including intensity of competition, product- and offer strategy, personnel selection and sector development. The complex influencing mechanisms of these additional factors could at least partially explain the lack of significance. The sample sizes for some modes are small which could also explain this lack of significance. With a low number of cases, there must be high absolute differences. Finally, a perception-based assessment of satisfaction can lead to a distortion of complex subject-matter.

Current mode and performance
Success is a measurement for the activity of a firm in general and in its foreign markets. With regard to mode switches, the question of whether one particular mode or a mode combination is particularly successful is of interest. For measuring success, first the satisfaction of the management with the success of internationalisation in the selected country is discussed and the turnover in this country is determined in comparison to the total foreign business turnover.

With the use of cross tabulation, the individual mode strategy in the most important foreign market is first set in comparison with the subjective satisfaction evaluation of the respective country. Then significant differences in satisfaction for the two groups

(Poor/Good) are examined in relation to the individual modes currently being employed. The original measurement with five-point scale (1=very good to 5=bad) was reduced to a two point scale: 1, 2 and 3 called good; 4 and 5 called poor.

Table 8.10 shows the current mode and the degree of satisfaction for the selected country. The figure shows the absolute number of modes used and the two categories of satisfaction about the result in the respective country. The two groups of "poor" satisfaction and "good" satisfaction are given. With regard to the two groups, there are no significant differences.

Table 8.7: Current mode and country satisfaction (N=178)

Current mode or mode combination	Country Satisfaction		Total N (%)
	Poor N (%)	Good N (%)	
Subsidiary	6 (14%)	37 (86%)	43 (24,2%)
Importer	3 (9,1%)	30 (90,9%)	33 (18,5%)
Multi-mode, without subsidiary	2 (10,5%)	17 (89,5%)	19 (10,7%)
Direct Export, with salesman	4 (22,2%)	14 (77,8%)	18 (10,1%)
Direct Export, without middleman	3 (17,6%)	14 (82,4%)	17 (9,6%)
Agents	2 (12,5%)	14 (87,5%)	16 (9%)
Multi-mode, with subsidiary	2 (15,4%)	11 (84,6%)	13 (7,3%)
Joint Venture	2 (40%)	3 (60%)	5 (2,8%)
Acquisition	1 (20%)	4 (80%)	5 (2,8%)
Others	1 (11,1%)	8 (88,9%)	9 (5,1%)
Total	26 (14,6%)	152 (85,4%)	178 (100%)
Anova	$F = 0.0879$	$P= 0.545$	

Note: This table includes switcher and non switcher

The subjective satisfaction assessments in relation to the currently employed mode show, overall, predominantly positive satisfaction values (85.4%) with regard to the most important foreign market. Of note here is that the assessment applies for all modes regardless of whether or not a switch has been made. With regard to the employed mode strategies, subsidiaries and importers were employed particularly often. For countries in which these strategies are employed, a particularly high degree of satisfaction was expressed by the companies surveyed (86% or 90.9%). Viewed in absolute terms, however, the countries with subsidiaries had the most frequent poor satisfaction values. It is also interesting that, frequently, mode combinations not employed for market entry are currently employed with predominantly positive satisfaction assessments. Joint ventures and acquisition are less frequently employed. Countries in which a joint venture is employed have, in relation, the most negative assessments.

Although 24.2% of the companies frequently choose subsidiaries as a single mode in the course of the internationalisation process (43 cases) or in combination with other modes (13 cases), the assumption cannot be made that this is the ideal mode with regard to the selected performance measurements and for assessment of the market operation. Also the mode of "importer" (33) is employed by 18.5% of the analysed sample as a final mode – the results on country satisfaction, however, show no significant differences. It may therefore be established that the assessment of satisfaction cannot be related to the operation mode.

In conclusion, it can be established that no significant influences of the operation mode on the success measurements of country satisfaction and relative country turnover could be established looking at the entire sample of switcher and non-switcher.

Therefore the initially formulated alternative hypothesis (H_2) can only be rejected:
  H_2: *Specific modes are more successful than others.*

8.5 Influence of corporate characteristics on performance

The characteristics presented in Chapter 7.3 for assessing the management style and the dividing factors of Growth factor, Mode factor, Risk factor and Specialist factor (previously defined in Chapter 7.4) are to serve as indicators. As specific company-relevant indicators – international experience, size of the company in the foreign market and turnover in the foreign market, can serve further indicators. For measuring company experience, the number of years in foreign business is used. For assessing the size of the company, the number of employees in the foreign market and the foreign turnover are used.

The dependent variable is the current company success in the selected foreign market. The company success is determined in the form of the relative country turnover against the export turnover, and the degree of satisfaction with the business in the selected country.

To analyse the influencing factors, the Pearson correlation test is used to find directions, strengths, and significances between pairs of corporate characteristics and management attributes.

Table 8.8 shows the correlation of corporate characteristics and the attributes of managerial style with country performance (turnover share).

Table 8.8: Descriptive correlation for corporate characteristics and country performance (turnover share)

Corporate Characteristics		Sales % of most important country of total export (Ln_PerrexpRatio)	
		Correlation	Sign.
Company figures			
Company in international business	Number of years	0.013	-0.109
International employees	Number of employees in foreign business	0.876	0.174
Managerial style			
Strategic planning	Planned strategy vs. luck and unexpected opportunities	-0.161	0.048**
Attitude towards risk	Risk averse vs. risk taker	0.096	0.242
Standardisation vs. differentiated approach	Standardised concept vs. individual concept	-0.003	0.968
Direction	Reduction of international activities vs. expansion of international activities	0.244	0.003***
Process	Incremental approach vs. ad-hoc approach	0.076	0.353
Rhythm	Continuous homogenous rhythm vs. discontinous rhythm of switch	0.159	0.053
Speed	Slow vs. fast changes	0.107	0.188
Intensity	Within mode switch vs. between mode switch	-0.007	0.934
Number of modes	Single mode vs. multi mode per country	-0.149	0.067
Mode strategy	Single mode strategy vs. multi mode strategy	-0.100	0.221
Factor influence			
Growth factor	Reduction of international activities vs. Expansion of international activities Slow vs. fast changes	0,172	0,036**
Mode factor	Single mode vs. multi mode per country Single mode strategy vs. multi mode strategy	-0,224	0,006***
Risk factor	Incremental approach vs. ad-hoc approach Risk averse vs. Risk taker	0,125	0,131
Specialist factor	Continuous homogenous rhythm vs. discontinous rhythm of switch Standardised concept vs. individual concept	0,106	0,201

Notes:
a) Detailed description of the indicators selected in Chapter 4.8 and 7.4.
b) * p < 0.1, ** p < 0.05, *** p < 0.01 (all two-tailed tests)

The analysis of influencing factors for corporate characteristics and management style with regard to country performance yields the results for the factors strategy (p=0.048) and direction (p=0.003). Weak significance is shown for rhythm (p=0.053) and number of modes (p=0.067). For country performance, the test for growth (p=0.036) and mode (p=0.006) also gave significant results.

The factors strategy, direction, rhythm and number of modes are significant influencing factors for country performance. Here, the significance of strategic planning to the success in foreign business is apparent. Companies which consciously select their internationalisation strategy and rely on a systematic strategic development are more successful with foreign business than companies which do not do this and who wait for coincidental opportunities. It is no surprise here that the international expansion significantly influences success with the foreign business as a fundamental driving force. It shows that international expansion more strongly influences performance than the reduction of foreign activities.

Also interesting is the influence of the time-related rhythm of international activities. In this result, the demand for a company's flexibility is expressed with regard to foreign activity. Depending on the requirements, changes are undertaken in the market operation at various time intervals without the organisation and management being overburdened. The number of modes employed per market has little signifigance. Particularly in highly dynamic segments, it may be necessary to employ not only one mode but several modes simultaneously in order to participate in attractive developments.

It should be established that there is no indication of the influence of the speed of internationalisation, the level of standardisation of the strategy or the intensity of resource allocation on the switch of foreign operation mode. Also, no significant differences could be found with regard to perception of risk.

There are also no indications of the significance of the duration of international presence, and thereby international experience and number of employees in the foreign market. At least, no significant differences could be found.

This means that for differentiating between variously successful companies, information on strategy, direction, rhythm and number of modes is particularly useful.

As a further measurement criterion, the assessment of the management can serve as a subjective judgement of their success in the foreign market. Table 8.9 shows the correlations for corporate characteristics and for the attributes of managerial style with country satisfaction.

The analysis of influencing factors of corporate characteristics with regard to country satisfaction yields the results for Number of Employees in international business (p=0.021), Turnover Export in 2006 (p=0.002) and Export ratio (p=0.039).

Firms with a higher number of employees in the foreign market and higher export rates are more satisfied with their foreign activities than companies with fewer employees and lower export rates.

There are no significant differences with regard to the influence of international experience on the level of satisfaction.

The measurement of the attributes of the management styles show significant influence of strategy, (p=0.015), standard (0.007), speed (0.015) and growth (p=0.025). Weak significance is shown for specialist (p=0.054).

Table 8.9: Descriptive correlation for corporate characteristics and country satisfaction

Corporate characteristics	Degree of Satisfaction - Mean		Diff.	Sign.
	Satisfied	Not satisfied		
Company figures				
Number of years of the company in international business	34.41	34.85	0.438	0.924
Number of employees in international business	231.26	59.22	-172.042	0.021**
Export Turnover in 2006	40.901	14.638	-26.2631	0.002***
Export ratio	46%	34%	-0.11937	0.039**
Managerial style				
Planned strategy vs. luck and unexpected opportunities	-1.37	-0.44	0.922	0.015**
Risk averse vs. risk taker	-0.56	-0.70	-0.144	0.645
Standardised concept vs. individual concept	1.55	0.48	-1.072	0.007***
Reduction of international activities vs. expansion of international activities	2.31	1.96	-0.346	0.174
Incremental approach vs. ad-hoc approach	-1.33	-1.15	0.179	0.651
Continuous homogenous rhythm vs. discontinuous rhythm of switch	1.3	1.04	-0.261	0.362
Slow vs. fast changes	0.17	-0.63	-0.803	0.015**
Within-mode switch vs. between-mode switch	0	-0.04	-0.038	0.902
Single mode vs. multi-mode per country	-0.69	-0.26	0.432	0.305
Single-mode strategy vs. multi-mode strategy	1.07	0.52	-0.555	0.152
Factor influence				
Growth factor	0.0593	-0.4152	-0.4745	0.025**
Mode factor	-0.0234	0.1317	0.1551	0.474
Risk factor	0.0279	-0.0897	-0.1177	0.585
Specialist factor	0.0534	-0.3579	-0.4114	0.054**

Notes:
a) Satisfaction was grouped from satisfaction level 1 very good until 3 ok
b) Dissatisfaction was grouped from satisfaction level 4 bad and 5 very bad
c) The attributes of managerial style are the result of a bipolar scale from -3 to +3
d) The identified factors are the result of the factor analysis from Chapter 7.4
e) * $p < 0.1$, ** $p < 0.05$, *** $p < 0.01$ (all two-tailed tests)

Strategic planning, however, showed significant influence. Companies which systematically planned their foreign business were more satisfied with the achieved results. Clearly higher satisfaction levels are achieved with individually, adapted strategies and approaches. With regard to the factor speed, companies which drive and develop internationalisation faster are more satisfied. The factor growth achieves higher satisfaction levels with companies which quickly expand their foreign operations. The factor specialist considers the influence of market-oriented actions on the level of satisfaction. Firms which carry out mode switches in response to irregular necessities in the foreign market, and which rely more on individual concepts, achieve higher satisfaction levels.

No indications of any influence on satisfaction between international experience and the number of employees can be found. There are also no significant differences with regard to risk perception, the process of the switch and resource allocation.

In summary of possible indicators on success (measured by the relative turnover share in the foreign market and the level of satisfaction), it becomes clear which attributes have a significant influence and which do not. For example, the results show that with strategic planning, not only a higher level of satisfaction can be achieved but also objectively better results.

The initially formulated alternative hypothesis (H_3) can be confirmed.

H_3: *Systematic decision-making to switch modes has a positive influence on international success.*

The results for the other indicators show a non-uniform picture. With regard to the initial hypothesis, it can, however, be assumed that certain company-specific characteristics are associated with success in the foreign market.

The initially formulated alternative hypothesis (H_4) can therefore partially be confirmed.

H_4: *Firm specific characteristics are associated with international success.*

8.6 Mode management and performance

The invested resources and strategies reflect the internationalisation process in the form of a strategic basic alignment. The question arises as to the effects of these activities on company success. In this section, and with the use of the mode clusters as an indicator, the effect on success of various strategies and resource applications is evaluated. The groups identified in Chapter 7.3 (C 1 to C 5) represent various typologies of strategy, resource allocation and behaviourisms in the market operation.

Measurement of country satisfaction with export business as a performance indicator was first collected with a five-point scale (1=very good to 5=bad) which was later reduced to a two-point scale (good: 1 very good to 3 satisfactory and poor: 4 ok to 5 bad). The effect of the switch on the identified clusters follows. Measurement criteria for this are the satisfaction assessments in the selected foreign market.

Table 8.10 shows the degree of satisfaction for the most important foreign market in respect to the identified five clusters. The results show no significant differences.

Table 8.10: Mode cluster and country satisfaction (N=176)

Mode Cluster	Country Satisfaction		Total
	Poor	Good	
1 Domination	6 (18%)	28 (82%)	34 (19%)
2 Low resources	8 (23%)	27 (77%)	35 (20%)
3 Control	5 (18%)	23 (82%)	28 16%)
4 Balanced	5 (13%)	34 (87%)	39 (22%)
5 Selective	1 (2,5%)	39 (97,5%)	40 23%)
Total	25 (14%)	151 (86%)	176 (100%)

Note: Using the binomial test there are no significances at the 5% level.

The observed cases do, however, present an interesting indication of a general high level of satisfaction with the result of the selected foreign market. Companies in Cluster 5 perceive the highest satisfaction, whereas Cluster 2 perceives the lowest satisfaction compared to all of the other clusters.

In Table 8.11, satisfaction with foreign business (in general) is presented according to the five clusters. The results show no significant differences.

Table 8.11: Mode cluster and satisfaction with international business (N=178)

Mode Cluster	Satisfaction with international business		Total
	Poor	Good	
1 Domination	8 (23%)	27 (77%)	35 (20%)
2 Low resources	14 (40%)	21 (60%)	35(20%)
3 Control	9 (32%)	19 (68%)	28 (16%)
4 Balanced	13 (33%)	27 (67%)	40 (22%)
5 Selective	10 (25%)	30 (75%)	40 (22%)
Total	54 (30%)	124 (70%)	178 (100%)

Note: Using the binomial test there are no significances at the 5% level. The discussion of the results for satisfaction are based on the relation between high satisfaction and low satisfaction, and only secondarily on the absolute frequency of the cases.

The best satisfaction results for the foreign business were achieved in Clusters 1 and 5; the poorest were found for Cluster 2. In contrast to the satisfaction assessment for the most important foreign market, the firms were less satisfied with their assessment of foreign business in general.

From the collected data, it becomes apparent that none of the identified clusters significantly differs from the others in terms of better results. It can therefore be established that certain patterns exist, but no dominating strategy can be identified. Some observed differences are, however, important to discuss.

Companies from Clusters 1 and 5 are particularly satisfied with the results of their foreign business. Cluster 1 represents larger companies with a higher number of foreign markets. For these companies, the international expansion is of very high importance. As a mode, subsidiaries are predominantly employed. Companies in Cluster 5 predominantly employ importers for market operation, prefer standardised concepts and can be classified as risk-averse. The subjective satisfaction assessment is based on a good relationship between benefit and expense/effort. Cluster 3 companies predominantly work with own sales personnel in combination with other forms of direct export. They are traditional and adapt their strategies to the requirements in the countries. The fact that they have the lowest level of satisfaction, however, might indicate a need for adjustment.

In Table 8.12, the satisfaction improvement is presented according to the five clusters in their averages for the specific country. The results present no significant differences.

Table 8.12: Performance improvement of mode switch for mode cluster

Mode Cluster	Change in satisfaction (N=79) – Mean (1 very good, 5 bad)	
1 Domination	1.4737	
2 Low resources	1.2308	
3 Control	1	
4 Balanced	1.5238	
5 Selective	2.2143	
Total	1.5063	
Anova	F = 1.233	p=0.304

There are, however, indications that mode switching creates value because improved performance can be achieved (Chapter 8.7). The observed cases show that Cluster 5 achieves a markedly higher improvement of satisfaction than all other clusters.

The annual turnover growth after mode switching (cp. Chapter 8.7, for operationalisation performance measurement see Table 4.6) shows no significant differences.

The satisfaction improvement for mode switching in the most important foreign market is shown for the five clusters in Figure 8.3. The results present no significant differences.

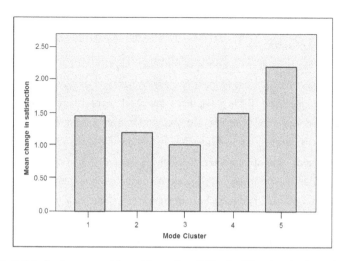

Figure 8.3: Satisfaction improvement (mean) for mode switching for different mode clusters in the most important country

t-Test for improvement between one and two switches show no significant results either (Change in satisfaction: 0.496)

With regard to these results, it can be established that specific patterns can be identified. As regards effects on company success, however, it was shown that successful market operations or export business could be undertaken with every cluster. No dominating patterns with regard to the effects on company success could be found. To what extent the individual clusters are responsible for increased performance is an important aspect for further research.

8.7 Mode switching performance

Mode strategy of switchers

The current foreign operation modes of the switchers (N=95) are shown. This is the mode which is achieved after at least one switch from the market-entry strategy and which is currently used. If the companies switched several times, the most recent mode selected was chosen for the analysis (the current mode). Single modes were taken into consideration as well as multi-mode combinations. With single modes, market operation was undertaken exclusively via a single, specific form (e.g. subsidiaries), while with multi-modes various modes were employed simultaneously (e.g. subsidiaries and importer). To elucidate the significance of subsidiaries, the presentation is made as single mode and multi-mode in combination with other foreign operation modes. Multi-mode combinations are divided according to modes with, e.g. importer with or without subsidiary or e.g. importer and direct export with sales person.

In Table 8.13 the distribution of the current modes among the sample companies is shown.

Table 8.13: Distribution of current modes

Current Mode	Frequency	Valid Percentage
Subsidiary	30	31.58%
Multi-mode combination, without subsidiaries	19	20.00%
Multi-mode combination, with subsidiaries	13	13.68%
Importer	9	9.47%
Direct export, without middlemen	9	9.47%
Agents	4	4.21%
Joint Venture	4	4.21%
Acquisition	3	3.16%
Others	4	4.21%
Total	95	100

Subsidiaries stand out as the clearly favoured single mode, appearing as a kind of target mode for almost 32% of all switches. In combination with other modes, the share of subsidiaries even lies at 45%.

Multi-modes as a simultaneous combination of modes are used in almost 34% of all switchers. It can be observed that 20% of the companies employed multi-modes without subsidiaries while in 14% of the cases subsidiaries were employed simultaneously with other modes.

Both direct export without middlemen and importers were employed as a current mode in 9.4% of the cases. Agents, joint venture or acquisition were the current modes in only three and four cases, respectively.

When the target mode is compared to the selected market-entry strategy, a clear intensification of resources and commitment becomes apparent. For the market-entry strategy, strategies with a low level of commitment and resource allocation dominate (1. importer 27%, 2. direct export without middlemen 19% and 3. agents 16.5%). This shifts, however, with one or several mode switches from a low-level resources strategy to the strategy of a subsidiary involving a high degree of commitment and resource allocation. Sales Office/Affiliates/Subsidiary seems for many companies to be an attractive form of foreign operation mode, achieved via various intermediate steps.

The frequency of mode combination as a final/current mode shows the flexibility with which the initial market-entry modes were developed. For example, the market-entry strategy of importer was supplemented by a subsidiary so that the importer's business could be gradually taken on and an independent operation could be carried out. The previous partnerships could not be switched without significant efforts. In addition, the management wanted to prevent turbulence on the market caused by the separation from the partner. Further reasons for mode combinations can lie in a more efficient market operation through presence in several sales channels or market segments at the same time. Depending upon the competence and strategic emphasis of the employed partnerships, mode combinations can, in their scope, achieve value-adding activities. The agent can primarily concentrate on extending the customer network while the subsidiary carries out training and service measures.

Mode switching performance

In this section the effect of the last switch to reach the current mode on company performance is analysed. As reference points, the various modes in the most important country market of the respondents were taken.

To equate this to performance, four measurements were used:

1. Immediate Turnover Growth – taken as the ratio of turnover three years after the switch to the turnover one year before the switch $((T_3-T_{-1})/T_{-1}$, assessed if growth ratio is >1)

2. Long-Term Turnover Growth by Year – the ratio of the current turnover (in 2006) to the turnover one year before the switch. This was also computed by dividing this ratio by the number of years since the switch $((T_{2006}-T_{-1})/T_{-1}/$number of years)

3. Immediate Satisfaction Improvement – the difference between satisfaction with performance in the country three years after the switch and satisfaction one year before the switch (Satisfaction 3y – satisfaction –1y).

4. Long-Term Satisfaction Improvement – the difference between current satisfaction with performance in the country (in 2006) and satisfaction one year before the switch.

The mean-performance measures of the different modes are displayed in Table 8.14.

Table 8.14: Current mode and mean performance measures(for switchers only)

Mode	N	Immediate turnover growth[1]	Immediate satisfaction improvement[2]	Long term turnover growth by year[3]	Long term satisfaction Improvement[4]	Time since last mode switch (year)
Subsidiary	30	9.21	1.83*	2.09	1.57*	10.53
Multi-mode, no subsidiary[5]	19	2.88*	0.90	0.74	0.24	5.26
Multi-mode, with subsidiary[6]	13	5.60	1.25*	2.63	0.08	6.85
Importer	9	2.67	2.00	1.21	1.50	8.56
Direct Export, without middlemen	9	2.77*	2.00*	0.96	0.43	5.33
Agents	4	5.60	3.67*	1.75	2.67*	1.50
Joint Venture	4	5.00	0.00	3.50	0.00	0.75
Acquisition	3	1.94	1.67	0.57	1.00	8.00
Others	4	6.42	1.33	1.27	0.33	9.00
Total	95	5.58	1.64	1.68	0.84	7.36

Notes:
a) [1]Immediate turnover growth shows the mean ratio three years after the switch
b) [3]Long term turnover growth shows the mean ratio by year
c) [2, 4]Valuation of satisfaction with the results of the mode performance was based on the difference between satisfaction level (the higher the result, the better improvement in degree of satisfaction)
d) [5]Multi-mode, no subsidiary: categories of mode combinations are used, but without the subsidiary mode
e) [6]Multi-mode, with subsidiary: subsidiaries are used together with other mode combinations
f) *is $p < 0.05$ then a significant difference exist
g) Export with own sales person could not be calculated due to missing values.

For a confidence interval of 95%, the employed t-test presents significance for immediate turnover growth with multi-modes (but no subsidiary) and direct export without middleman. Both show significantly lower-than-average performance. It is interesting to note that although it is not significant, the mode choice of subsidiary far outperforms all other modes with regard to immediate turnover growth. This might explain the significant satisfaction improvement of the mode.

Direct export without middlemen and agents were also both significantly above average in terms of immediate satisfaction improvement; and both represent a rather low-risk investment approach. Significantly low average immediate satisfaction improvement was reached with multi mode with subsidiary.

Finally, significantly above-average and long-term satisfaction improvement could be achieved with subsidiaries and agents.

It is observed that for the measurements of immediate turnover growth the switch to subsidiaries perform best, followed by mode combinations with subsidiaries and "agents". Acquisition has the lowest immediate effects on turnover, followed by importer and direct exports without middleman.

For short-term satisfaction increase, "agents" show the best improvement,, followed by importer and direct export without middlemen. The lowest short term effect on satisfaction improvement is shown with the joint-venture mode and multi mode without subsidiary.

The direct turnover effect achieved with subsidiaries might be owing to the circumstance that former mode-customer contacts can be used. Leads in the existing customer network can be utilised and intensified. Subsidiaries profit from previous efforts through the initially selected market-entry strategy. As a mode, they achieve higher turnover effects after the switch than all other modes of operation. This requires, however, that the separation from the previous mode is without negative effects for future cooperation. The management responsible for switch thereby seems to be a significant success factor.

With regard to long term turnover effects (annual turnover growth), the switch to joint venture performs best, followed by multi-mode with subsidiary and subsidiary as a single mode. The lowest annual turnover effect was shown by acquisition and multi-modes without subsidiaries. With regard to long-term satisfaction effect, the switch to "agents" shows the highest improvement followed by subsidiaries; whereas the lowest long-term satisfaction was observed with joint venture and multi-mode with subsidiary.

The variation for immediate turnover growth and long-term turnover growth by year from current mode perspective are shown in Figure 8.4 and Figure 8.5.

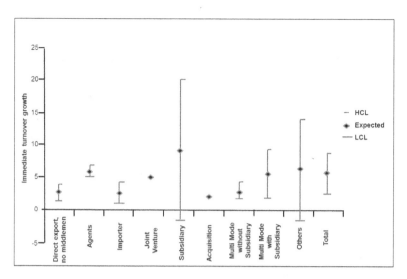

Figure 8.4: Variation of immediate turnover growth through mode switching (mean)

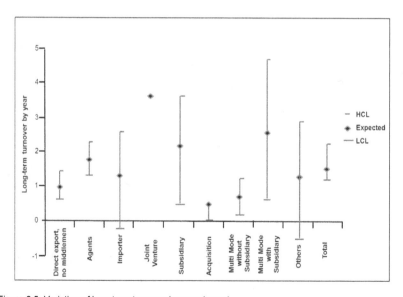

Figure 8.5: Variation of long-term turnover by year (mean)

The 95% confidence interval for the short-term turnover effects of the switch is 8.98 or 2.17 (mean value 5.58). The sample variances of the observed short-term turnover effects of the switch present, in particular for subsidiaries and mode combinations, show high variances. Extreme values for the effects of the switch are responsible for this. It could, for example, be observed that with the switch from importer to subsidiary, the turnover severely dropped in the short-term while, in another case, the replacement of an importer with a subsidiary caused a doubling of turnover. These extremes are certainly an element of business reality. However, a prognosis regarding the effect of the switch difficult to make with them.

Negative effects directly manifested in a loss of turnover and leading to a decrease in satisfaction could not be established. A possible reason lies in the survey time period of four years. Normally, companies immediately react to turnover losses and remove their causes. After a quick reaction, there is still sufficient time within four years to improve the results. A further reason lies in the fact that the internationalisation of the companies surveyed predominantly took place during phases of growth with accompanying advantageous frame conditions.

Although not all the presented results were statistically significant, certain mode performance differences could be identified. On the positive side, subsidiaries show above-average long- and short-term performance and satisfaction, as well as agent with average performance but far above-average satisfaction. Agents seem to represent the best compromise between investment risk and performance. On the negative side, multi-modes with no subsidiary and direct export without middlemen showed below-average performance. It is interesting to note that above-average immediate satisfaction improvement for direct export deteriorates strongly – probably due to the poor performance.

The success measurement for the effects of the switch resulted in at least partially significant results for the assessment of satisfaction. It can therefore be asserted that the switch to certain modes, such as agent, bears significant effects on success.

Therefore, the initially formulated alternative research hypothesis (H5) can partially be confirmed.

H5: Companies switching to single modes in one country are more successful then those switching to combination of modes.

Number of switches and performance

Now that it has been shown that a switch of foreign operation can have at least partially positive effects, there is the question of the effects of multiple switches.

The number of switches in the selected foreign market serves as an indicator. To measure performance, the changes in performance owing to the switches serve as an indicator. Changes in satisfaction and turnover are taken as the relevant measurement values.

Table 8.15 shows the changes in the satisfaction values one year after the switch in comparison to three years after the switch.

Table 8.15: Mode switching and performance improvement

Number of switches	Change in satisfaction – Mean (1 very good, 5 bad)	
1. Switch (N=96)	1.4082	
2. Switch (N=20)	2.1667	
3. Switch (N=1)	3	
4. Switch (N=1)	3	
Total	1.6032	
Anova	F=0.610	p=0.657

The analysis of variance for a significance level of 0.05 for the degree of satisfaction presents no significant differences. The subsequent Levene Test for assessing variance inhomogeneity between the first and second switch also presents no significant differences.

The results of the mean values show, in summary, an improvement of performance through the switch. The number of switches has no influence on the performance indicators assessed.

8.8   Interim conclusions: Switchers vs. Non-switchers

Though conditions clearly change after market entry and a once-selected operation mode is not necessarily optimal for the long run, it could be detected that 49% of the survey respondents did not changed their market-entry strategy. The status-quo is maintained because decision makers are satisfied with the current mode. Their perception of activities plays a significant role as does the comparison with their own experiences, expectations and intentions, and the subjective assessment of the business development of the foreign market. Companies which have switched, (51%), primarily do so in order to optimise the status quo. A switch is made because certain signals in the environment and its key actors call for such a change. In these cases, it is the motivation of the decision makers, influenced by their perceptions and interpretations of events, that seems to be decisive. Non-switchers, however, seem to be highly satisfied with the selected market-entry strategy (at least they say they are happy). A change of strategy is not necessary.

The most frequent non-switching modes are importer (N=24), direct export with own salesperson (N=19), subsidiaries (N=14), agents (N=12) and direct export without a salesperson (N=8). The most frequent switching modes from the view of the target or end mode are subsidiaries (N=30), and mode combinations with or without subsidiaries (N=13, N=19); if one groups the various modes according to the application of resources it becomes clear that, in 75% of cases, non-mode switchers currently use low-level export strategies. Such strategies are used by switchers in only 36% of cases. For non-switching companies, there seems to be no need to adjust after market entry. Switchers, on the other hand, align their initially selected market-entry strategy through a switch. Their resource allocation, engagement and commitment markedly increase after market entry, which becomes apparent in the high number of foreign subsidiaries.

With non-switchers, satisfaction with the most important foreign market is surprisingly lower than at market entry. Switchers, however, state nearly the same level of satisfaction as regards current satisfaction in comparison to the satisfaction at market entry. Only assumptions can be made as to the precise reasons for this. Non-switchers may lack alternatives with which they could carry out objective comparisons. On the other hand, increased knowledge of the foreign market can lead to a higher expectation value and thereby to a greater gap between expectation and the actually perceived performance of the mode employed.

The often-employed non-switcher mode of importer plays an important role in the sample – in particular in countries with low sales turnover. In countries with high sales turnover, however, direct export with and without middlemen, acquisitions and agents are employed. Switchers, on the other hand, take the strategy of subsidiaries in combination with other modes, and subsidiaries alone or with importers to achieve the largest single turnovers in the most important foreign market.

The reasons for the switch lie either in dissatisfaction with the partnership thus far ("under-performing") or in the expectation of a positive business development ("over-performing"). Non-switchers, however, maintain their strategies because they are satisfied or do not expect an advantage.

With regard to resource allocation and the commitment tied to this – switchers allocate more resources for market development while non-switchers rely on low-level export strategies. A comparison of the attitudes of the management regarding the internationalisation process shows that switchers tend to be more prepared to take higher risks. They are more growth-orientated, faster and consciously take risks when opportunities arise. Non-switchers are more passive and risk averse.

With regard to the corporate characteristics, such as experience in the foreign country, age of the company and export turnover, there were no significant differences between non-switchers and switchers.

A performance comparison between switchers and non-switchers does not present any significant differences. Both switchers and non-switchers can be successful in the foreign market. Also with regard to the type of mode it was shown that companies can be successful with all of the observed modes.

The assessment of the effect of the switch presented no uniform result. However, for certain modes, such as agents, it could be statistically shown that the switch had positive effects.

The various observations and types of behaviour are summarised in Table 8.16.

Table 8.16: Decision categories for non-switchers vs. switchers in the most important country

Categories	Non-switcher	Switcher
Point of reference	Most important foreign country	
Current mode used	Importer, Direct sales with own salesman and subsidiaries are mostly used	Subsidiaries and mode combinations with and without subsidiaries as main target mode
Modes gaining highest turnover	Acquisition Direct Export with salesman Direct Export without middleman Importer	Subsidiary in combination with other modes Subsidiaries Importer Mode combination (without subsidiary)
Satisfaction with entry mode	Higher satisfaction	Lower satisfaction
Reason for non-switching or switching	1. Happy with current situation 2. Not economical enough 3. Economic development in foreign market does not justify changes	1. Customer oriented & growth 2. Unhappy with partner 3. External factors
Resources and Commitment	Mainly low level export strategy (75%)	Partly low level export strategy (36%)
Dominant logic	Potential benefits one expected to be smaller than the potentially arising switching costs	Added value/benefit expected to be is greater than the potentially arising switching costs
Character	Fit between perception and expectation of decision maker about performance	To pass certain threshold of critical degree of dissatisfaction Advantageous option
Attitude	Passive, reactive mind set, risk averse	Proactive mind set, positive motivation, positive attitude towards risk
Performance	International success is not influenced by mode strategy or specific mode cluster Switching to single modes perform better than multi modes (Mode switching has an performance improvement effect)	

8.9 Pathways

In this section, the pathways of foreign operation strategies taken will be investigated. For the most important foreign market, the development of the operation strategy will be presented beginning with the entry mode and followed by the subsequent modes (Entry mode = 192 cases, Mode 1 = 98 cases, Mode 2 = 20 cases, Mode 3 = 1 case, Mode 4 = 1 case) up to the current target mode. Additionally, future mode switches will be analysed for further indications of planned mode switches. For this analysis, only cases in which a switch was undertaken are analysed. Non-switchers are not included here (N=94). For non-switchers, the market-entry strategy is the final mode.

It should be emphasised that the author first intends to document the individual cases and not formulate generalisations. The author is aware that the numbers of the identified cases after the second switch have a unique character. The intention here is to present actually observed behaviour. No more, but also no less.

From market entry strategy to first switch
As previously established, approximately half of the sample (51%) switched the selected market-entry strategy. It is then an interesting question as to which modes followed the market-entry strategy and whether certain patterns of sequential operation modes can be recognised.

First the market-entry strategy and the first subsequent mode are shown in Table 8.17.

The "Importer" mode served as the starting point for most pathways of internationalisation among the switchers (25 cases), followed by "agent" (18 cases) and "export without middlemen" (16 cases). In a total of 7 cases, "subsidiary" was the first strategy for operating in a new foreign market. Target mode for the first switch was predominantly "subsidiary" (34 cases), followed by "importer" (16 cases) and "own salesperson" (13 cases). Often a subsidiary was strived for with the first switch in order to replace the importer (in 10 cases) or the agent (in 6 cases).

313

Table 8.17: Most important entry modes and the subsequent 1st switching modes

Most important five entry modes		Most important five modes of first switch (frequency)						Total
		Subsidiary	Importer	Own sales-person	Agent	JV	Others	
Importer	repl.	10	6	1	1	1	1	25
	add.	2	1	1	0	1	0	
Agent	repl.	6	0	1	3	1	0	18
	add.	3	1	0	0	0	3	
No middle-men	repl.	2	3	3	0	2	2	16
	add.	0	1	0	2	0	1	
Own sales person	repl.	1	0	0	3	2	0	11
	add.	1	1	2	0	0	1	
Subsidiary	repl.	2	1	1	0	1	1	7
	add.	1	0	0	0	0	0	
Other	repl.	1	0	1	0	0	0	19
	add.	5	2	3	1	1	5	
Total		34	16	13	10	9	14	96

Notes:
a) repl.: means replacement - the old mode was replaced with the same or a new mode, i.e. agent replaced by subsidiary or old agent replaced by a new agent; add.: means additional - the new mode was used in addition to the old mode, i.e. importer and own salesperson
b) Answer: Only one answer was possible.

In 6 of the cases, existing importers were exchanged for new importers. In some cases, additional modes of market operation were added parallel to the previous options. This was particularly the case with agent (7 cases), importer (5 cases) and own sales personnel (5 cases). In most of the cases, an expansion of market activity was strived for via the investment of additional personal resources.

Table 8.17 presents the most frequently found internationalisation pathways for a one-time switch (Market entry, Mode 1) of foreign operation strategy.

Table 8.18: Most frequent internationalisation pathway for one-time switcher (N=96)[15]

Pathway: Entry Mode, First Switch	Cases
Importer replaced by Subsidiary	10
Agent replaced by Subsidiary	6
Importer replaced by Importer	6
Agent added by Subsidiary	3
Direct export without middlemen replaced by Importer	3
Direct export without middlemen replaced by own Salesperson	3
Own Salesperson replaced by Agent	3
Agent replaced by Agent	3

From first switch to second switch

All companies which undertook a second switch of operation mode are presented in Table 8.19 with their individual entry mode, mode 1 and mode 2.

Table 8.19: Internationalisation pathways: Entry mode, mode 1 and mode 2

Entry Mode	1. Mode	2. Mode					
		Subsidiary	Importer	Own sales person	Acquisition	Others	Total
Direct Export, with own sales person (5)	Agents	2	1				3
	Export Service Consultant			1			1
	Joint Venture	1					1
Direct Export, without middlemen (5)	Importer	3					3
	Joint Venture				1		1
	Subsidiary	1					1
Export Service Consultant (2)	Own sales person		1				1
	Importer		1				1
Agents (2)	Subsidiary	1					1
	Importer	1					1
Importer (2)	Joint Venture	2					2
Joint Venture(2)	Agents				1		1
	Direct export					1	1
Subsidiary (1)	Importer		1				1
Other (1)	Direct export			1			1
Number of switches		**11**	**4**	**2**	**2**	**1**	**20**

---

[15] The high difference (96-37=59) between the selected, particularly frequent pathways and the not listed paths results from the high number of observed individual paths. This shows that companies not only theoretically possess diverse options but also employ (in practical reality) individually various market operation modes subsequently, over the course of time.

9% of the surveyed companies switched their foreign operation mode a second time. In particular, the categories of "direct export without middlemen", "importer" and "subsidiary" were chosen (see Table 8.19 and Table 8.20). Market entry is made first without a middleman, in direct form. After a certain amount of time, an importer is then employed with the aim of having a local contact partner for intensified customer management. Cooperation with an importer is utilised to gather information about and knowledge of the market. Analysis and assessment of this information and the experience gained leads eventually to a termination of the importer's contract and the founding of an own subsidiary.

Multiple mode switches

In Table 8.20, the two cases from the sample group with three and four switches are shown along with the most frequent two-time switchers.

Table 8.20: Most frequent internationalisation pathways for multiple mode switches

Modes covered	Pathway	Cases
Entry Mode, First Switch, Second Switch (N=20)	Direct export without middlemen - Importer - Subsidiary	3
	Direct export with own salesperson - Agent - Subsidiary	2
	Importer – Joint Venture - Subsidiary	2
Entry Mode, First Switch, Second Switch, Third Switch (N=1)	Own Salesperson - Agent – Subsidiary - Subsidiary	1
Entry Mode, First Switch, Second Switch, Third Switch, Fourth Switch (N=1)	Subsidiary - Importer - Importer - Subsidiary - Acquisition	1

The three-time switch of mode took place via the pathway of "own salesperson", "agent", "subsidiary" and "subsidiary". Market entry was made first via an own area sales manager, who travelled the U.S. market for two years and then an agent employed as a local contact partner. After two further years, a subsidiary was added for commissioning and service of the systems. Two years after this, the agent's contract was terminated and an own subsidiary was founded for sales and engineering.

The four-time switch of mode via the pathway of "subsidiary", "importer", "importer", "subsidiary" and "acquisition" also occurred in the U.S. In this case, an own subsidiary was founded directly. The main motivations were the size of the country, the knowledge of approval procedures (FDA) and the intense consultation required with the medical products. After 11 years, the subsidiary was replaced by an importer, mostly all due to the high costs. Dissatisfaction with this importer led to his replacement by a new importer, who was then replaced by a subsidiary five years later. In a further strategic switch, the subsidiary was then closed after a drop in turnover and a local company was purchased.

Future mode switch

A further indication of the significance of mode switches and target modes are the statements made by the companies regarding planned mode switches in the future in this specific market. In a total of 21 cases, the companies stated that they planned on switching modes within the next four years. This would change the ratio of switchers to non-switchers from 51% to 61%. If the future target mode is observed, it is apparent that "subsidiaries" (38%) dominate as well as "export with own salesperson" (14%). One may conclude from this that a strategic change is often made from export via independent partners to an own form of market operation. The main motivations of more proximity to customers, more control and, above all, taking advantage of potential, support this assumption. It is also interesting to note that more than 70% of the companies which intend to switch in future have already changed their modes twice in the past. This might support the assumptions that experience with mode-switching bears a positive influence on readiness to undertake further switches.

Summary: Internationalisation pathway

In their internationalisation behaviour, the companies surveyed follow a process over time, which will be called pathway. In the following formula point of reference is the market-entry strategy and the subsequent modes.

$$m_{Pathway} = f\ (m_{entry},\ m_1,\ m_2,\ m_3,\ m_4\ )$$

Following the decision for market entry and a first phase of business activity, there was, in half of the cases, a switch of mode (N=96). In particular, the modes of "importer" (26%), "agent" (19%) and "direct export without middlemen" (17%) represented the starting point for the 1st switch. The first switch, "subsidiary" (35%), "importer" (20%) and "export with own salesperson" (23%) were mainly selected. Decisions revolving around market entry and mode switches are critical decisions that entail significant structural change with regard to operations on the foreign market. When these decisions are presented together, a certain pathway of action can be observed. For example, the companies frequently chose the pathway of "importer – subsidiary" (N=10). After a longer phase of stability and balance, the companies then switched modes a second time. The three-switch-pathway of "direct export without middlemen – importer – subsidiary" was, for example, chosen in three of the cases. In one case each, the mode was switched a third and fourth time.

To what extent these pathways influence foreign success can, however, not be answered here and should be subject to further research. The same applies to the assumption regarding possible influences of certain attitudes or management characteristics on the selected internationalisation pathway. This question will remain open as well.

8.10 Time related issues of mode switching

Duration until first switch

The next object of investigation is the length of time between market entry and the switch of the operation mode. Presented below in Figure 8.6 is the length of time which the initially selected market-entry strategy was switched. Following this, the length of time before the first switch is analysed from the perspective of the first target mode. And finally, the average time between the most common switching patterns are analysed.

The mean duration from entry-mode is displayed in Figure 8.6.

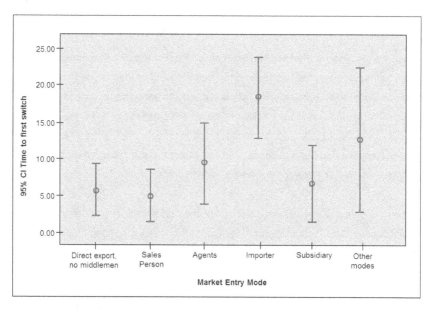

Figure 8.6: Mean duration until entry mode is switched (in number of years)
Note: ME_mode represent the most common entry mode of export without middlemen, export with own sales person, export with agents, export with importer, subsidiaries and other mode. The mean duration from market entry until first switch is given with 95%-confidence interval.

It can be established that the duration of time leading up to a switch of market entry strategy varies significantly, based on the type of the market entry strategy (ME-Mode). Switching away from importers, which is the most common market entry mode, takes the longest amount of time: 19 years on average. For the other four top entry modes, the first switch occurs on average after 5 to 10 years. The average time until the first switch is 11 years.

Possible reasons for the long maintaining of the importer mode include extensive and binding contracts with the partners which render a switch only possible on long term. Further reasons might be fears of losses, risk-aversion on the part of the decision markers, counter reactions to be expected, unclear and uncertain market conditions (resulting in little clarity and transparency regarding a market) or a change in management which bears effects over a long period of time leading up to the switch.

Possible reasons for the low dwelling time with direct export without middlemen and with own sales personnel could lie in the better quality of market information and the associated market transparency. Management increases its knowledge of market requirements and can more quickly decide on the optimal mode. Further reasons lie in the low level of binding to this mode which manifests itself in rather low switching costs. Reactions due to a business loss, by importers, are not to be expected here – this can also result in lower perceived switching costs.

When considering the destination mode of the first switch, the variations lose their significance. Only switching to a joint venture takes significantly less time, an average of 6 to 7 years, whereas all others take an average of 12 years. The underlying reason might be that the configuration of the target mode influences the time duration up until a switch to a lesser extent than the dismantling of the previous mode structures. Possible reasons could lie in the various interests of the actors tied to the previous mode structures and the resistance this involves.

With regard to the characteristics of successful internationalisation pathways, the influence of switching patterns on the duration of the selected modes will be analysed.

The findings for the four most frequent pathways for the first switch after market entry are shown in Figure 8.7.

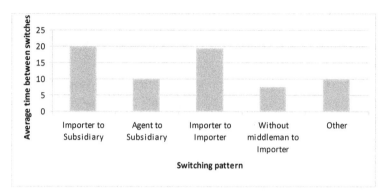

Figure 8.7: Mean duration from market entry until first mode switch for most frequent switching patterns (in number of years)

The most frequently taken pathway of "importer – subsidiary" has a mean duration of 20 years from market entry to the first switch. The pathway "agent – subsidiary" requires only half the time, and the pathway "importer – importer" requires nearly 20 years.

When considering the modes individually, there seems to be a much higher rigidity when it comes to switching from an importer than as with the other modes of operation. Having an importer as a basis for a pathway of internationalisation requires nearly twice the time to change than the other strategy options until the destination mode has been achieved.

From the perspective of the first mode switch (here target mode), however, the various modes present relatively little variations in time. This allows the assumption that, with regard to the length of time, it is irrelevant which mode is being strived for. What matters is which market entry strategy was initially selected. If, for example, a pathway begins with "importer", then the duration up until a switch is twice as high as with other forms of market entry, but this time can not be related to the target mode.

If one considers the most frequent target mode of "subsidiary", there are no significant variations in terms of time duration for the switch.

For the subsidiary mode as destination this also applies: the time depends on the previous mode.

However, with subsidiary as well it is of importance from which basis this mode is being strived for. In the sample group, there were time differences from "importer – subsidiary" and "agent – subsidiary" of over 10 years (Figure 8.7).

From these results, it seems that importers possess a higher rigidity than agents. The reasons for this could generally lie in the perception of higher switching costs. Agent relationships seem easier to dismantle because the relationship is less binding. The perceived switching costs are therefore lower with an agent than they are with an importer.

Dwelling time and performance
Furthermore, the question can be asked as to the influence of the period duration on satisfaction with market operations in the foreign market. The dwelling time in years after the time of market entry and the degree of satisfaction are examined as the main indicators.

It was examined as to whether there is a correlation between satisfaction in the most important foreign market, behaviour of the management and a switch of mode at a certain point in time. For measuring the dwelling time, the duration was formed into a six-point scale from less than one year to more than 12 years. In addition, a possible correlation between the dwelling time and satisfaction with the foreign business was analysed. Measurement of satisfaction as a performance indicator was first made with a five-point scale (1=very good to 5=bad) which was later reduced to a two-point scale (good: 1=very good to 3=satisfactory and poor: 4=ok to 5=bad).

As a test method, the Pearson correlation coefficient was used to find directions, strengths and significances in the relationship between pairs of variables and t-tests.

322

The aim is to find significant differences between means in the duration measures for the two distinct groups of satisfaction levels.

The statistical analyses however did not show significant differences between satisfied and dissatisfied companies and the dwelling time after market entry until a switch is made.

In the following two tables, the number of cases for the sample with regard to country satisfaction (Table 8.21) and satisfaction with the foreign business in general (Table 8.22) are presented.

Table 8.21: Duration after market entry until first switch and satisfaction

Duration after market entry until first switch	Country Satisfaction		Total
	Poor	Good	
0-3 years	11 (19%)	48 (81%)	59 (35%)
4-9 years	9 (11%)	72 (89%)	81 (47%)
10-12 years	1 (10%)	9 (90%)	10 (6%)
more than 12 years	2 (9.5%)	19 (90.5%)	21 (12%)
Total	23 (13.5%)	148 (86.5%)	171

Note. Using the binomial test there are no significances at the 5% level.

Table 8.22: Time after market entry until first switch and satisfaction

Duration after market entry until first switch	Satisfaction with international business		Total
	Poor	Good	
0-3 years	18 (30%)	42 (70%)	60 (35%)
4-9 years	26 (32%)	56 (68%)	82 (47%)
10-12 years	2 (20%)	8 (80%)	10 (6%)
more than 12 years	4 (19%)	17 (81%)	21 (12%)
Total	50 (29%)	123 (71%)	173

Note: Using the binomial test there are no significances at the 5% level.

The time period from market entry until the first mode switch bore, for the companies surveyed, no significant influence on the level of satisfaction. Based on the actual research subject of timing and the mode switch, the dwelling time and assumed relation to satisfaction offers no statistically significant explanation approach.

The question is whether objective indications for correct answering of the research question can even be achieved with the selected measurement values (Chapter 7.5). The measurement value of satisfaction is strongly influenced by the current mode, own expectations and individual perceptions of the internal and external situation. In the individual case, satisfaction provides interesting indications of performance. In comparison with other companies in the sample, it does not, however, give a valid picture of the opinion and behaviour. Furthermore, the measurement indicator of dwelling time in connection with satisfaction is apparently not suitable for providing an indication of time-related optimality of a certain action, such as the mode switch. Companies can switch modes both as a result of positive satisfaction and as a result of dissatisfaction.

In the alternative research hypothesis H_6 it was assumed that the decision-making period leading up to the switch influences success in the foreign country. The decision-making period is essentially defined as the time period from the first idea of a switch to the implementation (Chapter 6.1). The dwelling time is therefore the time period in which decision-making and implementation takes place.

No significant results could be found with regard to dwelling time and its influence on success (satisfaction).

Therefore, the initially formulated alternative hypothesis (H_6) has to be rejected.

> H_6: *The longer the mode switching decision process takes, the more positive the outcome is.*

Further indications regarding the question of the optimal timing of a switch can be found in the analysis of the survival times of the foreign operation modes up to the switch. This is discussed in the following section.

8.11 Time to switch foreign modes

In the following section, the question of the time to switch the market-entry strategy is explored. Using survival methods (Foster et al. 2006), the possible influence of certain sectors, countries and market-entry strategies will be analysed for their relationship to mode switching time. To predict the occurrence of such switches, the most important influencing factors will be assessed according to their survival probability (here, the maintaining of the market-entry strategy) for various sectors and country groups in a model.

In the survival analysis it will be examined how high the probability is that the companies surveyed will "survive" within the study time period without a switch of market-entry strategy. As a graphical aid for describing the events, the "survival plot" will be used. On the x-axis, the duration up to a switch of market-entry strategy (Time_to_1st_sw) and between first and second switch (time_1_to_2) are given in years. The y-axis gives the probability with which the event occurs. The event is the switch of market-entry strategy.

In the following section, the individual "survival functions" are classified by industrial sectors, countries and the market-entry strategy. Following the individual categories, the change of the risk to switch is shown within a certain time frame using the hazard function. The cumulative hazard function is the inverse of the survival curve. It gives the rate by which, to a certain time ("t"), companies "survived" without a switch to the point where they experience a change of the status quo ("momentary tendency to change status quo") and a switch of mode.

In Figure 8.8, the point in time when a switch was made is shown as well as the probability of the switch in the context of the industry sectors.

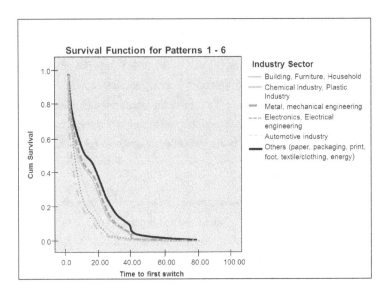

Figure 8.8: Probability to survive without switch and survival time for specific industry sectors (cumulated survival probability vs. survival time)

From the figure it becomes clear that for the sectors of Electronics / Electrical engineering and Chemical / Plastic there is a clearly higher probability of a switch of mode after market entry in comparison to other sectors. The probability that no switch of the market-entry mode is made within 20 years is approximately 0.15 for the sectors of Electronics and Chemical, 0.2 for Automotive, and 0.4 for Building. A possible reason for this could be the various sector dynamics. In sectors with traditionally lower development dynamics, there seems to be less of a necessity to switch the market-entry strategy. In highly dynamic sectors such as Electronics and Chemical the rapid adjustment of strategy and switch of market-entry strategy could be explained by these characteristics.

In Figure 8.9 the change of risk of switching a market-entry strategy is shown over time for the various industrial sectors.

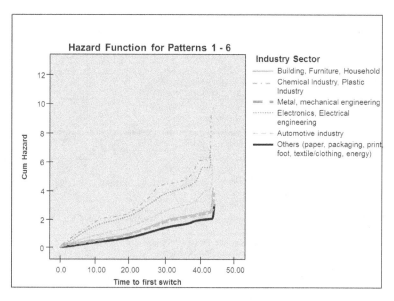

Figure 8.9: Estimation of probability to switch and switching time for selected industrial sectors

It can be established that the risk of switching the market-entry strategy after approximately 10 years is nearly twice as high in the Chemical- and Electronics sector than in the sectors Building/Furniture/Household. The risk of a switch in the Automotive Sector is higher than in the sectors Building/Furniture/Household and lower than in the sectors Chemical and Electronics.

Using the proportional hazard regression analysis by Cox (Bühl 2008), the variables are identified which influence the survival time (in this context, the maintaining of the present market-entry mode) for the sectors mentioned.
ne by using forward selection.

Table 8.23 shows the different covariates entered into the equation. The multiple regression was done by using forward selection.

Table 8.23: Predicted covariates in the equation influencing survival time

Covariates	Details
Growth factor (GF)	Reduction of international activities vs. Expansion of international activities Slow vs. fast changes
Mode factor (RF)	Single mode vs. multi mode per country Single mode strategy vs. multi mode strategy
Risk factor (RkF)	Incremental approach vs. ad-hoc approach Risk averse vs. Risk taker
Specialist factor (SF)	Continuous homogenous rhythm vs. discontinuous rhythm of switch Standardised concept vs. individual concept
Cluster (QCL)	- Cluster 1 - Domination - Cluster 2 – Low resources - Cluster 3 - Control - Cluster 4 - Balanced - Cluster 5 - Selective
Satisfaction of market entry (SatisfEntry)	Degree of market entry satisfaction (Very satisfied, Satisfied, Not satisfied)
Industry sector (Sector)	- Building, Furniture, Household - Chemical Industry, Plastic Industry - Metal, Mechanical Engineering - Electronics, Electrical Engineering (EDV, Electricity, Control, Medical instruments, Optic) - Automotive Industry (cars, lorries, supplier of parts)
Country groups (Country_group)	- Mature markets - Newly industrialised markets - Emerging markets
Market enry mode (ME_mode)	- Export without middlemen, Export with own sales person - Agents - Importer - Subsidiary - Others

Note: QCL represents beside the preferred mode strategy characteristic corporate data (e.g. size, experience, age) and the main attributes on management style.

The result shows a significant influence of the covariate Risk Factor ($p = 0.019$). For Risk Factor (RkF), the coefficient is $b = 0.266$, which means that a higher value of the covariant reduces the survival time.

Table 8.24 shows the influence of covariates on the industry sector survival.

Table 8.24: Influence of covariates on industry sector survival and omnibus tests of model coefficients

Covariates	Coefficient (b)	Standard Error	Sig.	Quality criteria
Growth factor (GF)	-.073	.152	0.632	-2 Log Likelihood: 678.304
Mode factor (RF)	-.150	.130	0.248	Chi-square: 13.604
Risk factor (RkF)	.266	.113	0.019**	P=0.125
Specialist factor (SF)	.012	.116	0.917	

Note: *p < 0.1, **p < 0.05, ***p < 0.01

The analysis of the covariate industry sector on survival probability showed no significance (p=0.125).

In Figure 8.10 the point in time at which a switch was made is visualised as well as the probability of the switch in the context of country groups.

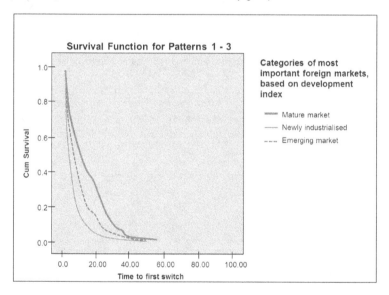

Figure 8.10: Probability to survive without switch and survival time for specific foreign markets (cumulated survival probability vs. survival time)

It is not surprising that there is a low probability of a switch of the market-entry strategy within the first few years. This applies to all foreign markets (Table 8.11). In this timeframe, the management is still giving the selected market-entry strategy time to take effect and to manifest itself. However, as of the fifth year after market entry,

329

clear differences become apparent. The probability that the company will not switch after 5 years is 0.78 in a mature economy, 0.18 in a newly industrialised economy and 0.35 in an emerging market. It can therefore be established that the selected market-entry strategy is more quickly switched in emerging markets than in mature and saturated markets. In mature markets, the companies surveyed switched very slowly. Here, the cumulative switch-probability (median survival time), which applies to half of all cases, lies at approximately 28 years. In view of the composition of the sample group and the average age of the companies surveyed (68 years), this comes as no surprise. Many German companies were already exporting to European foreign markets in the sixties; they participated in the boom phases in these markets over the course of several years. In many cases, a switch of mode was not necessary because the markets were developing positively. Market entry in newly industrialised and emerging markets, however, was made much later. The competitive environment in these countries was intense and characterised by a massive crowding out. This apparently had a much faster switch of operation mode as a result.

In Figure 8.11, the change of the risk for the switch of market-entry strategy is depicted over time in the country context.

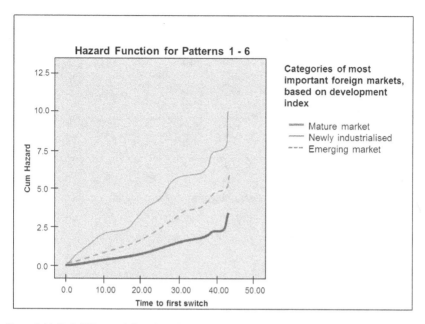

Figure 8.11: Probability to switch and switch time for selected country groups (mature, newly industrialised and emerging markets)

It can generally be established that the risk of switching the market-entry strategy increases over time. With consideration of the specific country environment, it can also be established that the risk of a switch in newly industrialised markets is nearly twice as high as in mature markets. Ten years after market entry, the risk of a switch in newly industrialised markets is nearly twice as high as in mature markets. The risk of a switch in emerging markets is higher than in mature markets, but clearly lower than in newly industrialised markets.

Table 8.25 shows the influence of covariates on country survival.

Table 8.25: Influence of covariates on country survival and omnibus tests of model coefficients

Covariates	Coefficient (b)	Standard Error	Sig.	Quality criteria
Growth factor (GF)	-.175	.153	.251	-2 Log Likelihood: 679.002
Mode factor (RF)	-.137	.120	.253	Chi-square: 14.189
Risk factor (RkF)	.187	.109	.085*	P=0.028
Specialist factor (SF)	.045	.118	.702	

Note: *$p < 0.1$, **$p < 0.05$, ***$p < 0.01$

The results of the survival analysis, however, show a significant influence of the covariant Risk Factor ($p = 0.085$). For the covariate Risk Factor the coefficient is = 0.187, which means that a higher value of the covariate reduces the survival time.

The analysis of the covariate "country" on survival probability also shows significance ($p=0.028$).

In Figure 8.12, the point in time at which the various market-entry strategies were switched is shown, as well as the probability of the switch for the individually selected market-entry strategy.

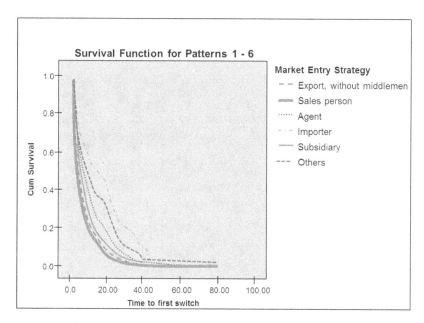

Survival Function for Patterns 1 - 6

Market Entry Strategy
- – – Export, without middlemen
- ▬▬ Sales person
- ······ Agent
- – · – Importer
- ▬▬ Subsidiary
- – – – Others

Figure 8.12: Probability to survive without a switch and survival time for specific entry modes

As can be seen in Figure 8.12, the market-entry strategy of "importer" is maintained longer than all other market-entry strategies and is not switched for a longer period of time. It becomes apparent that after ten years, the following modes survive without a mode switch: importers with a probability of 0.6, agents with a probability of 0.4, subsidiaries with a probability of 0.26, export strategy without middlemen with a probability of 0.22 and own salesperson with a probability of 0.18. For all modes, the probability then decreases over the course of market activity. The probability that the importer has not been switched after 20 years is approximately 0.38, for agents approximately 0.18 and for subsidiaries, export strategies without middlemen and own salesperson approximately 0.08. This means that for importers there is a twice-as-high probability of not being switched after market entry in comparison to agents and a four-times-higher probability in comparison to subsidiaries, export without middlemen and export with own sales personnel.

In Figure 8.13, the change of risk of switching a market-entry strategy is shown over time for the various modes.

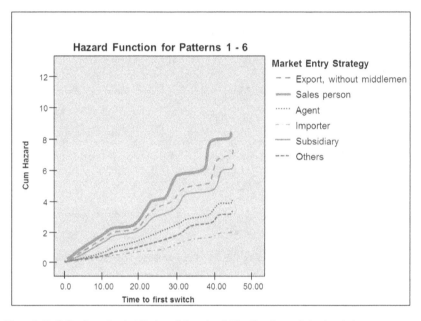

Figure 8.13: Estimation of probability to switch and switching time for market entry strategy

It seems that shortly after market entry there are already differences in the risk of a switch of mode. After 10 years of market operation, for example, the risk with own sales personnel is twice as high as in comparison to the importer. Over the course of market presence, this risk increases. After 30 years, the risk of a switch with own sales personnel is three times higher than switching importers.

Table 8.26 shows the influence of covariates on country survival.

Table 8.26: Influence of covariates on mode survival and omnibus tests of model coefficients

Covariates	Coefficient (b)	Standard Error	Sig.	Quality criteria
Growth factor (GF)	-.094	.150	.530	-2 Log Likelihood: 662.304
Mode factor (RF)	-.067	.129	.606	Chi-square: 21.208
Risk factor (RkF)	.184	.113	.103	P=0.012
Specialist factor (SF)	.002	.121	.990	

Note: *p < 0.1, **p < 0.05, ***p < 0.01

The analysis of the covariant mode strategy on survival probability show significance (p=0.012).

The results of the survival analysis, however, show no significant influence of the other covariates.

In Figure 8.14, the time between first and second switches depending on country group (mature, newly industrialised and emerging markets) is shown.

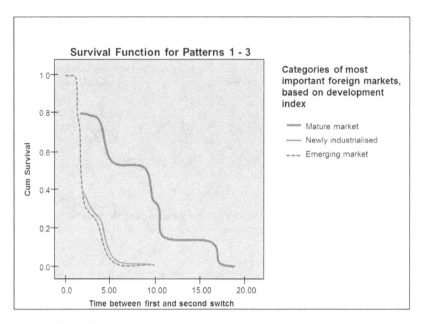

Figure 8.14: Probability to survive a second switch and survival time for selected country groups

As can be seen in Figure 8.14, there is a probability of 0.6 that a switch will not be made within five years after the first switch in a mature market. There seems to be no particular requirement to realign within the first five years after the first switch. After a further five years, however, the probability that a switch will not have been undertaken is very low at 0.2. In the other two country groups, the probability of not-switching is already very low after five years at 0.05. After ten years, there is scarcely a chance that the company would not have switched modes.

In Figure 8.15 the change of risk of a second switch after a first switch is shown for the specific country groups (mature, newly industrialised and emerging markets).

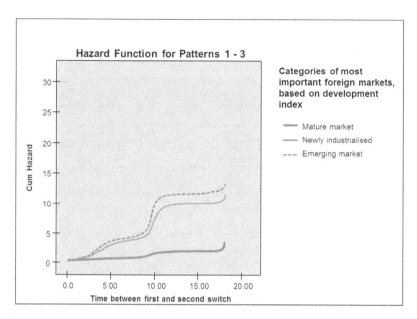

Figure 8.15: Estimation of probability to switch a second time for selected country groups

Changes in the risk of the second mode switch present differences between the three country groups. Compared to mature markets, there is a doubly high risk of a second mode switch five years after the first switch in newly industrialised economies and emerging markets. After another five years, the risk of a switch for the high-growth countries increases while it also increases for mature markets but to a significantly lesser degree in comparison to the other country groups.

Table 8.27 shows the influence of covariates for country groups on the second switch.

Table 8.27: Influence of covariates on country groups for the second switch and omnibus tests of model coefficients

Covariates	Coefficient (b)	Standard Error	Sig.	Quality criteria
Growth factor (GF)	.398	.485	.412	-2 Log Likelihood: 68.038
Mode factor (RF)	-.183	.391	.639	Chi-square: 6.929
Risk factor (RkF)	.922	.433	.033**	P=0.327
Specialist factor (SF)	.299	.360	.405	

Note: *p < 0.1, **p < 0.05, ***p < 0.01

The analysis of the covariate country group on survival probability show no significant differences (p=0.327).

The results of the survival analysis, however, show significant influence of the covariate Risk Factor (p=0.033) with the coefficient of b=0.922. This shows that companies which are more willing to take risks are more readily willing to undertake a further alignment in the form of a second switch.

It is also apparent that the second switch was made faster than the first switch (7.65 vs. 11.36 years, a significant difference at the 10% level (p=0.07). However, for the time it took between the first switch and the second switch, the difference is not statistically significant (7.65 vs. 5.55 years).

Table 8.28 shows the duration between market entry and first switch and the first switch until the second mode switch.

Table 8.28: Duration after 1st and 2nd switch occurs (in years)

Duration	All switchers	Companies with 2 switches
Time from entry to first switch	11.36	7.65
Time from 1st to 2nd switch	-	5.55

It can be established that the comparisons of the survival curves show significant differences for the selected country groups and mode strategies. After five years, a switch is made in newly industrialised markets with a more than three-times-higher probability and in emerging markets with a twice as high probability than in mature markets. A further interesting finding is a strong resistance of certain market-entry strategies in the observation period. The probability that an importer has not been switched after 20 years is two times higher than as with an agent, and four times higher than with subsidiaries, export without middlemen and own sales personnel.

The survival curves for industrial sectors, however, show no significant differences. With the exception of the "risk factor", there were no significant results for evaluating the predictability of the mode switch through selected variables.

As regards dwelling time after market entry, a critical influence of timing aspects on switching probability can be assumed with the result that alternative research hypothesis H_7 can be confirmed.

H_7: *The longer the duration/time after market entry the higher the probability to switch.*

The results also show an influence of management factors on the dwelling time after market entry. However, the significant results only refer to the influencing factor of risk. For all other factors, no significant influence could be found.

8.12 Probability of undertaking a switch

In the last section, the time period leading up to the first switch was analysed. Now, the derived factors influencing the probability of a mode switch are to be weighted using the regression approach (Backkhaus et al. 2008). The following questions are central:

- with what probability are certain modes switched?
- what influence do certain company-specific modes and groups for the management of foreign operations bear on the probability to switch?
- are there significant differences between these characteristics?

As main indicators for the analysis of the influencing factors – managerial style (Mode factor, Risk factor, Growth factor, Specialist factor), country groups, industry sector and mode strategy were selected. The indicators represent the assumed factors influencing the probability of a mode switch (or, rather, dividing factors between the two groups of non-switchers and switchers).

First the basic correlations between the assumed influencing factors of the mode switch will be determined as covariates. Then the logistic regression function will be estimated using the maximum likelihood method. The interpretation of the co-efficients, reciprocal relationships and "odds" conclude this section. An analysis of the total model and the characteristic variables conclude the logistic regression approach (Backkhaus et al. 2008).

In

Table 8.29, the results of the logistic regression for determining the probability of the first mode switch are summarised.

Table 8.29: Regression analysis on the determinants of mode switching (first switch)

Covariates	Coefficient (b)	Standard Error	Sig.	Exp(B)	Quality criteria
Growth factor (GF)	.617	.222	.006**	1.853	
Mode factor (RF)	.127	.190	.506	1.135	
Risk factor (RkF)	-.177	.205	.386	.837	
Specialist factor (SF)	.272	.191	.154	1.313	
Building, furniture, Household	1.148	.713	.108	3.151	
Chemical industry, plastic Industry	1.446	.721	.045*	4.246	
Metal, mechanical engineering	1.522	.640	.017**	4.582	
Electronics, electrical engineering (EDV, electricity, control, Medical instruments, Optic)	1.108	.670	.098	3.029	-2 Log likelihood 177.044
Automotive Industry (cars, lorries, supplier of parts)	2.551	.959	.008**	12.823	Cox & Snell R Square .257
					Nagelkerke R Square .345
Mature markets	-.296	.528	.575	.744	
Newly industrialised economy	-.977	.686	.155	.376	
Emerging market	/	/	/	/	
No middlemen	-.975	.717	.174	.377	
Sales person	-.501	.782	.522	.606	
Agent	-.237	.718	.741	.789	
Importer	-.946	.662	.153	.388	
Subsidiary	-.938	.767	.221	.391	
Satisfaction on market entry	.910	.230	.000***	2.484	

Note: *p < 0.1, **p < 0.05, ***p < 0.01

Table 8.29 shows the number of companies correctly classified on the dependent variable mode switch. 73.3 % of the mode switches can be predicted with the covariates used. The result shows a significant influence of the covariate Growth Factor (p=0.006) and Chemical Sector (p=0.045), Metal/Mechanical Engineering (p=0.017) and Automotive Sector (p=0.008). Satisfaction at market entry shows

341

significant influence as well (p=0.0001). Other covariates such as mode strategies or countries do not show any significant influence.

Table 8.30: Classification matrix of logistic regression on mode switching (first switch)

Observed	Predicted		
	Companies with 1 switch		
	Non switcher	Switcher	Percentage correctly classified
Non switcher	47	25	65.3
Switcher	19	74	79.6
Overall Percentage			73.3

Note: The cut value is 0.500

With regard to the strength and direction it can be established that the positive b-value 0.617 of the covariate "growth" indicates that an observation with a high assessment value belongs more to the group of switchers rather than the non-switchers. The situation is similar with sector classification. The positive b-values of individual sectors (Chemical, b=1.446; Metal/Mechanical Engineering, b=1.522; Automotive Sector, b=2.551) show that companies in these sectors belong to the group of switchers.

The results for the odds ratio as one measure of the association between the two variables mode strategy and switching/non-switching are interesting. For companies, the predictors of growth factor (odds ratio 1.853) and the different industry sectors, such as Chemical (odds ratio 4.246), Metal/Mechanical Engineering (odds ratio 4.582) and Automotive (odds ratio 12.823) were significantly associated with the mode switching.

On the other hand it is the high assessment value of satisfaction on market entry (b=0.910) that is another important determinant of switching behaviour of the non-switcher.

The results show that the growth factor, or the characteristics "internationalisation expansion" and "internationalisation speed", have dividing character. Correspondingly, the alternative research hypothesis H_8 which postulates that the observed variables of management style bear influence on the group division between non-switchers and switchers or switching probability can be confirmed.

H_8: *Specific management-styles pertaining to internationalisation are related to the probability of mode switching*

The results also show that the individual business environment in the foreign market plays an important role in the probability of a switch. In particular, the dynamic sectors of Chemicals, Engineering and Automotive require more alignments of market-entry strategies. The odds ratio that companies will switch after market entry is within the Chemical Industry, for example, approximately 4.2 times higher and in the Automotive sector approximately 12.8 times higher. This indicates the significance of external environmental influences within the sector, the resulting demands on the companies and the necessity of high flexibility of the management of foreign operations. It also shows, however, that not all sectors explain the switch of market-entry strategy or bear a significant influence. More traditional sectors, such as the Construction industry, do not present any significant influence between the groups of non-switchers and switchers.

Somewhat surprising is that the mode strategy bears no significant influence on the two groups of non-switchers and switchers for the first switch. The expectation that specific modes influence the probability of a switch could not be confirmed. Correspondingly, the alternative research hypothesis H_9 is to be rejected.

H_9: *There are specific modes which influence the switching probability more than other modes.*

Now that the probability of switching the market entry strategy and influencing factors on the first switch has been discussed, the question arises as to which factors influence the second switch of a foreign operation mode.

In Table 8.31 the results of the logistic regression for determining the probability of occurrence of a second mode switch are summarised.

Table 8.31: Regression analysis on the determinants of mode switching (second switch)

Covariates	Coefficient (b)	Standard Error	Sig.	Exp(B)	Quality criteria
Growth factor (GF)	.203	.444	.647	1.226	
Mode factor (RF)	.984	.450	.029**	2.675	
Risk factor (RkF)	.820	.348	.019**	2.270	
Specialist factor (SF)	-.165	.334	.620	.847	
Building, furniture, Household	-.299	1.379	.829	.742	
Chemical industry, plastic Industry	-.814	1.431	.569	.443	-2 Log likelihood 65.436
Metal, mechanical engineering	-.400	1.158	.730	.670	Cox & Snell R Square
Electronics, electrical engineering (EDV, electricity, control, medical instruments, optic)	-.046	1.226	.970	.955	.245
Automotive Industry (cars, lorries, supplier of parts)	-.985	1.547	.524	.373	Nagelkerke R Square .392
Mature markets	1.454	1.026	.157	.288	
Newly industrialised economy	2.756	1.359	.043**	.318	
Emerging market	/	/	/	/	
No middlemen	1.454	1.026	.157	4.279	
Sales person	2.756	1.359	.043**	15.730	
Agent	.255	1.128	.821	1.290	
Importer	-.810	1.091	.458	.445	
Subsidiary	-.222	1.449	.878	.801	

Note: *p < 0.1, **p < 0.05, ***p < 0.01

Table 8.32 shows the number of companies correctly classified in the dependent variable second mode switch. 85.1 % of the second switches can be predicted with the covariates used. The result shows a significant influence by the covariates Mode factor (p=0.029), the Risk factor (p=0.019), the country group of newly industrialised markets and the mode export with own sales person (p=0.043). Other covariates such as sector or other mode strategies do not show any significant influence.

344

Table 8.32: Classification matrix of logistic regression on mode switching (second switch)

Observed	Predicted		
	Companies with 2 switches		
	Non Second switcher	Second Switcher	Percentage correctly classified
Non Second switcher	74	2	97.4
Second Switcher	12	6	33.3
Overall Percentage			85.1

Note: The cut value is 0.500

With regard to the strength and direction of influence it can be established that the positive coefficient of 0.984 of the covariate "mode" factor and 0.820 of the covariate "risk" factor indicates that an observation with a high assessment value belongs more to the group of switchers than to the group of non-switchers. Companies with high mode diversity and thereby more mode experience tend to switch more than other companies. It is not surprising that companies which define themselves as risk-oriented are more likely to belong to the switchers group.

Regarding the influence of the country environment on the probability of a switch it may established that the positive b-value of the country group Newly Industrialised Economy (beta=2.756) indicates that companies in these countries rather belong to the group of switchers.

With the second switch, there are significant influences for the export strategy with own sales personnel. Regarding influence, the positive coefficient of 2.756 shows that companies which carry out foreign operations after market entry with own sales personnel are more likely to switch rather than to maintain this mode.

As regards the odds ratio, it can be established that the predictors of mode factor (odds ratio 2.675), risk factor (odds ratio 2.270) and the mode export strategy with own sales personnel (odds ratio 15.730) were significantly predictive of a second mode switch.

From the perspective of the research hypotheses, for the second switch, it can be established that certain management characteristics influence the probability of a

345

switch. With the second switch, however, know-how and mode experience are more the focus than international growth orientation. If there is mode experience in the form of various mode strategies then the probability is high that there will be a switch. If this is not the case then the mode will be maintained after market entry.

Correspondingly, the alternative research hypothesis H_8, which postulates that certain variables of the management style influence the switch, can be confirmed for the second switch.

> H_8: Specific management-styles pertaining to internationalisation are related to the probability of mode switching.

Considering the significant influences of the mode "direct export with own sales personnel", it can be established that research hypothesis H_9 might be at least partially confirmed. However, as the mode with sales personnel is only just significant at the 5% level and only for the second switch, one should be cautious about rejecting the null hypothesis 9. Overall there is insufficient evidence to conclusively accept the alternative hypothesis 9 that there are specific modes which influence the switching probability more than other modes.

In summary companies which internationally expand with a special focus on speed of growth in the foreign market are more likely to switch after market entry. Necessary environment adjustments in certain, dynamic sectors, such as Chemicals, Automotive or Engineering additionally increase the probability of a switch. The country classification to Newly Industrialised Markets also plays a significant role.

With the second switch – mode strategies, mode experience and know-how are more the focus and influence the switch. Risk-conscious managers and companies are of particular interest.

This chapter focused on the empirical evaluation of the research hypotheses by applying various quantitative methods.

With regard to the basic hypothesis, the assumption was confirmed that there is a relationship between mode switching and a company's success. A mode switch is an important option for success in foreign business. However, in the management of foreign operations, both switchers and non-switchers can be successful in the foreign country (see Chapter 8.4 and Chapter 8.6).

The question of whether the switch is worth it and increases company success showed significantly positive results with regard to short-term effects in a time period of three years after the switch (see Chapter 8.7).

The evaluation of the reasons for or against a switch shows that companies decide between two pools: "still good enough"/"not too good" or "not satisfied"/"very satisfied". A decision is made for a switch based on objective success measurements (economical aspects) and subjective assessments, judgments, preferences and valuations. Factual reports on company performance, such as country reports and perception-based assessments by managers mark the decision-making behaviour (see Chapter 8.3)

Time-critical aspects in decision-making behaviour, such as the duration of time until an opinion is formed or the speed of mode switching, showed no significant influence on company success (see Chapter 8.10 and Chapter 8.11).

Also no generalisable indications of the positive influence of certain mode strategies on company success could be identified. The same applies to the number of switches and the decision-making period as influencing factors for company success. In this sense, the success of a foreign mode operation is highly individual. No dominating success strategy could be identified (see Chapter 8.4, 8.5 and 8.6).

The probability of whether a switch will be made or not depends on specific attitudes relating to the management of foreign operations. For the first switch, international expansion and internationalisation speed dominate, as well as the influence of certain sectors, such as Automotive, and the country classification in Newly

347

Industrialised Countries. For the second switch, mode experience and know-how, as well as specific mode strategies, influence the probability of a switch.

The probability of a switch strongly depends upon the existing mode strategies. Specific modes are switched faster than others. Specific market-entry strategies are left significantly longer without adjustments. The significance of the market-entry strategy as the most important imprinting for the internationalisation process becomes very clear (see Chapter 8.11 and 8.12).

This chapter focused on the description and interpretation of the comprehensive result of the large-scale sample group of German companies and their behaviour in the management of foreign operations under special consideration of mode switching.

The focus of this chapter was the presentation of the results from the assessment of nine research hypotheses regarding the influencing factors of mode switching, timing, mode strategy and performance implication. With regard to the most important influencing factors of the switch, the decision-making process and the success in the foreign market showed significant findings.

In the following chapter, the main results will be summarised and the major contributions presented; limitations will be discussed and the most important implications for future research will be shown. The chapter closes with recommendations for management for mode switching.

Chapter 9 Core results, Limitations and Implications

Internationalisation is an important strategic option for the further development of firms. Many firms are already active in foreign markets and have successfully managed market entries. Analyses show, however, that the further development of foreign operation modes have been strongly neglected to date. The few approaches and theories on this research subject are predominantly of conceptual nature and the few empirical studies can not yet supply a uniform theoretical construct.

From this the primary aim of this study is derived: to theoretically and empirically analyse internationalisation and behaviour in the context of the mode switch. In the following, the selected conceptual methods and findings are summarised. Following this, the most important aspects of the empirical analyses will be presented and the work is placed in the context of existing research. Finally, implications for the management of foreign operations are derived and the author gives his concluding observations regarding the management of foreign operations and mode switching. The explanatory theory on foreign operation and mode switching is derived on the basis of the concept of path dependency. The aim is to create comprehensive understanding of the switch of a foreign mode between rigidity and impetus.

9.1 Conceptual results - selected theoretical results

To find a suitable theoretical basis and to explore relevant areas for examining internationalisation and mode switching a comprehensive literature review was first carried out for the three theoretical levels of internationalisation, mode switching and decision-making behaviour in the context of the mode switch. No single theory alone could answer the most important questions regarding the mode switch (Chapter 2).

It is apparent that the explanatory theories on internationalisation primarily concern themselves with the reasons and motives and also the success of the most promising market-entry strategy based on individual maximisation of profit, transaction costs and insufficient information. In the recent past, studies that focus on market exits owing to the failure of foreign market activity have added to this research area. The process-oriented theories on internationalisation, however, are more focused on the behaviour of the individual actors in the internationalisation process and thereby provide explanatory indicators regarding changes over time. With this, the more statically oriented internationalisation models of the new institutional economics and industrial economics are supplemented by the dynamic theories on international firm development. This lends the internationalisation a holistic perspective and is observed as a decision-making and learning process for the dimensions of internal and external environmental factors, change of foreign operation, structure, process and culture. The concept of path dependency with the core argument of self-reinforcing effects supplies explanatory approaches for the influence of patterns or schemes relating to past experience on today's actions.

The studies regarding important factors such as time, culture, success-factor research and performance have traditionally been focused on single aspects of internationalisation and their significance.

Based on the literature review, the decision-making behaviour relating to the switch was described and discussed on the basis of the theoretical concepts and discussed partial theories. From the identification of the most important context factors, such as switching conditions, switching barriers, switching motivators, switching cost, switching objectives and switching strategy a framework for analysis was derived for the qualitative part of the empiricism.

In summary, the literature review showed that no specific theory for analysis of the mode switch is preferred. Rather, several partial theories form the basis. Secondly, there is no established concept that explains how companies operate in the foreign country after market entry with regard to the foreign mode. Third, there is a lack of further evidence, particularly in the form of retrospective process-oriented studies which do not only derive empirical findings from exemplary case studies.

9.2 Key empirical results

9.2.1 Results from the qualitative research

For the qualitative analysis, the results of the expert interviews with 15 firms in Germany were examined (Chapter 5). In the evaluation, focus was placed on the uncovering of fundamental processes which trigger a switch of foreign operation mode and on the development of a framework for analysis for the quantitative section. With the aid of retrospective process-oriented studies, the change in behaviour ex post after market entry was documented and discussed for one significant country of the firms surveyed.

The qualitative section of this work supplies a comprehensive analysis framework for describing and evaluating the most important dimensions of the switch of foreign operation mode (Chapter 5). The process-oriented structure, beginning with the initial considerations regarding the main drivers of a switch and extending to a detailed description of the observed decision-making behaviour and the actual actions and establishment of foreign operations, promoted transparency and understanding of the research subject. The identified explanatory categories created a solid foundation and contributed important findings for the further development of the work.

The qualitative findings showed that foreign operation behaviour is influenced to a high degree by deficits in rationality. Socio-cultural, cognitive and resource based influencing factors including the positions and attitudes of the decision makers towards internationalisation and mode switching, experience with internationalisation, the mental state of decision-makers, the current interests of decision makers and key actors involved and the objectives/positions/attitudes with regard to power and risk. All these, plus further context factors, form a complex mixture of aspects amidst which internationalisation decisions are made.

Another important contribution is supplied by the analysis of the decision-making process tied to mode switching based on the phases of opinion building, negotiation and implementation (Chapter 6.1). In the first phase, decision makers formed an opinion regarding current information. At the end of the phase, a switch of mode and

351

the necessary measures are anticipated in principle. In the second phase negotiation with actors involved in both the old- and new mode follows. Adding to the ideal-typical process here is extensive discourse amongst key actors regarding interests, feasibility and the possible consequences of the switch. In the case of a positive decision, implementation follows. This can include the termination of a current partner's contract and the founding of a subsidiary with subsequent start of operations.

Based on the results, specific patterns of conceptual structuring and management of foreign operations could be identified (Chapter 6.2). Various dimensions, such as Direction, Order, Pathway, Speed, Duration and Intensity form the framework of the various options for taking action. The totality of the decisions for the individual dimension forms a characteristic profile – the strategic mode-switch profile.

The behaviour typologies identified with the aid of the critical incident method create transparency and consequently assist in an understanding of the influencing mechanisms tied to managing foreign operations (Chapter 6.3.1). It can explain how country- and sector conditions, motivation of key actors, target setting, power, barriers, feedback loops and reaction-decisions regarding the mode switch bear an influence over a longer development time.[16] The results show what kind of influences exist with regard to the mode switch and over the course of time after market entry.

The findings show that decision-making processes leading to implementation are complex, depending upon the mode context and mode profile. In certain situations, some modes seem "easier" to change than others. The reasons for this lie not only in extensive founding modalities or time-consuming terminations of contracts. The rigidity of some foreign operation modes, biases in the decision-making process, clashing interests, mental barriers, lack of experience with switches, dominating logic and persistent behavioural patterns also significantly influence the decision to switch.

---

[16] Foreign market entry analysed in the cases took place between 1980 and 1996. In the shorter period a switch was made after one year; for the longest period, a switch was made after 20 years. This indicates long development time.

A core result is the identification of evolutionary pathways and the description and subsequent discussion of seven switch-pathway patterns based on the decision-making behaviour of managers in the internationalisation process (Chapter 6.3.1). The subsequent discussion of the development pathways over the course of time shows the various styles of management and the effect of the mode decision on the development in the foreign market.

Further interesting findings resulted through the analysis of the mode-switch pathway. The 17 identified cases ascertained specific concentration on mode positions after market entry (Chapter 6.3.2). The connection of those mode positions indicate the existence of characteristic pathways that firms take for certain reasons and describes the path development based on the selected mode.

In summary, the qualitative part of the study showed that mode switching is an inherent element of internationalisation; however, it also showed that the decision to switch is highly unsystematic and seems to be a rather emergent response to specific foreign circumstances rather than a deliberate internationalisation-policy decision. This is not to say that there is no basic clarity as to the impact direction in the foreign market, but shows the kind of high flexibility with which the companies observed decide. It has become clear what kind of role certain development pathways and mode strategies play in successful foreign market operations.

9.2.2 Results from quantitative research

For the quantitative analysis, a total of 192 firms were surveyed. Before the empirical analysis is discussed, the results of the hypothesis tests are summarised in Table 9.1:

Table 9.1: Overview of hypotheses assessment on the subject of mode switching

Hyp.	Variable 1	Variable 2	Sig.	Comments
Basis Hyp.	Specific mode switching behaviour	International success	Partly sig.	see Chap. 7.4, 7.7 and 7.8.
1	Satisfaction of market entry strategy	Probability of mode switching	Yes	See Chap. 8.3 and 8.4.
2	Mode strategy	International success	No	No specific mode or mode cluster (except cluster 2, which show significant different performance) could be identified as statistically dominant strategy for success see Chap. 7.4, 8.4 and 8.6.
3	Systematic decision-making	International success	Yes	see Chap. 8.5.
4	Firm specific characteristics	International success	Partly sig.	see Chap. 7.4, 8.5 and 8.6.
5	Mode switching (Single mode switching)	International success	Partly sig.	see Chap. 8.7.
6	Length of decision time	International success	No	The observed behaviour may give a first indication that the speed of decisions has practical relevance, but to what extent it effects success in the foreign market must remain open. see Chap. 7.5 and 8.10.
7	Duration after market entry	Probability of mode switching	Yes	see Chap. 7.5 and 8.11.
8	Management style	Probability of mode switching	Yes	see Chap. 8.12.
9	Specific modes (e.g. importer)	Probability of mode switching	No	No significant influence was found on the first switch, only second switch show slight evidence at the 5%-level See Chap. 8.12.

Specific mode switching behaviour

The focus of the assessment was to describe the behaviour of the firms after market entry. To assess the dependency of company characteristics, management style and mode strategy – cluster analyses were carried out which categorised companies with the same or similar behaviour in the management of their foreign operation after market entry. This was undertaken through the assessment of specific factors (growth, risk, specialist and mode) which were divided, via a factor analysis, into (predominantly) independent dimensions (Chapter 7.4). Here, it could be established that, depending on the preferred mode structure (Table 7.7), the firms could be divided into five clusters and these clusters displayed significant differences in management behaviour (Table 7.11). A significant finding here was that (depending on their cluster assignment) the surveyed firms prefer specific mode strategies for foreign operations, something that indicates a specific mode competency (Chapter 7.8). Five clusters of characteristic behaviour in the management of foreign operations were identified (e.g. preferred mode, corporate characteristics, timing of mode decision, mode switching probability) and they were also be empirically supported (Chapter 7.4).

The evolutionary pathways after market entry were also descriptively presented based on the selected modes and assessed using the quality criteria (Chapter 8.9). Here, it was established that companies take different evolutionary pathways after market entry until they reach their current mode. This allows a quantitative confirmation of the pathways already discerned in the qualitative interviews.

Mode strategy and switching mode performance
What kind of influence the identified clusters have on the company success must remain open (Chapter 8.6). Specific patterns could be identified, but to what extent the individual clusters influenced company success could not be conclusively answered. Only Cluster 2, "low resources" with the preferred mode of direct export showed statistically significant effects on foreign-business success (Figure 7.8).

With regard to the individual mode strategies, it was noted that certain modes were used particularly frequently (Table 7.3) and that there were varying levels of satisfaction with modes being used. No mode, however, was statistically shown to be particularly successful (Chapter 8.4). A comparison of sectors showed that no specific mode could be established as particularly successful for a sector (Chapter 7.7). The same applies for the country comparison. Here, as well, no mode could be established as especially successful for a specific country.

Regarding the question of whether a company can improve its performance through a switch or not (before/after perspective), it can be established that some modes

355

achieve significantly better results after the switch than the average. For example, subsidiaries showed above-average improvement both on short- and long term. Below-average results, however, were found with multi-mode with no subsidiary and direct export without middlemen (Chapter 8.7, Table 8.14).

Regarding the question of how relevant for success the number of mode strategies in a country is, the findings show better results for single-mode strategies than for mode combinations (Table 8.14).

With regard to the effects of switching opposed to not-switching, both modes of behaviour can lead to company success in the foreign country. The finding that non-switchers are significantly more satisfied with performance than switchers is not surprising (Chapter 7.6, Table 7.10).

Furthermore the extent to which switchers differ in their management style from non-switchers was analysed. Here, significant differences in strategic planning (p=0.035), international growth (p=0.029), speed of the switch (p=0.031) and intensity of the switch (p=0.026) could be established (Chapter 7.3).

The examination of the number of switches after market entry and performance also did not present any significant differences (Chapter 8.7). The firms could have success with no switch, one switch and multiple switches.

Influence factor on mode switching
Reasons for or against a switch identified in the quantitative analysis were all to be assigned to the traditional rationality perspective, such as the means-ends relation (Chapter 8.3). Either a switch is made because the company is satisfied with performance thus far and an expansion of this positive development is expected through the switch (Growth) or a switch is made because improvement of the position is expected (Unhappy about performance) (Figure 8.2). Non-switchers do not switch because they are satisfied with performance thus far and a switch would hardly bring further positive business effects (Figure 8.2).

The influence of satisfaction as a driver of the switch resulted in significantly different results in the observation of switchers vs. non-switchers (Chapter 8.5). Non-switchers are retrospectively more satisfied with the selected mode of market entry (1.65 as opposed to 2.47, p > 0.001) than companies which have switched. Over the course of time, it could be observed that satisfaction assessments even out. The initially high level of satisfaction of the non-switcher decreases while the satisfaction assessment of the switcher remains the same. Satisfaction as a justification for the switch lies in a conflicting field between "underperforming" and "overperforming" (Figure 8.2).

The probability of whether a switch will be made or not depends upon specific attitudes of the responsible managers for the foreign operations (Chap 8.12). For the first switch, the variables of international expansion and internationalisation speed dominate, as well as the influence of certain sectors, such as automotive, and the country classification of newly industrialised country (

Table 8.29 and Table 8.31). For the second switch, mode experience and know-how influence the probability of a switch (Table 8.31). The first switch, different influencing factors are more important than as with the second switch. With the first switch, environment conditions in the country and the sector dominate. With the second switch, experience and know-how with regard to market operation is important. This indicates an adaptation of the strategy in which the market-entry strategy is adjusted to market and sector demands and, with the second switch, the strategy in detail forms the focus and is optimised.

Decision process for mode switching

The results for the subject of decision-making behaviour during the mode switch comprising the decision duration, the timing of the decision and the reasons for the switch or decision not to switch were described and assessed on the basis of the quality criteria. It can be concluded that the switch of mode in the foreign country occurs at least as frequently as non-switching after market entry, and that the mode switch thereby represents an important element of the international management of a company.

The description and discussion of decision-making behaviour per cluster (Chapter 7.8; Table 7.11), the characteristics and differences between switchers vs. non-switchers (Chapter 8.8, Table 8.16) and the timing of the mode decision (Chapter 7.5, Table 7.9) create clarity and transparency as to how companies and the management make their decisions. It can also be established that the systematic planning of activities in the area of foreign operations plays an important role for success. Clear causal connections were observed between systematic planning and success (Chapter 8.5).

Mode switching and timing
The aspects of time and dynamics, which have been long neglected in theoretical treatments of international management were explored. This work explores the influence that speed of decision making bears on the internationalisation of companies (Chapter 7.5). It is not surprising to learn that companies decide, negotiate and implement mode switches at different speeds (Figure 7.10, Table 7.9). Although not significant, it is important to note that companies take varying amounts of time to make their decision to switch modes. It could be observed that fast switchers take approximately a year to move from the decision to switch to implementation, while slow-switchers need approximately 3 years. The results also showed, however, that companies take the time they need to reach the right decision for the right situation. In this context, not only fast switchers can be successful, but also switchers who need longer for opinion-building, negotiations and implementation.

An analysis of various timing aspects with regard to mode switches was carried out. Differences were established with regard to how long the period is before a market-entry strategy is switched, how long it takes before certain modes are achieved and how long the timeframe is between switches (Chapter 8.10). To what extent the various dwelling times after market entry affect company success remains an open question. Significant differences could not be found with regard to dwelling times and the effect on success.

Results of the survival analysis showed that switches take place earlier in certain industry sector, such as the electronic and chemical industry, and that the probability of a switch is lower in saturated markets than in emerging markets (Chapter 8.11). With regard to the timing of the switch, it could be shown that certain modes, such as the importer mode, are maintained significantly longer without a switch and present higher rigidity against a switch in comparison to all other mode options (Figure 8.12). It was shown that the individual qualities of the management's attitude toward risk, the scope of resource transfer and commitment, the number of modes per country and the structure of the mode portfolio are of high relevance as directly influencing parameters with regard to switching probability.

When a switch will be made significantly depends on the currently employed mode. This important finding means that the chosen market-entry strategy, in particular, bears an important influence on all further decisions regarding future market operations.

In conclusion, the contribution of this study is summarised according to the areas of Theory, Methodology, Empire, Context and Substantivity.

Through the comprehensive analysis at the levels of internationalisation and mode switching, this work contributes to the theoretical explanation of the phenomenon of mode switching in the internationalisation process. The holistic perspective from the view of the company-management uncovers correlations and causal mechanisms tied to the strategic change. The most important determinants of the optimal timing of a switch and the key decision-making areas of the foreign-mode switch in their overall context (from the strategic- and behavioural perspective) are presented and discussed. The formulation of 14 propositions summarises the most important findings and form the theoretical contribution of this work to research in this field.

The use of a comprehensive quantitative analysis expands on the low number of quantitative works on mode switching and, in combination with the qualitative analyses undertaken before the quantitative analyses, an interesting change in perspective is achieved with regard to the subject study and the question of "how", "what", "why" and "how many". The use of mixed methods here in connection with the selected retrospective processual approach brings additional clarity and transparency. The selected research method also gives indications of how short-and long-term effects of a switch on a company's success can be analysed and measured in the future. This is a valuable contribution to the management and control of international operations.

With regard to the empirical findings and predictions of future actions in the management of foreign operations, the study shows a number of relationships and causal mechanisms which, until now, were only conceptionally assumed, such as the findings regarding success relevance of mode switching. Here, both the qualitative and quantitative results on the key influencing factors and their effects on success make an important contribution to previous knowledge. They also, however, show that mode switching is not a necessity for successful foreign business. It must be decided based on individual case analyses.

The future use of these research results for the management of foreign operations is multifarious. The results could be used in response to the demand for a rational decision-making process with concrete aims of internationalisation in the form of a target mode, to assess a foreign operation based on the value contribution of a switch, or to increase mode competence. These are only a few examples.

9.2.3 Contribution to theory

The main contribution of these findings lies in a broadening of the previous perspective from market entry to the entire internationalisation process, in particular the management of a foreign operation over time. The results here show how foreign operations can be successfully carried out and what is to be considered with a switch.

These findings show the high significance of the study subject for successful internationalisation and confirm previous research on the management of foreign operations and mode switching (Swoboda 2002; Pedersen et al. 2002; Fryges 2005;

Welch et al. 2007; Benito et al. 2009). They show the critical influence on a company's success and thereby confirm the assumption of Benito et al. (2009) and the results of Swoboda (2002) that the management of foreign operations – in this case, the mode switch – is critical for a company's success in a foreign market.

The results for the effects of the mode switch are very significant. This study has shown that the mode switch can bear positive influence. This represents a contribution to the existing knowledge (see Chapter 2.5) with regard to the effects of a switch in the foreign market over a certain period of time.

Benito and Welch (1994) and Petersen and Welch (2002) described the concept of mode combinations and the fields of application. This study ties in with the conceptual work of these researchers and, using the quantitative results, points out effects of switches on foreign operations to mode combination. The results show that mode combinations are frequently exercised strategy options (Oviatt et al. 2005; Gabrielsson et al. 2008). Compared to the impact of single modes, however, their contribution to corporate success in this study turns out to be less significant.

In this study, individual countries with single modes; and specifically, the modes subsidiaries and agents, achieve above-average success after the switch. The conceptual work of Benito et al. (2009) is thus complemented and empirical evidence provided regarding the relevance for success of the new (target-) form of foreign operation. Also from the perspective of the work of Swoboda (2002), who primarily examined characteristics of successful "Gestalten" in the internationalisation process without, however, explicitly addressing the success of individual mode of foreign operations after the switch, the study at hand provides interesting additional findings.

According to Petersen et al. (2000), Pedersen et al. (2002) and Welch et al. (2007), the "switching costs" as perceived possible costs of a switch are the reason for the change. This study, however, gives the satisfaction of the decision maker as the main reason for the change. Thus, the assumption by Petersen et al. (p. 49, 2000) regarding the influence of satisfaction on the switch, is confirmed. In addition to the general examination of the foreign intermediary (Petersen et al. 2000), this study deals specifically with particular mode strategies.

This subjective judgement comprises the business criteria, such as fulfilment of certain or previously agreed turnovers, as well as the interpretation and perception of environment conditions, specific expectations and own interests. The more business-focused aspect of switching costs is thereby broadened to include behaviourial characteristics. The influence of existing distribution structures in the domestic country on the choice and management of foreign operations (McNaughton and Bell 2000) is interesting but was not pursued in this thesis. As the sample companies had already achieved a high degree of internationalisation lower dependency on the domestic market can be assumed.

As one of few, this study with its results shows the differences between the influencing factors of the first and second switch (Swoboda 2002). This supplements the work of Freyges (2005) who showed the sector environment, internal resources, duration since market entry, product alignments and R&D activities as influencing factors for the probability of a switch. With the first switch, attitudes about internationalisation as a growth strategy and the sector environment play a particularly important role. With the second switch, mode experience and mode strategy, as well as the specific country environment dominate. Here, the conceptual assumptions of Benito et al. (2009) are partially confirmed; however, Benito et al. did not make any conceptual differences between the first and the second switch.

The findings confirm the results of Kaufmann and Jentsch (2006) that companies take certain positions in internationalisation and then leave certain positions over time to take new ones. Particularly frequent positions could be identified and tied together to pathways (Hutzschenreuter et al. 2007). Contrary to the results of Kaufmann and Jentsch (2006), particularly interesting pathways within the combinations of export strategies and of export strategies to subsidiaries could be found.

The analysis of decision making showed results similar to those previously published by Aharoni (1966). In this study, the decision-making process with its phases of opinion building, negotiation and implementation play an important role. This study, however, extended beyond the market-entry decision and observes the decision regarding strategy and change as part of a dynamic internationalisation process (Swoboda 2002; Jones and Coviello 2005; Benito et al. 2009).

Influencing factors of systematic planning and timing are of particular note with regard to the decision-making process and their effect on success in the foreign market. Contrary to McNaughton (2001), and similar to Calof's (1993) results, it can be shown that systematic planning has significant effects on success in the foreign market. This supports Pedersen et al. (2002) opinion that careful planning and the analysis of various mode options can improve the management of foreign operations.

As often assumed (Swoboda 2002, Hurmerinta-Peltomäki 2003, Jones and Coviello 2005) and empirically partially supported (Dibrell et al. 2005), timing aspects of the switch are critical for a company's success. This study's results for timing in the context of the decision-making process for a mode switch supplement the conceptual work by Jones and Coviello (2005) and show that both fast- and slow decision makers can be successful. The empirical results indicate that what counts is the efficient use of time in the form of a paced- or time-balanced process to learn effectively (Petersen et al 2002). The results show the importance of negotiating with key actors before deciding to switch modes and deciding what the timing and future strategy should be. This partially contradicts the popular research approaches of Born Global (Oviatt et al. 2005, Gabrielsson et al. 2008) or rapid internationalisation (Shrader et al. 2008) in which fast internationalisation should be pursued just shortly after a company is founded. The results of this study show the importance of a moderate position in which the internationalisation and management of the foreign operation have sufficient time and space for development and coordination in the sense of a co-evolutionary approach. The duration and right timing for the switch is observed as a product emerging from the co-evolution of internationalisation activities, corporate characteristics, mode strategy, management style and industry influences.

Further, it was shown that specific existing mode strategies are more rigid than others and need more time before they are switched. The assumed factor of "experience" (Swobada 2002, Benito et al. 2009) could not be clearly identified as the reason for this mode rigidity. To avoid bias based on past experience, however, the results support the demand for a rational decision-making process (Calof 1993; McNaughton 2001; Becker 2005) so that the potential negative effect of rigidity could be overcome and all potential options for a successful internationalisation strategy can be considered systematically.

On the other hand, the explanations by Williamson (1995) and analysis by Fryges (2005) are partly confirmed, as the rigidity of certain mode strategies indicates that the existing relationship is at least temporarily locked in by a high perceived switching cost.

Through identification of groups of homogenous behaviour with regard to mode strategies, decision-making duration, management style and corporate characteristics, the existing explanation of mode switching (Pedersen et al. 2002, Fyges 2005; Benito et al. 2005, Kaufmann and Jentzsch 2006; Petersen et al. 2006; Swoboda and Jager 2008) is broadened in its perspective. The observations of specific patterns show to what extent these factors can influence the mode switch in a country and within a country portfolio.

Finally, the integrated explanatory approach regarding mode switching with the theory of path dependency makes an important contribution to the existing literature (Eriksson et al. 2000; Hutzschenreuter et al. 2007). It shows that past decisions made for the management of foreign modes (Benito et al. 2009) and the achieved results play an important role for the internationalisation path of a company. The demand for a dynamic perspective is fulfilled and the actual market-entry decision is given high significance as a starting point for internationalisation because it is the basis for all further decisions and is mainly irreversible.

9.3 Limitations and implications for future research questions in international business

Although the analysis model for mode switching is based on theoretically-supported and management-specific research, the possibility cannot be excluded that one or several relevant criteria were not considered which would have been relevant for characterising decision-making behaviour with regard to the mode switch and which might determine the success of switching companies.

Despite this conceptional limitation, the main contribution of this work lies in the comprehensive review of the literature on mode switching and a consideration of these findings in the context of the mode switch and the proposition deduction. In addition, the work shows that various partial theories from established International Business literature seem well-suited for analysing behaviour of foreign management operations.

This work fulfils the need for a greater transparency of the influencing factors tied to the switch and their significance for the company's success which became apparent during the literature review and offers a contribution that develops a concept on the subject of decision-making behaviour in the context of foreign mode switches that is guided by theory and considers the specific internationalisation literature.

In the hypotheses formulation, a median position was often taken without a concrete reference object for measurement of optimality having been formulated. This could be criticised from the view of the quantitative analysis. What does one do with hypotheses which cannot be measured? For the author it is a matter of documenting assumed correlations, even if they are not directly measureable, in order to show that there cannot be any specific correlations of influence here with regard to optimality of the mode switch. Here, companies individually decide, take action and are subject to particular internal and external influences.

The qualitative section of this work primarily deals with behaviour in the past retrospectively assessed in the present by the interview partner. Recall bias, rationalisation of poor past decisions or also difficulties in clearly identifying cause and result are the epistemological disadvantages of this selected method. The visualisation of the most important events and multiple testing for thoroughness, sequence and time relation improve the presentation of results.

The concentration on a specific country (in this work, the foreign market with the highest relevance for the company) is of advantage as it can be assumed that sufficient information and knowledge will be available even on a retrospective basis. A disadvantage is that this focus excludes other countries where the company operates. The question of how foreign operations reciprocally influence each other in the country portfolio and what kind of effect this bears on decision-making behaviour with regard to future modes would be an interesting question for future research.

Also of note is that the country selection was undertaken by the interview partners. There was no control of the countries observed and therefore the assumption was that these were predominantly successful foreign markets. For this reason, a differentiation between success and non-success of modes can only be established to a limited degree. In the sense of the objective, an observation of the actual behaviour during the switch would be of preference.

For the quantitative data collection, one top manager per company was taken. Their statements also comprise subjectively perceived events and experiences which cannot be set in perspective by further statements of other company members. The inclusion of further interview partners per company would therefore be desirable for further studies in order to allow various perspectives.

For the construct operationalisation, the measurement for identification of a company's success represents a familiar problem – for this work, as well. The quantitative section of this work provides sensible indications of how short and long-term success can be measured over time. However, the problem of the judgement framework of the decision maker remains. The request for further, quantifiable indicators such as return on assets (ROA), return on sales (ROS), return on equity (ROE), sales growth, market share and return on investment (ROI) is understandable from the view of the author – however, more in the theoretical sense; it can, in most of the cases, most likely not be fulfilled, because managing directors are not always willing to give this information. The same applies to the degree of satisfaction as a measurement of success. For measuring success, future research should therefore focus more strongly on the combination of both objective and subjective measurement criteria.

Perception-related assessment of international competitiveness is dependent upon the mood and emotional situation but also on the underlying expectations. Obviously an exact replication is not always easy. To ensure the stability of the success criteria, this study not only evaluated success depending on the situation but also considered success from various perspectives such as long-term and short-term success, success of the switch itself, of the foreign market and of the overall export business. Precisely because the measurement of internationalisation success is a central element in international business research, there is a need for further research here. Accompanying single-case studies (in-depth field research, clinical case studies with longitudinal focus) may provide more insights into the relationship between mode switching and performance.

The operationalisation of the management style regarding mode switching could only be based on a few, existing empirically-tested operationalisations. Here, a factor-structure was shown that supplies indicators for relevant dimensions for describing attitudes and management behaviour. However, some single indicators had to be excluded due to too low factor loading. Here, the findings of this work can be used to further refine the measurement apparatus.

The ex-post form selected for the study subject makes it impossible to avoid a lack of sharpness in the result evaluation. Gaps in memories, lacking quality of information or rationalisation made after the fact render the data collection and make the result interpretation difficult. For future research there is the demand for a timely beginning, ideally before the switching process begins, and scientific accompaniment up until the perceived end of mode switching. This would have the advantage that results of the observed switching process are not yet known and an influencing of the research results through knowledge of the outcome is avoided. The enormous efforts tied to this approach are, however, not to be underestimated.

This work limits itself to German-speaking companies in a specific environment. To what degree these findings apply to other languages or cultural circles would also be an interesting research field. In analyses comparing countries and cultures, it could be assessed as to whether similar strategy types crystallise with e.g. Scottish or other companies of a different nationality. The results presented here apply only for German companies.

This study determines the effect of the switch on individual modes and mode combinations. The switch to single modes showed a tendency toward stronger positive changes in performance. One should not, however, necessarily conclude from this that single modes generally are the better strategy. Particularly during a phase of reorienting within a market, mode combinations can be a very expedient form of foreign operation which can reduce the emergence of conflicts with existing partners. Moreover, in many industries full market coverage cannot be achieved with a single mode, which in turn would be an argument for mode combinations. Future research should therefore more strongly consider the option of strategy combination within and outside a distribution channel, and examine the influence of mode combinations on international success.

An interesting future research area is the role of the "electronic" mode in combination with "physical" foreign operation modes. In this study, strategies of direct export (such as agent or importers) are mainly observed. Senior management, however, must have extensive knowledge of "electronic" aspects of international market operations in direct combination with traditional strategy forms.

A major requirement for increasing company success is the systematic evaluation of options for potential future strategies. For future research, and based on the findings of this study, there is the question of possible evaluation criteria and evaluation processes regarding the advantages of a switch in a country and in connection with other countries from a holistic perspective.

This study offers a number of interesting starting points for explaining and justifying behaviour during a mode switch. For future research, however, there is a continued need for more transparency in providing reasons for company actions and a stronger integrative perspective of individual explanatory theories.

9.4 Implications and recommendations for future management of foreign operations

In the following, some conclusions are drawn for the internationalisation of companies and the management:

The most important finding here is that both non-switchers and switchers can be highly successful in the foreign market and that the organisation of certain dimensions is relevant to success. During the analyses, it was shown how the individual companies can organise their strategy portfolio. At the same time, the individual descriptive dimension most relevant to success was emphasised. In this manner, a reflection on the structuring of company-internal factors with the behaviour modes of the identified typologies could give indications of corresponding changes.

Senior management has to make a number of complex internationalisation decisions which should harmonise with each other and also take the strategic force of the internationalisation and the requirements of foreign customers into consideration. In addition, reciprocal effects between different foreign markets must be considered. The aim of achieving international company success requires consideration of these interdependencies and reciprocal effects if decisions are to be made for structuring foreign operations after market entry. In this context, the findings of this work support a holistic perspective of the management of international activities which considers interdependencies and synergies between countries. The classic decision-making fields for the market-entry strategy and the management of the foreign operation are important areas for organisation. They should not, however, be treated as two separate entities that stand side-by-side and can be viewed in an isolated manner.

The analysis of the influencing factors clearly emphasised the importance of timing aspects. Certain market-entry strategies, such as the importer mode, are maintained for a longer period of time than other modes. For management practice, the necessity can be derived to think about possible pathways already at market entry so as to avoid unnecessary waste of time in achieving optimal market operations. The demand for long-term planning can be tied to this as a counter alternative to the concepts of "trial and error" or "wait and see". The success relevance of systematic planning, particularly in the area of international market research, supports this demand.

From the qualitative analyses, it was observed how complex the influencing factors are on the switch. To prevent influencing factors, such as loss of power, resistance to change, sunk costs, risk aversion or network dependencies from gaining the upper hand and allowing pathological decisions there should be the demand for stronger rationalisation of decisions involving the mode switch. Companies must increasingly base their decisions on objective criteria, document the course of decision making and the information used for it, and make the results of their decision transparent.

The results of the study illustrate the particular significance of the mode subsidiary for international success. For the management, the requirement to considerably increase knowledge and know-how regarding this type of strategy can be derived. Compared to single modes, mode combinations achieved only average results. This is all the more surprising in that in many instances, it is not until mode combinations are used that the kind of comprehensive market coverage is attained which a single mode alone could not achieve. Furthermore, it should be noted that direct export strategies without middlemen achieve rather poor results and thus appear more suitable for market entry. Early switching of this foreign mode, e.g. to subsidiary given due profitability, represents a strategic option for the management of foreign operations that is worth considering.

With regard to decision-making behaviour before and during the switch of a mode, it was shown how important the individual process phases for opinion building and implementation are. For the future, even more weight should be placed here and take the form of an active decision-making process so that companies can take best advantage of their potential in foreign markets. In practice, this can mean the use of relationship- and process managers who tend to be the stakeholders of switch decisions and actively manage. Systematic planning of foreign operations (with targets, milestones, external consultants and reviews) is also of particular importance because short-term targets are reduced in significance. This also includes tools for securing rationality, such as portfolio analyses or a net present value analysis. What can help further is the decision maker's self-commitment to institutionalised decision-making processes and certain standard mechanisms (review meetings, justifying decisions/non-decisions, openly presenting criteria, etc.) to reduce rationality deficits. This includes a strong willingness to learn and decision-making competence to reduce "decision costs" owing to delay.

A possible process in which a systematic decision (Becker, p. 175, 2005) can be brought about is shown in Figure 9.1.

The individual steps of degree of target achievement, benchmark between the current situation and the assessed potential, the discussion of alternatives, the assessment of the economic advantages and the determination of a positive value provide orientation as to how an assessment process for evaluating a switch of mode can be structured.

Through its system, the process ensures consideration of the advantage of a mode switch between the poles of resistance to change with some modes and maintaining flexibility in the internationalisation process.

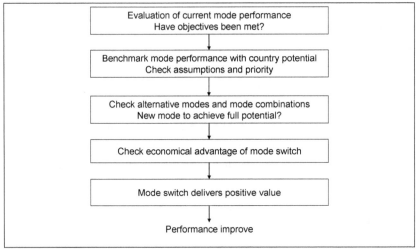

Figure 9.1: Evaluation of switching mode – systematic decision making process

The discussion of the path dependency of the decision also raises the demand for a significant improvement of the knowledge of options tied to foreign operation. To put it in simple terms, it is about more than the knowledge of classic market-entry strategies. It is about comprehensive know-how as to in what manner these strategies can be combined and how a successful switch can be undertaken both internally and externally so that possible reservations regarding a necessary further development of the company can be cleared out of the way. The terms of mode experience and mode competence repeatedly mentioned in this context are a first step but need to be expanded on by foreign operation competence.

For the successful management of a foreign operation, there is the necessity to integrate the concept of pathway dependency. It should be the primary goal in the internationalisation process to avoid rigid path dependencies and to recognize and further develop positive path dependencies. In this conclusion, this demand will be addressed with the development of an explanatory theory on the behaviour of firms during mode switching.

9.5 The case for path dependence - How history matters in mode switching

The concept of path dependency is to be used here because decisions and behavioural patterns in the past such as mode experience and their effects on future decisions and behavioural patterns play a major role in mode switching (Benito et al. 2009). Previous research on path dependency (Eriksson et al. 2000; Araujo and Rezende 2003; Schreyögg and Sydow 2003; Schreyögg et al. 2003; Sydow et al. 2005; Hutzschenreuter et al. 2007; Dievernich 2007) offers a good foundation for general explanations which will be expanded in perspective in the following through the internationalisation theories discussed and the empirical results. A further reason for selecting the concept of path dependency lies in the process perspective. In this manner, better understanding of the challenges involved in changing strategies and organisations over the course of internationalization and in particular after market entry can be gained.

First, the implication of the empirical results of this work regarding behaviour before, during and after the mode switch will be discussed. This will be based on the phases "path creating", "path shaping" and "path dependency". Then the fourth phase of "path breaking and path creating" will be introduced. The possibility and limitations of "path management" will be indicated with particular focus on the phenomenon of breaking path dependency as regards decisions on foreign operation modes. This section ends with key conclusions and the remaining challenges.

In Table 9.2 the most important influencing factors on the management of foreign operation and mode switching are presented based on the results of this work. The categorisation of the most important determining factors here is to be understood as an attempt to create a holistic explanatory model regarding the development of foreign operations.

The research subject of this study comprises, in particular, Phase 2 and Phase 3. The mode switch can only occur after completion of market entry. In Phase 1, market entry therefore represents the starting point. In the descriptions of Phase 2 and Phase 3, the empirical results for the behaviour of switchers and non-switchers from

Chapter 5 to 8 are integrated. Phase 4 comprises summarising recommendations for the successful management of foreign operations.

Table 9.2: Most important influencing factors to explain path dependency in internationalisation and mode switching

Phase	Process elements	Components	Indicators
1. Path creating	Market entry	Historicity, Small events	- Management style (management intention/strategic objectives/ management perception to risk and opportunity) - Company characteristics - Mode experience, mode competence - International experience - Mode strategy
Critical Juncture/ Critical Event		*Market entry as initial starting point: The market entry decision*	
2. Path shaping	Market penetration	Positive and negative feedback from internal and external environment	- Degree of satisfaction - Financial results (e.g. sales growth) - Mode learning, mode experience - Managerial style - Business environment
Lock-In		*Reduced strategy options (strategy diet)*	
3. Path dependence	Mode pathway (m_{entry}, m_1, m_2, m_3,..m_N)	Stabilising factors target/strategy ignorance inefficacy immunity	- Mode strategy, pathway identified - Performance, satisfaction of current mode - Time to switch - Influence factors on mode switching - Context factors (industry sector, country group, mode strategy) - Mode experience - Resistance to switch, risk averse - Conflict of objectives - Know-how, Capabilities - Unwillingness - Economically inefficient
Un-Lock		*Expanded strategy options*	
4. Path breaking and path creating	Path management, Mode flexibility	Open mind set Leadership by objectives Long-term oriented Sustainable development	- Short-term/local and long-term/system oriented decisions - Global mind-set - Personal objectives/Country objectives/Internationalisation objectives - Alternative generation (management recommendations path breaking and path creating by management intention) Recommendation to improve pathway performance

Note: the dark-colored area in the table comprises of the main research area on management von foreign operation and mode switching.

In the following, the most important findings will be discussed and expanded based on the model of path dependency previously introduced (Chapter 2.3.7).

9.5.1 Path creating: Decision for international expansion as point zero and market entry

The decision regarding international expansion represents the start of a foreign market operation. At this point, the company at least theoretically has a free choice of countries and market-entry strategy. In fact, however, the company begins in a specific environment of existing network structures in the home country and the foreign country, with experiences with other countries, successes and failures. Though all options seem open to decision makers at this point, they are nevertheless influenced by motivation, capability and their own perceptions regarding internationalisation, the already existing mode strategy, mode competence and experience with strategic changes in their home and foreign markets (Jones and Coviello 2005; Hutzschenreuter et al. 2007, Brouthers and Hennart 2007; Chirico and Nordqvist 2010).

Although it is a new foreign market – there are already organisational persistencies and stabilities which have crystallised from the internationalisation of the company to date and the internationalisation experiences of its decision makers (Buckley et al. 2007). Both a high and low degree of experience can limit the choices of market-entry decisions (Brouthers 2002). With extensive experience, the company relies on familiar patterns of action that have been successful in other markets. Market entry as an economic process is thereby, in its totality, not wholly without presuppositions. It is influenced by previous decisions and the perceptions tied to these (Winter 2000; Zollo and Winter 2002; Hutzschenreuter et al. 2007).

The structural and cognitive embedding of the company contributes to the successful initiation of the internationalisation process and mobilisation of resources. As a result, uncertainty is reduced and temporally limited stabilities are created. Small events in the form of first contacts with country experts, coincidental acquaintances, visits to trade shows, market-research results, the behaviour of competitors or also direct

375

contact with interested partners from the foreign country promote opinion building regarding future internationalisation and create the foundation for the market-entry decision. Small events as process-effective occurrences can be of accidental nature but can also come about consciously as intended management behaviour. Whether it was a accumulation of information or single ideas of particular significance for the market-entry decision can only be observed retrospectively; it cannot yet be ascertained during the actual decision-making phase. As precursors to the market-entry decision however, such small events are of high importance because they unintentionally narrow freedom of action.

At a certain moment, the market-entry strategy itself finally forms as a kind of big event, a "critical juncture" (Schreyögg and Sydow 2003). This is to be understood as the first emergence of an event that exerts sustainable, self-reinforcing effects and is thereby responsible for the persistence. The market-entry strategy as a critical event marks the transition to the phase of path creation.

The decision-making process regarding market entry is based on organisational structures that have emerged in the past (Holtmann 2008; Barreto 2010). It is not a fully autonomous decision. On the contrary, decision makers are predisposed based on past organisational decisions made for internationalization (Zollo and Winter 2002; Hutzschenreuter et al. 2007). The historically prominent mode strategy, the flowing processes and decisions from this determine the selected mode of operation and thereby internationalisation behaviour.

Once the decision regarding the market-entry strategy has been made, there is therefore a clear narrowing of the future field of action. For example, this study showed a particular frequency of switches to a subsidiary after market entry with an importer (market-entry decision as a big event). In this sense, the selection of the market-entry mode acts as an imprint for all further mode decisions which may follow and thereby reduces the initial result-openness to a few options.

9.5.2 Path shaping: Determination of foreign mode strategy

Once the market-entry strategy has been determined, there is a phase of relative stability (Kutschker 1996). First experience with market- and customer requirements is gathered and put into action. Uncertainty is reduced. First learning effects take place. Connections are made and, ideally, new customers are won.

Only the occurrence of "small events" brings movement again into the organisational system. These events are the triggers for the crystallisation of action (Schreyögg and Sydow 2003). Each new step, be it even the smallest change in internationalisation behaviour leads to feedback loops between the key actors, the organisation, the network and the cultural context (Jones and Coviello 2005). These influence the next action and decision. This can be a case of discrepancies between the target and status quo in the internal and external environment of the decision makers. Budget discrepancies, errors in delivery, failure to meet deadlines, poor reporting between partners, errors in project control, lack of knowledge of market developments or also the market entry of a new competitor, insolvency of an international customer, a previous strategy meeting or low level of success in the acquisition of new customers can all represent triggers for considering a change of the current market-entry strategy (Eisenhardt and Martin 2000). There is a "misfit" between expectations and reality. A switch of mode seems sensible in order to reduce discrepancies and to regain a "fit". A decision-making process begins regarding the question of switching modes. The observed results show a superordinate significance of the factor "satisfaction" as an indicator for or against a switch. If satisfaction is high then a switch is made so that further potential in the country may be utilised. If satisfaction is low then a switch is made with the hope of improving the current situation. The feedback loops do not necessarily have to be negative in this case. A highly positive market development, new projects, coincidentally acquired special knowledge regarding new requirements – all representing in their sum an "overfulfilment" of expectations – can also trigger, as small events, extensive changes in the foreign mode due to expansion plans.

The originally selected market-entry strategy can be switched but does not have to happen. It is possible that the current mode is maintained. The results clearly show

377

that success in the foreign country is not dependent upon whether companies switch or not. If a switch is not made then the market-entry strategy is maintained.

Of note, however, are cases in which the switch from an efficient to a more efficient mode is not made. Although the anticipated benefit is larger than the sum of expected switching costs, the switch is not undertaken. A switch to a new mode would be advantageous but is not initiated because, for example, the decision maker fears counter-reactions of the partner and negative repercussions. In another case, a switch is not made because the individual switching costs are too high (Weiss and Anderson 1992). Although, objectively viewed, the status quo is inefficient; the decision maker's personal view is that it is "bearable". Further reasons which may act to prevent a switch are low or unclear profit prospects but also lacking resources or lacking management capabilities (Teece at al. 1997; Winter 2003). Lack of motivation on the part of decision makers owing to non-ambitious goals, other interests, or loss- and risk aversion can also lead to a clinging to the foreign operation mode employed thus far. A lack of capability and knowledge on the part of decision makers as regards how a potential switch after market entry should be carried out and later managed might only end in a maintaining of the status quo. Loss aversion, risk aversion and sunk costs result in a selective perception that also makes it difficult to recognise the need to take measures (Bronner 2003). On the other hand, high satisfaction with the mode employed can also lead, as a positive feedback loop, to a resistance to change the originally selected market-entry strategy.

If the market-entry strategy is not switched, for whatever reason, as is often the case, feedback-loop effects are still created in the relevant foreign market and also for other countries where the firm operates. Not switching in a foreign market can mean that the resources not applied for the switch of activities are then available for other markets. If, however, the market-entry strategy is switched then feedback-loop effects are created which, in extreme cases, lead to a reproduction of this action for other countries.

If this perspective is followed then every switch of the initially selected market entry strategy is a "big event" because – at a certain point in time – the future type and form of market activity is decided. Mode switching thereby replaces the market-entry strategy as a critical juncture (decision of mode switching = critical juncture II after entry mode). The previous events and decisions take effect ex post and break the path for the decision on the mode profile (direction, order, intensity, switch pattern, timing, etc.).

Whether a critical juncture crystallises from these small events (meaning that the operation mode is changed) can only be determined retrospectively and not at the time of the event itself. Each investment decision leads to a certain degree of dependency as it binds the decision-maker to decisions made in the past. Whether a switch is undertaken or not, and which mode of operation is selected, depends upon the international business context and – in particular – the market-entry strategy thus far, the motivation of the decision makers, the capabilities and the perceptions. Although there are plenty of options, the factors mentioned above strongly limit the possibilities of future mode operation. In many cases, alternatives are dismissed because initial self-reinforcing mechanisms are already taking effect (Benito et al. 2009).

This situation is reminiscent of the discussion during the expert interviews regarding the mode of international operation of a medium-sized producer of dental products. With this supplier, export had been carried out exclusively via sales representatives. The company had very good experiences and results with this in the past. Concentration-processes in the European dental trade and new product developments, however, required an adjustment of the strategy. The decision makers, though, assessed the risks arising from a switch as being higher than the possible opportunities and maintained their current strategy. They did not want to change their organisation because they feared this would negatively affect short-term efficiency. It is rather unlikely that a single area sales manager in such an organisation would resist the system logic. Precisely because the decision makers are only interested in short-term optimisation or target achievement, innovative options for action are perceived as being a disturbance and not an occasion to reflect on a possible future mode. Other options, such as the founding of a branch office, are immediately ruled out. Habitual familiarisation with certain decisions creates a situation that limits perception and the possibility of recognising other alternatives. In the extreme case, no more decisions are made aside from those which reproduce the current decisions over and over. As long as the mode is successful, no necessity to switch presents itself to the company. A kind of mode competency establishes itself with the result that only certain mode-options are trusted in. This also includes certain formal and informal rules of conduct presented in the organisation as "rules of the game". They have the effect that a certain mode of behaviour not only firmly establishes itself but is also further expanded. Certain solutions and behavioural modes in market activity become all the more attractive, the more frequently they are used. Deviating from the mode of behaviour, or the rule, is "expensive". This prevents deviations from the development path and it comes to path dependency and the "lock-in" effect. On the other hand, not every structure that crystallises is a symptom of a beginning negative pathway dependency. The limitation of alternatives for acting with regard to foreign operation modes also has the advantage that these limited options are considered in greater depth and can be concentrated on by the actors.

9.5.3 Path dependency and switching lock-ins

Once the decision for the foreign mode operation has been made, the actors must gain knowledge, identify partners, establish models for cooperation, build up local structures, solicit customers, launch sales and marketing activities and implement the entire concept (roll-out). After a short time, internal and external structures and processes in the home- and foreign country stabilize (Kutschker 1996; Kutschker and Bäuerle 1996). Due to the paradigm of short-term efficiency increase and emerging feedback loops, the organisation solidifies. In this phase, switching to an alternative is tied to significantly more effort than if the alternative mode had been chosen directly from the start. A company may therefore retain a certain pathway even though it later becomes apparent that another alternative would have been the better choice (Hutzschenreuter et al. 2007).

The empirical findings show that certain market entry strategies, such as "importers", present clearly longer dwelling times until a switch is made than as is the case with e.g. "agents". The strategic change for specific modes thereby seems more difficult, which indicates a clinging in the sense of path dependency (Chapter 8.3, 8.10 and 8.11).

Certain dominating patterns of action crystallise which can be positive or negative in nature. Positive path dependency is of course welcome. What one wishes to prevent, are inefficient path dependencies.

Path dependency arises through the dominating strategic decision regarding the type and form of foreign market operation. Through self-reinforcing mechanisms, the market-entry decision provokes or induces future decisions. The market-entry decision and the subsequent switches as emerging event sequences form the development pathway. Self-reinforcing effects in the sense of mode strategies are (Werle 2007):

- Learning effects: beneficial experience with the mode improves and increases performance
- Satisfaction/Efficiency: positive feedback in the form of turnover increase, market-share growth and new-customer acquisitions lead to a remaining with the successful mode strategy
- Sunk costs/Quasi-irreversibility of investment: investments made for market entry and the establishment of the foreign operation are not to be lost. Therefore the decision maker decides to maintain the initial decision.
- Network: cooperation with actors from the market (suppliers, customers, middlemen, employees, etc) lead to a social binding in network structures with corresponding binding effects and the maintaining of established structures.
- Power: expansion of power or the risk of losing power lead to a maintaining of the status quo.
- Moral obligation: Value perceptions and relationships are formed on the basis of the mode which are not questioned as to their rational benefit and which thereby reduce uncertainty.
- Complementarity: Formal and informal rules of conduct regarding the mode strategy, "rules of the game" or operating procedures act as templates for

thinking and acting, and reciprocally strengthen each other. This leads to an increased stability and the maintaining of existing foreign operation structures.

Pathway-dependent processes are not self-correcting. On the contrary, they are predestined to solidify once-made errors. Self-reinforcing moments have had the result that each step along the direction initially taken is disproportionately rewarded by new advantages (Zollo and Winter 2002). In this manner, the direction taken becomes increasingly rigid, regardless of its quality. This renders internationalisation not the result of decisions regarding the mode and strategy of market operation but primarily a result of excluded alternatives.

An example of this is as follows: our company holds on to the agent organisation and decides against a switch to own sales representatives or a subsidiary. The company does this despite the fact that the agent is not close to the customer or is only interested in new products to a limited degree (in other words, despite the fact that the agent is ineffective). It could be that massive compensation payments will fall due after years of cooperation and the company is not willing to pay them. Often, key actors would like to change their pathways and switch but they cannot. Here, there are usually power- or interest-constellations that are not to be changed. This could include shares in the importer which one would not like to withdraw or dependency on the current sales partner in a country which, in the case of termination of contract, would have negative repercussions in another country. One company, for example, selected a large importer as its exclusive sales partner for China, Taiwan and South Korea. The planned founding of a subsidiary in China had to take this arrangement into consideration. There was the danger that if the contract was terminated in China the entire relationship would be massively affected. Business in northern Asia might be negatively influenced. For this reason, the company decided (after years of negotiations) to set up the subsidiary in parallel to the importer. Selective customer protection and combining of after-sales service were the main aspects of the agreement. The previous decision affects the later decision, not in the form of determinism in which no strategic exit exists, but more in the form of a strong limitation of possible options for action. In this context, the decision to work with a large importer for several countries at the same time results in self-reinforcing effects which, finally, either narrow down, in the extreme case, actually "lock-in" behavioural patters. The pathway then presents a high degree of path bonding. This is to be understood as a strongly narrowed "corridor" of action with an iterative decision-making processes.

Nevertheless, not every structure which establishes itself is a worrisome sign of path dependency or represents a "lock-in". Total lock-ins are rare and are the result of pathological decision circumstances (Dievernich 2007).

Positive pathway dependencies with replication of certain behaviour patterns in foreign business can protect the company from excessively complex structures. If a once successful path is used (on a non-reflected basis) for another market, there is the large advantage that mechanisms are known and implementation can thereby spare company resources and allow the company to remain flexible. In the negative case, a non-reflected transference of the market entry strategy in one country to another country can lead to a misfit, resulting, for example, from the lack of consideration of alternative sales channels.

It should be noted here that it can often come to a solidification of, for example, inter-organisational routines (Teece et al. 1997; Zollo and Winter 2002) in which similar decisions or behaviour modes are perpetually reproduced – but these are rarely without alternatives. With increased effort or higher order capabilities (Winter 2003), downtrodden pathways of mode decisions can be left and solidified structures can be broken up.

For successful internationalisation, it is not only important to identify switching lock-ins but also (and primarily) to break these locks, change the pathway and design specific pathways.

9.5.4 Path-breaking and switch de-locking

The goal of the pathway break is to reduce or avoid stringent path dependencies (Karim and Mitchell 2000; Hutzschenreuter et al. 2007). For this, feedback loops and self-reinforcing mechanisms resulting from emotional, cognitive, social or resource-related processes must be openly identified and their lock-in effect on possible foreign operation mode switches reduced. The reduction of the solidified structures that have evolved through repeated actions and routine play an important role here (Leonard-Barton 1992; Eisenhardt and Martin 2000). The aim is to maintain variability with regard to strategic and organisational decisions. Anomalies in decision making, aversion to change, clinging to once successful paths, exercising power or resource allocation are all factors which limit the innovative ability of the organisation and thereby its variability.

To loosen the organisation from its solidification, the company can either act consciously to free itself from the switching lock-in, or a situation may occur in the internationalisation environment which more coincidentally causes an opening of the pathway. In internationalisation practice, a conscious pathway break is made when, for example, a mode structure characterised by agents and importers is replaced by a sales subsidiary. This is a new mode of market operation with which the company has not yet gained experience. The positive developments in the foreign market thus far and the motivation of the decision makers to expand business prompt the switch of mode and the strategic change from export to direct investment. The release of the lock-in can, however, also be the result of unintended events occurring during the course of the internationalisation process. This includes, for example, the sudden contract termination of the agent, the financial weakening of a competitor which suddenly make an acquisition possible, or also the unexpected access to a major project resulting from the visit to an international trade fair.

Effective methods which result in a conscious pathway break of the internationalisation pattern thus far can be developed from the tool box of change management and strategic consulting (Gattermeyer and Al-Ani 2001) . Presenting alternative internationalisation options, stopping self-reinforcing processes through behaviour-related intervention (i.e. target agreement meetings with a long-term and short-term time horizon), the introduction of extensive transformation processes, the introduction of counter-paradoxes for breaking away from pathological pathways and systematic resource allocation are only a few of the possible measures. In general, the introduction of strategic structuring instruments with specific adjustments to the internationalisation is recommended. These will give the international management greater flexibility for taking action.

9.5.5 International path creation

Not only must there be a break or release from the path followed thus far, but also alternative pathways as options for action must be created (Hutzschenreuter et al. 2007; Dievernich 2007). For the decision maker there is therefore the clear necessity for further development, despite and also because of past internationalisation experience. Success concepts are not only to be conserved but also continuously developed. To stand still is to take a step backwards – translating this insight into action is what international path creation is about. An important aid for this is the introduction of a target mode. The definition of the desired for target mode already at market entry serves as orientation for those involved in the internationalisation and prevents, through its clear goal formulation, the pursuance of inefficient paths. In internationalisation practice, this would mean that the selected market-entry strategy is only temporary in nature and would be sooner or later switched to the target mode (for example, a subsidiary). For decision makers, the selection of market-entry strategy with this path perspective depends on other factors than as was the case with market-entry. It is now no longer a question of expected sales growth, market-entry costs or level of risk but more a question of factors such as easy changeability, information transfer to increase market knowledge or low switching costs.

Furthermore, focus is to be placed on international management development so that awareness of the system environment for internationalisation and mode switching will be achieved. Conscious reflection takes centre stage. The goal must be to avoid a limiting path dependency, to critically observe positive path dependencies or self-reinforcing mechanisms or to consciously further develop so that a solidifying path can be left.

Concrete measures for reducing aversion to change must first have as their goal that decision makers possess the necessary awareness and sensitivity, and be able to recognise the need to switch modes at all. The establishment of a systematic process for the positive value of switching facilitates perception of relevant factors (see Chapter 9.4,Figure 9.1). Decision makers must be able to assess the advantages of a switch. A lack of knowledge and high uncertainty with regard to unknown modes promotes and does not reduce aversion to change. To overcome rigidity, the lack of motivation as regards active internationalisation must be counteracted with the introduction of continuous benchmarking, an ambitious goal setting, repeated employee-/partner-/ and customer surveys, and a method of best-practice exchange. Such measures create transparency and force the management to justify results. They thereby counteract a dissonance-free adherence to the status quo. The overall probability of path dependency is strongly reduced and the management is rendered truly able to make decisions.

In summary, the development path is visualised in Figure 9.2 and is based on the ideas of Schreyögg et al. (2003). The aim is to make the company behaviour in a country visual. A change of market-entry strategy and multiple switches of mode are assumed (see Chapter 8.9).

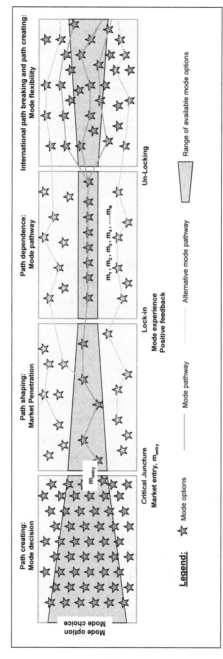

Figure 9.2: Explanatory model of path dependency in internationalisation and mode switching (with reference to Schreyögg et al. 2003; Sydow et al. 2005; Dievernich 2007)

The first phase is characterised by an undirected search process for market-entry options. The grey shadowing is to underline the historical influence of decisions. The transition from the first phase to the second is characterised by Critical Juncture. This is to be understood as the occurrence of the significant event, such as the market-entry decision. This decision and the market entry have sustainable effects and trigger self-reinforcing processes. The further process of foreign operation mode can, as of this point in time, take a pathway-like course; however, this is not essential. Firms can switch their market-entry strategy, or not as the case may be. The transition from the second to the third phase is finally the critical point in time which portrays the beginning of the lock-in and thereby the process-oriented, irreversible characteristic. Before this, every mode of foreign operation is still possible. With the lock-in, possible development processes are narrowed. The third phase portrays the sequentially pursued modes and possible mode switches. They are of stabilising character and constitute the mode pathway. The transition from the third to the fourth phase is characterised by a breaking away from existing development pathway. The number of possible mode options is increased and, in addition to traditional operation modes, strategic alternatives can be considered. In summary, there is high organisational flexibility in the fourth phase for mode innovations.

With the aid of path dependency theory, the influence of patterns or schemes of past experience with market operation on current actions was presented and solutions shown for improving performance in the internationalisation pathway and the management of foreign operations. This study supplies important empirical findings on the influencing factors of the switch, the company's success, the right timing and the decision-making behaviour tied to the switch. It was shown how the key management individuals' strategic ability to act can be achieved and expanded in a targeted way.

How a deviation can be made from an internationalisation pathway and whether it is possible to create something new and to consciously influence the internationalisation pathway was addressed in the phase of international path-breaking and path-creating. In this study, there are no direct empirical results for this; however, in the qualitative section, indications could be found that will be integrated here as a recommendation for management. In essence, firms investigate new possibilities of foreign operation and experiment with them. They create niches or protected spaces in the form of test markets in which the use of new mode strategies is tried out; the decision-making process is rationalised with the perspective of a "target mode".

The explanatory approach of path dependency and the integration of determining factors from the results of this work in a holistic theoretical framework are an attempt to explain how companies operate in foreign markets. The necessity of research with a deeper analysis of these determining factors in single-case studies is obvious and should therefore be mentioned here. Nevertheless, the explanatory framework supplies helpful indications for stabilising positive pathways, recognising negative path dependency, for breaking up paths and proceeding down new paths and for (in sum) for generally carrying out active path management. Although many questions still remain open in this context, a first and comprehensive explanatory approach has been formulated here that not merely explains past behaviour but can also aid active management of pathways in the future.

The results of the present study provide a valuable contribution to the management of foreign operations and questions revolving around mode switching. The aim of this study to further close theoretical gaps and derive useful recommendations for management can be considered fulfilled. The presentation of the empirical results for influencing factors of mode switching and effects on a company's success in a foreign country in particular provide orientation in the internationalisation of the business model.

In conclusion, the management of foreign operations and mode switching for companies is earning increasing respect. For companies after the market-entry phase, the phase of penetration as a third internationalisation phase of realignment and adaptation to a changed global reality will be of high importance. This study attempted to meet this challenge and provide a useful aid through conceptual and empirical research.

References

Adner, Ron and Levinthal, Daniel A.: What is not a real option: Considering boundaries for the application of real options to business strategy, in Academy of management review Vol. 29, No. 1, p. 74-85, 2004.

Aharoni, Y.: The foreign investment decision process, Harvard University, Boston, 1966.

Aharoni, Y.: In Search for the unique: Can firm-specific advantages be evaluated?, in: Journal of management studies, 30, No. 1, p. 31-49, 1993.

Ahlstrom, David and Bruton, Garry D.: International Management, Strategy and Culture in the Emerging World, Cengage Learning, South-Western, 2010.

Alajoutsijärvi, Kimmo, Möller, Kristian and Tähtinen, Jaana: Beautiful exit: how to leave your business partner, in: European Journal of Marketing, Vol. 34, No. 11/12, p. 1270-1289, 2000.

Albaum, Gerald and Duerr, Edwin: International Marketing and Export Management, 6 Ed., FT Prentice Hall, Harlow, 2008.

Albers, Sönke, Klapper, Daniel, Konradt, Udo, Walter, Achim and Wolf, Joachim: Methodik der empirischen Forschung, 2 Ed., Gabler, Wissbaden, 2007.

Amis, John, Slack, Trevor and Hinings, C.R.: The pace, sequence, and linearity of radical change, in: Academy of Management Journal, Vol. 47, No. 1, p. 15-39, 2004.

Amram, Martha and Kulatilaka, Nalin: Real Options – Managing strategic investment in an uncertain world, Harvard Business School Press, Boston, Massachusetts, 1999.

Ancona, Deborah G., Okhuysen, Gerardo A. and Perlow, Leslie A.: Taking time to integrate temporal research, in: Academy of Management Review, Vol. 26, No.4, p. 512-529, 2001.

Andersen, Poul Houman and Skaates, Maria Anne: Ensuring Validity in Qualitative International Business Research, in: Marschan-Piekkari and Catherina Welch: Handbook of Qualitative Research Methods for International Business, p. 464-485, 2004.

Anderson, Otto: Internationalisation and Market Entry Mode: A Review of theories and conceptual frameworks, in: Management International Review, 37, Special Issue 2, p. 27-42, 1997.

Andersson, Per and Mattsson, Lars-Gunnar: Timing of strategic actions in internationalization processes involving intermediares - a network perspective, EIBA Conference Paper, accepted as competitive paper, December, 2004.

Ansoff, H. Igor and McDonnel, Edward: Implanting Strategic Management, 2 Ed. New York, 1990.

Araujo, Luis and Rezende, Sergio: Path dependence, MNCs and the internationalisation process: a relational approach, in: International Business Review, Vol. 12, No. 6, p. 719-737, 2003.

Asmussen, Christian G., Benito, Gabriel R.G. and Petersen, Bent: Organizing foreign market activities: From entry mode choice to configuration decisions, in: International Business Review, 18, p. 145 – 155, 2009.

Auhagen, Elisabeth and Bierhoff, Hans-Werner: Angewandte Sozialpsychologie, 2003

Außenhandelsstatistik (Foreign trade statistics), Statistische Bundesamt (Federal Statistics Office), Fachserie 7, Reihe 1, p. 18., January 2009.

Axinn, Caterine and Matthyssens, Paul: Limits of internationalisation theories in an unlimited world, in: International Marketing Review, p. 436-449, 2001.

Axley, Stephen R.: Communicating Change: Questions to consider, in: Industrial Management, Vol. 42, Issue 4, p. 18-23, Jul./Aug. 2000.

Bach, M.: The world of Serendipity, Prentice-Hall International, London, 1970.

Backhaus, Klaus, Erichson, Bernd, Plinke, Wulf and Weiber, Rolf: Multivariante Analysemethoden, 11 Ed., Springer, 2006.

Bachmann, Anne: Subjektive versus objektive Erfolgsmaße, in: Albers, Sönke, Klapper, Daniel, Konradt, Udo, Walter, Achim and Wolf, Joachim: Methodik der empirischen Forschung, 2 Ed., Gabler, Wissbaden, p. 89-102, 2007.

Barkema, Harry G., Baum, Joel A. and Mannix Elizabeth A.: Management Challenges in a new time, in: Academy of Management Journal, Vol. 45, No. 5, p. 916-930, 2002.

Barreto, Ilídio: Dynamic Capabilities: A Review of Past Research and an Agenda for the Future, in: Journal of Management, Vol. 36, No. 1, p. 256 – 280, 2010.

Bartlett, C.A. and Ghoshal, S.: Managing Across Boarders: The Transnational Solution, Havard Business School Press, Boston, 1989.

Bartlett, C.A. and Ghoshal, S.: Internationale Unternehmensführung. Innovation, globale Effizienz, differenziertes Marketing, Campus, 1990.

Bartlett, C.A., Birkinshaw, Julian and Ghoshal, S.: Transnational Management, McGraw Hill, 4 Ed. New York, 2004.

Bazerman, Max H. and Chugh, Dolly: Decisions without blinders, in: Harvard Business Review, Vol. 84, Issue 1, p. 88-97, Jan. 2006.

Baum, Robert J. and Wally, Stefan: Strategic decision speed and firm performance, in: Strategic Management Journal, 24, p. 1107-1129, 2003.

Bausch, Andreas and Krist, Mario: The effect of context-related moderators on the internationalisation-performance relationship: Evidence from meta analysis, in: Management International Review, Vol. 47, 3, p. 319-347, 2007.

Beamish, Paul W. and Jiang, Ruihua Joy: Timing and performance of post entry foreign subsidiaries, in: Academy of management, best conference Paper 2004 IM:D1.

Becker, Marc: Controlling von Internationalisierungsprozessen, MIR-Edition, Gabler Wiesbaden, 2005.

Bell, Jim, Young, Stephen and Crick, Dave: Small Firm Internationalization and Business Strategy - an exploratory study of "knowledge-intensive" and "traditional" manufacturing firms in the UK, in: International Small Business Journal, Vol. 22 (1), 23-56, 2004.

Bell, Jim, McNaughton, Rod, Young, Stephen and Crick, Dave: Towards an Integrative Model of Small Firm Internationalisation, in: Journal of International Entrepreneurship, 1, p. 339-362, 2003.

Benito, Gabriel R.G., Pedersen, Torben and Petersen, Bent: Export Channel Dynamics: An Empirical Investigation, in: Managerial and Decision Economics, 26, p. 159 – 173, 2005.

Benito G.R.G, Petersen, B and Welch, L.: Towards more realistic conceptualisations of foreign operation modes, in: Journal of International Business Studies, 40, p. 1455 - 1470, 2009.

Benito G.R.G and Welch, L.S.: Foreign Market Servicing: Beyond choice of entry mode, in: Journal of International Marketing, Vol. 2, No. 2, p. 7-27, 1994.

Berenkoven, Ludwig, Eckert, Werner and Ellenrieder, Peter: Marktforschung: Methodische Grundlagen und praktische Anwendung, 11 Ed., Gabler, Wiesbaden, 2006.

Berger, Suzanne: How we compete, Currency Doubleday, New York, 2006.

Birkinshaw, J.: Entrepreneurship in multinational corporations: the characteristics of subsidiary initiatives, in: Strategic Management Journal, 18, p. 207-229, 1997.

Birkinshaw, Julian and Hood, Neil: Multinational subsidiary evolution: Capability and charter change in foreign-owned subsidiary company, in: Academy of Management Review, Vol. 23, No. 4, p. 773-795, 1998.

Birkinshaw, Julian: Publishing qualitative research in International Business, in: Marschan-Piekkari and Catherina Welch: Handbook of Qualitative Research Methods for International Business, p. 570-584, 2004.

Bierhoff, Hans-Werner: Sozialpsychologie, 5 Ed., Kohlhammer, Stuttgart 2000.

Bhaskar, Roy: A Realist Theory of Science, Leeds, 1975.

Böhler, Heymo: Marktforschung, 3 Ed., Kohlhammer Verlag, 2004.

Borghoff, Thomas: The capability of global evolutionary dynamics, in: Oesterle, Michael-Jörg: Internationales Management im Umbruch, Deutscher Universitäts-Verlag, 2007.

Bortz, Jürgen and Döring, Nicola: Forschungsmethoden und Evaluation, 4.Aufl., Springer, 2006.

Bronner, Rolf: Pathologies of Decision-making: Causes, Forms, and Handling, in: Management International Review, 2003/1, Vol. 43, p. 85-101, 2003.

Brouthers, Keith: Institutional, cultural and transaction cost influences on entry mode choice and performance, in: Journal of International Business Studies 33 (2), p. 203–221, 2002.

Brouthers, Keith and Brouthers, Lance: Why service and manufacturing entry mode choices differ: the influence of transaction cost factors, risk and trust, in: Journal of Management Studies 40 (5), p. 1179–1204, 2003.

Brouthers, Keith D. and Hennart, Jean-Francois: Insight from international entry mode research, in: Journal of Management, Vol. 33, No. 3, p. 395-425, 2007.

Brouthers, Lance E. and Nakos, George: The role of systematic international market selection on small firms`export performance, in: Journal of small business management, 43 (4), p. 363 – 381, 2005.

Buber, Renate and Holzmüller, Hartmut H. (eds.): Qualitative Marktforschung, 2. Ed. Gabler, Wiesbaden, 2009.

Buckley, Peter and Casson, Mark: The optimal timing of a foreign direct investment, in: The economic journal, Vol. 91, No. 361, p. 75-87, 1981.

Buckley, P.J. and Casson, M.C.: A theory of cooperation in international business, in: Cooperative strategies in international business, p. 31-55, 1988.

Buckley, P.J. and Casson, M.C.: The future of the multinational enterprise, 2 Ed. Macmillan, London, 1991.

Buckley, P.J. and Casson, M.C.: Models of the multinational enterprise, in: Journal of international Business Studies, 29 Jg., Nr. 1, p. 21-44, 1998.

Buckley, Peter J., Devinney M. and Louviere, Jordan J: Do Managers behave the way theory suggests? A choice-theoretic examination of foreign direct investment location decision making, in: Journal of International Business Studies, 38, p. 1069 – 1094, 2007.

Buckley, Peter J. and Ghauri Pervez (eds.): The Internationalization of the Firm: A Reader, London: Academic Press, 1994.

Bühl, Achim: SPSS 16, 11 Ed., Pearson, 2008.

Bundesministerium für Wirtschaft und Technologie (BMWI): Jahreswirtschaftsbericht 2007, Berlin, p. 19, Feb. 2007.

Burke, A.G.: Leading organizational change, in: S. Chowdhury (Ed.): Organisation, p. 291-310, Financial Times, Prentice Hall, 2002.

Byrne, B., M.: Structural Equation Modelling with AMOS, 2nd Ed, Taylor and Francis Group, Sussex, 2010.

Calof, Jonathan L.: The Internationalization Process: an Examination of Mode Change, Mode Choice, and Performance. Unpublished doctoral dissertation, University of Western Ontario, Western Business School, London, Canada, 1991.

Calof, Jonathan L.: The Mode Choice and Change Decision Process and its Impact on international performance, in: International Business Review, 2, No. 1, p. 97-120, 1993.

Calof, Jonathan L. and Beamish, Paul W.: Adapting to Foreign Markets: Explaining Internationalization: International Business Review, 4 (2), p. 115-131, 1995.

Cadogan, John, W., Diamantopouluos, Adamantios and Siguaw, Judy A.: Export-Market-oriented Activities: Their Antecedents and Performance Consequences, in: Journal of International Business Studies, 33, 3, p. 615-626, 2002.

Cavusgil, S.T.: Differences among exporting firms based on their degree of inernationalisation, in: Journal of business research, 12, p. 195-208, 1984.

Chetty, Sylvie and Agndal, Henrik: The impact of relationships on changes in internationalisation strategies of SMEs, in: European Journal of Marketing, Vol. 41, No. 11/12, p. 1449-1474, 2007.

Chetty, Sylvie and Champell-Hunt, Colin: Paths to internationalisation among small- to medium sized firms - a global versus regional approach, in: European Journal of Marketing, Vol. 37, p. 796-820, 2003.

Chetty, Sylvie and Blankenburg Holm, Desiree: Internationalisation of small to medium-sized mnufacturing firms: a network approach, in: International Business review, 9, p. 77-93, 2000.

Chetty, Sylvie and Champell-Hunt, Colin: A strategic approach to internationalization: a traditional versus a "born-global" approach, in: Journal of International Marketing, Vol.12, No.1, p. 57-81, 2004.

Child, John, Faulkner, David and Tallman, Stephen: Cooperative Strategy, 2 Ed. Oxford, 2005

Child, John, Hong Ng, Sek and Wong, Christine: Psychic Distance and Internationalisation, in: International Studies of Management & Organisation, Vol. 32, No. 1, p. 36-56, Spring 2002.

Chirico, Francesco and Nordqvist, Mattias: Dynamic capabilities and trans-generational value creation in family firms: The role of organizational culture, in: International Small Business Journal, Vol. 28, p. 487 – 504, 2010.

Clark, Timothy, Pugh, Derek S. and Mallory, Geoff: The process of internationalisation in the operating firm, in: International Business Review, Vol. 6, No. 6, p. 605-623, 1997.

Coase, Ronald H.: The nature of the firm, in: Economica, 4 Jg., p. 386-405, 1937.

Cohen, W.M. and Levinthal, D.A.: Absorptive Capacity: A New Perspective on Learning and Innovation, in: Administrative Science Quarterly, 35, No. 1, 1990, p. 128-152, 1990.

Copeland, Tom and Tufano, Peter: Komplexe Entscheidungen leicht gemacht, in: Harvard Business Manager, p. 74-87, Juni 2004.

Coviello Nicole E. and Jones Marian V.: Internationalization: conceptualising an entrepreneurial process of behaviour in time, in: Journal of International Business Studies, 36, 3, p. 284-303, 2005.

Coviello Nicole E. and McAuley, Andrew: Internationalization and the smaller firm: a review of contemporary empirical research, in: Management International Review, 39 (3): p. 223-256, 1999.

Cranach, M. von: Toward a theory of the acting group, in: E. White & J.H. Davis (Eds.): Understanding group behavior: Small group processes and interpersonal relations, New York, Lawrence Erlbaum, p. 147-187, 1996.

Czinkota, Michael R.: Export development strategies: US Promotion policy, New York: Praeger, 1982.

Czinkota, Michael R.: How government can help to increase U.S. Export performance,, 111th Congress, 2nd Session, Georgetown University Washington, 2010.

Czinkota, Michael R. and Ronkainen, Ikka A.: An international marketing manifesto, in: Journal of International Marketing, Vol. 11, No. 1, p. 13-27, 2003.

Cyert, Richard M. and March, James G.: A behavioral theory of the firm, New Jersey, 1963.

Cyert, Richard M. and March, James G.: Eine verhaltenswissenschaftliche Theorie der Unternehmung, 2 Auflage, Stuttgart, 1995

Daniels, John D. and Cannice, Mark V.: Interview studies in international business, in: Marschan-Piekkari and Catherina Welch: Handbook of Qualitative Research Methods for International Business, p. 185-206, 2004.

David, P. A.: Clio and the economics of QWERTY, in: American Economic Review, 75(2), p. 332-336, 1985.

De Wit, Bob and Meyer, Ron: Strategy – Process, Content, Context, 3th Edition, Thomson Learning, 2004.

De Geer, Hans, Borglund, Tommy and Frostenson, Magnus: Interpreting the international firm: Going beyond interviews, in: Marschan-Piekkari and Catherina Welch: Handbook of Qualitative Research Methods for International Business, p. 324-341, 2004.

Denbigh, K.G.: Three Concepts of Time, Springer-Verlag Heidelberg Berlin, 1990.

Denzin, Norman K. and Lincoln Yvonna S.: Handbook of Qualitative Research, London Sage, 1994.

Denzin, N. and Lincoln, Y.S.: Handbook of qualitative research, 2 Ed., London, Thousands Oaks, Sage, 2000.

Dhanaraj, Charles and Beamish, Paul W: A resource-based approach to study of export performanc, in: Journal of small business management, 41 (3), p. 242-262, 2003.

Dibrell, Clay, Davis, Peter S. and Danskin, Paula: The influence of Internationalisation on Time-Based Competition, in: Management International Review, Vol. 45, p. 173-19, 2005.

Dichtl, E, Köglmayr, H.-G. and Müller, S: International orientation as a precondition for export success, in: Journal of International Business Studies, Vol. 21, No. 1, p. 23-40, 1990.

Diekmann, Andreas: Empirische Sozialforschung, 20 Ed., rowohlt, Hamburg, 2009.

Dievernich, Frank, E.P.: Pfadabhängigkeit im Management, Kohlhammer, Stuttgart, 2007.

Dülfer, E: Internationales Management in unterschiedlichen Kulturbereichen, München, Wien 1992.

Dunning, J.H.: Trade, Location of economic activity and MNE: A search for an eclectic approach, in: Ohlin, Hesselborn and Wijkmann: The international allocation of economic activity, p. 395-418, 1977.

Dunning, J.H.: Explaining the international direct investment position of countries: towards a dynamic or development approach, in: Weltwirtschaftliches Archiv, 117 (Heft1), p. 30-64, 1981.

Dunning, J.H.: Explaining the international production, London, Boston, Unwin Hyman, 1988a.

Dunning, J.H.: The eclectic paradigm of international production: A restatement and some possible extensions, in: Journal of international business studies, Vol. 19, No. 1, p. 1-13, 1988b.

Dunning, J.H.: The globalisation of business, Routledge, London, New York, 1993.

Dunning, J.H.: The eclectic paradigm as an envelope for economic and business theories of MNE activity, in: International Business Review, 9, p. 163-190, 2000.

Eckstein, Peter P.: Angewandte Statistik mit SPSS, 6 Ed. Gabler, Wiesbaden, 2008.

Eisend, Martin: Weltbild und Forschungsfrage, in: Haase, Michaela: Kritische Reflektion emperischer Forschungsmethodk, Diskussionsbeiträge des Fachbereichs Wirtschaftswissenschaft, Freie Universität Berlin, p. 31, 5/2007.

Eisenhardt, Kathleen and Martin, Jeffrey: Dynamic Capabilities: What are they?, in: Strategic Management Journal, Vol. 21, p. 1105 – 1121, 2000.

Engelen, A., Heinmann, F. and Brettel, M.: Cross-cultural entrepreneurship research: Current status and framework for future studies, in: Journal of International Entrepreneur, 7, p. 163-189, 2009.

Eriksson, Kent, Majkgård, Anders and Sharma, D. Deo: Path dependence and knowledge development in the internationalisation process, in: Management International Review, Vol. 40, p. 307-328, 2000.

Eriksson, Kent, Majkgård, Anders and Sharma, D. Deo: Time and experience in the internationalization process, Zeitschrift für Betriebswirtschaft, 71. Jg., H. 1, p. 21-43, 2001.

Eisele, Jürgen: Erfolgsfaktoren des Joint-Venture-Management, Diss. Mannheim 1995.

Ellebracht, Heiner, Lenz, Gerhard, Osterhold, Gisela and Schäfer, Helmut: Systemische Organisations- und Unternehmensberatung, Gabler, Wiesbaden, 2002.

Flanagan, John C: The Critical Incident Technique, in: Psychological Bulletin, vol. 51, no. 4, p. 327-358, 1954.

Fletcher, Richard: A holistic approach to internationalisation, in: International Business Review, 10, p. 25-49, 2001.

Flick, Uwe, Kardorff, Ernst and Steinke, Ines: Qualitative Forschung, 4. Ed., Rowohlt, Hamburg 2005.

Flick, Uwe: Qualitative Sozialforschung, 3. Ed., Rowohlt, Hamburg 2005.

Fisch, Jan Hendrik: Establishing foreign subsidiaries as investments under uncertainty, Conference Paper, 30 th annual EIBA Conference, Ljubljana, Slovenia, December 5-8, 2004.

Fisch, Jan Henrik: Internationale Realoptionen, Aufbau von Auslandsgesellschaften bei Unsicherheit und Irreversibilität, Gabler Wiesbaden, 2006.

Fischer, Lorenz and Wiswede, Günter: Grundlagen der Sozialpsychologie, 2 Ed., Oldenbourg, 2002.

Foster, Jeremy, Barkus, Emma and Yavorsky, Christian: Understanding and using advanced statistics, Sage, 2006.

FAZ am Sonntag, Interview with CEO McKinsey Germany, 15.1.2005.

Frankfurter Allgemeine Zeitung, 20 goldene Regeln für die unternehmerische Entscheidung, 2.4.2006.

Frishammer, Johan and Andersson, Svante: The overestimated role of strategic orientations for international performance of smaller firms, in: Journal of international entrepreneur, p. 57-77, 2009.

Freidank, Jan: Managing transformational change, Dissertation, unpublished, San Diego, 1994.

Frey, Dieter and Irle, Martin: Theorien der Sozialpsychologie, Bd. 2, 2 Ed., 2002.

Fryges, Helmut: The Change of Sales Modes in International Markets – Empirical Results for German and British High-Tech Firms, Discussion Paper No. 05-82, Century for European Economic Research (ZEW), 2005.

Fujita, M.: Transnational Activities of Small and Medium-Sized Enterprises, Boston: Kluwer Academic Publisher 1998.

Gabrielsson, Mika, Kirpalani, Manek, Dimitratosd, Pavlos, Solberg, Carl Arthur and Zucchellag, Antonella: Born globals: Propositions to help advance the theory, in: International business review, 17, p. 385-401, 2008.

Gabrielsson, Mika and Kirpalani, Manek: Born global: How to reach new business space rapidly, in: International business review, 13, p. 555-571, 2004.

Gattermeyer, Wolfgang and Al-Ani, Ayad: Change Management und Unternehmenserfolg, 2 Aufl., Wiesbaden, 2001.

Gelbrich, Katja: Blueprinting, sequentielle Ereignismethode und Critical Incident Technique, in: Buber, Renate and Holzmüller, Hartmut H. (eds.): Qualitative Marktforschung, 2. Ed. Gabler, Wiesbaden, p. 617-633, 2009.

Gemser, Gerda, Brand, Maryse J. and Sorge, Arndt: Exploring the Internationalisation Process of Small Business: A Study of Dutch Old and New Economy Firms, in: Management International Review, Vol. 44, 2004/2.

German Chamber of Commerce/Deutscher Industrie- und Handelskammertag: Going International 2007, Experience and Perspectives of the German Business Abroad, Survey, Berlin, November 2007.

Gersick, Connie: Revolutionary Change Theories: A Multilevel Exploration of the Punctuated Equilibrium Paradigm, in: The Academy of Management Review 16(1): p. 10-36, 1991.

Ghauri, Pervez: Designing and conducting case studies in international business, in: Handbook of Qualitative Research Methods for International Business, edited by Rebbecca Marschan-Piekkari and Catherina Welch, Edgar Elgar Publishing, p. 109-124, 2004.

Ghemawat, Pankaj: Globale Expansion – kein leichter Weg, in: Harvard Business Manager, p. 82-94, Februar 2002.

Ghymn, Kyng-il, Liesch, Peter and Mattson, Jan: Australian import managers´ purchasing decision behavior: an empirical study, in: International Marketing Review, Vol.16, No.3, p. 202-215.

Gomes, L. and Ramaswamy, K.: An Empirical Examination of the Form of the Relationship between Multinationality and Performance, in: Journal of International Business Studies, 30 (1), p. 173-187, 1999.

Giddens, A.: Die Konstitution der Gesellschaft. Grundzüge einer Theorie der Strukturierung, Frankfurt a.M., 1988.

Gmünden, Hans Georg: Success factors of export marketing – a meta analytical critique of the empirical studies, in: New perspectives on international marketing, p. 33-62, 1991.

Greenwood, R. and Hinings, C.R.: Organizational design types, tracks and the dynamic of strategic change, Organisation Studies, 9, p. 293-316, 1988.

Greipel, Peter: Strategie und Kultur, Paul Haupt Verlag, Dissertation, Stuttgart, 1988.

Greif, Siegfried, Runde, Bernd and Seeberg, Ilka: Erfolge und Misserfolge beim Change Management, Hofgrefe Verlag Göttingen, 2004.

Grünig, Rudolf and Kühn, Richard: Entscheidungsverfahren für komplexe Probleme, Springer Berlin Heidelberg New York, 2004.

Guba, E.G. and Lincoln, Y.S.: Competing paradigms in qualitative research; in: Denzin and Lincoln: Handbook of Qualitative Research, p. 105-117, Sage Publication, 1994.

Guba, E.G. and Lincoln, Y.S.: Paradigmatic controversies, contradictions, and emerging confluences; in: Denzin and Lincoln: Handbook of Qualitative Research, 3 Ed., p. 191-215, Sage Publication 2005.

Gupta, A.K. and Govindarajan, V.: Cultivating a global mindset, in: Academy of Management Executive, 16, 1, p. 116-126, 2002.

Hall, Edward T. and Hall, Mildred Reed: Understanding cultural differences: keys to success in West Germany, France and the United States, Intercultural Press, 1996.

Haase, Michaela: Kritische Reflektion emperischer Forschungsmethodk, Diskussionsbeiträge des Fachbereichs Wirtschaftswissenschaft, Freie Universität Berlin, 5/2007.

Hammond, John S., Kenney, Ralph L. and Raiffa, Howard: The hidden traps in decision making, in: Harvard Business Review, p. 1-11, Sept-Oct 1998.

Heinen, Edmund: Unternehmenskultur, Oldenbuorg, München, Wien, 1987.

Hennart, Jean-Francois: A Theory of Multinational Enterprise, The University of Michigan Press, Ann Arbour, 1982.

Hinterhuber, Hans Hartmann: Strategische Unternehmensführung – strategisches Denken, Band 1 und 2, 7. Ed., de Gruyter, Berlin, 2004.

Hitt, M.A., Hoskisson, R.E. and Kim, H.: International Diversification: Effects on Innovation and firm performance in product diversified firms, in: Academy of Management Journal, 40 (4), p. 767-798, 1997.

Hofstede, Geert: Culture´s consequences, Beverly Hills, CA: Sage, 1980.

Hofstede, Geert: Cultures and Organizations: Software of the mind, London, McGraw-Hill, 1991.

Hofstede, Geert: Lokales Denken, globales Handeln, 2. Aufl., München 2001.

Hollensen, Svend: Global Marketing, FT Prentice Hall, 4. Edition, Harlow, 2007.

Holtmann, Jan Philip: Pfadabhängigkeit strategischer Entscheidungen, Kölner Wissenschaftsverlag, Dissertation, 2008.

Hurmerinta-Peltomäki, Leila: Time and Internationalisation, Dissertation, Turku School of Economics/Finland, 2001.

Hurmerinta-Peltomäki, Leila: Time and Internationalisation, in: Journal of International Entrepreneurship, 1, p. 217-236, 2003.

Hurmerinta-Peltomäki and Nummela, Niina: First the sugar, then the eggs...or the other way round? Mixed methods in international business research, in: Marschan-Piekkari and Catherina Welch: Handbook of Qualitative Research Methods for International Business, p. 162-180, 2004.

Hutzschenreuter, T., Pedersen, T. and Volberda, H.: The role of path dependency and managerial intentionality: a perspective on international business research, in: Journal of international business studies, 38, p. 1055-1068, 2007.

Hymer, S.H.: The international operations of national firms: a study of direct foreign investment, MIT Press, Cambridge, MA, 1976.

IHK Stuttgart: Going International, Stuttgart, 2004, 2007, 2008.

Johansson, Johny K.: Global Marketing: Foreign Entry, Local Marketing And Global Management, McGrawHill/Irwin, 2005.

Johanson, J. and Wiedersheim-Paul, F.: The internationalisation of the Firm – four swedish cases, in: Journal of Management Studies, p. 305-322, 1975.

Johanson, J. and Mattson, L-G.: Internationalization in Industrial Systems – A Network Approach, in: Strategies in Global Competition, edited by Hood and Vahlne, New York, p. 287-314, 1988.

Johanson, J. and Mattson, L-G.: Network positions and strategic action – an analytical framework, in: Industrial Networks: A new view of reality, p. 205-217, 1992.

Johanson, J. and Vahlne, J.E.: The internationalisation of the firm: A model of knowledge development and increasing foreign market commitments, in: Journal of International Business Studies, Vol. 8, Nr.1, p. 23-32, 1977.

Johanson, J. and Vahlne, J.E.: The mechanism of internationalisation, in: International Marketing Review, 7 (4), p. 11-24, 1990.

Jones, Marc T.: Globalisation and Organisational Restructuring A strategic perspective, in: Thunderbird International Business Review, Vol. 44 (3), p. 325-351, May-June 2002.

Jones, Marian V.: The Internationalisation of Small High-Technology Firms, in: Journal of International Marketing, 7, 4, p. 15-41, 1999.

Jones, Marian V. and Coviello Nicole: Internationalisation: conceptualising an entrepreneurial process of behavior in time, in: Journal of International Business Studies, 36, p. 284-303, 2005.

Jost, Peter-J.: Strategisches Konfliktmanagement in Organisationen, 2. Aufl., Wiesbaden 1999.

Jost, Peter-J.: Organisation und Motivation, Wiesbaden 2000.

Kappler, Ekkehard, in: Perspektiven der Strategischen Unternehmensführung, Theorie aus der Praxis – Zur Wirkung strategischer Unternehmensführung, p. 83, 2003

Karim, Samina and Mitchell, Will: Path-dependent and path-breaking change: Reconfiguring business resources following acquisitions in the U.S. Medical Sector, 1978 – 1995, in: Strategic Management Journal, Vol. 21, p. 1061 -1081, 2000.

Karlsen, Tore, Silseth, Pal R., Benito, Gabriel R.G. and Welch, Lawrence S.: Knowledge, internationalization of the firm, and inward - outward connections, in: Industrial Marketing Management, Vol. 32, p. 385-396, 2003.

Katsikea, Evangelia and Morgan, Robert E.: Exploring export sales management practices in small - and medium sized firms, in: Industrial Marketing Management, Vol. 32, p. 467-480, 2003.

Katsikea, Evangelia, Theodosiou, Marios, Morgan, Robert E. and Papavassiliou: Export Market Expansion Strategies of Direct-Selling Small and Medium -Sized Firms: Implications for Export Sales Management Activities, in: Journal of International Marketing, Vol. 13, No. 2, p. 57-92, 2005.

Katsikeas, C.S., Deng, S.L. and Wortzel, L.H.: Perceived export success factors of small and medium-sized Canadian firms, 5 (4), Journal of International Marketing, p. 53-72, 2003.

Katsikeas, Constanine S.: Determinants of export performance in a European context, in: European Journal of Marketing, Vol. 30, No. 6, p. 6-35, 1996.

Kaufmann, Lutz and Jentzsch, Andreas: Internationalisation Process: The case of Automotive Suplliers in China, in: Journal of International Marketing, Vol. 14, No. 2, p. 52-84, 2006.

Kinkel, Steffen and Lay, Gunter: Motive, strategische Passfähigkeit und Produktivitätseffekte des Aufbaus ausländischer Produktionsstandorte, in: Zeitschrift für Betriebswirtschaft, 74. Jg., H. 5, p. 415-440, 2004.

Kirchner, Martin: Strategisches Akquisitionsmanagement im Konzern, Gabler, Wiesbaden, 1991.

Knight, Gary A. and Kim Daekwan: International business competence and the contemporary firm, in: Journal of International Business Studies, 40, p. 255-273, 2009.

Kobi, Jean-Marcel and Wüthrich, Hans A.: Unternehmenskultur: Der Schüssel des Erfolgs, in: Output, Vl. 14, p. 23-28, 1985.

Krist, Mario: Internatiionalization and firm performance, Dissertation, Gabler Wissenschaft, Wiesebaden, 2009.

Koch, Jochen: Strategic Paths and Media Management – A Path Dependency Analysis of the German Newspaper, Branch of High Quality Journalism, Media Management, SBR 60, p. 50-73, January 2008.

Kogut, B. and Singh, H.: The effect of national culture on the choice of entry mode, in: Journal of International Business Studies, Vol. 19, No.3, p. 411-432, 1988.

Kornmeier, Martin: Kulturelle Offenheit -Auswirkungen psychischer Distanz im interkulturellen Marketing, 2002.

Kotter, J.P.: Leading Change, HBS Press, Boston, MA, 1996.

Kutschker, Michael: Evolution, Episoden und Epochen: Die Führung von Internationalisierungsprozessen, in: Engelhard, J. (Hrsg.): Strategische Führung internationaler Unternehmen. Paradoxien, Strategien, Erfahrungen, Wiesbaden, p. 1-37, 1996.

Kutschker, Michael: Kooperation: Grundlagen der sozialwissenschaftlichen Prozessforschung, in: Kooperationen, Allianzen und Netzwerke, Joachim Zentes/Bernhard Swoboda and Dirk Moschett (Hrsg.), Wiesbaden, p.234-254, 2003a.

Kutschker, Michael: Prozessuale Aspekte der Kooperation, in: Kooperationen, Allianzen und Netzwerke, Joachim Zentes, Bernhard Swoboda and Dirk Moschett (Hrsg.), Wiesbaden, p. 1055 – 1084; 2003b.

Kutschker, Michael and Bäuerle, Iris: Three + One: Multidimensional Strategy of internationalisation, MIR, 37 Jg., Nr.2, p.101-124, 1997.

Kutschker, Michael and Schmid, Stefan: Internationales Management, 5. Aufl. München, Wien 2006.

Kuemmerle, Walter: The Entrepreneur's Path to Global Expansion, in: MIT Sloan Management Review, p. 42-49, Winter 2005.

Knight, Gary A. and Cavusgil, Tamar, S. Innovation, organizational capabilities, and the born-global firm, in: Journal of International Business Studies, 35, p. 124-141, 2004.

Knight, Gary A. and Kim, Daekwan: International business competence and the contemporary firm, in: Journal of international business studies, p. 255-273, 2009.

Lamb, P.W. and Liesch, P.W.: The internationalisation process of the smaller firm: ref-framing the relationships between market commitment, knowledge and involvement, Management International Review, 42, 1, p. 7-26, 2002.

Lee, Chong S. and Habte-Giorgis, Berhe: Empirical approach to the sequential relationships between firm strategy, export activity, and performance in US manufacturing firms, in: International Business Review, 13, p. 101-129, 2004.

Leonidou, Leonidas C.: An analysis of the barriers hindering small business export development, in: Journal of small business management, 42 (3), p. 279-302, 2004.

Leonidou, Leonidas C., Katsikeas, Constantine S. and Coudounaris, Dafnis N.: Five decades of business research into exporting: A bibliographic analysis, in: Journal of international management, 16, p. 78-91, 2010.

Leonard-Barton, Dororthy: Core Capabilities and Core Rigidities: A Paradox in Managing New Product Development, in: Strategic Management Journal, Vol. 13, Special Issue: Strategy Process: Managing Corporate Self-Renewal, p. 111-125, 1992.

Lewin, K.: Group Decision and Social Change", in: E. Maccoby, E. Newcomb and E. Hartley (Editors): Readings in Social Psychology, New York, 1948.

Li, Lei/Li, Dan and Dalgic, Tevfik: Internationalization Process of Small and Medium-sized Enterprises: Toward a Hybrid Model of Experiental Learning and Planning, in: Management International Review, Vol. 44, p. 93-116, 2004.

Lichtenstein, Benyamin Bergmann and Lumpkin, G.T.: The role of organisational learning in the opportunity-recognition process, in: Entrepreneurship Theory and Practice, July, p. 451-472, 2005.

Link, Wolfgang: Erfolgspotenziale für die Internationalisation, Wiesbaden 1997.

Luostarinen, R.: Internationalization of the Firm, 3. Ed., Helsinki, 1989.

Lynch, Richard: Strategic Management, 5th Ed., Harlow, 2009.

Macharzina, K. and Engelhard, J.: Paradigm Shift in International Business Research: From Partist and Eclectic Approaches to the GAINS Paradigm, in: Management International Review, 31Jg., Special Issue, p. 23-43, 1991.

Macharzina, Klaus and Wolf, Joachim: Unternehmensführung – Das internationale Managementwissen, 5 Ed., Gabler, Wiesbaden, 2005.

Maitland, Elizabeth, Rose, L. Elizabeth and Stephen, Nicholas: How firms grow: clustering as a dynamic model of internationalization, in: Journal of international business studies, 36, p. 435-451, 2005.

Malhotra, Naresh K., Agarwal James and Ulgado Francis M.: Internationalization and entry modes: A multitheoretical framework and research propositions, in: Journal of international marketing, Vol. 11, No.4, p. 1-31, 2003.

Malik, Fredmund: Manager Magazin, March 2009.

Marschan-Piekkari, Rebbecca and Welch, Catherina: Handbook of Qualitative Research Methods for International Business, Edgar Elgar Publishing, 2004.

Macdonald, Stuart and Hellgren, Bo: The interview in International Business Research: Problems we would rather not talk about, in: Marschan-Piekkari, Rebbecca and Welch, Catherina: Handbook of Qualitative Research Methods for International Business, Edgar Elgar Publishing, p. 264-281, 2004.

McDonald, Frank, Krause, Jürgen and Tüselmann, Heinz-Josef: Cautious International Entrepreneurs: The Case of the Mittelstand, in: Journal of International Entrepreneurship,1, p. 363-381, 2003.

McKenna, Richard J. and Martin-Smith, Brett: Decision making as a simplification process: new conceptual perspectives, in: Management Decision, Vol. 43, No. 6, p. 821-836, 2005.

McNaughton, Rod B.: The export mode decision-making process in small knowledge-intensive firms, in: Marketing Intelligence & Planning, 19/1, p. 12-20, 2001.

Meissner, Hans Günther and Gerber, Stephan: Die Auslandsinvestition als Entscheidungsproblem, in: Betriebswirtschaftliche Forschung und Praxis, 32, No. 3, p. 217-228, 1980.

Melin, L.: Internationalization as a Strategy Process, in: Strategic Management Journal, Vol. 13, p. 99-118, 1992.

Meyer, Klaus E. and Skak, Ane: Networks, Serendipity and SME Entry into Eastern Europe, in: European Management Journal; April, Vol. 20, No. 2, p. 179-188, 2002.

Miles, B. Matthew and Huberman, Michael, A: Qualitative Data Analysis – an expanded sourcebook, 2. Ed., Sage, 1994.

Miller, Lawrence: American Spirit, Visions of a new corporate culture, Morrow New York, 1984.

Mintzberg, Henry, Raisinghani, D. and Theoret, A: The structure of unstructured decision process, in: Administrative Science Quarterly, Vol. 21, p. 246-275, 1976.

Mintzberg, Henry: The Rise and fall of strategic planning, Prentice Hall, Englewood Cliffs, New York, 1994.

Mintzberg, Henry, Ahlstrand Bruce W., Lamprel, Joseph: Strategy safari: A guided tour through the wilds of strategic management, The free press/Simon Schuster, New York, 1998.

Moen, Oystein and Servais, Per: Born Global or Gradual Global? Examining the export behavior of small and medium sized enterprises, in: Journal of International Marketing, Vol.10, No.3, 2002, p. 49-72, 2002.

Morosini, P. and Singh, H.: Post-Cross-Border Acquisition: Implementing "National Culture Compatible" Strategy´s to Improve Performance, in: European Management Journal, 12 (4), p. 390-398, 1994.

Morosini, P., Shane, S. and Singh, H.: National cultural distance and cross-border acquisition performance, in: Journal of International Business Studies, 29 (1), p.137-158, 1998.

Morris, Donald: A new tool for strategy analysis: the opportunity model, in: Journal of business strategy, Vol. 26, No.3, p. 50-56, 2005.

Morschett, Dirk, Schramm-Klein, Hanna and Swoboda, Bernhard: Decades of research on market entry modes: What do we really know about external antecedents of entry mode choice?, in: Journal of international Management, 16, p. 60 – 77, 2010.

Moser, Reinhard: Ausländische Direktinvestitionen, Gabler Wissenschaftsverlag, Wiesbaden 2008.

Müller-Stewens, Günter and Lechner, Christoph, in: Perspektiven der Strategischen Unternehmensführung, Strategische Prozessforschung – Grundlagen und Perspektiven, p. 58, 2003.

Neubert, Michael: Internationale Markterschließung, mi-Fachverlag, Redline, Landsberg am Lech, 2006.

Niedereichholz, Christel: Unternehmensberatung, Part 1 and 2, 2 Ed. München Oldenburg, 1996.

Newmann, Isadore and McNeil: Conducting survey research in social science, University Press, Boston, 1998.

Nippa, Michael and Petzold, Kerstin: Zur Anwendbarkeit des Realoptionenansatzes als Instrument zur Unterstützung strategischer Entscheidungsprozesse – Indizien kontingenz-theoretischer Bewertungsnotwendigkeiten, in: Strategische Prozesse und Pfade, p. 151-193, 2003.

Nummela, Niina, Saarenketo, Sami and Puumalainen, Kaisu: Global-Mind-Set - A prerequisite for successful internationalization?, in: Canadian Journal of Administrative Sciences, 21 (1), p. 51-64, 2004.

Oesterle, Michael-Jörg: Probleme und Methoden der Joint-Venture-Erfolgsbewertung, in: Zeitschrift der Betriebswirtschaft, 65, No. 9, p. 987-1004, 1995.

Oesterle, Michael-Jörg: Internationales Management im Umbruch, Deutscher Universitäts-Verlag, 2007.

Otto, Klaus-Stephan, Nolting, Uwe and Christel Bässler: Evolutionsmanagement, Carl Hanser, München, Wien, 2007.

Oviatt, M. Benjamin and McDougall, P. Patricia: Defining International Entrepreneurship and modelling the speed of internationalisation, in: Entrepreneurship Theory & Practice, Sept., p. 537-553, 2005.

Patton, Michel Quinn: Qualitative research and evaluation methods, 3 Edition, Sage Publication, 2002.

Pauwels, Pieter and Matthyssens, Paul: Strategic flexibility in export expansion: growing through withdrawal, in: International Marketing Review, Vol. 21, No. 4 and 5, p. 496-510, 2004.

Pedersen T., Petersen B. and Benito G.R.G Benito: Change of foreign operation method: impetus and switching costs, in: International Business Review, 11, p. 325-345, 2002.

Penrose, E. T.: Foreign investment and the growth of the firm, in: Economic Journal, 60, p. 220-235, 1959.

Petersen Bent, Welch, Denice Ellen and Welch, Lawrence Stephenson: Creating Meaningful Switching Options in International Operations, in: Long Range Planning, 33, p. 688-705, 2000a.

Petersen B., Benito G.R.G. and Pedersen T.: Replacing the foreign intermediary, in: International Studies of Management and Organisation, Vol. 30, No. 1, Spring, p. 45-62, 2000b.

Petersen, Bent and Welch, Lawrence: Foreign operation mode combinations and internationalization, in: Journal of Business Research, 55, p. 157-162, 2002.

Petersen B., Pedersen T. and Benito G.R.G : The termination Dilemma of Foreign Intermediaries: Performance, Anti-Shiring Measures and Hold-up Safeguards, in: Solberg, C.A.: Advances in international Marketing, Vol. 16, Elsevier, Amsterdam, p. 317-340, 2006.

Pettigrew, Andrew M: Longitudinal field research on change: Theory and practice in: Organization science, Vol. 1, No. 3, p. 267-292, 1990.

Pettigrew, Andrew M: The character and significance of strategy process research, in: Strategic Management Journal, Vol. 13, p. 5-16, 1992.

Pettigrew, Andrew M./Woodman, Richard W. and Cameron, Kim S.: Studying organisational change and development: challenges for future research, in: Academy of Management Journal, Vol. 44, No. 4, p. 697-713, Aug. 2001.

Prahalad, C.K. and Doz, Yves, L.: The multinational mission, Free Press, Macmillan, New York, 1987.

Pressey, Andrew and Tzokas, Nikolaos: Lighting up the "dark side" of international export/import relationships, in: Management Decision; Vol 42, No 5, p. 694-708, 2004.

Raeside, Robert, Adams, John and White, David: Research Methods, Napier Business School, Napier University, Edinburgh, 2004.

Raithel, Jürgen: Quantitative Forschung, 2 Ed., VS Verlag für Sozialwissenschaften, Wiesbaden 2008.

Ramaswamy, K.: Multinationality and Performance: A Synthesis and Redirection, in: Advances in: International Comparative Management, 7, p. 241- 267, 1992.

Ramaswamy K.: Multinationality, configuration, and performance: a study of MNCs in the US drug and pharmaceutical industry, in: Journal of International Management, 1, p. 231-253, 1995.

Teece, David J., Pisano, Gary and Shuen, Amy: Dynamic Capabilities and Strategic Management, in: Strategic Management Journal, Vol. 18:7, p. 509–533, 1997.

Reid, S.D.: The decision-maker and export entry and expansion, in: Journal of international business studies, Fall, p. 101-112, 1981.

Reinhart, Carmen and Rogoff, Kenneth: This time is different: Eight centuries of financial folly, Princeton University Press, 2009.

Riesenhuber, Felix: Großzahlige empirische Forschung, in: Methodik der empirischen Forschung, Albers, Sönke, Klapper, Daniel, Konradt, Udo, Walter, Achim and Wolf, Joachim, 2 Ed., Gabler, Wiesbaden, p. 1-16, 2007.

Roberto, Michael A.: Lessons from Everest: The interaction of cognitive bias, psychological safety, and system complexity, in: California Management Review, Vol. 45, No. 1, Fall 2002.

Roedenbeck, Marc: Individuelle Pfade im Management, Gabler, Wiesbaden, 2008.

Rogers, Everett M.: Diffusion of innovations, 5 th edition, the free press, 2003.

Rollinson, Derek: Organisational Behavior and Analysis - an integrated approach, 3rd Edition, FT Prentice Hall, 2005.

Root, F.: Entry Strategies for international markets, Lexington Books, Lexington, 1987.

Roth, Erwin, Heidenreich, Klaus and Holling, Heinz: Sozialwissenschaftliche Methoden, 5 Ed. Oldenbourg Verlag, 1999.

Roubini, Nouriel and Mihm, Stephen: Crisis Economics: A crash course in the future of finance, Penguin Press, 2010.

Ruigrok, Winfried, Wagner, Hardy: Internationalization and Performance: An Organizational Learning Perspective, in: Management International Review, Volume 43, p. 63-83, 2003/1.

Rugman, A.M.: New theories of the multinational enterprise: an assessment of internationalization theory, in: Bulletin of Economic research, 38 (2), p. 101-119, 1986.

Rugman, A.M.: The theory of multinational enterprise: the selected papers of Alan M. Rugman, Vol. One, Edward Elgar, Cheltenham, Brookfield, 1997.

Rugman, Alan M. and Verbeke Alain: Extending the theory of the multinational enterprise: internalization and strategic management process, in: Journal of International Business Studies, Vol. 34, p. 125-137, 2003.

Sachse, Uwe: Internationalisation of medium-sized enterprise, Verlag Wissenschaft & Praxis, Sternenfels, 2002.

Sachse, Uwe: Wachsen durch internationale Expansion – Wie Sie Ihre Auslandsgeschäft erfolgreich ausbauen, Gabler-Verlag, Wiesbaden, 2003.

Sachse, Uwe: Transcript explorative interviews, Internationalisation and mode switch, p. 1-88, February 2007.

Sachse, Uwe: Field notes, Internationalisation and mode switch, p. 1-14 , February 2007.

Sachse, Uwe: Exportleitfaden Aus- und Weiterbildung, for German Minister of Education and Research, December 2008.

Sakhalin-II, Socio economc issue, FAZ, 10.2.2009

Saldana, Johnny: Longitudinal qualitative research: Analysing change through time; Rowman & Littlefield Publishers, 2003.

Saunders, Mark, Lewis, Philip and Thornhill, Adrian: Research methods for business students, 3 Ed., Pearson/Prentice Hall, 2003.

Schmitt, Eckart: Strategien mittelständischer Welt- und Europamarktführer, Wiesbaden 1997.

Schein, Edgar: Coming to a new awareness of organizational culture, in: Sloan Management Review, Vol. 25, No. 2, p. 3-16, 1984.

Schoppe, Siegfried: Kompendium der Internationalen Betriebswirtschaftslehre, Oldenbourg, 1998.

Schreyögg, Georg: Organisation, Gabler, 4. Aufl., 2003.

Schreyögg, Jörg and Sydow, Jörg: Strategische Prozesse und Pfade, Managementforschung Band 13, Gabler Wiesbaden, 2003.

Schreyögg, Georg, Jörg Sydow, and Jochen Koch, Organisatorische Pfade – Von der Pfadabhängigkeit zur Pfadkreation?, Managementforschung 13, p. 257-294, 2003.

Schülein, Johann August and Reitze, Simon: Wissenschaftstheorie für Einsteiger, WUV, Wien 2005.

Schuh, Arnold: Fallstudien in der Strategieforschung, in: Buber, Renate and Holzmüller, Hartmut H. (eds.): Qualitative Marktforschung, 2. Ed. Gabler, Wiesbaden, p. 999-1017, 2009.

Schwarz, Sandra: Muster erfolgreicher Internationalisierung von Handelsunternehmen, Gabler Edition Wissenschaft, Dissertation, 2009.

Senge, P.M. The fifth discipline, Century Business, London, 1990.

Sharma, Deo D. and Blomstermo Anders: The internationalizaion process of Born globals: a network view, in: International Business Review, 12, p. 739-753, 2003.

Shrader, C. Rodney, Oviatt, Benjamin M. and McDougall, Patricia Phillips: How new ventures exploit trade-offs among international risk factors: Lessons for accelerated internationalisation of the 21st century, in: Academy of Management Journal, Vol. 43, No. 6, p. 1227-1247, 2000.

Simon, H.: The New Science of Management Decision, Harper, New York, 1960.

Simon, Markus Christian: Der Internationalisierungsprozess von Unternehmen, Dissertation, Deutscher Universitätsverlag, Wiesbaden, 2007.

Souchon, Anne L., Diamantopoulos, Adamantios and Holzmuller Hartmut H.: Export information Use: A Five-Country Investigation of Key Determinants, in: Journal of International Marketing, Vol. 11 Issue 3, p 106-128, 2003.

Söhnchen, Florian: Common method variance and single source bias, in: Albers, Sönke, Klapper, Daniel, Konradt, Udo, Walter, Achim and Wolf, Joachim: Methodik der empirischen Forschung, 2 Ed., Gabler, Wissbaden, p. 135-150, 2007.

Statistisches Bundesamt (Federal Statistical Office): Sonderauswertung der Umsatzsteuerstatistik 2004, by commission of IfM Bonn, Wiesbaden 2006.

Steiger, Thomas and Lippmann, Eric (Publ.): Handbuch Angewandte Psychologie für Führungskräfte, Springer Heidelberg New York, 2. Edition, 2003.

Steinke, Ines: Gütekriterien qualitativer Forschung, in: Flick, Uwe, Kardorff, von Ernst und Steinke, Ines: Qualitative Forschung, 4 Ed., Rowolth, Hamburg , p. 319-331, 2005.

Stopford, John and Wells, Louis: Managing the Multinational Enterprise. Organisation of the Firm, and Ownership of Subsidiaries, New York, 1972.

Strauss, Anselm and Corbin, Juliet: Grounded Theory Methodology. An Overview. In: Denzin, Norman K. and Lincoln, Yvonna S. (Hrsg.): Handbook of Qualitative Research, London: Sage, p.273-85, 1994.

Sullivan, Daniel: Measuring the degree of internationalization of a firm, in: Journal of International Business Studies, 2nd. Q., p. 325-342, 1994.

Svensson, Göran and Wood, Greg: The serendipity of leadership effectiveness in management and business practices, in: Management Decision, Vol. 43, No. 7/8, p. 1001-1009, 2005.

Swoboda B. and Jager: Investments und Divestments – Gründe für den Wandel der Betätigungsformen aus Managementsicht, in Moser (Hrsg): Ausländische Direktinvestitionen, p. 55-77, 2008.

Swoboda, Bernhard: Dynamische Prozesse der Internationalisierung: Managementtheorie und empirische Perspektiven des unternehmerischen Wandels, Gabler, Wiesbaden, 2002.

Sydow, Jörg: Organisationale Pfade: Wie Geschichte zwischen Organisationen Bedeutung erlangt, in Martin Endreß, Thoma Matys (Hrsg.): Die Ökonomie der Organisation – die Organisation der Ökonomie, Verlag für Sozialwissenschaften, p. 15-31, 2009.

Sydow, Jörg, Schreyögg, Georg and Koch, Jochen: Organisational paths: Path dependency and beyond, Free University Press, 2005.

Tarlatt, Alexander: Implementierung von Strategien im Unternehmen, Dt. Universitäts-Verlag, Dissertation, Wiesbaden, 2001.

Thiel, Christian: Gestaltung von Vertriebsstrukturen im Auslandsmarkt, Dissertation, Gabler Edition Wissenschaft, 2007.

Thomas, M.J. and Araujo, L.: Theories of export behavior: A critical analysis, in: European Journal of Makreting, 19, 2, p. 42-52, 1985.

Trompenaars, Fons: Riding the waves of culture – understanding cultural diversity in business, London: Brealey 1994.

Turcan, R. V.: De-Internationalization and the small firm, in: Wheeler, C. / McDonald, F. /Greaves, I.: Internationalization: Firm strategies and management, Houndmills et al., p. 208-222, 2003.

Umbeck, Tobias: Musterbrüche in Geschäftsmodellen, Dissertation, Gabler, Wiesbaden, 2009.

Vas, Alain and Ingham, Marc: Organisational change: open your eyes, use a wide angle lens, in: European business forum, Issue 16, p. 60-64, 2003/4.

VDMA: Verband Deutscher Maschinen- und Anlagenbau - German Engineering Federation, www.vdma.org, 2010.

Vernon, Raymond: International investment and international trade in the product cycle, in: Quarterly Journal of Economics, 80, No. 2, p. 190-207, 1966.

Vermeulen, Freek and Barkema: Pace, Rhythm, and Scope: Process Dependence in Building a Profitable multinational corporation, in: Strategic Management Journal, 23, p. 637-653, 2002.

Voropajev, Vladimir: Change management – a key integrative function of PM in transition economies, in: International Journal of Project Management, Vol. 16, No.1, p. 15-19,1998.

Volberda, H.W. and Lewin, A.Y.: Co-evolutionary dynamics within and between firms: from evolution to co-evolution, in: Journal of Management Studies, 40 (8), p. 2111-2136, 2003.

Weber, Petra: Internationalisierungsstrategien mittelständischer Unternehmen, Gabler Edition Wissenschaft, Wiesbaden 1997.

Weick, Karl E. and Quinn, Robert, E.: Organizational change and development, in: Annual Review Psychology, 50, p. 361-86, 1999.

Weiss, Allen and Anderson, Eric: Converting From Independent to Employee Salesforces: The Role of Perceived Switching Costs, Journal of Marketing Research, Vol. XXIX, p. 101-115, February 1992.

Welch, L and Benito G.R.G.: De-internationalization. Working paper, Department of marketing, University of Western Sydney, 5/1996.

Welch, L. and Benito G.R.G and Petersen, B: Foreign Operation Methods - Theory, Analysis, Strategy, 2007.

Welch, Lawrence and Luostarinen, Reijo: Internationalization: Evolution of a concept, in: Journal of general management, 14 (2), p. 34-55, 1988.

Welch. C.L. and Welch, Lawrence S.: Re-internationalisation: Exploration and conceptualisation, International Business Review, Vol 18 (6), p. 567-577, 2009.

Werle, Raymund: Pfadabhängigkeit, in Arthur Benz, Susanne Lütz, Uwe Schimank, Georg Simonis (Hrsg.): Handbuch Governance, Verlag für Sozialwissenschaften, p. 119-131, 2007.

Williamson, Oliver E.: Markets and Hierarchies – Analysis and Antitrust Implications. Free Press, New York, 1975.

Williamson, Oliver E.: The Economic Institutions of Capitalism. Firms, Markets, Relation Contracting. The Free Press, New York, 1985.

Winter, Sidney: The satisficing principle in capability learning, in: Strategic Management Journal, Vol. 21, p. 981-996, 2000.

Winter, Sidney: Understanding Dynamic Capabilities, in: Strategic Management Journal, Vol. 24, p. 991 – 995, 2003.

The World Bank:, World Bank national accounts data, and OECD National Accounts data files. Export of gods and services (% of GDP), http://data.worldbank.org, 2.8.2010

World Fact Book, www.cia.org, Central Intelligence Agency, 2010.

Yin, R.: Case study research: Design and methods (2nd ed.). Beverly Hills, CA: Sage Publishing, 1994.

Yip, George S./Biscarri, Javier Gomez and Monti, Joseph A.: The role of the internationalization process in the performance of newly internationalizing firms, in: Journal of International Marketing, Vol.8, No.3, p. 10-35, 2000.

Young, Stephen, Dimitratos, Pavlos and Dana, Leo-Paul: International Entrepreneurship Research: What scope for international business theories?, in: Journal of International Entrepreneurship, p. 31-42, 2003.

Zalan, Tatiana and Lewis, Geoffrey: Writing about methods in qualitative research: Towards a more transparent approach, in: Marschan-Piekkari and Catherina Welch: Handbook of Qualitative Research Methods for International Business, p. 507-528, 2004.

Zaltman, Gerald and Moorman, Christine: The importance of personal trust in the use of research, in: Journal of Advertising Research, 28 (3), p. 16-24, 1988.

Zentes, Joachim, Swoboda, Bernhard and Morschett, Dirk: Internationales Wertschöpfungsmanagement, Verlag Vahlen, München 2004.

Zollo, Maurizio and Winter, Sidney: Deliberate Learning and the Evolution of Dynamic Capabilities, in: Organization Science, Vol. 13, No. 3, May – June, p. 339 – 351, 2002.

Appendix

A. 1 Selected results of quantitative analysis

Table A. 1.1: Mean Value, Standard Deviation, Confidence-Intervalls of attributes in managerial style

	N	Mean	Std. Error	LCI	HCI
Planned Strategy vs. Luck and unexpected opportunities	183	-1,02186	0,094576	-1,20723	-0,83649
Risk averse vs. Risk taker	183	-0,4918	0,100401	-0,68859	-0,29502
Standardised concept vs. individual concept	183	1,147541	0,096634	0,958138	1,336944
Reduction of international activities vs. Expansion of intern. activities	182	1,659341	0,066774	1,528464	1,790217
Incremental approach vs. ad-hoc approach	183	-1,01639	0,106948	-1,22601	-0,80678
Continous homogenous rhythm vs. discontinous rhythm of switch	180	1,072222	0,084132	0,907323	1,237122
Slow vs. fast changes	183	0,092896	0,100054	-0,10321	0,289002
Within mode switch vs. between mode switch	181	0,005525	0,095155	-0,18098	0,192029
Single mode vs. multi mode per country	182	-0,52198	0,120132	-0,75744	-0,28652
Single mode strategy vs. multi mode strategy (-2,2)	182	0,862637	0,108467	0,650042	1,075233

Table A. 1.2: Descriptive statistics and correlation – Management style and performance (Perrexp Ratio)

Variable	Measure	1.	2.	3.	4.	5.	6.	7.	8.	9.	10.	11.	12.
1. Specific export country growth	Annual % growth												
2. Degree of satisfaction for entry mode	Scale 1 - 5	.200											
3. Level of systematic	Bipolar scale -3 to +3	-.123	-.042										
4. Risk perception	Bipolar scale -3 to +3	-.046	-.099	-.114									
5. Level of marketing standardisation	Bipolar scale -3 to +3	.151	-.002	-.030	.116								
6. Scope of international activities	Bipolar scale -3 to +3	.120	-.007	-.162*	.107	.126							
7. Level of incremental approach	Bipolar scale -3 to +3	.005	.137	-.175*	.301**	.077	.126						
8. Rhythm of change	Bipolar scale -3 to +3	-.064	-.002	-.030	.068	.208**	.136	.047					
9. Pace of internationalisation	Bipolar scale -3 to +3	-.035	.003	-.193**	.135	.064	.416**	.193**	-.036				
10. Scope of resources transfer	Bipolar scale -3 to +3	-.132	.129	-.081	.232**	.103	.156*	.345**	.036	.314**			
11. Number of modes per country	Bipolar scale -3 to +3	-.146	-.056	-.118	.209**	.027	-.024	.076	.103	.128	.205**		
12. Mode portfolio	Bipolar scale -3 to +3	.100	.096	-.139	.127	.284**	.099	.141	.288**	.201**	.390**	.290**	
13. No modes	????	.056	.160*	.051	.192*	.089	.071	.046	.215**	.135	.157*	.212**	.301**

Result of market operation in the selected export market (dependent variable: turnover share of the export market against the total turnover in foreign business, Perrexp Ratio)

* p < 0.1

** p < 0.05

*** p < 0.01 (all two-tailed tests)

410

A. 2 Details of variable coding, explanation and measurements

Table A. 2: Variable coding

Variable	Explanation	Measure
Company figures		
YEARIP	Number of years interview partner in this position	Years
YEARIC	Number of years interview partner in the company	Years
EXPERIENCELL	Number of years interview partner in international business	Years
SECTOR	Industry sector	Six different sector groups
YEARCI	Number of years company in international business	Years
EMPLOYEEG	Number of employees in Germany	Number
EMPLOYEEL	Number of employees in internal business	Number
FOUNDATIONC	Year of foundation of company	Year
TURNOVERT	Total Turnover 2006	Euro
TURNOVERE	Turnover Export 2006	Euro
EXPORT_RATIO	Share of export turnover of total turnover	In Percent
COUNTRY_GRO UP1	Categories of most important foreign markets, based on development index	Mature markets, Newly industrialised markets, Emerging markets
MANYC	Number of foreign countries doing business with	< 20 Countries; ≥20 Countries
Mode characteristics		
MKENTRYMODE	Market entry strategy	Group of entry strategies: Export, Contractual, Investment, Others
NOSWITCHES	Number of switches	1 to 4 switches
NO_MODES	Number of modes used in mode portfolio at the same time	Absolute figure, from 1 until 12
ENDMODE	Current mode or mode combination in most important country used	Direct export with middleman, direct export without sales man, agents, importer, JV, Subsidiary, Acquisition, Combination, etc.

Table A. 2: Variable coding (cont.)

Managerial Style		
STRATEGY	Planned Strategy vs. Luck and unexpected opportunities	Bipolare scale, - 3 until +3
RISK	Risk averse vs. Risk taker	
STANDARD	Standardised concept vs. individual concept	
DIRECTION	Reduction of international activities vs. Expansion of intern. activities	
PROCESS	Incremental approach vs. ad-hoc approach	
RHYTHM	Continuous homogenous rhythm vs. discontinuous rhythm of switch	
SPEED	Slow vs. fast changes	
INTENSITY	Within mode switch vs. between mode switch	
MODENO	Single mode vs. multi mode per country	
MODESTRAT	Single mode strategy vs. multi mode strategy	
Factors identified		
GF (growth factor)	Reduction of international activities vs. Expansion of international activities Slow vs. fast changes	Bipolar scale, - 3 until +3
RF (mode factor)	Single mode vs. multi mode per country Single mode strategy vs. multi mode strategy	Bipolar scale, - 3 until +3
RkF /risk factor)	Incremental approach vs. ad-hoc approach Risk averse vs. Risk taker	Bipolar scale, - 3 until +3
SF (specialist factor)	Continuous homogenous rhythm vs. discontinuous rhythm of switch Standardised concept vs. individual concept	Bipolar scale, - 3 until +3
Mode characteristic		
INTERNET	Internet/Electronic Mode	Share of export turnover in percentage, degree of satisfaction from 1 (highly satisfied) to 2 (not satisfied)
INDEXPORT	Indirect Export	
DIREXP	Direct Export without middleman	
DIREXPSR	Direct Export with sales rep	
ESC	Export service consultant	
AGENTS	Direct export with agents	
IMPORTER	Direct export with importer	
ALLIANCES	Alliances	
FANLIZ	Franchising, Licensing	
JV	Joint Venture	
SALESOFF	Sales office, Subsidiary, Affiliate	
FOREIGNBUY	Foreign acquisition	
OTHERS	Other mode	

Table A. 2: Variable coding (cont.)

Variable	Explanation	Measure
Performance for most important country		
IMMDTO	Immediate Turnover Growth	The ratio of turnover three years after the switch to the turnover one year before the switch.
LTTOYR	Long-Term Turnover Growth by Year	The ratio of turnover in 2006 to the turnover one year before the switch. This was also computed by dividing this ratio by the number of years since the switch.
IMMDSAT	Immediate Satisfaction Improvement	The difference between satisfaction with performance in the country three years after the switch and satisfaction one year before the switch.
LTSAT	Long-term Satisfaction Improvement	The difference between satisfaction with performance in the country in 2006 and satisfaction one year before the switch.
SATISCOUNTRY	Satisfaction with results in selected important country	Scale 1 (highly satisfied) to 5 (not satisfied)
SATCOUNTRY	Satisfaction with results in selected important country	Satisfied (good satisfaction) Not satisfied (poor satisfaction)
PERREXPRATIO	Share of most important export country	Share of most important country from export turnover (e.g. 300 Mio Export turnover/700 Mio Total Turnover = 0,42 * 20% share of important market= 0,086 share of important country from export turnover)
MKENTSAT	Degree of market entry satisfaction	Very satisfied Satisfied Not satisfied
LN_ANNUALTO	Annualised turnover increase	Natural log of annualised % turnover taken
Performance of international business		
SATISEXPORT	Satisfaction with results in international business	Scale 1 (highly satisfied) to 5 (not satisfied)
OVERALLPERF	Satisfaction with results in international business	Scale 1 (good) to 2 (bad)
PERREXPRATIO	Share of most important export country	Share of most important country from export ratio (e.g. 300 Mio Export turnover/700 Mio Total Turnover = 0,42 * 20% share of important market= 0,086 share of important country from export turnover)
INT_EXP (1)	Number of employees in foreign business	0 = ≤ 250 1 = > 251 to 1000 2 = > 1000

413

A. 3 Survey questionnaire: Internationalisation and mode switching

Translated version of German original (5 pages questionnaire, excluding one page of introduction and explanation)

1. Please provide the following information on your company and on your person

This information is important for the segmentation and formation of typologies.

Company	Name of interview partner	Position
Telephone	Email	Years in this position
In the company since	Overall experience in international business of interview partner	

Please provide at least approximate estimates:

What does your company mainly do? (main product/service)				Number of years the firm has been exporting
Number of employees in Germany	Number of employees in international markets	Year of foundation	Sales turnover (Euro) in 2006	Export turnover (Euro) in 2006

2. How did your foreign operation mode develop?

Please assign your company a value between the two extreme positions (3). Marking the middle value (O) represents a neutral characterisation. The term "switch" refers to the change of foreign operation mode (e.g. agent, importer, sales officer, subsidiary, licensee etc.).

Our success is the result of a <u>consciously chosen</u> <u>strategy</u>.	③②①⓪①②③	To be honest, our success has had a lot to do with <u>luck, chance and the taking of unexpected opportunities.</u>
We are more careful in the foreign market and only take very <u>low risks</u>.	③②①⓪①②③	We're willing to <u>take risks</u>, as long as there's the corresponding profit.
For foreign market operations, we always follow the same concept.	③②①⓪①②③	We decide on a <u>case-by-case basis</u> what the best market-entry strategy would be.
We have <u>reduced</u> our number of foreign activities in the last five years.	③②①⓪①②③	We have <u>expanded</u> our foreign activities in the last five years.
We prefer a <u>step-by-step approach</u>, such as 1. Agent, 2. Own sales rep, 3. Sales office	③②①⓪①②③	If we sense that it's worth it, then we found a <u>direct</u> foreign sales branch/company.
A mode switch is undertaken normally at the same, regular time intervals.	③②①⓪①②③	The switch of mode takes place irregularly, sometimes at shorter, sometimes at longer intervals.
The number of foreign activities develops <u>very slowly</u>, e.g. a new agent/distributor in five years.	③②①⓪①②③	The number of foreign activities is growing very rapidly. Every 6 months or so there is at least one new agent/distributor in the foreign market.
We always switch at the <u>same level of intensity</u>, e.g. the agent is replaced by a new agent.	③②①⓪①②③	When we switch modes, <u>we jump from one level</u> <u>of intensity to another</u>, for example, an importer is replaced by a sales subsidiary.
We only use <u>one mode</u> per country, for example with an agent	③②①⓪①②③	We <u>combine several modes</u> per country, for example, importer and sales subsidiary simultaneously.
We always use the <u>same mode</u> for all countries (e.g. exclusively agents).	③②①⓪①②③	We always use <u>different modes</u> for a market.

414

3. How do you assess the following questions regarding your mode for foreign business?

In how many countries do you work simultaneously?	□ < 1- 2 Countries	□ 3 – 5 Countries	□ 6 – 10 Countries	□ 11 - 20 Countries	□ 21 - 40 Countries	□ > 40 Countries
How long after market entry does it normally take for you to change the mode?	□ < 1 Year	□ 1 – 3 Years	□ 4 – 6 Years	□ 7 - 9 Years	□ 10 - 12 Years	□ > 12 Years
How long do you normally need for your opinion-building process from the first idea to switch to the decision to switch?	□ < 1 Day	□ < 1 Month	□ 1 – 6 Months	□ 7 – 12 Months	□ 1 – 2 Years	□ more than 2 Years
How long is the time duration between the decision to switch and the beginning of implementation?	□ < 1 Day	□ < 1 Week	□ < 1 Month	□ 1 – 6 Months	□ 7 – 12 Months	□ more than 1 Year
How long is the time duration from the beginning of implementation until the new mode is functional?	□ < 1 Week	□ < 1 Month	□ 1 – 6 Months	□ 6 – 12 Months	□ 1 – 2 Years	□ more than 2 Years

4.a. Which modes of foreign operation do you employ for internationalisation (in percent)? *(Column 2, estimated percentage)*

4.b. How would you assess the level of satisfaction with the modes listed below? *(Column 3, satisfaction with the result)*

Type of foreign mode	Question 4.a. Estimated share of foreign turnover (%)	Question 4.b. Satisfied with result (1 – very satisfied, 5 – not satisfied)				
Internet based foreign business/E-commerce		①	②	③	④	⑤
Indirect export (with exporter located in Germany)		①	②	③	④	⑤
Direct export of the firm, direct without middleman		①	②	③	④	⑤
Direct export with own sales reps		①	②	③	④	⑤
Using export service consultant		①	②	③	④	⑤
Direct export with agents		①	②	③	④	⑤
Direct export with importer		①	②	③	④	⑤
Strategic alliances/partnering		①	②	③	④	⑤
Franchising/Licensing		①	②	③	④	⑤
Joint Venture		①	②	③	④	⑤
Foreign representation, sales branch, sales subsidiary, affiliate		①	②	③	④	⑤
Acquisition in foreign market		①	②	③	④	⑤
Other (please state which)		①	②	③	④	⑤
	100%					

5. Please state your <u>most important</u> foreign market and describe the development of the foreign operation mode <u>after</u> market entry. Choose between the mentioned list of type of foreign modes

Please state, when there was a mode switch and was the new mode was about, please state also when you exchanged or added to your previous foreign partner. Naturally, it is of interest to us if there was a mix of several activities (several entries) or whether one single mode was favoured. <u>Start with the first switch, define the target mode, the year of switch, indicate replacement or additional mode and assess the degree of satisfaction to the results of that switch. Do it for all changes of your</u>

Please select your most important foreign market (country name):	Most important foreign country	Estimated share of foreign sales (%):

Mode list as example: *(1) Internet based foreign business/E-commerce; (2) Indirect export (with exporter located in Germany); (3) Direct export of the firm, direct without middleman; (4) Direct export with own sales reps; (5) Using export service consultant; (6) Direct export with agents; (7) Direct export with importer; (8) Strategic alliances/partnering; (9) Franchising/Licensing; (10) Joint Venture; (11) Foreign representation, sales branch, sales subsidiary, affiliate; (12) Acquisition in foreign market;(13) Other (please state which)*

Market Entry Strategy (1-13) – How do you realised the first sales turnover?	Reasons for this strategy	Year of entry	Degree of satisfaction with the results of the strategy mode (1- highly satisfied, 5 – not satisfied)				
			①	②	③	④	⑤

First switch of entry mode – selected type of strategy	Year of switch	Either as replacement of old mode or additional to old mode: replaced: ☐ additional: ☐	Reasons for switch

	One year before the first switch (-1)	During the year of switch (0)	1. year after the first switch (+1)	2. year after the first switch (+2)	3. year after the first switch (+3)
Please estimate your sales development (turnover in Euro)					
Please state your degree of satisfaction with the results (1- highly satisfied, 5 – not satisfied)					

Second switch of entry mode – selected type of strategy	Year of switch	Either as replacement of old mode or additional to old mode: replaced: ☐ additional: ☐	Reasons for switch

	One year before the second switch (-1)	During the year of switch (0)	1. year after the second switch (+1)	2. year after the second switch (+2)	3. year after the second switch (+3)
Please estimate your sales development (turnover in Euro)					
Please state your degree of satisfaction with the results (1- highly satisfied, 5 – not satisfied)					

Third switch of entry mode – selected type of strategy	Year of switch	Either as replacement of old mode or additional to old mode: replaced: ☐ / additional: ☐		Reasons for switch

	One year before the third switch (-1)	During the year of switch (0)	1. year after the third switch (+1)	2. year after the third switch (+2)	3. year after the third switch (+3)
Please estimate your sales development (turnover in Euro)					
Please state your degree of satisfaction with the results (1- highly satisfied, 5 – not satisfied)					

Fourth switch of entry mode – selected type of strategy	Year of switch	Either as replacement of old mode or additional to old mode: replaced: ☐ additional: ☐		Reasons for switch

	One year before the fourth switch (-1)	During the year of switch (0)	1. year after the fourth switch (+1)	2. year after the fourth switch (+2)	3. year after the fourth switch (+3)
Please estimate your sales development (turnover in Euro)					
Please state your degree of satisfaction with the results (1- highly satisfied, 5 – not satisfied)					

Future mode planned	Year of switch	Either as replacement of old mode or additional to old mode: replaced: ☐ additional: ☐	Reasons for switch

6. Companies without switch after the initial market entry - Why did you not switch at all?

Guideline: Please give a mark from 1 – 5 how relevant the different statements are for your company, Rating of 1 means least important and rating 5 means most important.

Why did you not switch:	Degree of satisfaction with the results of the strategy mode (1- less important, 5 – most important)				
Uncertainty about the consequences	①	②	③	④	⑤
Cost too high	①	②	③	④	⑤
Not enough resources	①	②	③	④	⑤
Just not the right time	①	②	③	④	⑤
Expected economical development of foreign market does not look promising enough	①	②	③	④	⑤
Management capabilities are missing	①	②	③	④	⑤
Switching might not be economical enough	①	②	③	④	⑤
Happy with the current situation	①	②	③	④	⑤
No experience with other modes	①	②	③	④	⑤
Other (please state which)	①	②	③	④	⑤

7. Please state the development of turnover for this selected country market?

	2002	2003	2004	2005	2006
Estimated sales development (in Euro) in selected foreign market					

8. How was on average your own development compared to industry sector development in selected foreign market?

	Much better than sector growth	Better than sector growth	same	Lower than sector growth	Much lower than sector growth
Own development compared to sector development (in growth percentage) from market entry until today	❑	❑	❑	❑	❑

9. How satisfied were you with the development of this country market over time?

	Very good	Good	Satisfactory	Sufficient	Insufficient
Satisfaction with the internationalisation results in this selected foreign market	❑	❑	❑	❑	❑

10. How do you assess the overall turnover share from your foreign business?

	Very good	Good	Satisfactory	Sufficient	Insufficient
Satisfaction with the results of internationalisation so far	❑	❑	❑	❑	❑

11. What would you recommend to other firms who are considering a switch of mode? What would you particularly emphasise?

_____

12. May we contact you if you switch modes in the future or if you are currently planning to switch, so that we may receive a "best practice"- example?

Yes	No

13. Would you like to receive a copy of the research study report?
(will most likely be completed at the end of 2007)

Yes	No

Thank you for your support and your time to improve international business behaviour!

GPSR Compliance
The European Union's (EU) General Product Safety Regulation (GPSR) is a set
of rules that requires consumer products to be safe and our obligations to
ensure this.

If you have any concerns about our products, you can contact us on

ProductSafety@springernature.com

In case Publisher is established outside the EU, the EU authorized
representative is:

Springer Nature Customer Service Center GmbH
Europaplatz 3
69115 Heidelberg, Germany